CD-BUY-756

MANUAL AND INDUSTRIAL EDUCATION AT GIRARD COLLEGE, 1831–1965

This is a volume
in the Arno Press collection

AMERICAN ETHNIC GROUPS:
THE EUROPEAN HERITAGE

See last pages of this volume
for a complete list of titles

MANUAL AND INDUSTRIAL EDUCATION AT GIRARD COLLEGE, 1831–1965

An Era in American Educational Experimentation

LOUIS A. ROMANO

ARNO PRESS

A New York Times Company

New York • 1980

Editorial Supervision: Steve Bedney

First publication in book form 1980 by Arno Press Inc.

AMERICAN ETHNIC GROUPS: THE EUROPEAN HERITAGE

ISBN for complete set: 0-405-13400-2
See last pages of this volume for titles

Manufactured in the United States of America

Library of Congress Cataloging in Publication Data

Romano, Louis A
Manual and industrial education at Girard College, 1831-1965.

(American ethnic groups)
Originally presented as the author's thesis, New York University, 1974.
Bibliography: p.
1. Girard College, Philadelphia--History.
2. Industrial arts--Study and teaching--Pennsylvania--Philadelphia--History. 3. Manual training--Pennsylvania--Philadelphia--History.
I. Title. II. Series.
TT167.G57R65 1980 607'.74811 80-1075
ISBN 0-405-13450-9

Sponsoring Committee: Professor Henry J. Perkinson, Professor W. Gabriel Carras and Professor Elsie A. Hug

MANUAL AND INDUSTRIAL EDUCATION AT GIRARD COLLEGE, 1831-1965: AN ERA IN AMERICAN EDUCATIONAL EXPERIMENTATION

Louis A. Romano

Submitted in partial fulfillment of the requirements for the degree of Doctor of Education in the School of Education of New York University

1974

In Memory of

ELVIRA ROMANO (1891-1971)

TABLE OF CONTENTS

PREFACE

One of the most unusual chapters in American educational history has been that of the Girard College of Philadelphia, a private school founded by the generous benefaction of the merchant philantropist Stephen Girard. This study had its origin in the difficulties I encountered in obtaining a satisfactory account of Girard College and its history, particularly with reference to manual and industrial education in the United States. As a school founded to care for orphaned boys, it seemed logical that Girard College would develop pragmatic programs which imparted occupational and/or vocational skills, and this would have been congruent with much of the private charitable educational endeavor in behalf of the 19th century poor. However, on this facet of the Girard experience, little information was available.

The studies that had been done on Girard College were largely institutional histories, *e.g.*, Cheesman A. Herrick, *History of Girard College* (1927); Ernest Cunningham, *Memories of Girard College* (1942); or specialized monographic studies dealing with delimited facets of the Girard experience, *e.g.*, James D. White, "The Needs and Problems of Girard College Graduates" (1949); Wilfred B. Wolcott, "Background of the Educational Provisions of the Will of Stephen Girard" (1948).

My dissertation proposes a dimensionally comprehensive study of manual and industrial education at Girard College, the genesis of articulated programs and the vicissitudes of changing curricula.

Most of my research was done at Girard College with the use of archives largely restricted hithertofore. I am particularly indebted to President Karl R. Friedmann of Girard College who allowed and supervised my use of the Girard College archives and who arranged those necessary permissions for my use of other archives deposited at the offices of the Trustees of the Estate of Stephen Girard. Further necessary permissions were obtained through the offices of the solicitor for the Estate, Thomas J. Gaffney, to whom I am also indebted. Additionally, I am particularly grateful for the time and effort extended in my behalf by Joseph W. Anderson, Assistant Secretary to the Trustees of the Estate of Stephen Girard. I owe a particular indebtedness to Margaret E. McFate, Head Librarian of Girard College, who patiently allowed me the use of her office and extended all of the resources of the library, and her knowledge of the college archives for a successful completion of the dissertation.

There are many others at Girard College to whom I am obligated; beyond those already mentioned, others who were particularly helpful included: John C. Donecker, Assistant to the President; Creel W. Hatcher, Head, Department of Mechanical Instruction; Caswell E. MacGregor, Director of Secondary Education; Emil Zarella, Director of the Office of Admissions and Student Relations; and Alfred Moscariello, Business Manager.

This dissertation was begun under the aegis of Professor William P. Sears, Jr. who extended invaluable advisements as it progressed; both Professors Elsie A. Hug and Frederick L. Redefer who, with Professor Sears constituted the original Dissertation Committee, were equally invaluable as supportive resources as the work progressed. Professor Henry J. Perkinson, with whom I had had work in American educational history assumed the chairmanship of the Dissertation Committee upon Professor Sears' retirement. I am indebted to both Professor Perkinson and Professor W. Gabriel Carras (who replaced Dr. Redefer on his retirement) for continued support during completion of the work. My introductions to Girard College and its administrative officers were largely facilitated by Professor Francesco Cordasco of Montclair State College who continued as an invaluable resource during the dissertation's progress; I can only inadequately acknowledge his encouragement and guidance.

L. A. R.

A Note on the Girard College Governance and Presidential Succession

Governance

The following chronology skeletally profiles the evolving pattern of governance of the Girard College. [See, for further detail, *infra*: 41-43; 78-79; 173-174; 282; 286]:

[1832] Philadelphia granted authority by Pennsylvania legislature to implement Girard will. The Select and Common Councils were empowered to appoint agent and officers.

[1833] Philadelphia City Councils appoints Board of Commissioners of the Girard Estates and Board of Trustees of Girard College.

[1841] Board of Trustees abolished.

[1847] Board of Directors of Girard College by the Philadelphia City Councils.

[1869] Pennsylvania Legislature amended the Act incorporating the City of Philadelphia by creating a Board of Directors of City Trusts charged with administering charitable trusts.

[1870] Supreme Court of Pennsylvania affirmed constitutionality of 1869 amendment which had created a Board of Directors of City Trusts charged with administering charitable trusts.

[1959] By decree of the Orphans Court of Philadelphia the Board of Directors of City Trusts was discharged as trustee of the estate of Stephen Girard. Management of the estate was placed under the charge of the Trustees of the Estate of Stephen Girard, Deceased, whose members were appointed by the Orphans Court of Philadelphia.

[1968] The Board of City Trusts of Philadelphia resumed control of the estate of Stephen Girard.

Presidential Succession

For detailed discussion of the presidential succession and tenures, see, *infra*: 55-56; 67; 82-83; 148; 151; 171-172; 185; 220-221; 262; 279-280; 286.

[1836-1841] Alexander Dallas Bache

[1848-1849] Joel Jones

[1850-1863] William H. Allen

[1863-1867] Richard Somers Smith

[1867-1882] William H. Allen

[1883-1910] Adam H. Fetterolf

[1910-1939] Cheesman A. Herrick

[1940-1954] Merle M. Odgers

[1955-1957] E. Newbold Cooper

[1957-1968] Karl Friedmann

[1969-] Gayle K. Lawrence

CHAPTER I

INTRODUCTION

THE PROBLEM

The problem of this research was to describe and analyze the history of manual and industrial education at Girard College, founded in Philadelphia in 1831, as a privately endowed free boarding school for white, indigent, fatherless boys between the ages of six and eighteen, and to relate this history to the mainstream of manual and industrial education in the United States, 1831-1965.

The subordinate problems inherent in the main problem are listed below:

1. To review the genesis and founding of Girard College in 1831 to the advent of its opening in 1848, and to relate it to the educational setting of the early 19th century United States.
2. To review manual and industrial education at Girard College from 1848 to 1876 and to relate to it the development of industrial education in the United States in a period of the expansion of both industry and education.
3. To review manual and industrial education at Girard College from 1876 to 1917 and to relate to it the development of industry and education in the United States in a period of new emphases and change.
4. To review manual and industrial education at Girard College from 1917 to 1965 and to relate to it the development of industry and education in the United States in a period of marked social and educational change.
5. To note the trends in manual and industrial education at Girard College and to relate these to the mainstream of manual and industrial education

in the United States.

DEFINITION OF TERMS

As used in this research, certain specific or technical terms are defined as follows:

Apprenticeship Education: A type of training commonly provided youth preparing for a trade before the advent of the factory system; usually possessed three distinguishing characteristics: (a) the binding of the apprentice to a master for a term of years, often 7; (b) the contracting of the master to train and initiate the apprentice in a trade; and (c) the custom of lodging the apprentice in the house of the master.[1]

Girard College: A privately endowed, free boarding school for white, indigent, fatherless boys between the ages of six and eighteen, located in Philadelphia. It is not an institution of higher learning.

Industrial Education: Instruction which is planned for the purpose of developing basic manipulative skills, safety judgments, technical knowledge and related occupational information for the purpose of fitting young persons for initial employment in industrial occupations and of upgrading or retraining workers employed in industry.[2]

Manual Education: A historically-oriented term which includes the evolution of manually-directed activities in its many evolving forms as a means of mental training, manual training, mechanic arts instruction, manual arts instruction, and industrial arts education.

(a) Mental Training - An outgrowth of early sense-realism philosophy which held that "doing led to knowing."

---

[1]Carter V. Good, (ed.), Dictionary of Education, p. 34.

[2]Roy W. Roberts, Vocational and Practical Arts Education, p. 285.

(b) Manual Training - An earlier type of school shop activity usually restricted to fixed exercises in woodwork, metalwork, and mechanical drawing; strong emphasis was placed on tool exercises and manual skill; gave way first to manual arts and later to industrial arts.[3]

(c) Mechanic Arts - A type of school shopwork (predominant during the latter part of the nineteenth century) designed to teach the trades and related science; a substitute for apprenticeship taken in school while studying mathematics, science and engineering.[4]

(d) Manual Arts - One of the early terms used to identify shopwork involving design and hand construction in various mediums with the purpose of developing art appreciation and manual skills.[5]

(e) Industrial Arts - Those phases of general education which deal with industry--its organization, materials, occupations, processes and products--and with the problems resulting from the technological nature of society.[6]

Practical Arts Education: A general term used to denote a type of functional education of a manipulative nature on a nonvocational basis; usually includes agriculture, business, homemaking, and industrial arts.[7]

---

[3]Carter V. Good, *op. cit.*, p. 576.

[4]*Ibid.*, p. 41.

[5]*Ibid.*

[6]Gordon O. Wilber, *Industrial Arts in General Education*, p. 2.

[7]Carter V. Good, *loc. cit.*

Vocational Education: That part of an individual's (age indeterminable) education which prepares him for occupational efficiency and well-adjustment in gainful employment in a socially desirable calling.

DELIMITATIONS

The following delimitations were placed upon the research in order to circumscribe and confine the problem:

1. This study was delimited to the years from 1831, the founding of Girard College, to 1965.

2. Only that part of the curriculum of Girard College that has been concerned with manual and industrial education was covered by this study, with necessary concomitant evolving references to the general curriculum in which industrial education was a part.

4. No attempt was made to assess definitively the organization and success of manual and industrial education in meeting the prescribed aims and objectives structured and stipulated in the will of the founder, Stephen Girard.

BASIC ASSUMPTIONS

Although the assumption is not of itself necessary, it is felt that there is need for its statement: Any educational institution, as a necessary extension of the social fabric, reflects the society's major aims, objectives, and evolving form.

BASIC HYPOTHESIS

Girard College, in its foundation as a school for orphaned boys, both in its curriculum and its major educational commitment, epitomized over a century of experimentation in manual and industrial education which, *pari passu*, reflected the broad patterns of an evolution of practical arts and industrial education in one significant sphere of American educational history.

SIGNIFICANCE OF THE STUDY

Girard College is a particularly interesting institution to the historian of education because it was founded in that period of United States history when formal, carefully structured, and organized instruction of a practical nature was almost non-existent for a major portion of the citizenry and nearly non-existent for the lower classes.[8] The school was founded in Philadelphia in 1831 by the will of Stephen Girard and opened on January 1, 1848. It is a privately endowed, free boarding school for fatherless boys, and maintains and educates free of charge as many boys as the income from the endowment will permit. Under the provisions of Stephen Girard's will, the school was founded for

> . . . poor white male orphans, between the age of six and ten years, . . . [who would] be instructed in the various branches of sound education . . . [and] scholars, who shall merit it, shall remain in the college until they shall respectively arrive at between fourteen and eighteen years of age; they shall then be bound out by the Mayor, Aldermen and citizens of Philadelphia, or under their direction, to suitable occupations, as those of agriculture, navigation, arts, mechanical trades, and manufactures, according to the capacities and acquirements of the scholars respectively; consulting, as far as prudence shall justify it, the inclinations of the several scholars, as to the occupation, art, or trade, to be learned.[9]

---

[8]Girard College is set in the context of educational theory that was largely dominated by monitorial and Lancasterian theory which attempted the mass education of the poor only in the most basic rudiments of literacy. The monitorial schools which were largely the results of the efforts of Joseph Lancaster (1778-1838) and Andrew Bell (1753-1832) had a wide influence in early nineteenth century America. See John F. Reigart, _The Lancasterian System of Instruction in the Schools of New York City_ which includes considerable material on the history of the Lancasterian system in America. See also David Salmon, _Joseph Lancaster_ and David Salmon, (ed.), _The Practical Parts of Lancaster's Improvements and Bell's Experiment_.

[9]"The Will of the Late Stephen Girard, Esq.," Article XXI. The text of Stephen Girard's will is most conveniently found in a verbatim transcript in Henry W. Arey, _The Girard College and Its Founder_, pp. 57-85.

Girard's commitment to apprenticeship and his preference that "I [he] would have them taught facts and things, rather than words or signs . . ."[10] largely provided the educational principles upon which practical education was to be founded in his college.

It must be realized that Stephen Girard was neither an educator nor an educational theorist, but his multi-faceted educational benevolence reflected an awareness of and a concern for the educational problems of his time.[11] His philosophy, theory, and plan for education as reflected in his life and, even further, through his last will and testament do not provide the opportunity for a categorization or a general schema but do suggest rather an eclectic humanitarian design, altruistic by its very nature, aware of the practical needs and basic educational competence of the less fortunate. Although Girard's life spanned a time in history fraught with educational reform, new theory and practice, interacting with changing religious, social, economic, and political conditions, no direct causal-relationship may be drawn between Girard's view and any significant educational thought or, more important, any other educational institution. The college outlined by Girard was to be unique among educational institutions. Even his use of the term "college" within the prescribed age limits was without precedence. Invariably, his plan for the college was his response to the educational and social system in 19th century Philadelphia and,

---

[10] Ibid.

[11] Girard's will provided land and $2,000,000 for the establishment of his college with continuing funds to be supplied from the final residuary funds derived from stock dividends; $10,000 to the comptrollers of the public schools for the city and county of Philadelphia for the use of schools upon the Lancaster system; and $6,000 for the establishment of a school in Passyunk Township in the county of Philadelphia for poor white children. (Girard hoped that the townspeople would make additions to this founding fund). See Henry W.Arey, Ibid., pp. 57-85, passim.

in an extended sense, for the United States.[12]

In the early days of the founding of the college, the curriculum was planned largely within the guidelines set by Lieber's A Constitution and Plan of Education for Girard College for Orphans[13] and Bache's Report on Education in Europe.[14] Its evolving form has led to a dual curriculum, for the college meant to serve both general and practical educational needs. This dichotomy of purpose is reaffirmed in the current curriculum which

> . . . offers him [each boy] an elementary school education and a comprehensive secondary school course, providing the credits in academic subjects required for entrance to college, together with vocational training along either business or trade shop lines.[15]

The success of Girard College as an eleemosynary institution was generally affirmed in the early years of its founding. Siljestrom, a representative of the Swedish government, reported in 1853 that

> . . . it [Girard College] is perhaps the only orphan asylum in the world that no traveller would venture to pass by unnoticed. Besides the great interest which the institution has in the eyes of the philanthropist and the observer in consequence of its object, it has the further attraction of being one of the "lions" [quotation marks in the original] of America.[16]

---

[12]The vast changes in social and economic history in the early decades of nineteenth century America are noted in V. T. Thayer, Formative Ideas in American Education, particularly pp. 63-84. See also Edward Everett, The Importance of Practical Education and Useful Knowledge.

[13]Francis Lieber, A Constitution and Plan of Education for Girard College for Orphans.

[14]Alexander D. Bache, Report on Education in Europe to the Trustees of The Girard College For Orphans.

[15]As quoted in most recently published school brochure, Girard College [1967], p. 1.

[16]P. A. Siljestrom, The Educational Institutions of the United States, pp. 273-274.

Soon after the opening of the college's mechanical school building in 1884,[17] the school's success in meeting its practical educational purpose was equally affirmed.

> He [Girard] also expressed a desire that "they shall be taught facts and things rather than words and signs." These directions of the Founder have been carried out in a well-planned eight years' course of study; and although no special trades are taught, a Mechanical Hall, containing workshops with the requisite machinery and steam power, has been erected, and instruction is given in the handling of tools and the working of wood, iron, and steel. The boys thus taught find ready employment in machine shops and manufactories at double the wages they could otherwise have obtained.[18]

Prior to World War II, Fee made this cogent analysis:

> In observing the transition from manual labor to more recent developments in industrial education, Girard College represents the development of a financially independent institution, able to command the best available educational program desired to fit each boy into the surrounding industrial world upon reaching maturity.[19]

And of the school in general, the historian Grizzell wrote:

> The Girard College for Orphans indicates a pioneer educational contribution to the boy of the great middle and lower middle class, a population group that could, in Girard's day, ill afford education in an independent boarding school. . . .
>
> The total educational program suggested for the college was a century in advance of the early nineteenth century. . . .
>
> Although Girard probably did not visualize his institution as being concerned with preparation for further education, his curricular plans were so flexible that boys with intellectual

---

[17] Cheesman A. Herrick, History of Girard College, p. 236. The chronological history of Girard College is best sketched in the official institutional history of Herrick.

[18] James P. Wickersham, A History of Education in Pennsylvania, p. 435.

[19] Edward M. Fee, The Origin and Growth of Vocational and Industrial Education in Philadelphia to 1917, p. 103.

> aptitudes and interests have had no difficulty in meeting the requirements of higher institutions with the most rigorous standards.[20]

Today, more than ever, the topics of "dual" curriculum or 'comprehensive" schools dominate the educational scene. Polemical arguments on these topics arise from all quarters and the general problem has remained a perennial one. Should occupational and practical education be given in all high schools? Should all high school students receive instruction in practical subjects? Are the schools responsible to prepare all students for the world of work? What courses should be taught?

There are no ready answers to these questions and their multitude of counterparts, and there is a dire need for scholarly research to help meet the many problems. The report, Education for a Changing World of Work, epitomizes this need.

> If vocational education is to meet the needs of training in this rapidly changing world, it must adapt itself to changing conditions. Its patterns of organization must fit into the evolving educational structure of the Nation. Its curriculum content must be in line with technological and social needs. Its methods of instruction must be in keeping with the latest and best understanding of how people learn and how they can be taught most effectively. If vocational education programs are to provide adequately for the needs of a State or of a Nation as a whole, or if specific programs are to be effective, much more information is needed than is now available. This is the task of research--

---

[20] E. Duncan Grizzell, "The Place of Girard College Among Educational Institutions," Educational Outlook, XXII (November 1948), pp. 32-38. This entire issue of the Educational Outlook is given over to various facets of the Girard experience. As a further point of reference S. Herman Macy writes an article on "The Plan, Philosophy, and Objectives of Girard College," in which he observes: "This [objective to teach boys to think intelligently as far as their abilities permit] can be realized by providing differentiated courses, procedures, and objectives for individual differences; by integrating standards and methods at certain ages and periods; by emphasizing mastery of fundamentals in all classes; by stressing quality of performance and discouraging the superficial in accomplishment; by developing intellectual honesty; and by fostering independence in thinking, discouraging the practice of thinking in the patterns of either habit or groups." loc. cit., p. 9.

> on a broad scale--from specific studies of detailed problems to nationwide studies of problems involving the whole country.[21]

A study of manual and industrial education at Girard College, of course, has not provided answers to the numerous problems that have arisen or will arise in industrial education. This investigation has sought, however, to present a view of manual and industrial education at an institution which has had a unique curriculum and which, being privately endowed, has had the means to implement and to modify the curriculum as seen in light of its student needs, independent of local, state, or federal fiscal policies. The study is not only important as part of the overall educational history of the United States but also as a mirror of manual and industrial education in the United States.[22] In a sense, Girard College's commitment to a dual program provides insight into the many problems that have faced a dual curriculum school and the manner in which this institution has and does meet them. The raison d'être for such a study has been cogently expressed by Sears who states:

---

[21]Report of the Panel of Consultants on Vocational Education, Education for a Changing World of Work (Washington: U. S. Department of Health, Education, and Welfare, 1963), p. 194. This report defined vocational education to mean ". . . all formal instruction for both youth and adults, at the high school, post-high school, and out-of-school levels which prepares individuals for initial entrance into and advancement within an occupation or group of related occupations." (p. 5).

[22]See in this connection, Melvin L. Barlow, History of Industrial Education in the United States, who notes that among the myriad problems he encountered in providing a history of industrial education, the lack of information on the contributions of individuals and of industrial schools proved a major obstacle. Of schools in particular, he noted: ". . . the schools of industrial education are not delineated in such a way as to represent their full story. Some schools are mentioned merely because they were related to a particular fact of the history under review, but other fine, continuously strong contributions of many schools were of necessity not detailed. The story of the schools of industrial education, like that of the people, must await another day for review in history." (pp. 6-7)

> Many of the agencies offering practical education are of sufficient age to merit studies that might reveal the problems that they faced in their development and the ways they went about solving them. Their histories will reveal their strengths and weaknesses. Trends will emerge from such studies, and the story of the past may, if critically studied, help present workers in the field to develop solutions to the problems they face. Research into the history of the field need not result in musty, dust-gathering tomes but may very well present the field with lively, effective, and useful knowledge that can be applied to present situations.[23]

RELATED STUDIES

Extensive preliminary research into the related literature indicated a large assortment of diversified materials which fall into the following categories: (A) General works which are closely related to the history of Girard College. (B) Works that are general histories of manual and industrial education in the United States. (C) Institutional histories which have attempted the study of a specialized curriculum in a unique educational setting. (D) Sources closely related to a significant aspect or area of this research.

(A) General Works Which Are Closely Related To The History of Girard College

The earliest attempt to trace the life of Stephen Girard and to assess Girard's provisions for the education of indigent youth was written by Simpson,[24] a former clerk in Girard's bank. His ambivalent treatment of Girard is presented with a view to ". . . neither gratify his [Girard's] friends, who thought him infallible, nor satisfy his enemies, who believe

---

[23] William P. Sears, "Analytical Procedures for Scientific Research," Research in Industrial Arts Education, Ninth Yearbook of the American Council on Industrial Arts Teacher Education (1960), p. 63.

[24] Stephen Simpson, Biography of Stephen Girard.

him to have been everything that is frail."[25] While some of Simpson's sources may be considered suspect, the value of the book lies in Simpson's views of Girard's behest as it would respond to educational needs as perceived.

Soon after the opening of Girard College in 1848, Arey,[26] as Secretary of the Board of Directors of the Girard College for Orphans, wrote a short biography of Stephen Girard and a history of Girard College. Although Arey had access to the volumes of Girard papers in repository at the College, much of his material appears to have been taken from Simpson's earlier work, but with a marked favorable disposition toward Girard.

Another favorably disposed biography was written in 1884 by Ingram,[27] the great grandson of Stephen Girard's brother John. Like Arey, he makes little use of the Girard papers but structures his biography using official documents concerning the life of Girard (birth certificate, baptismal papers, etc.); the lawsuits attempting to break the Girard will; the papers of Professor William Wagner, a former apprentice and later agent of Stephen Girard; and family letters. Ingram's purpose is to present ". . . openly and accurately the intimate facts of a life which has been so grossly misrepresented. . . [by Simpson]."[28]

No adequate biography of Stephen Girard appeared until the Board of Directors of City Trusts of Philadelphia contracted with McMaster.[29] His

---

[25]Ibid., p. vi.

[26]Henry W. Arey, The Girard College and Its Founder.

[27]Henry A. Ingram, The Life and Character of Stephen Girard.

[28]Ibid., p. xii.

[29]John B. McMaster, The Life and Times of Stephen Girard.

two-volume work represents the official, authoritative, and definitive life of Girard. As a recognized American historian, McMaster writes the first full-dress historical biography of Girard, invaluable in its uses of sources afforded by the Girard papers, presenting vignette pictures of the social and economic context of Girard's world with, unfortunately, little but passing reference to Girard College. However, Herrick,[30] then president of the college, felt that McMaster (as well as the other biographers of Girard) had not captured Girard "the man" or "the founder." Herrick's volume is intended to meet that need as well as to provide the students at the college with a reasonable, ingenuous version of their benefactor's life.

Herrick's treatment of Girard might well be compared with that of Wildes,[31] the most recent of the Girard biographers, who appears to have had time to go beyond Girard's fifty-thousand personal documents in repository at the college and listen to a few wives' tales.

The only full-length history of Girard College was written by Herrick.[32] As an institutional history concerned with a total picture of Girard College, Herrick, of necessity, points up only the highlights in a rapid chronological commentary. Because of Herrick's official connection with the college and because it was an institutional history, Herrick does not attempt any critical assessments but writes instead an orthodox chronicle.

(B) Works That Are General Histories of Manual and Industrial Education in the United States

An early history of vocational education was written by McGrath[33] in 1913. McGrath traced vocational training through the early centuries,

---

[30] Cheesman A. Herrick, Stephen Girard, Founder.

[31] Harry E. Wildes, Lonely Midas: The Story of Stephen Girard.

[32] Cheesman A. Herrick, History of Girard College.

[33] William J. McGrath, "History of Vocational Education" (unpublished Ph.D. dissertation, New York University, 1913).

covering both the Eastern and Western World, placing particular emphasis upon the occupational adjustments each society made in the light of changing social and industrial conditions. Using this background as a rationale, McGrath presented in summary a broad program for needed vocational education for the United States in view of its own changing conditions.

Smith[34] traced the development of manual training in the United States. He presented those factors which introduced and accelerated the manual training movement as well as those obstacles which retarded its growth and the effect of manual training upon American education. Smith, like McGrath, was interested in seeing the establishment of a broad program of vocational training at all levels within existing educational aims and tendencies discerned.

Significant pioneer work in the broad area of the historiography of manual and industrial education have been provided by Bennett[35] and Sears.[36] Bennett's work is a detailed, chronological history of manual and industrial education which is the fullest account presently available. As a repository of material, Bennett remains an excellent source but only as an encyclopedic capsule for any period, individual, or educational curriculum. Almost inevitably, Bennett is a starting point for continued and extended investigation.

Sears, on the other hand, details a complete overview of the origins and beginnings of vocational education. He establishes with ample cogency that industrial education is largely a response to the needs of society,

---

[34]Ross H. Smith, Development of Manual Training in the United States.

[35]Charles A. Bennett, Manual and Industrial Education Up to 1870. See also his History of Manual and Industrial Education, 1870 to 1917.

[36]William P. Sears, The Roots of Vocational Education.

the conduct of which will find its cource in industry, education, legislation, and social progress.

(C) Institutional Histories Which Have Attempted The Study of a Specialized Curriculum in a Unique Educational Setting

Institutional histories are necessarily varied and reflect the various patterns of development. One of the most valuable of these is that of Chittenden[37] who, as long-time director of the Sheffield Scientific School, has written a model institutional history with considerable attention to the history of higher education in America and the emergence of the scientific school, and with detailed attention to social forces, change, patterns of industrialization, and the history of scientific thought, all with reference to the part that the Sheffield Scientific School plays in the process. Actually, it becomes a vast repository of the social history of nineteenth century America which cuts across the lines of education at all levels and in this connection is invaluable in discerning broad patterns of influence and educational philosophy.

Still another history, from a similar vantage point, is that of Coates[38] who wrote the history of a famous manual training high school. The origin and development of the institution is traced within the mainstream of early manual and industrial education in the United States which was suggestive for the approach employed in this history of manual and industrial education at Girard College.

On a broader tableau, Smith[39] attempted an historical account of

---

[37]Russell H. Chittenden, History of the Sheffield Scientific School of Yale University, 1846-1922.

[38]Charles P. Coates, History of the Manual Training School of Washington University.

[39]Herbert E. Smith, "The Historical Development of Technical Education in the First Nine Colleges Founded in the United States, 1636-1862" (unpublished Ph.D. dissertation, New York University, 1940).

the development of technical education (both undergraduate and graduate) in the nine colleges and universities before the American Revolution. The growth of technical education is traced from its early beginnings in science and applied science and further attention is paid to the forces that have played a part in their growth. Technical education is discerned largely as an outgrowth of education in applied science. Attention is given to the history of manual and practical arts below the college level.

With particular reference to the development of a special curriculum in a teacher preparatory institution is the work of Fink[40] who traced the development of the industrial arts teacher-training curricula and the development of the industrial arts and vocational education summer programs at the Oswego State Normal School. However, no marked attempt was made to set the development of the curricula or summer programs within the mainstream of the industrial arts or industrial vocational movement in the United States.

A recent model institutional history is the history of the School of Education at New York University by Hug[41] who demonstrated the practicability of the history of an institution whose genesis was largely due to the discernment of basic needs and converging social forces.

(D) Sources Closely Related to a Significant Aspect or Area of This Research

Studies which were closely related to the work of the investigator

---

[40] Eugene D. Fink, "History of the Development of Industrial Education and of Industrial Arts Education at the Oswego State Normal School" (unpublished M.A. thesis, New York University, 1933).

[41] Elsie A. Hug, _Seventy-Five Years in Education: The Role of The School of Education, New York University, 1890-1965_.

are perhaps most exemplitively noted in the works of Fee[42] and White.[43] Fee has traced an invaluable history of vocational-industrial education in Philadelphia with particular reference to apprenticeship education with detailed references to the long history of the apprenticeship commitment at Girard College. White's study was an investigation of the needs and problems as reported by Girard College graduates which allows insight into the general effect of the Girard curriculum and, in a measure, an assessment of the achievement of its aims and objectives. It was limited to the fifteen classes graduated between 1936 and 1943 inclusive.

On a broader scale, but with direct relevancy to many of the investigator's interests, is Wickersham's[44] work which is a standard history of education in Pennsylvania for the period that it surveys and in which can be traced many educational developments and concerns which directly impinge on the history of Girard College.

As a detailed assessment of the educational provisions of Stephen Girard's will, the study of Wolcott[45] provides a valuable assessment of the educational provisions of the will of Stephen Girard seen against the backdrop of Girard's life and the philosophic ideas that the author was able to discern both from Girard's life and the major educational currents of early nineteenth century America.

---

[42]Edward M. Fee, The Origin and Growth of Vocational Industrial Education in Philadelphia to 1917.

[43]James D. White, "The Needs and Problems of Girard College Graduates" (unpublished Ph.D. dissertation, University of Pennsylvania, 1949).

[44]J. P. Wickersham, The History of Education in Pennsylvania.

[45]Wilfred B. Wolcott, "Background of the Educational Provisions of the Will of Stephen Girard" (unpublished Ph.D. dissertation, University of Pennsylvania, 1948).

PROCEDURE IN COLLECTING AND TREATING DATA

In the application of the historical method and such other research techniques which the data required for analysis and interpretation, the researcher was guided by the works of such recognized authorities as Barzun and Graff,[46] Gottschalk,[47] and Good and Scates;[48] the criteria established by Brickman in his Guide to Research in Educational History was particularly noted.[49]

Primary source materials were used wherever their use was required; the data were examined for internal and external consistency in order to establish their validity for the purposes of the study; and the data collected were classified and organized in a manner designed to facilitate orderly collation, synthesis, description and evaluation. In general, bibliographical and factual data were organized chronologically, except that some data were also classed by author and organization, where such treatment was appropriate to the problem.[50]

---

[46]Jacques Barzun and Henry F. Graff, The Modern Researcher.

[47]Louis Gottschalk, Understanding History.

[48]Carter V. Good and Douglas E. Scates, Methods of Research.

[49]See particularly his "Applying the Historical Methods of Research To Education," pp. 91-190. William W. Brickman, Guide to Research in Educational History. Brickman discusses in considerable detail the historical method, the classification of sources, external and internal criticism, and the determination and interpretation of facts.

[50]See in this connection, passim, William W. Brickman, Ibid., particularly his admonition and observation, "He [the historian] draws inferences and generalizations which remain tentative until he has completed his study. All hypotheses have to meet the tests of logical consistency and agreement with fact. If an hypothesis, for example, is based upon such fallacious reasoning as post hoc, ergo propter hoc and other logical errors, then it is valueless. Similarly, the hypothesis which does not conform to observed facts can hardly be considered adequate. The historian must also be careful not to make his hypotheses too simple. Excessive generalizations and oversimplifications have weakened many an historical report." (pp. 97-98).

Criteria For The Selection Of Data

To insure objectivity and validity of data, whether bibliographical or factual, the following criteria were applied wherever their use was indicated:

1. If factual, are the data representative of the condition they describe?
2. Does the authority have recognized standing in the field?
3. Is the publication a significant contribution to the literature of the field?
4. If a primary source is cited, has it been examined in its original form by the researcher? Is such examination possible?[51]

The criteria stated above were applied regularly in the collection of data for this study.

Sources of Data

For the early phases of the origin and development of Girard College as indicated in subproblem I, a wealth of material allowed the delineation of the educational context and social history in which Girard College knew its origin.[52] The origin, however, was cast against this historical background with the extensive use of primary material relating to the founding

---

[51] See William W. Brickman, "External and Internal Criticism," _Ibid._, pp. 93-95.

[52] See the general historians of American education which are available, _e.g._, R. Freeman Butts and Lawrence A. Cremin, _A History of Education in American Culture_; Ellwood P. Cubberley, _Public Education in the United States: A Study and Interpretation of American Educational History_; H. G. Good, _A History of American Education_; Adolph E. Meyer, _An Educational History of the American People_; and Paul Monroe, _Founding of the American Public School System_, Vol. I.

of Girard College, its aims and objectives.[53]

For subproblem II, III, IV, V, the primary materials (noted in Footnote #53 infra) formed the bulk of continuing reference and anchorage, but the historical context into which the history of the facets of the investigation proposed in subproblems II, III, IV, and V, were drawn (as in subproblem I) from the materials already noted as available.[54]

---

[53]Primary materials (holograph of Girard's will; annual reports of the College's Board of Directors, the Philadelphia Board of Directors of City Trusts, and the President of the College; official curricula; and dejecta membra of an archivistic nature) are in a closed deposit collection at the College which have been made available to the investigator. The annual reports of the president are a rich source of curricular and organizational information of which the following is representative: "Manual Training still continues to be an important feature of education in Girard College, as well as elsewhere. . . . We are pleased to report that our Sloyd school is coming up to our highest expectations. During the past year the boys have shown a steadily growing interest in Sloyd work, as well as a marked development of skill in the use of tools. The work is conducted along the lines of general education rather than as a means of special development of technical skill. To this end the instructor has followed pretty closely the course of models as developed by years of study in the best Sloyd training schools. The characteristic feature of this course is the progressive series of exercises continuing through the entire course. Each model depends upon the one preceding, and is in turn a preparation for the succeeding one. The models are useful, serviceable, and in most cases familiar objects, calculated to arouse the lively interest of the pupil. The exercises, as well as the tools employed, are arranged with reference to the worker's growing power, calling for a gradual increase of effort, step by step, while the first exercise with each tool is calculated to give a correct effective impression of its typical use. . . . We believe the time has come when the Sloyd work should be extended, both in sending more boys and in giving more time. Under our present curriculum only one lesson of two hours each per week is given. The experience of other schools and that of our best educators convinces us that two lessons of two hours each per week would result in no loss whatever in the work of the regular branches, while the progress in Sloyd would be proportionately much greater than at present." Adam H. Fetterolf, "Girard College President's Report for 1899," Thirtieth Annual Report of the Board of Directors of City Trusts for the Year 1899, pp. 113-115. All of the Presidents' Reports were available to the investigator and were used whenever appropriate material presented itself within the purview of the study.

[54]See Footnote #52, supra.

CHAPTER II

BACKGROUND AND FOUNDING OF GIRARD COLLEGE (1800-1848)

I

In his study of the American common school, Lawrence Cremin discerned its emergence and development during the early 19th century (1815-1850) as a response to four basic social and intellectual trends in the early life of the Republic: (1) the democratization of politics; (2) the growth of the struggle to maintain social equality; (3) the change in the conception of man and society; and (4) the rise of nationalism.[1] Within this context, the varied educational institutions which the society created are better understood as responses to broad cultural changes, and the founding of Girard College takes on relevancy within the history of the period.

The early national period (ending at about 1830) witnessed a struggle to adapt an educational structure to the political, economic, and social needs of the new republic. Following the Revolution, prominent statesmen and educators placed great importance upon the idea that the welfare of the new nation depended on the enlightenment of the people, and the need to educate its youth.[2] The political and educational views of the French liberals were well known in America with their emphases on lay and national education, and these ideas were the formative nexus out of which the

---

[1] Lawrence A. Cremin, _The American Common School: An Historic Conception_, p. 1, _ff_.

[2] See particularly Merle Curti, _The Social Ideas of American Educators_, pp. 50-100.

generating principles of American education evolved.[3]

Early educational theory is best exemplified in Franklin and in Jefferson who responded to the complex of forces and needs. As early as 1749, in discussing his plans for the Philadelphia Academy, Franklin had observed: "It would be well if they [the students] could be taught everything that is useful, and everything that is ornamental."[4] For the poor, Franklin accepted the practice of the charity school, and viewed morality and moral training as the indispensable foundation of a good society.[5] Drawn from his own experiential background, his utilitarian and commercial interests, Franklin was strongly influenced by empiricism and the scientific knowledge of the Enlightenment. Jefferson was convinced that the primary requisite of a free society was a continuous system of public education and his _A Bill For The More General Diffusion of Knowledge_ (1779) which he presented to the Virginia Legislature is to be contrasted with Franklin's Academy in that Jefferson's proposal removed the stigma of pauperism and charity from elementary education.[6] Although widespread interest continued for improved public enlightenment, serious discussion of the idea of a tax supported system of education did not reappear until the early decades of the 19th century.[7]

Underlying much of the early educational struggle is the concept of

---

[3]A. O. Hansen, _Liberalism and American Education In The Eighteenth Century_. A restatement of much of the liberal sentiment of the French _philosophes_ is in the periodical literature of the period. See _e.g._, _American Journal of Education_, Vol. I (January 1826), _et ff_.

[4]Benjamin Franklin, _Proposals Relating to the Education of Youth in Pennsylvania_, pp. 7-8.

[5]See Thomas Woody, _Educational Views of Benjamin Franklin_.

[6]Charles F. Arrowood, _Thomas Jefferson and Education in a Republic_.

Federal versus State education. Both the Land Ordinance of 1785 and the Northwest Ordinance of 1787 early affirmed Federal interests; conversely, as late as 1800, only seven state constitutions mentioned education. Although a number of state plans for the administration of education were adopted,[8] the problem of support of state systems was a major one. The colonial pauper school idea proved to be tenacious, and progress in building a free universal school system in the old and new states was slow, with all the issues of class and sectional conflict.

The issues of sectional and class prejudice are reflected in much of the educational thought and practice of the early national period. In Massachusetts, a law of 1827 made the district school mandatory, but many of the districts were too poor to support schools and in the weakening of the abortive attempt to establish public schools, many parents sent their children to private schools; in New York the schools were free only to the very poor; the Pennsylvania Constitution of 1790 required the legislature to provide such facilities "that the poor may be taught gratis;" both in New Jersey and Delaware, pauper-schools were largely adopted; in the South public school laws were largely abortive attempts; and in the Western states the desire to democratize education and remove the marks of Eastern social stratification from the school in the interest of democratic citizenship remained strong.[9]

Between the Revolution and 1830, educational provisions for the common

---

[8] Plans were adopted in New York (1784); Connecticut (1810); Virginia (1815) and in Michigan (1817-1837). See R. Freeman Butts and Lawrence A. Cremin, _A History of Education in American Culture_, pp. 241, _ff_. See also Newton Edwards and Herman G. Richey, _The School in the American Social Order_, pp. 217, _ff_.

[9] See generally R. Freeman Butts and Lawrence A. Cremin, _op. cit._ For many of the early statutes and practices, see E. W. Knight and C.L. Hall, _Readings in American Educational History_.

people were no better than they were in colonial times. The apprenticeship system had declined.[10] Free education was largely limited to paupers. Private and church schools were in the main the only ones available, and the impetus to provide education was furnished by a humanitarian and a social reform motive. Infant schools, monitorial schools, and secular Sunday schools were organized to meet burgeoning needs. The monitorial system introduced by Joseph Lancaster in 1818 was widely adopted,[11] and remained popular because it reduced the costs of education. Some experimentation occurred with the manual-labor schools, popularized by Fellenberg, a disciple of Pestalozzi; but among the most significant efforts were those of the philanthropic "free" or "public" school societies which were organized in many of the larger cities.[12]

---

[10]P. H. Douglas, American Apprenticeship and Industrial Education, p. 54.

[11]The Free School Society of New York used the Lancasterian monitorial system from 1806 until 1853. The Lancasterian, or Monitorial, system of instruction was one in which the master taught directly several of the older children and these, in turn, taught the others. See John F. Reigart, The Lancasterian System of Instruction in the Schools of New York City.

[12]See particularly, William O. Bourne, History of the Public School Society of the City of New York. The educational situation in Pennsylvania at this time was essentially what follows. The Pennsylvania Constitution of 1790 provided for the establishment of pauper schools at the convenience of the legislature. In 1802, the first pauper school act was passed which provided tuition for children to attend a private school if the parents declared themselves as paupers. Subsequent pauper school acts were passed in 1804 and 1809. In 1824, an optional free-school act had been passed but was replaced in 1826; the pauper school act of 1809 continued in force. In Philadelphia, in 1818, due largely to the efforts of "The Society for the Promotion of a Rational System of Education," a system of city schools based upon the Lancasterian system was organized for the children of the poor. Joseph Lancaster was employed as Principal of the Model School. Another prominent society at work in Philadelphia was "the Philadelphia Society for the Establishment and Support of Charity Schools." See generally James P. Wickersham, A History of Education in Pennsylvania. The best contemporary treatment of poverty and of the pauperism which was characteristic of American cities is by Joseph Tuckerman, On the Elevation of the Poor.

II

In essence, the patterns of American education that evolved throughout the colonial period and that of the early Republic reflected largely the inherited European educational aims and practices which--not unlike other institutional and cultural patterns--had been reproduced or modified in varying forms to meet the needs and conditions of the individual New World colonies. The apprenticeship system was one such educational system which had been transplanted to the New World. The colonists retained the characteristic old world economic, class, humanitarian, and religious motives but ". . . broadened [its scope] to such an extent that it became a new and peculiarly American institution."[13] Traditionally, the English apprenticeship system had been established by guilds to control the quantity and quality of goods and services, affording the master craftsman comparative economic security.[14] In its early practice it had become the prime education for middle class youth.[15] However, with the passage of the English Act of 1562, apprenticeship became a national system and in 1601, the Poor-Law was passed which allowed church wardens and overseers to "bind out" all poor children which did not necessarily mean to learn a trade or be educated, but rather to be maintained through an indenture.[16]

---

[13]Robert F. Seybolt, Apprenticeship and Apprenticeship Education in Colonial New York, p. 107.

[14]Jonathan F. Scott, Historical Essays on Apprenticeship and Vocational Education, pp. 50-58.

[15]Charles A. Bennett, History of Manual and Industrial Education Up To 1870, p. 21.

[16]Robert F. Seybolt, op. cit., pp. 20-21.

In the American colonies, however, apprenticeship was a town and colony directed system, with no gilds or craft organizations.[17] Like their English forbears, they, too, used laws to regulate apprenticeship. But there was no precedent for the use to which they applied their apprenticeship laws: to provide the basis for a compulsory education which is best exemplified by the famous Massachusetts Act of 1642.[18] Although the early laws concerning apprenticeship generally found in the colonies were contained in Poor-Laws, the legislative provisions for the kind of education to be given were applied to voluntary apprentices as well as to poor apprentices.[19] In this sense, colonial apprenticeship became the major source for an elementary education as well as the principal form of trade instruction. In the early life of America when hand production formed the basis for the industrial system and the level of technology was low, apprenticeship met the basic needs.

Notwithstanding this, however, certain inherent defects of the apprenticeship system brought about a decline in its use long before the industrial revolution. In itself, the period of apprenticeship was too long and in many cases involved more "chore" work for the apprentice rather than experience at the trade.[20] In its diminishing practice, the "father and son" relationship

---

[17]See in this connection, Charles A. Bennett, op. cit., p. 268, particularly his provocative statement: "In its [America's apprenticeship system] development it had the advantage of being directly under the town and colony authorities, for there were no gilds or craft organizations as such in the colonies."

[18]Robert F. Seybolt, op. cit., pp. 36-51.

[19]American apprenticeship largely assumed two types: voluntary apprenticeship where the apprentice made a voluntary agreement to being apprenticed, usually motivated by the youth's desire to learn a trade; and compulsory or forced apprenticeship which as a rule involved poor children who were bound out by town authorities for the providing of their maintenance. Compulsory apprenticeship was also used as a punishment for debt and a penalty for idleness. See in this connection, Robert F. Seybolt, Ibid., pp. 22, 32; and Paul Douglas, op. cit., pp. 42-44.

[20]Paul Douglas, op. cit., pp. 50-51.

was lost when the traditional educational institutions in order to reduce the antiquated obligations that in themselves tended to bring about the decline of the entire system.[21] Even further, with the advent of the factory system in America in the early nineteenth century, the small craftsman shop became a factory based upon specialized skills, creating a greater demand for labor than could be met by apprenticeship which in its last vestiges was misused by many employers in an exploitation of labor.[22]

With the decline of apprenticeship many substitutes evolved in American society. A primary causal factor for not only the decline of apprenticeship but the advent of new forms was the introduction of the factory system which created new social patterns and technologies. The factory system particularly influenced those educational institutions which had taken shape by 1800 and continued to develop in the early decades of the nineteenth century.[23] Two educational forms that singularly illustrated this shift are the mechanics institute and the lyceum. Both were attempts as part of an overall effort made by the common people to obtain more "useful education" in order to

---

[21]Bernard Bailyn, Education in the Forming of American Society, pp. 30-31.

[22]See in this connection, Mechanics Free Press, [Philadelphia] November 29, 1828, quoted in John R. Commons, et al., A Documentary History of American Industrial Society, Vol. V, pp. 70-72, particularly, "The practice of many master mechanics in this city, in employing none but apprentices in their manufacturing establishments, is an evil severely felt by the journeymen of all denominations; for whenever this is a greater number of mechanics than the demand of labor requires, it is evident the surplus must be thrown out of employ. There are men of this city who have from 15 to 20 apprentices, who never or seldom have a journeyman in their shops; but to supply the place of journeymen, and to monopolize to themselves trade and wealth, as one apprentice becomes free, another is taken to fill up the ranks." (p. 70)

[23]Charles A. Bennett, op. cit., pp. 270-329. See also in this connection, William P. Sears, Roots of Vocational Education, pp. 138-151; and Paul H. Brooks, The Effects of the Industrial Revolution on Industrial Education in America Between 1775-1875 (unpublished M.A. thesis, Kansas State Teachers College, 1955).

elevate their social and economic status.[24] The earliest institute was organized in New York City in 1820 by the General Society of Mechanics and Tradesmen which had been formed in 1785 to provide ". . . mutual aid, assistance in case of sickness or distress, and care for the widows and orphans of those who should die without property."[25]

In 1820, the society opened a library for apprentices and a mechanics' school which provided an elementary education for the children of indigent members. Equally important was the founding of the Franklin Institute of Philadelphia in 1824. In order to provide its members with a knowledge of mechanical science, it provided lectures, models and an elementary school for the children of its members.[26] Many institutes were founded, all with a view ". . . to meet the breakdown of the apprenticeship system."[27] While the institutes were found in the cities, the lyceums were organized in small towns and the country to provide meetings and lectures covering a host of social, vocational and scientific subjects. The movement was stimulated by Josiah Holbrook in 1826 following the publication of his plan of popular education, American Lyceum of Science and the Arts, but the lyceum is noted in existence as early as 1797.[28]

---

[24]Charles A. Bennett, _op_. _cit_., p. 328.

[25]_One Hundred and Twenty-Fifth Annual Report of the General Society of The General Society of Mechanics and Tradesmen of New York City_, _1911_, quoted in Charles A. Bennett, _op_. _cit_., p. 317.

[26]Charles A. Bennett, _op_. _cit_., pp. 318-319.

[27]John S. Brubacher, _A History of the Problems of Education_, p. 270.

[28]"The name 'lyceum' was used to designate a society that applied to the trustees of the University of Pennsylvania, in 1797, for permission to use a room in the college for its meetings." See in this connection, James Mulhern, _A History of Secondary Education in Pennsylvania_, p. 472, who refers to _Minutes of the Trustees of the University of Pennsylvania_, Vol. V, p. 56.

While the institute and the lyceum reflected the "nonschool"[29] or "informal"[30] attempts to extend useful knowledge, there were, at the same time, continued arguments to broaden (as well as to extend) the common school and "secondary school" curricula to provide a more practical and functional offering. An education with a practical value derived support from educational reformers in that it would help meet the problem of providing an ". . . education for ordinary everyday living, [as well as] . . . for moral adequacy, and . . . for the intelligent and responsible exercise of citizenship."[31] The contemporary literature indicates how the economic value of this type of education provided a "cash value" rallying cry for the labor parties of the 1820's and how educators who were also attempting to popularize education were quick to capitalize on this point.[32]

Apart from its economic dimension, educators generally saw an educational value in this practical design for both a common school and a "secondary" curriculum but based their value on a multiplicity of forms. For some, this value became ". . . more of a learning--from--books--about--more--useful--things, [providing] . . . a *more practical* education [italics in the original] . . . ."[33] For others it was based on the idea that manual activity

---

[29]See R. Freeman Butts and Lawrence A. Cremin, *op. cit.*, p. 240.

[30]See John S. Brubacher, *op. cit.*, p. 357.

[31]See in this connection Lawrence A. Cremin, *op. cit.*, p. 63.

[32]R. Freeman Butts and Lawrence A. Cremin, *op. cit.*, p. 214; also Lawrence A. Cremin, *op. cit.*, pp. 62-66. Much of the literature of the period is generously sampled in Frank T. Carlton, *Economic Influences Upon Educational Progress in the United States* and Philip R. V. Curoe, *Educational Attitudes and Policies of Organized Labor in the United States*.

[33]R. Freeman Butts and Lawrence A. Cremin, *op. cit.*, pp. 221-222.

was a means of mental training,[34] while still others believed that the addition of practical subjects would ". . . make education more directly useful."[35]

The genesis of Girard College is particularly understood against not only a background of the development of a practical education but especially in terms of the development of a tripartite framework: (1) industrial schools for poor or orphaned children; (2) the manual labor movement; (3) private-venture schools and academies. Each of these forms was concerned with a practical education which becomes clarified in terms of a social determinism to which (albeit with a lesser or greater degree of recognition) they were responding.

Early nineteenth century America had sustained the interest in human welfare that had been stimulated by earlier intellectual movements and continued (in keeping with old world practice and the new world humanitarian _animus_) to support schools for orphans and paupers. Although education as a public function and expense had already been somewhat accepted, many of the schools that were founded during this period for underprivileged children were due to philanthropic efforts.

The earliest school for orphans or poor children in America was endowed by Dr. John de la Howe in 1797 for an agricultural or farm school in Abbeyville, South Carolina, which was to be modelled after a plan proposed in the _Columbian Magazine_ for the month of April, 1787. Aside from the usual academic subjects, the children were to be taught all the subjects that would

---

[34] Charles A. Bennett, _op. cit._, pp. 72-127. See also Lewis E. Anderson, _History of Manual and Industrial School Education_, pp. 135-154.

[35] R. Freeman Butts and Lawrence A. Cremin, _op. cit._, p. 214.

make them superior farmers (or farmers' wives).[36] Another pioneer school was the Farm and Trades School which was established in 1814 by private philanthrophy for the orphans of Boston providing instruction and opportunities for manual work.[37]

Traditionally, in the founding of schools for the children of the poor, it had not been uncommon to provide a practical education which in many instances also provided a means of self-support to relieve the burden of maintaining the schools. Whether in attempting to provide individual economic sufficiency or institutional support, it is in these schools that are found some of the earliest institutions to afford systematic training in agricultural or industrial occupations.[38]

The first real industrial school for the poor had been conducted by Pestalozzi at Neuhoff from 1775 to 1780.[39] He provided practical pursuits in order that these poor children might become economically independent as well as providing ". . . a commensurate cultivation of the head and the heart."[40] While the experiment at Neuhoff had been a financial failure, it successfully demonstrated the possibility of "regenerating" the children through education.[41]

---

[36]Charles A. Bennett, op. cit., pp. 93-95.

[37]Ibid., p. 242.

[38]Lewis F. Anderson, op. cit., pp. 76-77.

[39]William P. Sears, op. cit., p. 85.

[40]Lewis F. Anderson, Pestalozzi, p. 102. For a general consideration of Pestalozzi's theory of vocational education, see Debendra Chandra Dasgupta, "The Place of Vocational Education in Modern Educational Theory from the Sixteenth to the Twentieth Century." (unpublished Ed.D. dissertation, University of California, 1932).

[41]Charles A. Bennett, op. cit., p. 112.

Closely related to Pestalozzi's attempts was Fellenberg's academy at Hofwyl in 1817 which was characterized by its emphasis on manual labor. The organizational and administrative success of Fellenberg provided an impetus for agricultural, industrial reform, and manual labor schools.[42] In America, the manual labor movement had begun during the years 1825-1830, reached its height about 1834 and had subsided by 1840. For American advocates, manual labor was a means of preserving the health of students and a means of defraying the expenses of schooling.[43]

The private-venture school had been borne out of the need for a different secondary education that was being offered by the Latin Grammar School.[44] It was an attempt to meet the theoretical, technical instruction demanded in occupations other than for farmers, artisans, and handicraftsmen, which could be learned through apprenticeship.[45] Unlike town schools, the private-venture schools were free to originate and practice ideas which were in anticipation of the vocational needs of a developing colonial economic life.[46] While meeting a transitional need, many of the private schools became an academy, English school or English Grammar School to widen their general offerings.[47] Of these, the academy was to receive greater prominence in that it attempted to combine the value and content of the Latin schools and the English schools into one institution, providing a compromise between a practical education and a traditional one.[48] However, the practical education provided was large-

---

[42] Ibid., p. 128.

[43] Ibid., pp. 182-183.

[44] Robert F. Seybolt, Source Studies in American Colonial Education: The Private School, p. 53.

[45] Ibid., p. 35.

[46] Ibid., pp. 100-101.

[47] Ibid., p. 53.

[48] Theodore R. Sizer, The Age of the Academies, p. 19.

ly an intellectual one: rather than training for practical skills (which was only found occasionally), the education provided was in the main, a "book learning" one.[49]

III

> And whereas I have been for a long time impressed with the importance of educating the poor, and of placing them by the early cultivation of their minds, and the development of their moral principles, above the many temptations, to which, through poverty and ignorance; they are exposed; and I am particularly desirous to provide for such a number of poor male white orphan children, as can be trained in one institution, a better education as well as a more comfortable maintenance than they usually receive from the application of the public funds. . . . (Stephen Girard's Will)[50]

Stephen Girard (1750-1831), mariner, merchant, financier, philanthropist, was born near the city of Bordeaux, France. Of his childhood, relatively little is known except that Etienne or Stephen was the second child and eldest son of a family of ten; received a meagre education for which he paid a part from his own earnings at sea; and had begun his seafaring life at the age of fourteen as a cabin boy. By the age of twenty-six, Stephen Girard had left the sea. In twelve years he had taken his captain's license; sailed in a dual role of mariner and merchant; and, due to a fortuitous storm, had entered Delaware Bay and anchored in Philadelphia.

In Philadelphia, he was no longer a mariner; he turned to mercantile interests. His characteristic business foresight prevailed on him to engage only in the buying and selling of goods during the British blockade of the port in 1776 and 1777. Philadelphia had become his home and in 1777 he was

---

[49] Ibid., pp. 31-32.

[50] Article XX. The text of Stephen Girard's will is most conveniently found in Henry W. Arey, The Girard College and Its Founder, pp. 57-85. The investigator has examined the holograph will which is deposited in the Girard Archives at the college. All quotations are from the holograph instrument. See Appendix A, pp. for excerpts from the will.

married to a Philadelphia girl, Mary Lum. The year following he took the oath of allegience and fidelity to Pennsylvania. The war being over, he set himself to promote shipping between his home and the markets of the West Indies.

Girard was pertinacious in overcoming obstacles and achieving success; he had not spent the first twenty-six years of his life idly. He knew the sea; he knew mercantile operations; and he knew men, especially those he would select as captains and supercargoes. While all his ventures were not profitable, the successful ones outweighed by far his losses. Success in his trade with the West Indies and instinctive business acumen brought him to expand his trade to Europe, later to South America, and Asia.

It is not known to what degree he was a rich man by the turn of the nineteenth century (one biographer suggests that he was worth over half a million dollars); his later involvement in banking is generally alluded to as the means by which he accumulated his vast fortune; however, by 1815, he was recognized along with John Jacob Astor as one of the two richest men in America. But his financial genius, particularly his participation in the Bank of the United States; his efforts in the financing of the War of 1812; and his ammassing of a great fortune were by no means the sole reason for his place in American history. In a sense, perhaps he was best known during his life (and remained revered posthumously) for his humanitarian services during the yellow fever epidemics of 1793, 1797, and 1798 that occurred in Philadelphia during which he had exposed himself fearlessly as a superintendent of the Bush Hill Lazaretto. Beyond his administrative duties he had even helped to perform the distressing and revolting duties necessary to the care of the sick, not discounting the financial aid he extended from his own fortune. Beyond even this, perhaps his own prophetic words shed light on what was to become his most famous patrimony: "My deeds must be my life.

When I am dead, my actions must speak for me."[51]

These deeds became crystallized in his will in which he left ample detail, carefully structured in its minute directions (as had been his custom of providing in all his business instructions), to set into being the complicated execution of what were to be his final but continuing benevolent acts. In his will, Girard had provided $30,000 to the Pennsylvania Hospital; $20,000 to the Pennsylvania Institution for the Deaf and Dumb; $10,000 to the Orphan Asylum of Philadelphia; $10,000 to the City of Philadelphia for the use of the schools based upon the Lancaster system; $10,000 to the City of Philadelphia to purchase fuel to be distributed ". . . amongst poor white housekeepers and roomkeepers, of good character, residing in the City of Philadelphia;" $10,000 to the Society for the Relief of the Poor and Distressed Masters of Ships, their widows and children; $20,000 to the trustees of the Masonic Loan for the use and benefit of the Grand Lodge in Pennsylvania; $6,000 to named trustees to be used for the erection of a school building in Passyunk Township; $500,000 as a fund for the development of the Water Street and Delaware Avenue area of Philadelphia; and $300,000 to the State of Pennsylvania for improving canal navigation; and modest gifts and

---

[51]A brief account of Girard's life is given only to establish a continuing focal point of reference, since this investigation is not primarily biographical in nature. Considerable biographical material is available. The best brief account is available in William E. Lingelbach's article in the Dictionary of American Biography. Other brief accounts are available in Meade Minnigerode, Certain Rich Men, pp. 3-30; and Theodore J. Grayson, Leaders and Periods of American Finance, pp. 115-127. The sketch of Girard written by the patrician historian James Parton, Famous Americans in Recent Times, pp. 223-257, is perhaps the most graphic especially since he derived much of his material from the "lips and from the papers" of Girard's legal advisor, William J. Duane. Another short sketch is also found in Henry W. Arey, The Girard College and Its Founder, pp. 5-31. For full length biographies see Stephen Simpson, Biography of Stephen Girard; Henry A. Ingram, The Life and Character of Stephen Girard; John B. McMaster, The Life and Times of Stephen Girard; Cheesman A. Herrick, Stephen Girard, Founder; Harry E. Wildes, Lonely Midas: The Story of Stephen Girard. For a general analysis of the major biographies see supra, pp. 11-13.

annuities for relatives, employees and friends.[52]

It is also out of this will that are found the immortal provisions through which the complex founding of Girard College takes form. Even in his life, Girard had carried on what might be termed a "practical philanthropy." Among the many anecdotes which his biographers recount, perhaps the following vignette by Herrick has relevancy:

> . . . he [Girard] came upon a poor carter whose horse dropped dead in the street and that a curious crowd of sympathizers were standing by expressing vain regrets. Sizing up the situation, Girard took out his purse, extracted a bill, and as he gave it to the man said to the company, "I am sorry five dollars' worth. How sorry are you?"[53]

For the educational needs of ". . . poor male white orphan children, . . ." Girard provided "two millions of dollars" which were to be used to erect

> . . . a permanent college with suitable out-buildings, sufficiently spacious for the residence and accommodation of at least three hundred scholars, and the requisite teachers and other persons necessary in such an institution, and in supplying . . . decent and suitable furniture, as well as books and all things needful to carry into effect my [his] general design.[54]

In the plans for the building of the college, Girard was most meticulous and exacting. "The said college shall be constructed with the most durable materials, and in the most permanent manner, avoiding needless ornament, and attending chiefly to strength, convenience, and neatness of the whole."[55] Girard then gave specific directions as to the length, breadth, and the height of the building. Even further, he provided directions for the vaulting of the interior; materials to be used; methods to be used in fastening; thick-

---

[52]Articles I through XXIII, *passim*. Holograph will.

[53]Cheesman A. Herrick, *Stephen Girard, Founder*, p. 119.

[54]Article XXI, para. 1. Holograph will.

[55]*Ibid.*, para. 2.

nesses of walls; heating and lighting the building; the size of rooms and doors; and for the general topography of the grounds immediate to the building.[56] "In minute particulars not here noticed [in the will], utility and good taste should determine."[57] The only directions provided for the erection of ". . . at least four out-buildings [were that they be] . . . in such positions as shall at once answer the purposes of the institution, and be consistent with the symmetry of the whole establishment. . . ."[58] He also directed that the entire college ". . . be enclosed with a solid wall, at least fourteen inches thick, and ten feet high, capped with marble and guarded with irons at the top so as to prevent persons from getting over."[59]

Having blocked out the design for his college, Girard proceeded to direct its regulation.

> When the College and appurtenances shall have been constructed and supplied with plain and suitable furniture and books, philosophical and experimental instruments and apparatus, and all other matters needful to carry my general design into execution; the income, issues, and profits of so much of the said sum of two millions of dollars as shall remain unexpended, shall be applied to maintain the college according to my directions.
>
> 1. The Institution shall be organized as soon as practicable. . . .
>
> 2. A competent number of instructors, teachers, assistants, and other necessary agents shall be selected; . . . but no person shall be employed, who shall not be of tried skill in his or her department, [and] of established moral character. . . .
>
> 3. As many poor white male orphans, between the age of six and ten years, as the said income shall be adequate to maintain, shall be introduced into the college as soon as possible. . . .
>
> 4. On the application for admission, an accurate statement should be taken in a book. . . .
>
> 5. No orphan should be admitted until the guardians [or those concerned] . . . shall have given power to the [administrators]. . . .

---

[56] Ibid., *passim*.

[57] *Ibid.*, *para*. 2.

[58] *Ibid*.

[59] *Ibid.*, *para*. 3.

6. . . . a preference shall be given--first, to orphans born in the city of Philadelphia; secondly, . . . any other part of Pennsylvania; third, . . . the city of New York; and lastly, the city of New Orleans. . . .

7. The orphans admitted into the College, shall be there fed with plain but wholesome food, clothed with plain but decent apparel, (no distinctive dress ever to be worn) and lodged in a plain but safe manner; Due regard shall be paid to their health, and to this end their persons and clothes shall be kept clean, and they shall have suitable and rational exercise and recreation; They shall be instructed in the various branches of a sound education, comprehending, reading, writing, grammar, arithmetic, geography, navigation, surveying, practical mathematics, astronomy; natural, chemical and experimental philosophy, the French and Spanish languages, (I do not forbid, but I do not recommend the Greek and Latin languages)--and such other learning and science as the capacities of the several scholars may merit or warrant: I would have them taught facts and things, rather than words or signs; and especially, I desire, that by every proper means a pure attachment to our Republican Institutions, and to the sacred rights of conscience, as guaranteed by our happy constitutions, shall be formed and fostered in the minds of the scholars.

8. [If] . . . any of the orphans . . . from malconduct, have become unfit companions for the rest,. . . they shall no longer remain therein.

9. Those scholars, who shall merit it, shall remain in the College until they shall respectively arrive at between fourteen and eighteen years of age; they shall then be bound out by the Mayor, Aldermen and citizens of Philadelphia, or under their direction, to suitable occupations, as those of agriculture, navigation, arts, mechanical trades, and manufactures, according to the capacities and acquirements of the scholars respectively, consulting, as far as prudence shall justify it, the inclinations of the several scholars, as to the occupations, art or trade, to be learned.[60]

While necessarily leaving many details to the Mayor, Aldermen, and citizens of Philadelphia, Stephen Girard prescribed further restrictions on his "primary object," the college. Of these, the following is perhaps the most famous.

---

[60] Ibid., passim.

> . . . I enjoin and require that no *ecclesiastic*, *missionary*, *or minister of any sect whatsoever shall ever hold or exercise any station or duty whatever in the said College*; *nor shall any such person ever be admitted for any purpose*, *or as a visitor*, *within the premises appropriated to the purposes of the said college*:--In making this restriction, I do not mean to cast any reflection upon any sect or person whatsoever; but as there is such a multitude of sects, and such a diversity of opinion amongst them, I desire to keep the tender minds of the orphans, who are to derive advantage from this bequest, free from the excitement which clashing doctrines and sectarian controversy are so apt to produce; my desire is, that all the instructors and teachers in the College, shall take pains to instill into the minds of the scholars, *the purest principles of morality*, so that, on their entrance into active life, they may *from inclination and habit*, evince *benevolence toward their fellow creatures*, and *a love of truth*, *sobriety*, *and industry*, adopting at the same time, such religious tenets as their *matured reason* may enable them to prefer.[61]

Stephen Girard left an estate of well over six million dollars. The continuing funds for the college were to be supplied from the final residuary funds which were to be placed in trust, with the income to be applied ". . . to the further improvement and maintenance of the aforesaid College. . . ."[62]

> But, if the said City shall knowingly and wilfully violate any of the conditions hereinbefore and hereinafter mentioned, then I give and bequeath the said remainder, and accumulations, to the Commonwealth of Pennsylvania, for the purpose of internal navigation; excepting, however, the rents, issues, and profits of my real estate in the city and county of Philadelphia, which shall forever be reserved and applied to maintain the aforesaid College, in the manner specified in the last paragraph of the XXIIst clause of this Will; And if the Commonwealth of Pennsylvania shall fail to apply this or the preceding bequest to the purposes before mentioned, or shall apply any part thereof to any other use, or shall, for the term of one year from the time of my decease, fail or omit to pass the laws hereinbefore specified for promoting the improvement of the City of Philadelphia, then I give, devise, and bequeath the said remainder and accumulations (the rents aforesaid always excepted and reserved for the College as aforesaid) to the United States of America, for the purpose of internal navigation, and no other.[63]

---

[61]*Ibid.*, para. 6. [Italics retained as found in the original]

[62]Article XXIV; para. 2; section 1. Holograph will.

[63]Ibid., para. 2. Direct quotation from the will has been made insofar as it affords historical perspective for the founding of the

It is obvious that the will prescribed strict and almost immediate compliance: While the "poor white male orphans" had become his primary heirs, the citizens of Philadelphia (not discounting the greater view) and the citizens of the United States had become his residuary legatees. Stephen Girard died on December 26, 1831. As early as January 7, 1832, the executors of the last will of Stephen Girard sent a letter to the Mayor of the City of Philadelphia, presenting a certified copy of the will and a rent roll of Girard's real estate.[64] This communication was then forwarded to the Presidents of the Select and Common councils. In council on January 9, on Mr. William J. Duane's motion, which was adopted by the councils, it was resolved that a committee consisting of five members of each council including the respective presidents be appointed to consider and report on ". . . what measures ought to be adopted in order that the Mayor, Aldermen and citizens of Philadelphia may promptly and faithfully execute the trusts created by the late Stephen Girard."[65]

The committee reported on January 12, and the Councils adopted the following resolution:

> . . . that the President and Clerks of Councils, he directed to transmit to the Speakers of the Senate and House of Representatives of this commonwealth [of Pennsylvania] certified copies of the will of Stephen Girard, together with a letter stating the existence of a committee upon this subject, and the intention of councils to make further communications as soon as they shall have an opinion upon the character of the Laws which may be necessary to ask for in order to carry the provisions of the will into effect.[66]

---

college. Necessarily, there is in the will considerable material which has little or no relevancy to this investigation.

[64] Hazard's Register of Pennsylvania, IX, No. 2 (January 14,1832), p. 27.

[65] Minutes of the Select Council October 15, 1832, to June 8, 1832, pp. 147-9. William J. Duane (1780-1865) had been a confidante and friend of Stephen Girard as well as his solicitor. Duane had drafted the final will and had also been nominated as an executor and actively engaged in the settlement of the estate.

[66] Ibid., pp. 152-153.

The next day, the Presidents of the Select and Common Councils addressed the Pennsylvania Legislature and requested the necessary authority to act in accordance with the will.[67] On January 14, a committee was appointed by the House of Representatives of the Commonwealth of Pennsylvania, "to confer with the constituted authority of the City of Philadelphia, as to what course may be necessary to enable the state to receive the benefit of the bequest made by the late Stephen Girard, Esq."[68]

The committee from the House of Representatives met with the City Council on January 26.[69] Subsequent meetings of this committee with the "Girard Fund" committee of the City of Philadelphia and the executors of the estate provided the basis for the initial legislation needed to carry out the provisions of the will.[70] On March 24, the legislature passed "an act to enable the Mayor, Aldermen and citizens of Philadelphia to carry into effect certain improvements and execute certain trusts."[71] A supplementary act was passed

---

[67]Cheesman A. Herrick, History of Girard College, p. 5. Herrick's institutional history is without any specific documentary reference to the sources which he used with the exception of general references to the annual reports of the presidents, directors, or trustees of the college. However, it is obvious that Herrick had available to him much archivistic material, the provenance of which he does not cite and much of which may no longer be extant.

[68]Hazard's Register of Pennsylvania, IX, No. 5 (February 4, 1832), p. 66. This committee was primarily concerned with the necessary legislation to enable the Commonwealth of Pennsylvania to receive the $300,000 bequeathed by Girard ". . . for the purpose of internal improvements by canal navigation . . ." (Article XXIII. Holograph will). The acts passed by the legislation providing the City of Philadelphia with power to carry out the provisions of the will necessarily provided the power to establish Girard College.

[69]Ibid., p. 69.

[70]See in this connection "Girard's Legacy," Hazard's Register of Pennsylvania, IX, No. 8 (February 25, 1832), pp. 127-128.

[71]Laws of the General Assembly of the State of Pennsylvania Passed at the Session 1831-1832 in the Fifty-Eighth Year of Independence, pp. 176-182.

on April 4, authorizing ". . . the election or appointment of such officers and agents as they may deem essential to the due execution of . . . the will. . . ."[72]

On the 19th of the same month, William J. Duane, as Chairman of the Committee on the Girard Fund, noted that since the Legislature of the Commonwealth had now provided the necessary powers, recommendations for the administrator and execution of the estate were now appropriate.[73] The recommendations of Duane and his committee provided the guidelines for the earliest plan for the management of the vast estate which was passed by the Councils on September 15, 1832. This Ordinance for the Management of Girard Trusts provided that the Select and Common Councils should elect a Board of Directors

---

[72] Ibid., p. 275.

[73] The report is to be found in Hazard's Register of Pennsylvania, IX, No. 17 (April 28, 1832), pp. 265-267. In the preface to the report, the committee noted that in order ". . . to digest a plan for the general management of the bequests of the late Stephen Girard, . . . it was especially necessary to consider the amount devised and bequeathed, the objects of the testator, and the means or agents for accomplishing these objects." (p. 265) Of the amount, the committee was still unable to determine an accurate estimate of the estate which they believed was probably near seven million dollars. Of the objects of the testator, they recounted the major intent of the provisions of the will. But in their review of the means or agents for carrying those objects into effect, they noted, perhaps even more perceptively than realized, how "practical" Girard had given his will the strength to withstand the future administrative difficulties that might arise, e.g.: "When we consider, the magnitude of the estate thus devised and bequeathed--the deep anxiety which the testator manifested for the strict execution of his designs--and his characteristic caution and prudence in his transactions through life, we cannot but regard, as very remarkable, his omission to designate specifically the agents, who should execute his designs, or the manner in which those agents should be created or continued. Without doubt, difficulties, in relation to any prescribed organization, presented themselves to a mind, which never contemplated any subject imperfectly, and rarely, if ever, failed to overcome obstacles; but, in relation to the duties to be performed, after his demise, instead of endeavoring to establish any particular plan, or to guard against abuses and perversions, he solemnly transferred all responsibility of that kind to the community which was to be so deeply concerned in the result: What compliment could be greater than this, to those with whom he had lived? What can be a stronger incentive than this, to future communities and their agents, faithfully to perform all that the testator desired?" (p. 265)

of the Girard Trusts who, while under the direction of the Councils, would be charged with the management of the estate and the execution of the trusts which were to be executed by the City of Philadelphia or its authority.[74]

But this plan was to be shortlived, for on December 13, it was noted in Council that a radical change in the Ordinance was necessary since investigation had shown that the plan provided for by the Ordinance was impractical. To remedy this, two further ordinances were presented for discussion.[75] As a result, "A Further Ordinance for the Management of the Girard Estates" was passed on January 10 of the following year which repealed major sections of the previous ordinance, and provided instead that the Mayor and four selected members of each of the City Councils would form a Board of Commissioners of the Girard Estates.[76] A second ordinance was passed on January 31. This was "An Ordinance for the Management of the Girard College" which provided for a Board of Trustees consisting of the Mayor of the City, the presidents of

---

[74]See in this connection, Hazard's Register of Pennsylvania, IX, No. 12 (September 22, 1832), pp. 190-192.

[75]See in this connection, Hazard's Register of Pennsylvania, IX, No. 25 (December 22, 1832), pp. 393-398. The major shortcoming of the Ordinance passed on September 15 as noted in this investigation was the great extent of power delegated to the Board of Directors. It was contended that "The Trusts created by the will of Stephen Girard are of incalculcable importance to this whole community. Involving interests of the highest and the most permanent value, they require for their management, the utmost prudence and foresight, and a constant reference to the presentation of those interests against every possible or probable contingency; according as that management, shall be judicious or the reverse, according as the generous intentions of the Testator shall be promoted or frustrated, must the splendid provisions of his will, prove a blessing or a curse to the city of Philadelphia. It is deeply important now, when those first steps are to be taken, which must in a greater or less degree influence the whole future progress, the constituted authorities of the city should place themselves under the guidance of such principles, and listen to the dictates of best experience." (p. 393). Important to this end, it was believed that the agents should be authorized to act only in an executive nature and that specific appropriations should only be assigned under the direction of the Councils.

[76]Ordinances of the Corporation of the City of Philadelphia Passed Between November 22, 1832 and September 22, 1836, pp. 475-479.

the councils, and fifteen members who were to be elected by the city councils.[77] A board was elected on February 11, and the members, in conformity with the ordinance governing their regulation, elected one of their own number to be president--Nicholas Biddle.[78]

Earlier on June 14, 1832, a Committee on the Building Plan for Girard College had been appointed and had proceeded to advertise for plans for the Girard College for Orphans, offering premiums as compensation.[79] On February 12, 1833, the first premium of $400 was awarded to Thomas U. Walter, Professor of Architecture in the Franklin Institute of Philadelphia.[80] On March 21, the City Councils passed "An Ordinance Relative to Building the Girard College for Orphans." The ordinance directed that a building committee composed of four members of each council should meet with eight members of the Board of Trustees along with an architect to determine the plan for the building of the college. It was further directed that the plans approved by the building committee were to be referred to the City Councils for final approval.[81] On March 28, Thomas U. Walter was elected the architect for the college.[82]

---

[77] Ibid., pp. 481-484.

[78] Hazard's Register of Pennsylvania, XI, No. 8 (February 23, 1833), p. 126.

[79] Hazard's Register of Pennsylvania, IX, No. 24 (June 16, 1832), pp. 393-399.

[80] Hazard's Register of Pennsylvania, XI, No. 8 (February 23, 1833), loc. cit.

[81] See in this connection, Ordinances of the Corporation of the City of Philadelphia Passed between November 22, 1832 and September 22, 1836, pp. 485-487.

[82] Hazard's Register of Pennsylvania, XI, No. 20 (May 18, 1833), p. 313.

On April 25, Nicholas Biddle, on behalf of the Joint Committee of the Select and Common Councils and the Trustees of the Girard College, submitted to the Select and Common Councils the report of a sub-committee on the plan of the buildings for the college, an estimate of the cost by the architect, and a resolution passed by the Board of Trustees of the college recommending that the plan be ratified by the councils. In the report on the plans for the buildings, it was noted that while the proposed building had been confined to the dimensions set by Girard, correct taste suggested that a portico be made in front of the building, and ". . . to a purpose at once useful and ornamental [to extend] . . . the columns of the portico around the flank of the building, so as to relieve the walls of a part of the pressure, so as to render the whole building perfectly secure."[83] The cost of the college with its out-buildings was estimated by the architect at $900,000, requiring six years for the completion of the construction.[84] The plan was approved by the Councils and the building committee was instructed to proceed with as little delay as possible.[85] Excavation began on June 3 and the cornerstone of the main building was laid on July 4, 1833.[86]

Very clear observations on the educational significance of the event were articulated by Nicholas Biddle who, in a major discourse, and particularly when, in speaking of the "branches of education" recommended by Girard, observed:

---

[83] Hazard's Register of Pennsylvania, XI, No. 25 (June 22, 1833), p. 390.

[84] Ibid., pp. 391-392.

[85] Ibid., p. 411.

[86] Hazard's Register of Pennsylvania, XII, No. 1 (July 6, 1833), p. 16.

> This excludes nothing--nay, it embraces everything necessary to form a well-educated man. How far this instruction is to be carried--whether, when the degrees of talent and disposition come to be analyzed, some are to be instructed up to the point of their appropriate capacity, while the more intelligent and more diligent are to be carried into the higher regions of science, are questions of future administrators, to be decided by experience. But it is manifest that all the means of education, thorough, perfect education, are to be provided; that every facility for the acquisition of knowledge should be at hand; nor is there any reason why the Girard College--liberally endowed beyond all example--should not be superior to any existing establishment, in the talents of its professors, or the abundance of its means of instruction; and with the blessing of God, so it shall be. There shall be collected within these walls all that the knowledge and research of men have accumulated to enlighten and improve the minds of youth. It will be the civil West Point of this county, where all the sciences which minister to men's happiness, and all the arts of peace, may be thoroughly and practically taught. Its success will naturally render it the model for other institutions--the center of all improvement in things taught, no less than in the art of teaching them--the nursery of instructors as well as pupils--thus not merely accomplishing the direct benefit of those to whom its instruction extends, but irradiating by its example the whole circumference of human knowledge.[87]

Concurrent with the early attempts to provide the plans for the buildings for the college in 1832, a premium of four hundred dollars was offered in the local newspapers for an acceptable system of education and government for the college that would conform to the provisions stated in the will.[88] Aside from the advertisement for such a plan, the Board of Trustees of the college invited Francis Lieber, a resident of Philadelphia at that time to submit one as well.[89] Lieber accepted the invitation and submitted his report

---

[87]Nicholas Biddle, Address. Together with an account of the Proceedings of Laying the Corner Stone of the Girard College for Orphans, pp. 17-18.

[88]Cheesman A. Herrick, History of Girard College, p. 6.

[89]Francis Lieber (1800-1872), the encyclopedist and political and social scientist, had already demonstrated his educational expertise at the New York educational convention held in 1830 at which the plans for the proposed University of the City of New York had been discussed. See in this connection, Frank Friedel, Francis Lieber: Nineteenth Century Liberal. See particularly

in December, 1833.[90]

Lieber's "Constitution and Plan of Education for Girard College For Orphans was divided into five parts: Part I set out extractions from the will which contained the directions and provisions for the college: Part II gave a list of constitutions, reports, histories, etc. for charitable institutions as well as for public, polytechnic and manual schools found chiefly in France and Germany; Part III contained his introductory report which formed the general principles for the proposed college; Part IV contained the constitution embodying 269 articles; and last, Part V provided a series of rules and regulations for the college.

Lieber saw Girard's bequest as one of historical importance. Girard had not simply wanted a pauper-school: "In short, he [Girard] demands a better than common, a sound, and, as circumstances may warrant, a superior education."[91] This education, Lieber believed, would provide an example for others to follow, raising the general standard of education.

> I am convinced that Girard College will offer some branches of education, superior to that which can now be obtained in any other institution in this country. . . . But children who have not been bereft of their parents, or who are possessed of property, will [also] profit by the college. . . . If you raise the standard of education for a certain class, and certain branches, by the system you will establish in the college, it will have the most salutary effect on the whole community at large.[92]

Friedel's observation that "The Directors [of the Girard Trusts] first commissioned Lieber in 1832, then decided upon a public competition for a $400 premium. When the Directors gave way to a board of Trustees, it withdrew the competition and renewed the offer to Lieber." (p. 105). See also Frank Friedel, "A Plan For Modern Education in Early Philadelphia," Pennsylvania History, XIV, No. 3 (July, 1947), pp. 175-184. Beyond Friedel, another important source of information on Lieber's life is Lewis Harley, Francis Lieber: His Life and Political Philosophy.

[90] See in this connection, Francis Lieber, Constitution and Plan of Education for Girard College for Orphans.

[91] Ibid., p. 43.

[92] Ibid., p. 47.

The school that would provide this best, in Lieber's view, was a polytechnic and teacher-training institution.

> . . . it is, if I understand the testament right, the distinct demand of Mr. Girard, to form a polytechnic school. The sciences which he enumerates as being desirable to be taught in the college, and the occupations which he mentions, as those for which the scholars should be proposed in the same, are such as essentially constitute and require a polytechnic school. . . .
>
> But the great diffusion of knowledge and the consequent demand for it--for they go always hand in hand, has created another kind of institutions [sic] in our time, which we do not possess, and which yet are allowed on all sides to be highly desirable for us--for us perhaps more so than for those countries in which they already exist: I mean seminaries for the education of teachers.[93]

Lieber believed that the education of the orphans should be moral and religious, practical and scientific, political, and physical. While Girard had excluded the entrance of ecclesiastics, missionaries, or ministers, Lieber did not believe that this also excluded the teaching of religion. Girard had desired that ". . . pains should be taken to instill into the minds of the scholars the <u>purest principles of morality</u>. . . ."[94] "But," Lieber queried, "who instils [<u>sic</u>] the purest principles of morality into the tender minds of youth without founding them on religious principles and without cultivating at the same time religion in their hearts?"[95] Lieber knew of none and felt that it would have been an absurdity to ascribe this to "practical" Girard. Rather, Lieber believed, that Girard had intended to eliminate those agitations that might be necessarily aroused by sectarian controversy.[96]

---

[93]<u>Ibid</u>., p. 55.

[94]See Article XXI. Holograph will.

[95]Francis Lieber, <u>op</u>. <u>cit</u>., p. 35.

[96]It is of interest to note on this point that Lieber felt that ". . . The framers of the Constitution of the University of the City of

Of course, in order to provide for a practical and scientific education, it would be necessary to provide all the courses that are necessary in preparation for a practical life or for further study, but in order to provide a better or superior education, it should include the specific branches of language (the art of expression); drawing, mathematics, history; natural sciences; natural history; foreign languages and their literature; statistics; geodesy; and technology in all its branches. In addition to this wide host of courses, Lieber would make full use of workshops, laboratories, and even recommend the erection of an astronomical observatory. In particular reference to the use of workshops he noted:

> Respecting mechanical education you will find that I recommend to erect some workshops. I understand that it was the intention of Mr. Girard to give directions to that purpose. However, this may be, I consider them of great importance in education, not in order to instruct in some special arts for their practice in after life; all that possibly can be learned in this respect in a college, may be learned much quicker, and more conveniently at a later period, when the scholar is bound out. But the reasons why I have always considered the cultivation of mechanical skill of importance are the following:
>
> 1. If properly selected and judiciously used, mechanical arts are conducive to health, afford a convenient recreation, and being a great amusement to the scholars, also, by the prohibition to practice them, an equally convenient punishment.
>
> 2. They give a general skill, an art to help ourselves, which to the latest period of life is of much use.
>
> 3. They give a general practical knowledge of the principles of mechanical arts, which on many occasions of our life whether we are engaged in the practical arts or not, is called for, and which always will form a ready nucleus for much valuable information, to which, without that knowledge we remain strangers.

New York had a similar exclusion of religious excietment in view, though indeed, they did not resort to similar means to obtain their object." (*Ibid.*, p. 39). The religious controversy in the founding of the University of the City of New York is delineated in Theodore F. Jones, *New York University, 1832-1932*, particularly pp. 3-21. (The University of the City of New York has become New York University.)

4. It is another means by which we place ourselves in contact with the world around us--an object. . . highly desirable in education.[97]

Girard had indicated that he desired that ". . . a pure attachment to our republican institution be formed and fostered in the minds of the scholars." Lieber readily concurred, suggesting that the scholars be instructed in the political character of man and given a clear insight into republican institutions through the operation of the college, incorporating the scholar's practical exercise of his political duties. Important to this would be the teaching of American and English history as well as the organization of governments as found in other nations. Lieber suggested that this training for citizenship was especially necessary in a free country if the country was to remain free.

Equally important would be the implementation of a physical education program through the use of gymnastic exercises and sports. An ardent follower of Frederick Lewis Jahn, the founder of modern gymnastics,[98] Lieber maintained that the physical education of the scholars should be promoted by cleanliness, wholesome diet, recreation in the open air, and the teaching and practice of gymnastics in a natural progression.

According to the plan for the organization of the college, the college was to be divided into three schools: a preparatory school for those between the ages of six and ten; a common school for those between the ages of ten to fourteen; and a high school for those between the ages of fourteen and eighteen. In the lower levels, Lieber suggested that it would be advisable to adopt the Lancasterian method in order to teach the first rudiments of learning in the shortest possible time. Beyond work that utilized the

---

[97]Francis Lieber, <u>op</u>. <u>cit</u>., p. 12.

[98]Frank Friedel, <u>Francis Lieber, Nineteenth Century Liberal</u>, p. 19.

monitorial system and was primarily concerned with rote learning or memorization, he believed that the maturing minds of the scholars should be trained in higher mental processes of ideas and theories, so necessarily so in a sound education.

Yet, before Lieber would have the Trustees decided upon a specific plan, he recommended sending ". . . a proper and well-prepared person to Europe, in order to inspect the most important polytechnic schools, and other establishments where a great number of orphans are educated. . . ."[99] The qualifications which Lieber deemed necessary for the person to be well-prepared included a knowledge of the language spoken in the country to be visited and a sound knowledge of education. A mission of this kind, Lieber believed, had a basis in similar studies made, such as by Cotter, Dupin, Cousin and Toqueville. Even further, this person could purchase books and instruments for the use of the college, meeting the needs of a library as mentioned in the will as well as necessary if the college should succeed.[100]

Lieber had described himself as the person for this mission as well as for the position of the president of the college. He had long desired to secure a foreign mission and has been encouraged by Nicholas Biddle,[101] who later suggested at a meeting of the Committee on Scholastic Education of the Board of Trustees in October 1834 that Lieber should be chosen and sent immediately to Europe on this mission. It is interesting that Lieber was not chosen. One of his biographers, Freidel, notes that a majority of the commitee considered the mission not within the provenance of the will[102] and in an

---

[99]Francis Lieber, _op_. _cit_., pp. 145-146.

[100]_Ibid_.

[101]See in this connection, Lewis Harley, _Francis Lieber: His Life and Political Philosophy_, pp. 61-62.

[102]Frank Freidel, _Francis Lieber, Nineteenth Century Liberal_, pp. 112-113.

earlier discussion of Lieber's plan suggests, perhaps, another reason:

> The plan, which so delighted intellectuals, made no impress upon the practical Philadelphia politicians who were to control the Girard legacy. Even when sponsored by native-born Americans, German educational ideas were slow to win acceptance among the nationalistic American public which saw a taint in anything introduced from abroad. Had Lieber been another Horace Mann, his task would have been difficult, laboring under a thick accent and a turgid, Germanic writing style, he found it impossible.[103]

Another plan for the college was presented in 1834 by Daniel McLure of Philadelphia. This same plan was republished in 1838 in an abbreviated form under the same title of _A System of Education for the Girard College For Orphans_ together with _A Brief Exposition of the Philosophic Principles Upon Which the System of Education for the Girard College For Orphans Is Founded_. This publication included replies from persons to whom initial copies of his _System of Education_ had been sent for reaction. While many letters were commendatory, there is little or no evidence of the influence of the report on the planning for the institution.[104]

A major influence of the Lieber report is evident in the action taken by the Committee on Scholastic Education of the Board of Trustees on June 1, 1836, in a report made to the Board suggesting that a competent person should be chosen as the presiding officer over the institution in order to prepare

---

[103] _Ibid._, p. 107.

[104] See in this connection, David McClure, _A System of Education For The Girard College For Orphans_. McLure proposed that the college be formed in four departments: an Infant Department for children of six to ten years of age who would spend the first two years in a French Infant class and the remaining two years in a Spanish Infant class; a Grammar Department for children of ten to fourteen years where they would be taught the Latin and Greek languages and the ordinary preparatory courses for a collegiate course; a Scientific Department for children of fifteen and sixteen years of age who would best succeed in a practical course rather than a collegiate one as indicated by their work in the Grammar Department, and a Collegiate Department for children of fourteen to eighteen years of age who had successfully passed the Grammar Department.

himself for the opening of the college which was believed to be the following year. This appointment, they believed, was necessary before the course of instruction for the college could be fixed. As necessary to the presiding officer's preparation, they suggested that he ". . . should enjoy the advantage of examining other similar institutions in foreign countries, so as to furnish the Board of Trustees the benefit of the latest improvements in the substance and the modes of public instruction."[105] Upon presentation of the committee's report, the Board of Trustees adopted the following resolution:

> Resolved, That the President of this Board be requested to apply to Councils to authorize this Board to appoint, at this time, a presiding officer of the Girard College for Orphans, at a salary of four thousand dollars per annum; and permission for said officer to visit Europe, for the purpose of examining the several institutions for education of the kind contemplated by the Will of Stephen Girard, making arrangements for procuring books and philosophical and experimental instruments and apparatus, and making report to this Board: the expense of his voyage to be defrayed out of the funds of the College.[106]

Soon after, John Sergeant, the counsel for the city and the Girard estate, notified Nicholas Biddle, President of the Board of Trustees, that having examined a copy of the resolution as passed, he was ". . . satisfied that the preparatory measure it proposes is within the authority given by the Will, and is in itself wise and expedient."[107] The propriety of the mission, Sergeant maintained, was sustained by an _a priori_ argument suggested by the

---

[105]"Report of Committee on Scholastic Education, June 1, 1836," _Reports of Committees, Resolutions, . . . , Relative to the Organization of the Girard College for Orphans, 1839_, pp. 3-4.

[106]_Reports of Committees, Resolutions, . . . , Relative to the Organization of the Girard College for Orphans_, 1839, p. 5.

[107]Letter from John Sergeant, Esq., to Nicholas Biddle, Esq., President of the Board of Trustees of the Girard College for Orphans. Philadelphia, July 12, 1836, in _Reports . . . Girard College for Orphans_, p. 5.

success of the West Point Academy which had been largely ascribed to the measure of sending the head of the school abroad to make inquiries thereby enabling him upon his return to devise and execute a successful plan.[108] On July 14, 1836, Nicholas Biddle notified the councils of the Board's request for sanction to carry out the proposed measure. The urgency of the matter was based on the tentative opening of the college within a year and the Board's belief that on the important choice of a presiding officer ". . . the character, and to a great degree, the ultimate fate of the Institution must depend; . . . [and] the Board believes that they have it now in their power to select a citizen eminently qualified for that station, and they are anxious to connect him with the Institution before other claims may call him elsewhere."[109] An ordinance pursuant to this was passed by councils on the same day.[110]

On July 19, 1836, Alexander Dallas Bache was elected President of Girard College.[111] Having been a member of the Board of Trustees for the college at

---

[108]Ibid., p. 6.

[109]Letter from Nicholas Biddle, Esq., to Select and Common Councils of Philadelphia. Philadelphia, July 14, 1836, in Reports . . . Girard College for Orphans, p. 7-9.

[110]See in this connection, "A Supplement to the Ordinance for the Management of the Girard College for Orphans," in Reports . . . Girard College for Orphans, p. 10. The ordinance was in essence the resolution adopted by the Board of Trustees, but did not fix the salary of the president, leaving it to the discretion of the Board.

[111]Merle M. Odgers, Alexander Dallas Bache, p. 34. Alexander Dallas Bache (1806-1867), educator and physicist, was the great grandson of Benjamin Franklin and the grandson of Alexander J. Dallas, Secretary of the Treasury under President Madison. Odger's work remains the standard biography of Bache. Among the many sketches available, George V. Fagan, "Alexander Dallas Bache," The Barnwell Bulletin, XVIII, No. 75 (April 1941) and Franklin Spencer Edmonds, History of the Central High School of Philadelphia, point up best Bache's educational accomplishments at the Central High School, with necessary reference to his presidency of Girard College.

that time, he resigned from his position on the Board to assume the post of presiding officer.[112] In terms of Lieber's qualifications for the person to make the European survey, one of Bache's biographers and a later president of the college, Merle M. Odgers, points out that "it would seem unlikely that the person was Bache."[113] Recall that the person described by Lieber should have been well-prepared in foreign languages and have a sound knowledge of education: Odgers suggests that since Bache had not been an accomplished linguist and had only eight years of experience in education as a university professor, he probably would have been considered unprepared for his new post by Lieber.[114] Rather, Odgers maintains: "It is understandable that the Board turned to one of its own number who had distinguished himself in education, in research, and in the local learned societies, and who had Bache's rich Philadelphia heritage. Nor was its choice unwise."[115]

On September 8, 1836, the City Councils appropriated $6,000 to pay the president's salary and his expenses to Europe.[116] On the 19th of the month, Bache received instructions from the Committee on Scholastic Education under the pen of the committee's chairman, Nicholas Biddle, Beyond reminding Bache of his appointment, Biddle outlined the scope of the mission broad. "Your object then is to visit all establishments in Europe similar to the Girard College: and as these are found principally, if not exclusively, in England, Scotland, Ireland, France, Belgium, Holland, Switzerland, Italy, Austria,

---

[112] See in this connection, _Journal of the Select Council Beginning October 16, 1835, Ending October 6, 1836_,. p. 193.

[113] Merle M. Odgers, _op. cit._, p. 30.

[114] _Ibid._, p. 30-33.

[115] _Ibid._, p. 33.

[116] _Journal of the Select Council Beginning Friday, October 16, 1835, Ending Thursday, October 6, 1836_, p. 275.

Prussia, and the rest of the State of Germany, these countries will form the limits of your tour."[117] While leaving the general points of information to Bache's discretion, Biddle enumerated those items that the board was especially desirous of knowing of the institutions to be visited:

1. Its history, general administration, and the nature and extent of its funds.

2. Its interior organization and government; the names, titles and duties of all the persons employed in it.

3. Who are admitted to it, and the forms and terms of admission, and where it is professedly for the education of orphans who are considered orphans.

4. The number and classification of the scholars, and their term of residence.

5. Their course of studies, in the minutest detail, from the commencement to the end of their residence in the institution, with the text-books and other works used.

6. As a part of that course, specially important to the Girard College, we should desire to know the regulations or the practice by which, among a large body of scholars, a portion, after continuing for some time in the institution, are permitted to begin their active career in life--while others, with greater aptitude or greater willingness to learn, are carried up to the higher branches of education. The nature and the mode of that discrimination would be highly interesting--as we would also be--

7. The precise extent to which moral and religious instruction is proposed to be given, and is actually given, and also by whom and in what form that instruction is conveyed.

8. The mechanical arts taught--the mode of teaching them--the models, tools, and implements of all kinds employed--and the manner in which the practice of these arts is mingled with the routine of studies.

9. The system of rewards and punishments in regard to studies or personal conduct.

10. The general police and discipline of the school.

11. The amusements--gymnastic exercises--games of all kinds, uniting instruction with agreeable relaxation--together with the number

---

[117] Letter from Nicholas Biddle, Esq., to Alexander Dallas Bache. Philadelphia, September 19, 1836, in Alexander D. Bache, _Report on Education in Europe to the Trustees of the Girard College for Orphans_, p. iv.

and extent of the vacations, pecuniary allowance, or personal indulgence to the scholars.

12. The diet and clothing of the scholars.

13. The regulations in regard to health, hours of study and rest, arrangement as to sleeping and eating, and the whole routine of each day's employment.

14. The expenses of the school, including salaries and all incidents, the average annual expense of each scholar.

15. The structure of the buildings, the arrangements of dormitories, rectories, play-grounds, and work-shops, illustrated drawings, where they can be procured.

16. As a proper foundation for similar statistical inquiries in this country, you will collect all the information you can in respect to the proportion of orphans to the rest of the community.[118]

While Biddle also indicated that the Board was anxious to open the college as soon as possible, no time limit was set for the mission; the importance of a good beginning for the college clearly meant that no date was fixed for Bache's return or for his report. To this beginning, Bache was further ordered to prepare from his "examination and reflection" of the institutions he would visit a plan for the government and instruction for the college.[119] The instructions of the board being clear, Bache sailed for Europe in late September, 1836, completing his tour and returning in October, 1838.[120]

The report that Bache submitted to the Board of Trustees may be considered one of the outstanding chapters in the Girard College experience. Its importance is not limited to that ascribed an archivistic educational document; beyond its merit as a pioneer study in comparative education, it is recognized as one of the reports on European education that helped to create general

---

[118]*Ibid.*, pp. iv-vi.

[119]*Ibid.*, p. vi.

[120]Alexander D. Bache, *Report on Education in Europe to the Trustees of The Girard College For Orphans*, p. 1.

interest in public education in America.[121] Bache's report in published form required an octavo volume of 666 pages. Beyond his introductory remarks, he devoted three chapters to a description of "Institutions for the Education of Orphans, or Other Destitute Children, the advantages of which are Sometimes Extended to Other Classes." To a description of "Institutions for Education in General," he devoted a major portion of the report. This section contained thirteen chapters describing infant, primary, and elementary schools; schools of the elementary class intended to prepare for some particular occupation in life; seminaries for the preparation of teachers of primary schools; secondary schools; and superior schools (a term Bache used to describe schools which prepared students for occupations requiring a special knowledge).

But even from such a wealth of material, Bache could not suggest a plan for the government and instruction of the college. Like Lieber, he realized that Girard ". . . intended no ordinary Orphan Asylum to be created."[122] Among the institutions he had visited, he had not found any institution which could serve as a prototype for the college. His concluding remarks to the report suggested a curriculum which would have to be drawn from many institutions to allow for the varying social and political differences as well as for the unique instructions of the testator, advising the Board that "The trustees of the college have appealed to the experience of Europe to furnish data necessarily wanting in a new country, and it remains for them to apply the experimental deductions thus obtained from the old world with the vigour

---

[121] See in this connection, Newton Edwards and Herman G. Richey, _The School in the American Social Order_, pp. 306-309; and Ellwood P. Cubberley, _Public Education in the United States_, pp. 354-366.

[122] Alexander D. Bache, _op. cit._, p. 2.

characteristic of the new."[123]

Whatever plans Bache might have realized for the college never reached fruition. Bache's return in 1838 and the publication of his report in mid-year 1839 came at a time of heightened anxiousness about the delay in the opening of the college. While the building of the college had begun with celerity, the six-year completion date set by the architect had been unattainable. Although the first report of the architect and the Building Committee on the state of the work had suggested meeting the early opening date,[124] the actual opening of the college was to take place nearly a decade beyond the projected date due to a multiplicity of factors.

Of the building of the college, a cause for delay might be attributed to the desire to provide a permanency and durability to a structure that was not a common one. The Building Committee, in order to provide this, had suggested ". . . that more than one story of the college should not be constructed in any one year. . ." in order to provide maximum strength to the arches.[125] This was not an uncommon building practice of the time and was followed. To this might also be added the later depreciation in value of some of the investments of the Girard legacy caused by the financial panic of 1837 which affected the reinvestment of funds, thereby limiting appropriations for building purposes.[126]

---

[123] _Ibid._, p. 606.

[124] See in this connection _Report of the Building Committee of the Girard College for Orphans to the Select and Common Councils of Philadelphia; Together With a Report to the Building Committee by Thomas U. Walter, Architect._ [_Report_ for 1833]

[125] _Report of the Building Committee of the Girard College for Orphans to the Select and Common Councils of Philadelphia; Together With a Report to the Building Committee by Thomas U. Walter, Architect._ [_Report_ for 1834], p. 3.

[126] Cheesman A. Herrick, _History of Girard College_, p. 18.

It is difficult to ascertain specifically what caused the delay, but a delay was evident. So much so that even while Bache had been in Europe on his mission, an attempt was made to provide an opening of the college before all the buildings had been completed. The reason for this was suggested by a committee of the Board of Trustees who reported:

> If it be practicable to open the College immediately, the benefits of instruction will be immediately imparted to many orphans, who may soon outgrow the limits prescribed by the Will; while, if the Institution cannot be soon organized, it will release the Board of Trustees and the Select and Common Councils from all responsibility for the apparent delay, and ascribe it to the true cause--an inherent difficulty in the Will of Mr. Girard.[127]

On April 26, 1838, a letter from Nicholas Biddle as President of the Board of Trustees, was presented in Councils requesting authority to begin instruction at the College in October, 1838.[128] But this authority was not provided; for on June 21, the Commissioners of the Girard Estate presented to the Councils an opinion of John Sergeant, the counsel for the estate[129] who believed that the problem impinged on one basic question: "The question, then, is--whether, according to the Will of Mr. Girard, orphans can be admitted and instructed before the College edifice is completed, so that they may be received and instructed within its walls?[130] On the basis of the particulars enumerated in the will which established a definite order for the organization of the college he held, ". . . my opinion is that the duties of the college

---

[127]"Report of Committee Appointed to Inquire and Report . . . " (

[128]See in this connection, letter from Nicholas Biddle to Select and Common Councils of the City of Philadelphia. Philadelphia, April 25, 1838, in Reports . . . Girard College for Orphans, p. 12.

[129]Journal of the Select Council Beginning October 13, 1837, Ending October 5, 1838, p. 108.

[130]Ibid., Appendix, p. 84.

cannot now be commenced."[131] The opinion that the opening of the college should be postponed until the buildings were completed and furnished was similarly held by Horace Binney, the prominent Philadelphia lawyer.[132]

Bache, however, saw some good in the delayed opening: it would afford time to make experiments. The plan for the college would necessarily be made of the best features of the institutions he had visited as well as some features that would be his own. For the plan to be practical, it would have to be tried and teachers would have to be trained to carry it out. When this had been accomplished, Bache felt that all the orphans who would apply could be admitted safely to the college; whereas without experimentation only a few could be admitted due to difficulties that would be encountered in an untried organization.[133]

The merit of such a plan was realized by the Board of Trustees. Relevant to this, Biddle proposed to the City Councils that a small model school be formed. The economy of the measure was based on the saving of the expense of experimenting on a large scale when the college would be completed, admitting a large group of orphans. Together with his own communication, Biddle forwarded the opinion of Horace Binney and John Sergeant, both of whom concurred favorably with such a plan.[134] A further endorsement was made by the

---

[131] Ibid., Appendix, p. 86.

[132] See in this connection, "Opinion of H. Binney, Esq., December 6, 1838," in Reports . . . Girard College for Orphans, p. 19-29.

[133] Letter from A. D. Bache to N. Biddle, Esq., Philadelphia, November 22, 1838, in Reports . . . Girard College for Orphans, pp. 34-39.

[134] See in this connection, letter from N. Biddle to the Select and Common Councils of the City of Philadelphia. Philadelphia, March 12, 1839; Letter from N. Biddle to Horace Binney, Esq. Philadelphia, January 28, 1839; Letter from Horace Binney, Esq. to N. Biddlê. Philadelphia, January 30, 1839; Letter from John Sergeant, Esq. to Horace Binney. Washington, February 4, 1839. All items are in Reports . . . Girard College for Orphans, pp. 40-55.

Commissioners of the Girard Estate and was submitted to Councils on April 11. In view of Binney's suggestion that the funds could be supplied from the ". . . residuary interest [of the estate] as is given to diminish the burden of taxation. . ."[135] of the City of Philadelphia, thereby not violating the will, the Commissioners offered a resolution that would appropriate six thousand dollars from the city treasury for the use of the Board of Trustees of the college to use in organizing and maintaining a preparatory school for one year.[136]

While this attempt to commence instruction in the college failed, in 1840 other attempts were made to provide for an experimental school. Not only did these attempts also fail but led to far-reaching ramifications. The year 1840 had been accompanied by sharpened criticism of the delay in the completion of the buildings of the college. Herrick notes that "The long delay in opening the college resulted in a growing public impatience and an increasing distrust of the councilmanic management of the Girard Trust."[137] On July 16,

---

[135]Letter from Horace Binney to N. Biddle, Esq. Philadelphia, January 30, 1839, in _Reports . . . Girard College for Orphans_, p. 54.

[136]See in this connection, "Appendix to the Journal of the Select Council," _Journal of the Select Council of the City of Philadelphia, Beginning October 12, 1838, Ending October 3, 1839_, pp. 54-59.

[137]Cheesman A. Herrick, _History of Girard College_, p. 18. See also in this connection, the editorials that appeared in the _Public Ledger_. Philadelphia, relevant to the growing restiveness of the public on this point. See particularly the editorial of February 7, 1840, which is representative of the tenor of the editorials which appeared, _e.g._, "We should be glad to know when those who have charge of this institution propose to take any active steps toward accomplishing the wishes of the founder, and the reasonable expectations of the public. Several years have already passed since the college edifice was commenced, and several more will probably pass before it is completed; and meantime, so far as we can perceive, nothing is likely to be done in furtherance of the great object--the education of orphans in whose behalf it was endowed. Efforts, it is true, have been made in the Councils to procure the passage of an ordinance appropriating a sufficient sum for a preparatory school but these have failed and the subject is again slumbering." Further editorials in the Public Ledger pursued the same attack,

it was noted by the councils that they had received a communication and had referred it to a special committee for a report.[138] On August 27, the committee made its report. The Board of Trustees had notified the councils of [First] ". . . a statement of their proceedings in fulfillment of what they conceived to be the purpose of their appointment; [Second], their views in relation to the future measures best calculated to give effect to the wishes of Mr. Girard, in the concern submitted to their charge; [and Third] reminded Councils of the fact that considerable sums are due on account of the expenses of the Board, the salaries of officers, and the purchase of books and apparatus."[139]

In order to prepare a scheme of "government and instruction" for the college, the Board noted that they had divided themselves into committees to collect material out of which a satisfactory plan for the college could be formed. Having no success in America in finding suitable materials which had been tried in practice, they thought it best to send a capable person on a mission to Europe to collect information on institutions of the proposed kind

---

e.g.: An Editorial of April 25, 1840, questioned the legitimacy of Bache's tour within the design of the will and called for an enlightenment of the public as to the amounts paid to architects, superintendents, teachers, etc., noting that other newspapers, the Inquirer and the Pennsylvanian, also called for information on the plans and purposes of the estate: an editorial of May 4, 1840, questioned whether the design of the testator had been met; and an editorial of May 6, 1840, listed allegations made by various groups which suggested that the building of the college had been unnecessarily protracted; money had been unwisely spent in experimentation and large salaries had been paid. The editorial demanded that a major question be answered: "When will the Girard School be ready for the reception of pupils?"

[138] Journal of the Common Council of the City of Philadelphia Beginning October 11, 1839, Ending October 8, 1840, p. 161.

[139] Communication from the Board of Trustees of the Girard College for Orphans to the Select and Common Councils of Philadelphia [Dated July 10, 1840]. Presented July 16, 1840, p. 3.

which were already in operation. Not wishing to be premature, the Board had waited until June, 1836, to send someone who on his return could assume the office of presidency of the college. This, they believed, was understood by Mr. Sergeant in his opinion allowing for the mission to take effect. Surprisingly so, they were not prepared for his subsequent decision, not allowing the board to open the college until all the buildings had been completed.

Not wishing to question the legal authority found in Sergeant and Binney, the Board had given up all expectation of being able to bring about the regular organization of the college. "But the President, on his return from abroad had brought with him such a fund of materials, and an amount of personal experience, which it was deemed of the utmost to secure for the benefit of the institution; as, if these should now be lost, the whole expense of the mission to Europe would have been incurred in vain."[140]

Bache, the Board noted, had suggested a preliminary school and to this both Binney and Sergeant gave full approval to the measure. The benefit of a small beginning was evident and the Board believed it would forestall a loss of time if an untried program would fail notwithstanding the large amounts of money that would be saved in such a useless expenditure. The funds for such a project could be applied from the general funds of the city, not even mentioning out of the Girard Trust itself. In conclusion, the Board hoped that they had not overstepped their authority vested in them by Councils, but felt that in all good conscience, they could not give an "Assent of silence" to any further postponement of the beginning of instruction at the College.[141]

The Special Committee report was particularly unfavorable to the idea of a preliminary school suggesting that it was an attempt merely to retain Bache as President. Even further, the committee contented that no plan for

---

[140] _Ibid._, p. 10.

[141] _Ibid._, pp. 3-20, _passim_.

organizing and conducting the school had been furnished by the Board, notwithstanding, any estimate of the sum needed to continue and advance the school which might be expected to last until the college was finally opened. The report attacked the idea of the experimental school on every conceivable ground: the experiment on a small scale would not be adequate to the objectives sought; the funds supplied would be in violation of the trust; boys in the experimental school would be over age by the time of the opening of the college and could not be admitted; no part of the college could be used until officially opened, thus necessitating using other facilities; and, if the city were to assume the financial burden of the school, it would add to its already existing debts.

Of the trustees, the committee felt that since the organization of the Board in February, 1833, no plan for a system of government and instruction for the Girard College had been submitted to councils, a duty which was considered first in the order of commitments. Beyond recounting the narrative supplied by the trustees of their own progress in attempting to supply a satisfactory system for the college, the committee felt displeasure in the idea that even after the Board had procured all the information that America and Europe could supply, they were not able to suggest a plan from their united "reflection and experience" and would need to obtain it in an experimental school, suggesting that much of the previous expenses had been in vain.

The committee also voiced disapproval of any attempt to complete the college in a short time since it would lessen the capital for the endowment of the college while the fund could be increased by interest, accumulations, if time were taken to complete the buildings. This was necessary since the original estimate of $900,000 had already been exceeded by $300,000 and it had been estimated that another $1,097,000 would be needed for the completion of the college with all its appurtenances. For the sake of economy, the committee recommended to dissolve the Board of Trustees and the office of the President of the College.[142]

Bache's letter of resignation to the Board of Trustees was received by the City Councils on October 8, 1840, together with the resignation of the Secretary of the Board.[143] Bache had been active for over a year in the reorganization of the Central High School of Philadelphia, with no apparent remuneration, and had now been asked by the Controllers of the Public Schools to enlarge his services. Accordingly, Bache requested permission from the Board to assume these duties until he might be needed for the proposed experimental school for the college or for the college itself.[144] However, on December 23, 1841, an ordinance was passed by Councils which repealed the Ordinance of January, 1833, and July, 1836, which had established the Board of Trustees and the office of president of the college respectively.[145]

Bache's loss to the college is assumed to have been the gain of the Central High School of Philadelphia. Odgers notes that Bache used the results of his report on education in Europe as the basis for his organization of the Central High School.[146] Herrick even further suggests that "While Bache did not work out in detail the educational scheme for the college, we may accept the plan which he did work out for the Central High School as an indication

---

[142] _Ibid._, pp. 200-242, _passim_.

[143] _Journal of the Common Council of the City of Philadelphia, Beginning October 18, 1839, Ending October 8, 1840_, p. 172.

[144] Appendix No. LXXIV, _Journal of the Common Council of Philadelphia, Beginning October 18, 1839, Ending October 8, 1840_, pp. 246-247.

[145] _Journal of the Common Council of Philadelphia, Beginning October 16, 1840, Ending October 7, 1841_, p. 100.

[146] Merle M. Odgers, _Alexander Dallas Bache_, p. 102.

of what he would have done, had he actually begun the work at the college.[147] As a result of his European tour, Bache had been influenced by the Prussian schools and believed that the Central High School should correspond to the "Gymnasia" and the "Real Schools" preparing students for either professional study or active business life. Like Lieber, he also believed that moral and physical education should be made a part of the functions of education.

Essentially, the curriculum provided by Bache for the Central High School followed three courses of study: A Principal Course of four years which prepared students for trade, commerce, and business as would be found in the "Real School" [realschule]; an Elementary Course for those students who could only afford two years of high school study; and a Classical Course which replaced the French and Spanish languages of the Principal Course with Greek and Latin and was designed as a preparatory course for college or university. The subjects embracing the Principal Course included Languages (English and modern or classical); geography and history; mathematics; mechanical and natural history; morals and evidences of Christianity; writing; and drawing.[148]

In passing, it should be noted that Bache had been placed upon the horns of a dilemma in the controversy between the city councils and the Board of Trustees. Herrick notes that Bache resigned out of self-respect.[149] Yet, even while Bache had been under attack in his role in the Girard College administration, he was praised for his work with the Central High School.[150]

---

[147] Cheesman A. Herrick, History of Girard College, pp. 136-137.

[148] Franklin S. Edmonds, History of the Central High School of Philadelphia, pp. 61-66.

[149] Cheesman A. Herrick, History of Girard College, p. 27.

[150] See in this connection, the editorial on the Central High School in the Public Ledger, Philadelphia, May 2, 1840, particularly, "We observe

And although Bache had officially severed his official connections with the college, he was held in high regard by the city councils and allowed continued use of a small frame building that had been erected in 1839 on the college grounds as a Magnetic Observatory.[151] Bache's loss to Girard College had been best expressed by Odgers in commemorative exercises held at the college on February 15, 1941:

> It is a pity, indeed that circumstances did not permit him [Bache] to leave his influence upon Girard College. If the civic authorities and more members of the early boards of control had had the cosmopolitan spirit and broad vision of a Bache, a spirit and vision that Girard himself would have applauded, Girard College would not have waited a half century to take its place among America's great schools and it would long have enjoyed a wide reputation commensurate with its size and resources and the importance of its work.[152]

Continued efforts to open the college reached climactic proportions in 1842. On October 28, 1841, a Joint Special Committee was appointed in councils ". . . to inquire into the practicability and expediency of opening the

---

that the Board of Controllers have recently adopted and ordered to be published a series of resolutions, expressive of their thanks to Mr. Bache, President of the Girard College, for his services in arranging and regulating the discipline of the High School. It gives us pleasure to notice this testimonial of approbation, as from all the information we can gather on the subject, Mr. Bache has fully earned the highest praise that can be bestowed upon him, by his zealous and well-directed efforts in this behalf; and his claims to consideration are not a little enhanced by the fact that his labors have been both voluntary and gratuitous."

[151]See in this connection, "Minutes of the Common Council, January 20, 1842," in Journal of the Common Council for 1841-1842, Beginning October 15, 1841, Ending September 29, 1842, pp. 65-66; Appendix No. XXII, p. 63. Beyond Bache's work at the Central High School and his subsequent superintendency of the Philadelphia city schools, Bache made observations at the college observatory until 1845. The importance of this work no doubt became a major factor in Bache being appointed as superintendent of the United Coast and Geodetic Survey in 1843.

[152]Merle M. Odgers, "Bache As An Education," Proceedings of the American Philosophical Society, Vol. 84, No. 2, (May, 1941), p. 170.

Girard College for orphans."[153] On February 17, 1842, the committee submitted its report which in substance did not consider it practicable to open the college in an unfinished state. While urging a rapid completion, the committee felt that a system of wise economy and retrenchment should be used in applying funds; that to sacrifice some of the residue funds for an overly hurried completion would impair the college fund since the securities which would have to be sold to achieve this would actually be sold at a sacrifice price (due to the occurring depression).[154] On March 24, the committee was discharged from further consideration of the subject.[155]

Concurrently, however, the councils of Philadelphia were notified by the House of Representatives of the Commonwealth of Pennsylvania that a Select Committee was being sent to Philadelphia to determine "whether the authorities of the City of Philadelphia have knowingly and wilfully violated any of the conditions of the will of Stephen Girard, late of the City of Philadelphia."[156] The Select Committee sat in Philadelphia from February 24 through March 3 receiving testimony from a host of witnesses. The cost of the building of the college was a major concern and testimony was pointed to that end. The committee heard testimony from architects, contractors and workers involved in the building of the college, attorneys-at-law (including William J. Duane), and a member of the city council.[157]

---

[153] _Journal of the Common Council, Council of Philadelphia, Beginning October 15, 1841, and Ending September 29, 1842_, p. 15.

[154] _Ibid._, p. 75. See also "Appendix to the Journal of the Common Council," No. XXIX, pp. 122-126.

[155] _Journal of the Select Council Beginning October 15, 1841 and Ending September 29, 1842_, p. 70.

[156] "Minutes of the Select Council for February 23, 1842," _Journal of the Select Council Beginning October 15, 1841, Ending September 29, 1842_, p. 60.

[157] See in this connection, "Testimony: Minutes and notes of the investigations into the Girard Trust, of the Committee appointed for that subject,

The report filed by the majority of the committee listed ". . . a series of abuses and wrongs, almost without parallel."[158] They offered the legislature two alternatives: if the legislature found that the will had been broken and violated and proceeded to have the estate reverted to the commonwealth, it would, in fact, be punishing the orphans in order to punish the Mayor, Aldermen, and citizens of Philadelphia; and, if the legislature found that there was evidence that funds had been squandered or misappropriated "not knowingly or wilfully," then there was recourse by law to deal out "even-handed justice."[159]

A minority report was also filed in opposition to the majority report. While concurring that there was evidence that the councils had erred in some of its judgments, ". . . no matter how gross may have been the violation of the will by the City Councils--by the terms of the will itself, if it were not violated wilfully and knowingly the State of Pennsylvania has no right to interfere, and the city of Philadelphia cannot be legally disturbed in the enjoyment of its trusteeship."[160] No evident action was ever taken by the legislature.

Beyond the year 1842, until the ultimate opening of the college in 1848, there were no further attempts to open the college before all the buildings were completed. As to the building of the college the work was subjected to

---

by the Legislature of Pennsylvania," Reports of the Majority and Minority of the Select Committee Relative to the Estate of Stephen Girard, Deceased, 1842, p. 19-47. Duane's testimony describes in detail the writing of the will and gives his assessment of the college buildings in view of what he believed to be Girard's taste. For the text of his testimony, see Appendix D, pp.

[158]"Majority Report," Reports . . . Estate of Stephen Girard, Deceased, p. 18.

[159]Ibid., pp. 16-17, passim.

[160]"Minority Report," Reports . . . Estate of Stephen Girard, Deceased, p. 51.

added delays. In the midst of the earlier controversy about the delay in opening, the architect had noted in his report for 1839 another reason for the slowness of the work: the difficulty in finding experienced stonecutters. To this end the architect had noted that advertisements had been placed in Boston, New York, and Baltimore, which provided only three additional workers.[161] Further delay was evident in 1840 which saw the beginning of reduced appropriations which reflected the policy of the councils to employ economic practices in order not to sacrifice the value of the stocks set apart for constructing the college. The reduced appropriations continued through 1844 when financial conditions allowed for the appropriations to be greatly increased. The increased appropriations continued until the final completion of the buildings in 1847.[162]

Confident that the buildings would be completed early in the year 1847, the City Councils passed a resolution on October 22, 1846, to direct the Commissioners of the Girard Estate ". . . to devise and report to councils a plan for opening the college in conformity with the will of the late Stephen Girard, as soon as possible after the completion of the buildings,

---

[161] Seventh Annual Report of the Building Committee of the Girard College For Orphans to the Select and Common Councils of Philadelphia, together with a Report to the Building Committee by Thomas U. Walter, Architect [Report for 1839], pp. 14-15.

[162] See in this connection, the Annual Reports of the Building Committee and the architect for the year 1840, et ff. See particularly, the Report for 1844 which indicated that the price of material and labor would be greatly reduced commencing with the year 1845. The reduction of expenses is evident when comparing estimates for construction in 1846 to those of 1839. Appended to the annual report of 1838 was the "Opinion of John Sergeant, Esq., on the Subject of Wall to Enclose the College Grounds." Sergeant had been asked by the Building Committee whether, in terms of the will, the entire site of the college had to be enclosed by a wall or whether it was sufficient to enclose only the portion upon which buildings were located. Sergeant was of the opinion that the entire estate was to be surrounded by a wall. The architect's estimate of the wall to enclose the whole forty-five acres was $125,000, to which was added $20,000 for the gates and lodges. In his report for 1845, the architect estimated that the expenses for the same were now estimated to cost only $66,000.

and the necessary arrangements of the premises."[163] And, on January 28, 1847, the Commissioners of the Girard Estate were authorized by the City Councils to make application to the Pennsylvania legislature for such acts that would enable the Mayor, Aldermen, and citizens of Philadelphia to carry out the intentions of Stephen Girard in connection to the organization of the College.[164]

On February 27th following, the Legislature of Pennsylvania passed "An Act Relative to the Girard College For Orphans." Under the provisions of the act the Guardians of the poor were empowered to indenture orphans to the Mayor, Aldermen, and citizens of Philadelphia, as trustees under the will of Stephen Girard; the indenture was not to express the terms of binding, but to expire before the age of eighteen years or at the pleasure of the trustees; there was to be relief in case of breach of duty; the Mayor, Aldermen, and citizens of Philadelphia were empowered to indenture orphans after leaving the college in suitable occupations, but the term of indenture was to close at or before the age of twenty-one years, and in the case the master of an apprentice should die, the said Corporation was to have the authority to bind such orphan again; the Corporation of the Mayor, Aldermen, and citizens of Philadelphia were to be the guardians of such orphan child and to take charge of the property of the orphan and to take care and account for the same; and and the Corporation was to have the power to cancel and annul indentures made.[165]

On the basis of the resolution made by the City Councils on October 22, 1846, the Commissioners of the Girard Estates referred the matter to a Com-

---

[163] _Journal of the Select Council of the City of Philadelphia, Beginning October 16, 1846, and Ending October 7, 1847_, p. 9.

[164] _Ibid._, pp. 45-46.

[165] See in this connection, "Appendix No. XVIII," _Ibid._, pp. 81-83.

mittee of three who reported on April 15, 1847. The report is interesting historically as showing a general plan in mind at that time, together with the breadth of view, particularly as what was then outlined became reality later on. Obviously, the first consideration was to determine ". . . by whom shall that organization be made and carried into effect?--By the City Councils directly, or by a board of Regents?"[166] The committee advocated that the college should not be governed directly by the City Councils for two major reasons: an educational institution should not be liable to frequent or sudden change and if under the control of the City Councils the college would be subject to all those causes which may temporarily change the character of city government; and that the history of public institutions had proven that when an interest or institution had been left to the care of officers who had been chosen primarily for other purposes, neglect, or mismanagement, was usually the rule.

While the councils were to be dissuaded from a direct control, the committee felt it necessary, however, to remind them of their moral and legal duty to carry out the wishes of Stephen Girard. That while others may be committed by the councils to execute their wishes, the councils should not forget that "They, and only they, are the Trustees."[167] If a regency idea was acceptable to the Councils, it was recommended that a medium-sized board of sixteen members representing appointments of both councils be instituted on a rotative basis allowing an appointment of two regents annually thereafter.

As to the plan of organization for the college, the committee pointed out the provision of the will limiting the age of admission between six and

---

[166] Report of a Special Committee to the Commissioners of the Girard Estate, on the Subject of Opening the Girard College For Orphans, April 15, 1847, p. 3.

[167] Ibid., p. 4.

ten which dictated that there could be no "college" as such for several years after the opening of the school. There would be no need for studies in the higher branches, nor professorships or expensive scientific apparatus. While these would ultimately be needed for the orphans, immediate attention would have to have been given to obtain primary teachers, nurses, slates, pencils, table-cards, and spelling books. Before the orphans would study in the higher branches, ". . . they must be washed and combed, and taught their letters and their multiplication table."[168] Under the terms of the will the extreme limits of attendance at the college embraced a period of twelve years, which could be conveniently divided into three portions of four years each designated as a Primary, an Intermediate, and a Collegiate department. The Primary department would contain studies of an elementary nature for students of six to ten years of age; the Intermediate department would contain studies of the common English branches for students from ten to fourteen years of age; and the Collegiate department would contain those courses that corresponded to an ordinary college course for students from fourteen to eighteen years of age. Since some students who enter the Primary department would never advance further due to "vicious habits or helpless dulness [*sic*]" and that all students would not remain until eighteen years of age, it was estimated that the number of pupils in the Primary department would always be greater than the number in the Intermediate, and that the Intermediate would always be greater than in the Collegiate department. On this basis the first school to organize would be the primary school.

On May 27, 1847, the City Councils passed "An Ordinance to Provide For the Organization and Management for the Girard College For Orphans."[169] This

---

[168] *Ibid.*, p. 7.

[169] *Journal of the Select Council of the City of Philadelphia, Beginning October 16, 1846, and Ending October 7, 1847*, pp. 102-107.

ordinance was essentially the bill that had been referred to Councils by the Commissioners of the Girard Estates who had been guided by the Special Committee mentioned previously. Minor changes had been made, in particular, the Councils had substituted the word "Directors" for "Regents." This ordinance was preeminently concerned with the election and function of the Board of Directors, providing guidelines for the extent of their jurisdiction. As part of their duties, it was ordered that a plan of a system of government and instruction be prepared and submitted to councils. If the plan were approved, it was further ordered that twenty days public notice of the intended opening date be given in order to make selections of instructors and other officers of the college.

On July 1, 1847, the Councils received a communication from Joseph R. Chandler, President of the Board of Directors of Girard College for Orphans, which contained a sketch of a plan for opening the college.[170] For the present needs, the board was of the opinion that only a Primary department would be required for the first year of the college. "This will be treading upon the safe and beaten path; and will afford sufficient time for the consideration of all those important and more expensive undertakings, that the plan of the liberal Founder contemplates. It must be recollected that the Girard College has no prototype."[171] To aid in preparation of the details of the

---

[170] _Journal of the Common Council of the City of Philadelphia, Beginning October 16, 1846, and Ending October 7, 1847_, p. 130.

[171] _Communication from the Board of Directors of the Girard College for Orphans to the Select and Common Councils_. June 29, 1847, p. 2. This document is generally unknown and no references to it have been found in the literature, but it is important not only as a set of basic principles for the opening of Girard College, it is equally an epitome of educational practice in the cities of mid-nineteenth century America, _e.g._, "It will be a school, in which shall be taught those branches of learning that receive attention in the Primary, Secondary, and Intermediate Schools, of what is familiarly known as the Public School system in the First District of Pennsylvania; and

college, the Board recommended the election of a President and a Matron. Beyond these principal officers, it was suggested that in accordance with the will that the furniture, books, and appropriate apparatus be provided and that a suitable number of instructors and agents be selected with their number and qualifications determined by the number and physical and mental condition of the pupils to be admitted.

Beyond this overarching summary, the Board devised a plan of three parts: Government, Instruction, and Maintenance. The administration and supervision of the school was to be vested in a chief executive officer styled as the President of the College who would be the governor as well as the father of the boys. In addition to the President it was recommended that a Matron should be in the Department of Government to assist the President in scholastic and parental relations. The Department of Instruction would be divided into three parts corresponding to the Primary, Principal, and Collegiate Departments.

> That of primary education, which would embrace spelling, reading, writing, the ground rules of arithmetic, and some elementary portions of grammar, geography, history, and physical science.
>
> The Principal Course, which would probably commence with pupils of eleven, and continue until they reached fifteen years of age; and

---

the instruction in which is given almost exclusively by female teachers. The complete success that has attended the labours of such teachers, both here and elsewhere, has induced the Board to adopt them for this department; and independently of the fitness of females to take charge of pupils of such tender age, their services can be commanded at more moderate salaries than those of men equally well qualified. . . . .
. . . .
While the President of the College shall give a general attention to the manners of the pupils; this branch of their education shall be specially cared for, by the Matron. By a prudent mingling among them, during their hours of study, and recreation, and at their meals, and by occasionally admitting them to her society as visitors; she may effect much by the influence of her example, and in case of need, by direct admonition or advice. The isolated, and conventional life of the pupils, without such advice and training, would lead to that unfitness for mingling with society, that is to be found too often in the graduates of our best Colleges." (pp. 1,9). For the full text of the report, see Appendix F, pp.

> embrace Grammar, Geography, History, Arithmetic, Drawing, the principal branches of Geometry, and Mathematics, and their applications to Surveying and Navigation; Original Composition, the French, German, Spanish, and Latin languages, and full courses of Lectures on the Physical sciences, and Technology, and an elementary course on Moral science. In this department ought also to be taught, in connection with History, the political Constitutions of the several principal nations of Europe, and very much at large the Constitution and Laws of the United States, and of the several states of the Union.
>
> The Collegiate Department, in which the studies of the principal department should be extended; the Greek, Latin and Hebrew Languages, and the higher departments of the Mathematical, Physical and Moral Sciences, be prosecuted; and, indeed, all the branches of study pursued in a University, ought to be within the reach of those pupils that may be qualified for such advanced instruction.[172]

On the basis of admitting one hundred pupils, it was believed that the instructional staff should commence with one principal female teacher and two female assistant teachers. In addition, four governesses would be required for hours of reflection, recreation, and sleep. In two years (1849) it would be necessary to enlarge the department to include a principal male teacher and one male and two female assistant teachers.

The maintenance of the College would be in the charge of a steward whose main function would be to supply plain and suitable food and overseer for the duties of the janitor, gardener, and domestics of the Institution. In connection with the maintenance of the institution it was further proposed that two physicians ought to attend its needs.

On the basis of this plan, the City Councils passed "An Ordinance to Provide for the Opening of the Girard College for Orphans" on September 16, 1847.[173] Essentially the plan submitted by the Board of Directors, it also directed that the Building Committee deliver possession of the college

---

[172] Ibid., p. 5.

[173] Journal of the Select Council of the City of Philadelphia for 1846-1847, Beginning October 16, 1846, and Ending October 7, 1847, pp. 138-142.

to the Board of Directors. On November 13, 1847, Mr. Isaac Elliot, the senior member of the Building Committee, delivered the keys of the College building to Joseph R. Chandler, President of the Board of Directors, in a formal ceremony held in the Main building at the college.[174]

The future of the Girard College for Orphans now seemed relatively assured: with a plysical plant after much argumentation agreed upon, and with a seemingly endless disagreement now closed, and with an endowment fund of an enormous proportion, but with a basic philosophy of instruction that had itself not fully formed, Girard College received its first students in January, 1848.

---

[174] "An Account of the Final Transfer of the College Buildings & Grounds to the Board of Directors," Final Reports of the Building Committee and the Architect of the Girard College for Orphans, . . ., 1848, pp. 83-92.

CHAPTER III

MID-CENTURY TO THE PHILADELPHIA CENTENNIAL

I

> Fellow citizens, we are about to enter upon the execution of a scheme of education, in some respect important. The foundation of it is a charity, munificent in its provisions, comprehensive and noble in its objects, and far-reaching in its results. Should it merely fail, we suffer the loss of a great good. Should it ever be perverted, we may incur great evils; but should it be made to accomplish the benevolent designs of the Founder of the College, we shall secure to many orphans, a better inheritance than riches.[1]

The Journal of the Select Council records the following: "The Board of Directors have . . . admitted (after due notice in the public papers) ninety-five poor male orphans, within the age of six and ten years; and on Saturday the first instant [January 1, 1848] the Board proceeded to open the College, with a few simple exercises appropriate to the character of the Institution so that the Girard College for Orphans may be not considered in a condition to fulfill in time, the philanthropic views of its Founder."[2]

From its very outset, a number of crosscurrents as to educational aims and objectives affected the early history of the college. While the college would be unique among educational institutions, it would, however, be neces-

---

[1] Joel Jones, "Address," Addresses Delivered on the Occasion of Opening the Girard College for Orphans, January 1, 1848, pp. 12-13.

[2] "Minutes of the Select Council for January 6, 1848," Journal of The Select Council of the City of Philadelphia for 1847-1848, Beginning October 15, 1847, and Ending September 28, 1848, p. 30, Appendix, p. 20. Notice of the opening of the college had appeared on December 1, 1847. The public was provided with an explanation of the college and an application for admission. The full text of the notice, explanation, and application for admission as found in the Public Ledger, [Philadelphia] December 1, 1847, are to be found in Appendix G, pp.

sarily confronted by the perennial problems of education. Traditionally, the problems facing educational institutions have arisen in the determination of the method of support; the type of control; the identity of the students; and the programs of the students whom it serves. For Girard College, the problem of support had been adequately provided for with the Mayor, Aldermen, and citizens of Philadelphia as trustees of the college. As for the students, Girard's will had stipulated a whole set of criteria which would have to be met if the children were to be eligible for entrance and the projected educational program: they were to be poor white male orphan children between the ages of six and ten years whom were to be fed, clothed, and lodged in plain manner; given suitable and rational exercise and recreation; to be instructed in the various branches of a sound education; taught facts and things, rather than words or signs; with those who merit it, to remain in the college until between fourteen and eighteen years of age, thereby to be bound out in suitable occupations. Underpining the intellectual and physical dimensions of the curriculum, Girard had further desired that a pure attachment to our Republican Institutions be formed and fostered in the minds of the scholars and that pains should be taken to instill into the minds of the scholars, the purest principles of morality.[3]

While Stephen Girard's will had provided the theoretic construct for a master plan for the college, its actual implementation had been left to those agents he had named for this program. In the planning for the institution and no less in the early years of the school's opening, there was continued evidence that while all efforts were made to carry out the design outlined in the will, there were honest contravening opinions as to the aims of the

---

[3]The criteria here have been extrapolated out of the will itself for which see Articles XX and XXI. Holograph will.

school. The pressing problem, with the opening of the college, was what the curriculum was to be, and this continued as a recurring problem, despite the extensiveness of the discussion which had preceded the formal opening.[4]

The college opened with a beginning class whose age group required only those subjects necessary to provide the ordinary branches of a common school education, evidently including instruction in the alphabet, spelling, reading, writing, arithmetic, geography, and grammar.[5] Within a week of its opening, Joseph R. Chandler, President of the Board of Directors, notified the City Councils that the President of the College, Joel Jones, was ". . . devising plans for extending the benefits of the Institution by appropriate modes of instruction."[6] What plans Jones had in mind were not realized since he left his office in June, 1849.[7]

---

[4]*Cf*. the discussion of the proposals of Lieber, pp. 50-55, and Bache, pp. 61-62. Lieber had recommended the establishment of a polytechnic and teacher-training institution. Bache, on the other hand, never submitted an actual plan, but if one agrees with Herrick (p. 71, *supra*) that Bache's plan for the Central High School was the crystallization of his views drawn from his report in Europe, Girard College would have embodied a Prussian Gymnasium and "Real School" curriculum.

[5]No actual record of the first courses have been available to the investigator; the subjects listed have been extrapolated from the *Second Annual Report of the Board of Directors of the Girard College for Orphans for the Year 1849*, p. 6.

[6]"Minutes of the Select Council for January 6, 1848," *loc. cit*.

[7]*Second Annual Report of the Board of Directors*, *op. cit*., p. 8. Cheesman A. Herrick, *History of Girard College*, p. 140, notes: "The fact that he was one of the founders of Lafayette College, indicated Judge Jones's interest in education. His educational ideals, however, appear not to have won the full support of the Board of Directors of Girard College. Perhaps these were not wholly practicable for the institution." A delineation of President Jones' ideals for the college are not to be found· only available are his observations of the chief characteristics of Girard's plan, e.g., "The most prominent, perhaps, of these, is its great comprehensiveness. It was the benevolent design of the Founder of this college, to sequester the poor orphan, at an early age, from the temptations and adverse influences incident to his condition, and at the close of his minority, to present him to society a virtuous, industrious,

The presidency remained vacant until January 1, 1850, when William H. Allen, a former Professor of Mental Philosophy and English literature at Dickinson College was installed as president.[8] By this time, 215 orphans had been admitted into the Primary department of the college and were divided into two schools, Primary 2 for incoming students and Primary 1 for students who had been promoted. The curriculum of the Primary 1 school continued instruction in both the elementary and the advanced branches provided during

---

well-educated man. It comprises the education of the family, of the school, of the college, of the ship, of the workshop and of the farm. It comprises also the training of the social and moral affections to the habits and practices of virtue--of the mind to the investigation of truth--of the hand, and of the physical powers of the body, to the exercises of the laborious and useful enjoyments of life. He did not propose, indeed, fully to attain all these objects within the walls of the College. Some of them must necessarily be pursued elsewhere; but the groundwork is to be laid here, and the course of discipline and instruction must be shaped with reference to the whole design. The peculiarity of this plan does not consist in the introduction of any new element into the education of youth for we see all these objects attained with eminent success, by well known and familiar means. We have only to open our eyes on the intelligent community in which we live, to have ample proof of the excellence of our educational systems. The peculiarity of the plan consists rather in the combination of all these objects under our arrangement, to be wrought out by one great system of means. Here, allow me to add, lies the chief difficulty to be apprehended in the way of the successful execution of the plan; it is the difficulty of properly constituting and maintaining, at all times, a large and complex agency, which shall not only be effective, but precisely suited to all the ends designed. Connected with this, is the further difficulty, already alluded to, of framing a proper system of economics and discipline to regulate the action of the whole." Joel Jones, "Address," _op. cit._, pp. 13-14. Soon after leaving the presidency of Girard College, Joel Jones (1795-1860) was elected the Mayor of Philadelphia. He served for one term. See in this connection, John H. Frederick's account of Jones in the _Dictionary of American Biography_.

[8] _Second Annual Report of the Board of Directors_, _op. cit._, p. 8. The report also notes that the presidency of the college had been offered to Frederick A. Packard, but that he had declined the appointment. Packard, a later director of the college, had in 1838 as the recording secretary and editor of publications of the American Sunday School Union, attacked Horace Mann for his refusal to introduce into Massachusetts' libraries certain books published by the Union. For an examination of the Packard Episode, see Raymond B. Culver, _Horace Mann and Religion in the Massachusetts Public Schools_, pp. 55-110. See particularly Culver's note that an anonymous reprint from the _Philadelphia Quarterly Observer_ entitled "Thoughts on the Condition and Prospects of Popular Education in the United States" has been attributed to Packard by the Yale Library (p. 71). Although undated, it is assumed to have been written before 1837 and represents an argument for public schools.

the first year along with the elements of History, English, composition, and Algebra.[9] By an ordinance of January 10, 1850, the Board of Directors had received permission from City Councils to admit an additional one hundred orphans during the year 1850 which would increase the total number to over three hundred orphans receiving instruction at the college. The Ordinance of January 10th also provided for the organization of the Principal Department of Instruction.[10] To this end, instructors had already been added in the

---

[9] Ibid., p. 3.

[10] Digest of the Acts of Assembly and Ordinances of Councils Relating to the Girard College for Orphans: With the By-Laws of the Board of Directors, the Rules and Regulations of the Institution, and the Will of Mr. Girard, 1851, pp. 27-30. This ready reference affords abundant evidence of the various lines of authority and the rules and regulations which governed the conduct and government of Girard College in its early years. Examination of the documents bearing on the growth and development of the college in its formative years clearly illustrates the attempts of both the City Councils and the Board of Directors to provide a continuing circumspect administration of the trust.

In brief review, the officers, instructors, and agents of the college held their offices ". . . during the pleasure of the Board of Directors" (Ordinance of September 16, 1847, Ibid., p. 13); and the Directors, in turn, were obliged to act ". . . in conformity with the Will of Stephen Girard, and with such Ordinances and Resolutions as the Select and Common Councils . . . enact[ed] and adopt[ed] in relation thereto" (Ordinance of May 27, 1847, Ibid., p. 2). From its inception, the Board of Directors functioned largely through the use of standing committees which were annually appointed by the President of the Board, e.g., Committee on Accounts, Library Committee, Committee on Instruction, Committee on Household, and Committee on Admission and Discharge of Pupils. (See the By-Laws of the Board of Directors in their "Report of the Board of Directors of the Girard College for Orphans to the Select and Common Councils, June 17, 1847," Journal of the Select Council of the City of Philadelphia for 1846-1847; Beginning October 16, 1846, and Ending October 7, 1847, Appendix, pp. 106-108). A committee on Morals was added through the By-Laws adopted on April 1, 1851 (Digest, op. cit., pp. 35-39). The City Councils, for the most part, relied upon the judgments and recommendations of the Mayor and Council members who comprised the Commissioners of the Girard Estate and were charged with the management of the estate. This is evident from the not infrequent reference found in the Minutes of the City Councils as indicated by the following extract: "Which was read and referred to the Commissioners of the Girard Estate." (e.g., "Minutes of the Select Council for December 6, 1849," Journal of the Select Council of the City of Philadelphia for 1849-1850: Beginning October 12, 1849 and Ending September 26, 1850, p. 43). This commission had been established by "A Further Ordinance for the Management of the Girard Estates" on January 10, 1833, as found in Ordinances of the Corporation of the City of Philadelphia

French and Spanish languages, in Drawing, and in Natural History and Psychology.[11] At the inauguration of President Allen, Joseph R. Chandler, President of the Board of Directors, noted the significance of the new department: "For two years past, we have been employed in instructing a primary department. We are now about to advance the most forward, the best qualified of that number, to another grade, and thus commence a new era in the proceedings of the college."[12] In the Annual Report of the Board of Directors, Chandler elaborated on its importance:

> The change in the ancient system of apprenticeships, will render it necessary for us to retain our pupils a few years

---

Passed Between November 22, 1832, and September 22, 1836, pp. 475-479. Throughout their hegemony (1848-1869), the Councils focused their attention mainly to the making of appropriations for the college; however, copious, variegated references to the college in the Minutes of the Journals of the City Councils and the appended reports and anniversary addresses found previous to the adoption of the Consolidation Act of 1854 indicate the attention of the Councils to the detail of and concern for conditions at the college. (The Consolidation Act of 1854 greatly enlarged the boundaries of the City of Philadelphia and required the solution of accompanying problems, apparently affording less time in Councils for attention to minute details of the college). Particularly suggestive of the Councils' concern was the passage of the Ordinance of November 9, 1848, which provided for a standing committee of Visitation to the college, viz:

"Section 1. Be it ordained and enacted by the Citizens of Philadelphia, in Select and Common Councils assembled, That the members of the Select and Common Councils shall constitute a Standing Committee of Visitation of the Girard College for Orphans; and the Presidents of each Council shall, immediately after the passing of this bill, and annually hereafter, on the organization of Councils, divide the members of their respective Councils into four sub-committees of eight members each; four of whom shall be of the Select, and four of the Common Council, who shall serve for two months in the order in which they are constituted as aforesaid.

Section 2. And be it further ordained and enacted by the authority aforesaid, That it shall be the duty of the said sub-committees to visit the Girard College for Orphans at least once in each month, and examine the condition thereof, and report the same to the Standing Committee of Visitation, or to Councils, at their discretion, at such times as they shall deem expedient." (See Digest, op. cit., pp. 20-21).

[11] Second Annual Report of the Board of Directors, op. cit., pp. 6-7.

[12] Joseph R. Chandler, "Address," Addresses Delivered on the Occasion of the Inauguration of President Allen, January 1, 1850, p. 8.

> longer than would have been requisite if they could be transferred to the home of a master, who, as in former days, would be responsible for their moral guidance, as well as their instruction in an art or trade.
>
> Our pupils having in all instances lost their fathers, and many of them being deprived of both parents, will need a better preparation both by age and education, for meeting the trials and temptations of life, than those who may, to a greater or a less extent, rely upon parental counsel and aid.
>
> We must, therefore, strive to make them desirable apprentices, and so to furnish them, mentally and morally as to command the best places, and at those rates of wages which may, under the new system, suffice for their respectable support until they attain majority.
>
> Such will be the purpose of the Principal Department: its graduates will have a thorough education in English and Mathematics--in Mental and Moral Science--the French, Spanish, and other modern languages--Natural History, Physiology, Chemistry, and Mechanical Philosophy in the most extended sense of both terms--Drawing, Practical Mechanics, Engineering, Agriculture, Navigation, &c., &c. Thus prepared, we may anticipate for them that improved lot in life which it was the cherished purpose of the founder of the Institution to secure, and for the attainment of which he made such munificent provision.[13]

President Allen outlined his views on the subject of a Principal department in a major report submitted to the Committee on Instruction on September 3rd of the same year.[14] In keeping with the design set out in the ordinance that provided for the commencement of instruction, he saw all incoming students entering into the Primary school. Each student would enter a class according to his level of knowledge, remaining in the Primary school until the age of eleven or twelve. Of all departments, primary, principal, or collegiate, he believed the Principal department to be the most important. Unlike the Primary school where some studies were given all students, the instruction in the principal department would be more individualized and flexible, ". . .

---

[13]Second Annual Report of the Board of Directors, op. cit., pp. 7-8.

[14]William H. Allen, Report of the President of Girard College to the Committee on Instruction, September 3, 1850.

for it will be the nursery from which the scholars, whose minds are susceptible of the highest cultivation, will be transplanted to the collegiate classes, and from which the others will be removed to the occupations of industrial life."[15]

In an earlier report to the Board of Directors he had simply enumerated a scheme of studies which he thought appropriate for the Principal department.[16] In the later report, he marked out a two-year general course for this department arranged among five departments of study, allowing for deviations that would necessarily be suggested by the individual case. The two-year general course is of such interest that it is skeletally subjoined:

I.-ENGLISH DEPARTMENT.

1. English Grammar.
2. English Composition.
3. Reading--(Narrative, Rhetorical and Poetical.)
4. Vocal Music.
5. Book-keeping, including practical exercises in keeping accounts, posting, balancing, drawing bills, notes, receipts, &c.
6. Universal History.
7. Constitution of the United States and Pennsylvania, with an exposition of the rights and duties of citizens.
8. Elements of Moral Science.
9. Drawing--(Architectural and Mechanical.)

II.-MATHEMATICS.

1. Arithmetic.
2. Elementary Algebra.
3. Elementary Geometry.
4. Elementary Trigonometry.
5. Mensuration of surfaces and solids, especially of Artificers' work.
6. Theory of Logarithms and their applications.
7. Laws of Perspective.

III.-LANGUAGES.

1. French--Colloquial phrases and narrative reading. French Composition.
2. Spanish--Colloquial phrases and narrative reading. Spanish Composition.
3. Latin commenced.

---

[15] _Ibid._, p. 3.

[16] William H. Allen, _Report of the President of Girard College to the Committee on Instruction, January 23, 1850_, pp. 3-4.

IV.-GENERAL PHYSICS.

1. Elementary Natural Philosophy, with Lectures and Experiments.
2. Elementary Chemistry, with Lectures and Experiments.

V.-SPECIAL PHYSICS.

1. The connexion and dependence of the Mineral, Vegetable, and Animal kingdoms of Nature.
2. Classification of Animals, Plants, and Minerals.
3. Popular Zoology.
4. Economical Natural History, including the properties and uses of the various articles known in commerce, and used in the arts.[17]

Upon completion of the course of study provided in the Principal department, whereupon the students would be between thirteen and fourteen years of age, President Allen believed that three divisions would be possible: a division of "scholars whose application, capacity, and moral character may entitle them to admission to the Collegiate department;" a second division to include all those ". . . orphans who ought to be bound out to suitable occupations as soon after as they shall have attained the age of fourteen years as eligible situations can be obtained for them," who would be determined ". . . by their physical development, their capacity to profit from continued instruction in the college and their general character, disposition, and habits;" and a third division of those students of "good character and fair capacity" who might profit from further instruction ". . . whose strength may not be equal to the hardships of a laborious occupation," and should be allowed to remain for one, two, or three years longer.[18]

His actual plans for a Collegiate department epitomized the feelings of those who believed that Girard College should be an institution of higher learning. His rationale for this department makes this point eminently clear:

> Mr. Girard did not bequeath his property to support a mere Asylum for Orphans, nor to endow a Primary School or an Academy

---

[17]William H. Allen, Report . . ., September 3, 1850, pp. 4-5.

[18]Ibid., p. 11-12.

> for their instruction, but to found a College. He intended to place within the reach of the "poor white male Orphans" of this City and Commonwealth, every aid and instrument which wealth could furnish for the study of the highest branches of knowledge. To provide raiment, food, and shelter for so many destitute children, through all coming time, would indeed have been a benefaction worthy of a great and liberal mind. But while the plan of Mr. Girard includes the foster home, the common school, and the high school, these are not the ultimate results of his bequest, but the means of reaching forward to higher and nobler results. While the preparatory courses of instruction will render available to society whatever is fit for use in inferior minds, they will also give opportunity for talent and genius to crop out and show their vein. They will enable the teacher to discover among the shells and pebbles of ocean, the "gem of purest ray serene," and to cull from weed and bramble the flower which else had "blushed unseen, and wasted its sweetness on the desert air."[19]

President Allen would devise the Collegiate department within four classes, the fourth corresponding to the Freshman of English and American colleges, the third to Sophmores, the second to Juniors, and the first to Seniors. Again, the studies would be divided into five departments as in the Principal department, but on a higher order than previously mentioned, *e.g.*,

FOURTH CLASS

I.-English Department.

1. English Grammar.
2. Elocution.
3. Dramatic Reading.
4. History.
5. Composition.

II.-Mathematics.

1. Arithmetic, (finished.)
2. Algebra, (finished.)
3. Geometry, (commenced.)

III.-Languages.

1. French, (continued.)
2. Spanish, (continued.)
3. Latin, (Cornelious Nepos and Caesar.)

IV.-General Physics.

1. Primary and Secondary qualities of bodies.
2. Laws of Motion and force.
3. Mechanical Powers.
4. Laws of the motion of falling bodies.
5. Theory of the Pendulum.

---

[19] *Ibid.*, p. 11. (Italics retained as found in the original).

V.-Special Physics.

1. Human Anatomy and Physiology.
2. Comparative Anatomy and Physiology.
3. Animal Mechanics.
4. Natural Theology--Evidences of Design.

THIRD CLASS

I.-English Department.

1. Composition.
2. History, (continued.)
3. Philosophy of the Intellect and Sensibilities.
4. American Constitution.

II.-Mathematics.

1. Geometry, (finished.)
2. Plane and Spherical Trigonometry.
3. Navigation.
4. Orthographic and Sterographic Projections.

III.-Languages.

1. Spanish, (continued.)
2. German, (commenced.)
3. Latin--Virgil and Cicero's _Orations_.

IV.-General Physics.

1. Pneumatics.
2. Acoustics.
3. Hydrostatics.
4. Hydraulics.
5. Construction of Machines.

V.-Special Physics.

1. Systematic Zoology.
2. Vegetable Organography.
3. Vegetable Physiology.
4. Systematic Botany.

SECOND CLASS

I.-English Department.

1. Logic.
2. Rhetoric.
3. Selected Declamations.
4. Composition.
5. Parliamentary Usage.

II.-Mathematics.

1. Surveying with field practice.
2. Analytical Geometry, including Conic Sections.
3. Differential Calculus.

III.-Languages.

1. German, (continued.)
2. Latin--Cicero, _De Officiis_.

IV.- General Physics.

1. Theromotics.
2. Light and Optics.
3. Electricity.
4. Magnetism.
5. Inorganic Chemistry.

V.-Special Physics.

1. Mineralogy.
2. Geology.

FIRST CLASS

I.-English Department.

1. Moral Philosophy.
2. Political Economy.
3. Original Declamations.
4. Written and Extemporaneous Discussions.

II.-Mathematics.

1. Integral Calculus.
2. Analytical Mechanics.
3. Civil Engineering, including Topographical Drawing.

III.-Languages.

1. Latin,--Germania, Agricola and Histories of Tacitus.
2. French, Spanish, and German (reviewed.)

IV.-General Physics.

1. Organic Chemistry.
2. Chemistry applied to the Arts.
3. Agricultural Chemistry.
4. Astronomy.
5. Physical Geography and Meteorology.

V.-Special Physics.

1. Hygiene.
2. The Application of Anatomy and Physiology to the treatment of wounds, drowning, cases of poisoning, and accidents from foul air, in the absence of a regular practitioner.[20]

---

[20] Ibid., pp. 13-16. In addressing the committee in reference to the choice of a course of studies, President Allen's general commentary on college courses deserves note: "In making out the course of study for the Collegiate Department, the committee will doubtless consider: First, What can be accomplished between the age of fourteen and eighteen by the best scholars, with their utmost diligence, under the most skillful instruction; and Second, What branches of study, and what order in taking them up, will most perfectly combine useful and practical knowledge with sound mental culture. They will also probably see reason to depart from the ancient usage of Colleges, which requires all students whatever their capacity or inclination, to pass through the same routine of studies. It is hoped that the time is not far distant when this bed of Procrustes, which requires the stretching of some minds

In projecting upon the dates when all classes would be finally realized according to his plan, President Allen saw January, 1855, as the time when ". . . all the Collegiate classes will be organized and the time of the Professors will be wholly occupied with the duties of their respective chairs.[21] Also, as soon as financially feasible, he recommended adding a permanent department for instruction in Drawing and the Arts of Design.

In order to allow the plan for the Collegiate department to function properly, Allen saw an imminent problem that would have to be overcome: A sufficient number of pupils would have to be admitted annually in order to insure that an adequate number sould be available for the higher departments in general. While the prescribed limits of six and ten years had already been fixed, he argued that there would be greater advantage in admitting the pupils at the more advanced rather than the earliest possible age.

> There is, undoubtedly, a moral advantage in receiving the orphans at the earliest allowable age, before their habits and characters have been formed. But they derive little benefit, intellectually, from so early an admission; for it is believed that two boys of equal age and capacity, both ignorant of the alphabet when admitted, and one being received at six years of age and the other at eight, will be found in the same class at fourteen. The benefits of the institution will be extended to a greater number of Orphans, its expenses will be diminished, and an adequate supply of scholars will be provided for the principal and collegiate classes, by receiving the Orphans, whenever this may be practicable, at the most advanced age allowed by the will.[22]

President Allen's report, a major statement of policy, was also concerned with the idea of manual labor. He notes that he had been asked by the Board of Directors to make his views on the subject known to them. In the opening

---

beyond the symmetry of nature, and the curtailing of the fair proportions of others, will be flung into the lumber garret of obsolete ideas. I submit that while the scheme of studies should come up to the highest standard attainable by the best students in their limited time, no scholar should be compelled to learn nothing, in the attempt to learn everything."

[21] Ibid., p. 20.

[22] Ibid., pp. 22-23.

days of the college, the President of the Board of Directors had indicated:

> Considerable labor will be necessary to put the Grounds in a situation appropriate to the Institution. Some ornamental portions will be considered requisite. Extensive gardens for the use of the household will be proper, and a portion must be set apart for the exercise and amusement of the pupils.
>
> It is expected that much which, for the present, is done by persons hired on the place may be performed by the pupils, to the diminution of the expenses of the College and the health and improvement of the habits of the boys.[23]

Allen's views on manual labor appear to have been in accord with those held by the Board. This is evident from his following statement:

> While Mr. Girard does not expressly provide for the employment of the pupils in manual labor, the college is undoubtedly authorized to employ them in that manner for recreation and rational exercise.
>
> After the age of ten years, the pupils may be usefully employed a few hours each week, in the following occupations, without encroaching upon school and study hours: (1) In certain personal services for themselves, such as brushing their own clothing, cleaning and polishing their own boots, &c. (2) In such agricultural and horticultural work as may be adapted to their strength and intelligence. (3) In keeping the walks in good order, and making improvements upon the grounds. In these occupations they should be under the direction of the Janitor, Prefects, Gardener or Steward.
>
> When the pupils shall have attained the age of twelve years they may be employed, during a part of their time of recreation, in the workshops, under the charge of a Prefect or of the Carpenter. They should be furnished with tools and materials for the manufacture

---

[23]"Minutes of the Select Council for January 6, 1848," loc. cit. See also in this connection First Annual Report of the Board of Directors of the Girard College for Orphans for the Year 1848, p. 6, particularly, "An Attempt was made to employ a part of the children's time in a small garden, during the spring and summer; the plan will be employed next year, and a portion of scholars will spend part of their time in assisting to keep the cultivated portion of the grounds in order. And the time of the boys, as they gain more strength by age, will be trained to a proper account, so that their habits may be formed for the pursuits of life, to which they are destined." The Second Annual Report of the Board of Directors, op. cit., p. 4, noted further: "The proper cultivation of the grounds--a portion of which it is proposed to lay out for a kitchen garden, while other parts of them will be appropriated to general husbandry and to ornamental culture--will, with the playground and swimming pool, give the means for a gradual introduction of the children to labor, and afford amusement and healthful occupation in the open air."

> of playthings, and for the construction of gymnastic apparatus. Materials may also be provided for such as may desire to manufacture salable articles for their own profit. After the payment of the materials used in such manufacture, each maker should receive half of the profits of his work, that he may learn the value of industry and the uses of money, and the other half should be reserved and paid over to him whenever he leaves the institution, to teach him the advantages of accumulation.[24]

By January, 1851, three hundred and five pupils were receiving instruction and maintenance in the college. The Principal department was to be organized on April 1st based upon the schema suggested by a report submitted on February 19th by a Joint Committee composed of the Committees on Household and Instruction and which had been adopted by the Board of Directors.[25] Of particular note, the schools of the College were to be divided into a Primary department and a Principal department with the Primary subdivided into two schools of Primary 2 and Primary 1, the Primary 2 being the lowest in the rank. The pupils of the Primary 2 school were to be those "of least age and attainments" and were to receive "such instruction therein as may be suited to their capacities." The "more advanced pupils" were to be placed in the Primary 1 school and were to receive instruction generally corresponding to the branches that were presently being taught and to ". . . be carried to such extent as a thorough preparation for the Principal department may require."[26]

---

[24]William H. Allen, _Report . . ., September 3, 1850_, p. 24.

[25]_Third Annual Report of the Board of Directors of the Girard College for Orphans for the Year 1850_, pp. 4-5.

[26]_Ibid._, p. 6. The results of these changes are seen in the subsequent _Fourth Annual Report of the Board of Directors of the Girard College for Orphans for the Year 1851_, pp. 4-5. The curriculum was noted as follows: Primary 2--Spelling, Reading, Writing, Grammar, Arithmetic, Etymology, Notation and Tables; Primary 1--Spelling, Reading, Writing, Grammar, Geography, Arithmetic, Etymology and History; and Principal--Geometry, Algebra, Arithmetic, Natural Philosophy, History, Geography, Grammar, Reading, Spelling, and Trigonometry. Although not listed in their tabular statement of courses, French, Spanish, Drawing, Writing, and Bookkeeping, were also part of the Principal course of studies.

In further detail, another provision set forth that "it should be the duty of the Gardener give instruction in useful and ornamental Horticulture and general Husbandry, to such number of the pupils, and at such times as the President may direct."[27] Worthy of mention is the conspicuous absence of any mention of a "collegiate" department which had been discussed at much length by Allen.[28]

With the organization of the Principal department, the division of the school into Primary 2, Primary 1, and Principal schools reflected the three-school division suggested by Lieber in his Constitution and Plan of Education for Orphans.[29] (This tripartite division was essentially continued until 1860). As for the scholastic instruction, it appeared to be a settled question except for the procurement of suitable apparatus and a laboratory for the study of chemistry which together with mathematics, the Board of Directors believed to be ". . . the first steps in any thorough course of practical education."[30] An urgency was expressed by the Board on this point since they

---

[27] Ibid., p. 7.

[28] In speaking of this early period, Herrick comments: "There were, however, differences of opinion as to the function of Girard College in both the Board of Directors and the City Councils. In all its early history there were two parties on the question of the purpose of the college. One party sought to make it a "college" in the usual sense of the term, that is, an institution for liberal culture. The other sought to make the institution an "orphanage" a place for the rearing and physical care of boys, with less regard for the more liberal aspect of their education." See in this connection, Cheesman A. Herrick, op. cit., p. 149.

[29] See supra, p. 52.

[30] Third Annual Report of the Board of Directors, op. cit., p. 11. For this same point in a fuller context, see Benjamin Gerhard, Address at the Third Anniversary of the College, January 1, 1851, particularly, "A new era has now sprung up. The immense and important discoveries in science within the present century, have astonished the philosopher and realized the imagery of the poet, while their practical applications have made vast additions to the sum of human enjoyment. With 1200 miles of Pennsylvania rail-roads, and

believed, "It is not consistent with the welfare of this [Principal] department of the college, to postpone the procuring of suitable apparatus and furnishing a Laboratory, until another year."[31]

The urgency in this matter was not limited to the Board of Directors. President Allen in a report to the Board noted: "Professor Stephens alludes, in his report, to the expediency of introducing the study of chemistry into the Principal department on the first of September next [1851]; and as a part of the boys of that school will probably be bound out that year, it is important that they should begin the study of that science before the close of the present year."[32] And in a later report, President Allen noted further: "It is desirable that the apparatus should be purchased and the laboratory fitted up as early as the first of September [1851], in order that the boys who will be bound out next spring may have the advantage of a course of lectures upon that science."[33]

---

about the same length of canals, not to speak of our other internal improvements, and of our navigable waters; and with our numerous iron works, our mines of coals, iron, copper, and lead; our manufacturing laboratories, and the numerour other branches of mechanical art; scientific engineers, manufacturers, machinists, and mechanics, who combine practical skill with scientific knowledge have unlimited ranges for employment open to them in our city and state; some of which I hope will be occupied with high distinction by the present and future pupils of the Girard College. Let them become thoroughly good draughtsmen, practical geologists, practical chemists, and let them be well versed in mechanical and natural philosophy--directing the education of each according to his tastes in regard to his future occupation of life, and you will remove all uncertainty as to the productiveness of his future industry." (p. 27)

[31]Third Annual Report of the Board of Directors, loc. cit.

[32]"Extract from the Monthly Report of the President," June 11, 1851, p. 2, as found in Report of Three Members of the Committee on Admission and Discharge Relative to Binding Orphans to Suitable Occupations, March 24, 1852, p. 4.

[33]"Extract from the Monthly Report of the President," July 9, 1851, p. 1, as found in Report of Three Members of the Committee on Admission and Discharge Relative to Binding Orphans to Suitable Occupations, March 24, 1852, p. 4.

Although the chemistry equipment and laboratory had not been provided for the September course, the problem of binding out the students now assumed a more significant importance. The question as to what length of time the boys should remain in the college had still not been definitely answered. The will had provided "Those scholars, who shall merit it, shall remain in the College until they shall respectively arrive at between fourteen and eighteen years of age;"[34] and many of the boys would be attaining fourteen years of age during the following year. To this there was evidence that there were differences of opinion as to when the boys should be bound out. President Allen had outlined his views on the age at which the pupils should leave the college in his Report to the Committee on Instruction in 1850.[35] On October 2, 1851, he reiterated his views subsequent to a disturbance among some of the pupils on September 4.[36]

> It is my opinion that all vicious, disorderly, and discontented pupils, who discover no signs of amendment, should be bound out as soon as practicable after the age of fourteen, and that all scholars of good capacity, application and character, should be retained in the Institution, to prosecute a higher and more extended course of study. I submit that pupils of superior ability and virtuous habits, have a stronger claim than others, to all the aids which the College can give them; and that a few of these, thoroughly educated, will accomplish more for society, and reflect more credit upon the Institution, than can be expected from a much larger number of inferior minds.
>
> I send herewith a paper marked (A), containing the names of the pupils who will become fourteen years of age anterior to January 1st,

---

[34]Article XXI, para. 9. Holograph will.

[35]See *supra*, pp. 86, *ff*.

[36]For a discussion of the disturbance of September 4, 1851, see the Report of A Special Committee of the Board of Directors of the Girard College for Orphans, Appointed September 10, 1851. This sixteen-page report typifies the attention to detail in the early years of the school's opening given to matters at the college including problems of discipline. Of particular note in the report is the resolution of the committee that four of the boys in question were considered ". . . improper companions for the pupils, and should be removed therefrom in compliance with the 21st Section, 8th Clause of the Will of Stephen Girard." (p. 16).

> 1853. * * * I have marked thus * the names of such boys, as from present indications, ought not to be retained in the College after the age of fourteen. It is desirable that places should be found for the oldest of these boys, without delay.[37]

Soon after the receipt of this report, on October 8, the Board of Directors authorized the Committee on Admission and Discharge to ". . . consider and report what measures ought to be adopted by the Directors, respecting the orphans who, from time to time, may arrive at between fourteen and eighteen years of age."[38] The committee reported to the Board on February 27, 1852, finding it necessary to first explain their delay in completing their charge before making their report. The reasons for their tardiness were based upon three considerations: first, the wording of their charge did not suggest prompt attention, implying that their duty was a grave one requiring sufficient time; second, the committee was awaiting the decision of the city councils in providing the necessary permission, which, as yet, had not arrived; and third, there would have been no report admitting to the delay if it were not for an impression prevailing in the college--one that

---

[37]"Extract from the Monthly Report of the President," October 2, 1851, p. 2, as found in Report of Three Members of the Committee on Admission and Discharge Relative to Binding Orphans to Suitable Occupations, March 24, 1852, pp. 4-5. In an earlier report to the Board, President Allen had suggested that the problem of student truancy from the institution could be better prevented if the penalty for such an offence were but a slight one. He repeated his request made some months previous to the communication that the Board authorize him, at his own discretion, ". . . to refuse to receive again as a pupil, without a new order of admission, any boy who may have run away three times. I request also, that if such power can be legally exercised, that I be permitted to the proper measures to place any boy in the House of Refuge, who, in addition to running away three times is incorrigibly vicious: provided that his friends refuse to cancel his indentures and take him away." See in this connection, William H. Allen, Report to Frederick Fraley, Esq., President of the Board of Directors of the Girard College for Orphans, p. 7.

[38]Report of the Committee on Admission and Discharge Relative to Binding Orphans to Suitable Occupations, February 27, 1852, p. 1. For the full text of this historically important development in the history of American education, see Appendix H, pp.

the committee held to be erroneous--that orphans who were fourteen years of age were to go out in the spring.[39]

> If this is an erroneous impression it ought at once to be removed, for it disturbs the feelings and minds not only of the orphans, but of their mothers and friends; and on the other hand, if orphans are of the age are to be bound out in the spring, the change ought to be announced by those who are competent to make it.[40]

For this reason, the committee felt it necessary to make its report before the decision of the councils had been received.

In rapid order, the committee reviewed the events leading to the inquiry at hand. In doing this, the committee called attention to the fact that none of the boys had attained fourteen years of age before December 1851. This being so, the Directors had confined their attention to only the maintenance and education of the orphans since there had been no previous necessity for closely examining the provisions of Stephen Girard's will which related to the binding of orphans to suitable occupations. However, in the autumn of 1851, while the Board of Directors had not taken action on this, various suggestions had been made.

> By some it seemed and still seems to be supposed, that the operation of binding the orphans may be regulated according to their ages: Others appear to regard the age of fourteen as the proper period for binding them: And so confident is even the President of the College, on the subject, that, in his report to the Directors, made on the 12th of February, he says, "I deem it important that situations should be engaged, with as little delay as possible, for the boys who are to go out in the spring."[41]

---

[40]*Ibid*., p. 2. Subsequent to the appointment of this committee, Samuel Norris, President of the Board of Directors, sent to the City Councils a communication accompanied by a preamble and resolution relating to the binding out of the orphans when they shall respectively arrive at between fourteen and eighteen years of age. See in this connection "Minutes of the Select Council for November 21, 1851," *Journal of the Select Council of the City of Philadelphia for 1851-1852, Beginning October 17, 1851 and Ending October 7, 1852*, p. 25. Apparently, this was a request for permission relative to the binding of orphans since the *Report of the Committee on Admission and Discharge*, *op.cit*. p. 1, mentions that ". . . the Directors had asked the attention of the City Councils to that omission [of provision by law or ordinance]."

[41]*Ibid*., pp. 2-3.

In contemplation of this, the committee realized that while there might not have been a present necessity in determining Girard's intentions or the duties of the Directors in the operation of binding the orphans, they did believe ". . . it is discreet to consider what is the true character of those intentions and duties, so that doubt may no longer exist, and that future operations may be advisedly conducted."[42] The committee's analysis of the will brought them to mark out what they thought to be the essential parts of Girard's plan of education: moral training, physical training, and intellectual improvement. The committee maintained that in these areas, as in all matters of importance, Girard provided directions ". . . not merely in clear, but mandatory terms; and his trustees in accepting his estate, solemnly undertook to execute their duty according to those terms."[43] On this basis, the committee observed, "If, therefore, the orphans who may be capable of receiving a thorough education, shall not be thoroughly educated, and if those orphans, whose facilities may be so limited that they cannot acquire a thorough education, shall not receive all the instruction which they may be capable of, the trustees will be accountable."[44]

The age limits set by Girard were considered by the committee as a sliding scale to allow each orphan to profit according to his own capacity and while a particular term of instruction had not been precisely defined, they concluded a fairly-declared term to be eight years. In practical terms, the committee held that of six orphans who had finally attained fourteen years, five had only received four years of instruction and the sixth was only approaching his fourth year as well. Also, they questioned whether any of these scholars had received instruction "in the various branches of a sound

---

[42]<u>Ibid.</u>, p. 3. [43]<u>Ibid.</u> [44]<u>Ibid.</u>, pp. 3-4.

education," especially since the college was still lacking "the philosophical and experimental instruments and apparatus" which Girard had noted would be available at the college's opening.

The committee took this opportunity to allude to suggestions made by Professor Stephens whose views the committee held to be cogent arguments for their strictures against President Allen whom they believed had not only proposed but had decided to bound out boys in the Spring. Professor Stephens, upon hearing that some boys were to be bound out in the Spring had noted to the Board: "The elder classes in the school are now reaching the age and the period in study, when boys can first be expected to have an insight into the value of education; and this incentive will, of course, gain strength as they advance to the practical scientific studies, which are a leading feature in Mr. Girard's requirements."[45] Beyond this, Professor Stephens had pointed out the fact that students who were being admitted into the Central High School of Philadelphia averaged more than fourteen years of age.[46] Expanding

---

[45] _Ibid._, p. 7.

[46] _Ibid._ The Central High School of Philadelphia was founded in 1838 by means of the Pennsylvania School Law of 1836. For the context in which it was founded, see George H. Cliff, "The Central High School of Philadelphia: An Historical Sketch," _The Semi-Centennial Celebration of the Central High School of Philadelphia_, particularly, "During its early years the public school system was very generally regarded in the light of a public charity, an impression not easy to dispel. At the time of the passage of the Act of 1836, there were no public high schools of a high order in the city of Philadelphia, and such as then existed were just emerging from the odium of charitable institutions. There was a general awakening to the need of better and more advanced educational facilities, the public mind being doubtlessly largely moved in this matter by the magnificent bequest of Stephen Girard." (p. 4.) Of the early years after the school's opening, it has been noted: "The first teaching of the High School was sound and thorough, but it lacked unity in the curriculum and cohesion in the courses. . . . As the school increased in popularity, however, and the number of students mounted into the hundreds, the defects of such an organization became apparent. It was fortunate that there was in Philadelphia at that time an educator of distinguished merit [Alexander Dallas Bache] who was temporarily without definite work." See in this connection Franklin Spencer Edmonds, _History of the Central High School of Philadelphia_, p. 43. For Bache's connection to the Central High School, see also Chapter II, footnote 144 _ff._

upon this point, the committee remarked:

> It seems, therefore, that the intelligent fathers of the pupils in the High School agree with Stephen Girard, not only in the anxiety to give a sound education, but as to what a sound education is; and it further appears, that in sustaining the High School, the community in which it exists sanctions the principles on which it is conducted. The fathers of the pupils in it, although their sons may be above the age of fourteen years, wisely prefer to have them fully instructed, to binding them out, when half instructed, to occupations, for which, owing to ignorance, they may be unfit. They do not stop their sons when in pursuit of knowledge, because they may be above the age of fourteen years; but they cheer and encourage them in their course. And yet, although the founder of the Girard College provided for at least such an instruction of the orphans therein, as may be had in the High School, Professor Stevens appears to doubt, whether it may not be the desire of Stephen Girard's Trustees, or of the Directors of the College, to make the College a mere grammar or primary school.[47]

---

[47] Ibid., p. 7-8. The tendency on the part of some to note under a common heading the work done at the Central High School and that at Girard College is found in the following analogy: "The controllers of our public schools announce with just pride that no graduate of the High School has been the subject of a penal accusation; and if the directors of Girard College can, fifteen years hence, point to the assembled alumni of their institution with the same boast, will it not indicate the means of preventing much of that depravity which we attempt, too often in vain, to cure in expensive penal establishments. They are to be working men; and if, when they shall have entered upon the duties of active life, they find a painful difference between their brothers, sisters and uneducated shopmates, and themselves, pure morality, benevolence towards their fellow-men, and the love of truth, will impel them to exert all their powers as men and citizens in behalf of those from whose ranks they came and with whom they will be identified. Education, in any enlarged degree, has hitherto been the privilege of wealthy few, and educated men have generally engaged in professional pursuits. Manual labor has been associated in most minds with coarseness and ignorance, and our republican experience has seemed to almost justify the contempt in which the laborer was held in feudal times. We have not yet accepted mind and character as the standard by which invariably to judge the man. The High School and our excellent grammar schools are doing much to remedy these evils, and the College will do much more." See in this connection William D. Kelley, "Anniversary Address," Address at the Fourth Anniversary of the Girard College for Orphans, January 1, 1852, p. 9. While the Report of the Committee on Admission and Discharge had also attempted an analogy in order to contrast (or compare) the work done at the institutions, one member of the Board of Directors held a different view: "We cannot admit any such analogy as the report suggests, between the High School and Girard College. The principles on which the two institutions are conducted are too diverse to justify it. The pupils and care-takers of the High School are not restricted by the provisions of a charity-foundation, and the whole reasoning on such an analogy is as irrelevant as it is inconclusive." See in this connection Private Document--Board of Directors of Girard College, [April, 1852], p. 15.

By arguments such as these, the committee sought to make clear their firm belief that the age of fourteen did not call for the automatic binding out of orphans. Even beyond this, they contended that the only consideration for binding out until even seventeen years of age could be whether or not the student had received as full an instruction as his faculties would enable him to receive. With this view in mind, the committee submitted four resolutions which they asked the Board of Directors to adopt. This report is both appropriate and relevant in the presentation of a singularly informative view of apprenticeship in mid-nineteenth century Philadelphia and is quoted _in extenso_:

> They [the committee] will not, however, close their report, without briefly adverting to an obstacle in the way of binding out orphans to suitable occupations, which the founder of the College could not have forseen. Formerly the operation of binding apprentices by indenture was almost universally adopted in Pennsylvania. The home of the apprentice was in the house of the master; who not only instructed the apprentice in his operative duties, but was the conservator of his morals. Within the twenty years which have elapsed since the death of Stephen Girard, however, the relationship previously existing between masters and apprentices has been almost wholly superceded, in the city and districts of Philadelphia at least, by a practice, which the committee believe to be highly injurious not only to the parties immediately concerned, but to society at large. Owing to the selfishness of masters, to combinations among journeymen, and to the necessities of unfortunate parents, the ancient and useful operation of binding by indenture has been almost abandoned. Masters in general, in order to be released from the responsibility of providing homes for apprentices, and of making the apprentices good workmen, hire boys from their parents at weekly or monthly wages, and the parents assent to those loose bargains, through ignorance of the consequences to their children, or under the pressure of a sad necessity. The committee trust that this practice is not long to prevail, and that in other parts of Pennsylvania it is unknown. But if these hopes are unfounded, still the committee do not despair of finding in Pennsylvania, masters willing to take apprentices by indenture from the Girard College. The orphans of that institution, if the injunctions of its founder shall be faithfully followed by his Trustees, will have had such a moral, physical and scholastic training, as to render them acceptable apprentices to all masters who truly understand their own true interest, and who at the same time have a just sense of their duty to society. Let the Trustees and Directors act their own parts well, and the future may be awaited without responsibility or apprehension.

> The resolution which the committee respectfully ask the Directors to adopt, are the following:
>
> 1st. Resolved, that all orphans who are capable of receiving the sound education defined in the seventh clause of the twenty-first article of Stephen Girard's Will, shall be instructed according to his requirements.
>
> 2d. Resolved, that orphans, whose faculties may not qualify them to receive the full education contemplated in the clause aforesaid, shall nevertheless be fully instructed in all the branches of education, which they may be able to master.
>
> 3d. Resolved, that the time, at which an orphan between fourteen and eighteen years of age should be bound out as an apprentice should be determined not according to his age, but to his fitness for the change.
>
> 4th. Resolved, that a book suitable for a register shall be provided and carefully kept in the College; that in it, from time to time, the names of orphans, as they shall severally arrive at the age of fourteen years, shall be entered; and that thereafter a faithful record shall be kept of the capacity, progress and standing of each of the said orphans as a scholar, as well as of his morals and health.[48]

The report had been presented to the Board of Directors on March 10, 1852, and had been laid on the table. At the meeting the Chairman of the Committee on Admission and Discharge suggested that ". . . any member who might not concur in the reasonings or conclusions of the report, would [should] put his views also in black and white, so that they might be examined and compared, and an intelligent judgment formed of their soundness."[49] On March 24, a minority report was presented by three members of the Committee on Admission and Discharge who did not concur in the report submitted on March 10. Their terse dissent reads as follows:

> The undersigned, members of the Committee of Admission and Discharge, Report: that they do not concur in the report submitted by three members of the Committee, who were a

---

[48]*Ibid.*, pp. 10-11.

[49]*Private Document--Board of Directors of Girard College*, [April 1852], p. 1.

majority at a meeting when it was considered. They think that it was Mr. Girard's intention to educate poor white male orphans after they become fourteen years old, so far as the Trustees of his estate believe it to be conducive to the interest of the boys. They believe that the Trustees, or their agents, are the sole judges of the amount of education after that period, that is likely to benefit the orphans, and that their deliberate act will not be questioned. In their judgment all boys over fourteen years of age should be bound out as soon as suitable places can be found for them, except where there are such developments as to induce the belief that a further education is likely to be decidedly beneficial. Believing that the views of President Allen would be misapprehended by all who read the report of the Committee, a copy of said report was sent to the President, with the request that he would give his views in writing. His reply, including extracts from all his reports touching this matter, is submitted as a part of this report.

Girard College, March 20th, 1852.

WILLIAM WELSH, ESQ.

My dear Sir,--I have the pleasure to acknowledge the receipt of your esteemed note of the 17th instant, inclosing a copy of a report recently submitted to the Board of Directors of this Institution by the Chairman of the Committee on Admission and Discharge.

In reply to your inquiry, whether my views are correctly represented in that report, and whether I ever expressed a wish to bind out boys who manifest an anxiety to receive an education, I have to state:

First.--That so far as my views are represented in that report to be adverse to retaining in the College boys of good character and fair capacity after the age of fourteen years, so far they are not correctly represented.

Second.--That I have never expressed a wish to bind out boys who "manifest an anxiety to receive what the founder of the College said they shall have," nor have I "proposed that such boys should be bound out in the ensuing spring," nor have I considered it "as decided that they are to be bound out at that time."

Third.--That "I have deemed it important that situations should be engaged with as little delay as possible, for the boys who are to bo out in the spring, "having presumed to believe that some boys, who ought not to remain in the College a day after they can be removed peaceably, would be bound out at that time. But I have never recommended the binding out of any boys BECAUSE they were fourteen years of age, but because, being fourteen, and therefore legally removable from the College, they were in other reports unfit to remain in it.

> I send inclosed copies of such parts of my reports as refer to this subject, in order that you may be in possession of the views which I have actually expressed, and that you may compare them with the views, which, probably through misapprehension, we are attributed to me. These extracts prove that I have uniformly recommended that all orphans of good havits and fair capacity, who wish to remain in the College, should be permitted to remain and enjoy all the advantages which the Institution has power to confer.
>
> Permit me to add that I learned, for the first time, from this report, the differences of opinion on this question exist between Professor Stephens and myself. I had inferred from the conversations we have had, and from his monthly reports, that we were agreed on this, as we are on all matters of importance relating to the instruction of the pupils. But, even if our views really differ, I do not perceive that any good can result from setting our opinions in array against each other in an official report to the Board. We are both here to obey the orders, and carry out the instructions of the Directors.
>
> Truly and respectfully yours, &c.,
> W. H. ALLEN [50]

In closing this argument, they offered the following resolution for the consideration of the Board of Directors: "Resolved, That the Committee of Admission and Discharge be requested to notify the Committee of the Commissioners of the Girard Trust, that the draft of an Ordinance submitted for

---

[50] _Report of Three Members of the Committee on Admission and Discharge, Relative to Binding Orphans to Suitable Occupations, Made to the Board March 24, 1852_, pp. 1-3. For cited extracts from the presidential monthly reports see pp. 99-100. See also in this connection "Extract from the Monthly Report of the President," March 10, 1852, as found in _Report . . . March 24, 1852_, _supra_, pp. 5-6, "He [Professor Stephens] closes with the remark that "these objections to the early removal of our pupils are intended to apply only to boys of fair abilities and general good conduct." This reservation enables me to coincide entirely with Professor Stephens' views, as it places them in perfect harmony with all the opinions which I have expressed to the Board on this subject in former reports."

"The point upon which I have always insisted is simply this: That the poor white male orphan, A, who has enjoyed the benefits of Mr. Girard's bequest, from seven, eight, nine, or ten, to fourteen years of age, but who, from bad habits or incapacity, is deriving little advantage from that bequest, has less claim for support and instruction, one, two, three or four years longer, than the poor white male orphan, B, under ten years of age, who with better habits and capacity, might derive more benefit from the bequest, but who, though an applicant, has never been admitted into the Institution, and, if A be continued, never can be."

consideration is approved by this Board."[51]

The request of the Chairman for added views also brought forward the views of a member of the Board of Directors who presented a different construction of the will than had been presented in the majority report of the Committee on Admission and Discharge. The immediate significance of the document lies in the pivotal questions the author posed that would have to be answered before attempting to formulate procedural guidelines in the binding out of the students and no less in the structuring of adequate curricula for the college, e.g.,

> The question presented to the Board (as I understand it) is, whether Mr. Girard's purpose will be most effectually accomplished by giving a useful education to the largest possible number of orphans, and not attempting to provide for the prolonged instruction of any; or by giving the ordinary advantages of the college to the mass of pupils, and providing means for the prosecution of the higher branches of science, for such as have the capacity and are disposed to pursue them.
>
> Did Mr. Girard intend that the pupils received into his College should be retained after fourteen for the purpose of being instructed in the higher branches of science?
>
> For what is their College course to prepare them?[52]

The majority report had been based on one major principle: That fitness for change and not age should determine the time at which the scholars should be bound out. In opposition to this, the later view was couched in his interpretation of the language used by Girard:

---

[51]Ibid., p. 6. Of particular note is the first section of the proposed ordinance: "Section 1. Be it ordained and enacted by the Citizens of Philadelphia, in Select and Common Councils assembled, That every orphan child in the Girard College, upon attaining the age of fourteen years, shall be bound out as directed by the will of Mr. Girard, in the manner hereinafter mentioned, except such thereof as, in the opinion of the Board of Directors and the Commissioners of the Girard Estate should remain in said College for the purpose of receiving a more extended course of instruction."

[52]Private Document--Board of Directors of Girard College, [April, 1852], pp. 2, 7.

> As many as said income shall be adequate to maintain (not to educate) shall be introduced to the College, and the number is to be increased as ability from the income (not as theprogress or grade of education) may warrant. And again--My design and desire being that the benefits of said institution shall be extended to as great a number of orphans (not as can be thoroughly educated, but) as the limits of said square and buildings therein can accommodate. Language could not more clearly express a desire and design to make the charity available to the largest number, not to the greatest literary advantage, of different individuals. And no argument is necessary to show, that the continuance of one pupil in the College after the legitimate advantages, both physical and intellectual, have been enjoyed, works the exclusion of some one from a 'comfortable maintenance,' as well as from a 'better education' than he could receive from the public funds.[53]

The idea that the benefits of the college should be extended to a great number led directly to the measure of education to be given. Referring back to the will, the author believed, "In respect of the design of the testator, it was 'to raise the pupils above the many temptations to which through ignorance and poverty, they are exposed.' This end can be accomplished by a very limited acquaintance with most of the branches [enumerated by Stephen. Girard]. . . ."[54] Also, it was noted that if an advanced education for a few pupils was given, it would require a disproportionate share of the income of the college--an error that was to be avoided in recalling an analagous situation: "We should thus make the same mistake inside as some persons conceive to have been committed outside--the expense of the portico, or the extra work, would be sadly out of proportion that of the main building."[55]

No less significant in this argument are the author's analysis of the educational needs that he believed that Stephen Girard had been aware of at the time of drafting his will and in particular Stephen Girard's intention that the orphans should receive ". . . a better education as well as a more

---

[53]Ibid., pp. 5-6.

[54]Ibid., p. 6.

[55]Ibid., p. 7. For the relevancy of this remark, see p. 45, supra.

comfortable maintenance than they usually receive from the public funds. . ."[56]

To this the author added in some detail the following:

> The education usually received from the public funds, we all know, was very limited as the date of Mr. G.'s will, very much more so than it is in the country at large at the present time. Many children who had past through the public schools of Pennsylvania, were not qualified for the simplest branches of business.; and hence boys and girls who were indentured at fourteen, usually stipulated for one or two winters' schooling. Mr. Girard had opportunities to know how very superficial and unprofitable this education by the public funds then was; and he also doubtless knew how common it was then, as it is now, through the pressure of poverty, to cut short this brief and meagre opportunity of learning, so soon as the child becomes capable of contributing by his labour (no matter how little) to the family sustenance. The cupidity of poor and ignorant parents prompts them to regard the advantages of schooling as quite unimportant, when set over against a dollar or two a week from a child's labour in a factory or shop. The grade of instruction which would be considered as '<u>better</u>' than that which is usually received from the public funds, then, is altogether exceeded in extent and value by the present plan of instruction in our College. Every pupil here of ordinary capacity and diligence, will have a better education for all the purposes of life at fourteen, than is possessed by one in a thousand, or even ten thousand, in the country at large, who are schooled up to that age at public expense.
>
> But Mr. Girard knew that the same narrowness of means which prompts inconsiderate parents to abridge the little opportunity their children enjoy at school is felt in their food, lodging and apparel, and hence he wished to connect an improvement in their school privileges with the comforts of a well furnished home. This branch of the charity has no counterpart in the community at large as the schooling has, for the public school funds are never applied to the 'comfortable maintenance' of children. If we take this object by itself therefore, separate from an independent of intellectual education, we cannot doubt that Mr. G. would wish to have the largest possible number partake of his bounty. The child who enters at six years of age, becomes <u>forthwith</u> a full sharer of the means of a 'comfortable maintenance.' His food, lodging, apparel &c., are as good then as they will be at fourteen or eighteen, and there can be no pretext for continuing him, with this purpose only in view, beyond the earliest period fixed for indenture. The sooner his cot in the dormitory and his seat at the table are vacated, consistenly with the terms of the will, so as to make room for a waiting applicant, the more perfectly we carry out Mr. G.'s benevolent design, so far as a 'more comfortable maintenance' is concerned. The boy who is indentured

---

[56] Article XX. Holograph will.

> to a good home at fourteen, passes from a 'comfortable maintenance' here, to a 'comfortable maintenance' with his master; and the vacancy is forthwith filled by one who, until then, is a stranger to any comfort at home or abroad. Now if we take into view the whole scope of the charity, the impression is not easily to be avoided, that a deliverance from the evils and temptations of 'poverty' was quote as much in the testator's mind, as a deliverance from the evils of 'ignorance;' and in this view, no one can doubt that the more rapid the succession of beneficiaries, the more diffusive would be the charity.[57]

In general, the author was most counterdisposed to the report of the committee. Rather than supplying a plan for the binding out of the orphans, the author hypothesized that a better title for the report might have been found in "Reasons for not binding out Girard College boys."[58] Each position held by the committee was analyzed at length and for the most part held to be in error or in need of revision. In this sense, his remarks on the conditions of apprenticeship are offered as a digest of his general comments:

> I have a word or two to say about the 'obstacle in the way of binding out orphans,' to which the Report adverts, (p. 10). I do not think any material change has taken place in the domestic relations of masters and apprentices since Mr. Girard's death. The practice of keeping apprentices with the master at his house had become nearly obsolete before that time. And considering the intercourse of Mr. Girard with this class of men, we can scarcely suppose him to be ignorant of it. But my main object is to put the boot on the right leg. It is neither the 'selfishness of masters,' nor 'combinations among journeymen,' nor 'the necessitites of unfortunate parents,' that has caused 'the ancient and useful operation of binding by indenture to be almost abandoned.' It is rather to be ascribed to the cupidity and pride and weakness of parents--to the general spirit

---

[57]Private Document, op. cit., pp. 3-5. Lest his argument be misunderstood the author took particular pains to emphasize the fact that he did not intend Girard College to become a mere orphan asylum: "Should any one be disposed to regard this view as disparaging to the grandeur of Mr. Girard's charity, by making the College little more than an immense victualiing house for poor children, he will greatly misapprehend me. I am disposed to put as high an estimate on the culture of the mind as any man in this Board or out of it, but I esteem the culture of the affections--of the moral nature--of the heart, as of far higher importance; and I am quite sure, that one of the most formidable obstacles to the culture of these is the pressure of poverty--of hunger and nakedness and homelessness." (p. 5).

> of independence and insubordination which characterizes our age and time and country--to the impatience of restraint, and a determination on the part of our youth to take the reins into their own hands. Apprentices envy journeymen, and journeymen envy masters. Masters feel that their interests are not regarded by the apprentice, and that every opportunity will be seized to take advantage; and apprentices and their parents regard the master with anything but a complacent spirit. It was not so formerly.
>
> . . . .
>
> And in this view it may be very questionable, whether the training we pursue here is not essentially defective. If we wish our boys to be patient, obedient, docile apprentices, should we not cultivate in them a very different spirit from that which most boys of their age manifest? Can we expect that they will fall into the rank of 'youngest apprentices' on a farm, in a workshop, or factory, or on the deck of a ship, and readily fulfil the appointed but often repulsive and humiliating offices of that station, if they have been accustomed to life in a palace, with servants to wait upon them, and their wishes not only gratified, but anticipated by those who have the care of them? And we must not forget, that whatever embarrassments may be met on this score by the present arrangements of the institution, it would be much increased by the retention of any considerable number of pupils, for any cause, beyond the age of fourteen. At that period of life a transition from an institution like this to the care and service of a master under indentures, may be made without comparatively little hazard; but when such a youth finds another cubit added to his stature, or another twelvemonth to his age, he takes a yoke with more reluctance, and especially if his self-esteem has been fed by commendations of his scholarship, or by being admitted to the privileges of a pet. We cannot evade the obligation to bind our pupils out at some time between fourteen and eighteen. This is not an open question. In the whole progress of their College course, therefore, reference should be had to the formation of those habits and the acquisition of that knowledge which (to use the expressive language of the Report) will make them 'covetable' apprentices. I submit, that so far as such habits and acquirements are needful for this end, they are easily attainable by or before the age of fourteen.[59]

It is not known what action--if any--was taken by the Board of Directors subsequent to the meetings held in March and in April, but the "Minutes of the Common Council for June 3, 1852," note that the Common Council had concurred in the following resolution passed by the Select Council:

---

[59] *Ibid.*, pp. 19-21.

> Whereas, The Time has arrived at which, in the opinion of the Councils, it has become proper and necessary, that some definite arrangement should be made as to the proper mode of disposition of such of the pupils of the Girard College as may be sufficiently matured for such future position in life as their capacity and inclinations may warrant, and Whereas, it is particularly desirable that by the earliest equitable arrangement in this particular, other pupils may be admitted (from the very large number of applications now pending) to participate in the advantages of the Institution; therefore,
>
> Resolved, That the Directors of the Girard College be requested to take into consideration the adoption of a proper system to be observed in relation to the appropriate manner and time, at which the pupils of that Institution are to be placed in such situations as their respective capacity and inclinations may warrant, and report the result of their deliberations to Councils.[60]

On July 8 following, the Select Council received from the Board of Directors a draft of "An Ordinance to provide for the binding out of the Orphans of the College" which the Council in turn referred to the Commissioner of the Girard Estates.[61] On November 4, the Common Council noted that they had been informed by the Select Council that the Commissioner of the Girard Estates had forwarded to them a bill entitled "An ordinance to provide for the binding out of orphans in the Girard College" and thereupon proceeded to a consideration of the bill. In the consideration of the bill amendments were proposed. A non-concurrence to amendments between the Councils led to the appointment of a Committee of Conference and a necessary postponement of discussion.[62] One week later, on November 11, the Committee was discharged from further consideration of the subject since the committee had been unable to agree on the

---

[60] Journal of the Common Council of the City of Philadelphia for 1851-1852, Beginning October 17, 1851 and Ending October 7, 1852, pp. 164-165.

[61] Journal of the Select Council of the City of Philadelphia for 1851-1852, Beginning October 17, 1851 and Ending October 7, 1852, p. 171.

[62] Journal of Common Council of the City of Philadelphia for 1852-1853, Beginning October 15, 1852, and Ending September 29, 1853, pp. 27-31.

proposed amendments.[63] On the same date, another amended draft of the ordinance was proposed in the Common Council and was passed;[64] however, on November 24, the Common Council was notified that the Select Council had passed the bill with further amendments to which the Common Council non-concurred. Another Committee of Conference was then appointed.[65] On December 2, 1852, "An Ordinance to Provide for the Binding out of Orphans in the Girard College" was passed; its interest lies in affording a long range view of the evolution of the changing thought in the very critical and continuingly difficult program of the binding out of the students. It is this ordinance which clearly demonstrates a significant departure in the history of Girard College, and it is to a consideration of this ordinance, the whole concept of binding out, and its subsequent influence on the program of studies at Girard College with which the following section is concerned.

II

The text of the ordinance is as follows:

> SECTION 1. _Be it ordained and enacted by the Citizens of Philadelphia, in Select and Common Councils assembled_, That every orphan child in the Girard College, upon attaining the age of fourteen years, or as soon thereafter as an appropriate place can be secured, shall be bound out as directed by the will of Stephen Girard, to suitable occupations, as those of Agriculture, Navigation, Mechanical trades and Manufactures, in the manner hereinafter mentioned: _Provided_, He has been instructed in the various branches of a sound education in accordance with the will of Stephen Girard: _And provided_, That where there are such developments as to induce the belief by the Board of Directors of said college, that a further education is likely to be decidedly beneficial, and the Board of Commissioners of the Girard Estates shall approve thereof, such child shall not be bound out, but remain and receive such further education as may be deemed expedient.[66]

[63] _Ibid._, p. 32, Appendix pp. 4-5. [64] _Ibid._, p. 34.

[65] _Ibid._, pp. 49-53.

[66] _Ordinances of the Corporation of the City of Philadelphia: Passed Between January 1, 1850, and June 6, 1854_, p. 1320.

The passage of the ordinance, however, did not resolve the differences of opinion that had previously existed. In their report to the Select and Common Councils on February 17, 1853, the Committee of Visitation for the months of November and December 1852, noted:

> During the period, or term, for which your Committee was appointed, the most important event which has yet occurred in the history of the College took place, in the passage of an ordinance by Councils, to authorize the binding out of a portion of the pupils. In view of the difficulties connected with this subject, and having reason to believe that considerable difference of opinion existed with regard to the construction of this ordinance your Committee deemed it their duty to inquire of the Board of Directors whether, in their judgment, any alteration or amendment of it was necessary, in order to enable them to bind out, at the present time, a portion of the pupils. Your Committee, through its Chairman, on their visit in December, submitted a resolution on this point to the Board of Directors; and on the tenth of this month, they received from J. Cowperthwait, Esq., Chairman of the Committee on Instruction, a reply which is herewith annexed.
>
> . . . .
>
> Philadelphia, February 10, 1853.
>
> My Dear Sir:--I called several times at your office, for the purpose of submitting to you the opinion of the City Solicitor, respecting the doubtful provisions of the ordinance recently passed by Councils, to provide "for the binding out of Orphans in the Girard College," without the pleasure of seeing you.
>
> The opinion of Mr. Olmsted seems to remove all obstructions to carrying out the ordinance; and at the stated meeting of the Board of Directors held yesterday, a resolution was adopted, directing the Standing Committee of the Board to proceed at once to carry out its several provisions. I hope this will be as satisfactory to the Committee of Visitation as it is to
>
> Yours, very truly and respectfully,
> Your obedient servant.
> J. COWPERTHWAIT.
> Chairman of the Committee on Instruction.
>
> A. G. Waterman, Esq.,
> Chairman of the Committee of Visitation.[67]

Beyond the legal aspects of the ordinance, a special committee of the

[67] Journal of the Select Council of the City of Philadelphia for 1852-1853: Beginning October 15, 1852 and Ending September 29, 1853, p. 105; Appendix pp. 194-196.

Board of Directors had been appointed on January 26, 1853[68] to report to the Board their reply to ". . . a series of inquiries involving the general economy of the institution--the course and extent of instruction to be given--the principles to be adopted in the admission and discharge of pupils, and indeed the whole design and scope of the charity."[69] Their purpose, the committee believed, was ". . . to secure landmarks, or to establish a few leading principles that should [would] determine the general policy of the Board in the future direction of the college."[70]

The inquiries posed to the committee totalled thirteen substantial sections and turned on a central question of the practibility of binding out students at the age of fourteen and how the termination of a student's enrollment at this age as well as other advanced ages would graphically influence the curriculum and other provisions at the college. In essence, the inquiries were addressed to the following areas of concern or discussion attendant to the major questions: (1) the possible enrollment depending upon a general binding out age of fourteen; (2) the effect of the enrollment age on the moral interests of the institution; (3) the extent of further education needed to sustain pupils who should remain beyond the age of fourteen; (4) an interpretation of the will of Stephen Girard with a view to determine the largest number of pupils to be retained beyond the age of fourteen; (5) the age required to retain the pupils in order that they be educated in the manner prescribed; (6) an evaluation of the will in order to postulate judgments as to whether the comprehensive education prescribed by Girard would obtain more eligible indentureships for the pupils than might be received at the

---

[68] Report (Board of Directors of the Girard College for Orphans, June 15, 1853, This report was submitted on June 8, 1853, and reflected the considerations of a Committee which had been convened on January 26, 1853).

[69] Ibid., p. 5.

[70] Ibid.

age of fourteen; (7) an attempt to determine whether the intent and design of the testation would be met best by keeping pupils beyond the age of fourteen or by receiving a comparable amount of new pupils; and lastly, (8) their view of the appropriations for the college.[71]

Of all the facts to be considered, the financial concern appears to have been the underlying key to the central problem. On this point, and in overview of the problem, the committee noted:

> . . . there can be but one opinion as to the leading purpose of the founder of Girard College. It was to furnish a desirable and safe home, a useful education and the knowledge of a good trade or business to the largest number of beneficiaries that the term of the will would admit, and the income of the trust-fund would maintain. And we are persuaded that, could the appropriated fund have been preserved for the use of the College, with its natural accumulation and without loss or abatement, or even if no more had been absorbed in the College structure than the original estimate contemplated, few of the perplexing questions which have embarrassed the administration of the charity would have been raised. The views of those who insist on a thorough and liberal course of education, for all the pupils who have the capacity and inclination to pursue it, might then have been fully met, without conflicting with the views of others, who would be disposed to educate the largest number in a more limited degree.[72]

Closely connected to this same issue, the tenth inquiry and the reply submitted by the committee brings into sharp focus the difficulty of the committee in attempting to resolve satisfactorily a basic philosophic consensus of the whole problem of apprenticeship:

> The <u>tenth</u> inquiry asks for an opinion on a point which the Committee regard as of grave importance. If the terms of the will, or the condition in which the trust is placed by a reduction of its value, leaves it in any degree discretionary with the trustees or their agents, to what extent the education of the pupils shall be carried, it is obviously their first duty to inquire what course will be most advantageous to the beneficiary. Now the question submitted to us is,
>
> "Whether there is good ground to believe that the most comprehensive education which the terms of the will allow would be likely to secure for the pupils, generally, a more eligible

---

[71] <u>Ibid.</u>, p. 5.

[72] <u>Ibid.</u>, p. 5.

> indentureship to <u>any such occupation as the testator contemplated</u> (taking into view the pupils advanced age and corresponding maturity of good or evil habits, principles, &c.) than they would have obtained at fourteen, or as soon thereafter as suitable places could be provided for them?"
>
> The Committee have considered the various bearings of this question, and are of the opinion that if the terms of the will clearly required, and the condition of the trust-fund would unquestionably warrant the instruction of the pupils in all the branches named in the will, so far as their capacities would admit, up to the full age of eighteen years, it would rather embarrass than facilitate their introduction, as indentured apprentices, to most of the occupations which the testator contemplated. At the same time the Committee concede that some few pupils, of peculiar capacity, might be retained in the institution till eighteen years of age, and instructed thoroughly in certain branches for which they have a strong predilection, and reap great advantages from it--<u>provided</u> at the end of the time a place were in reserve for them, which all this peculiar training is fitting them to occupy. Were there, for example, in our country, government-schools for the training of lads to the various departments of the marine service; and if a high degree of education would secure for a pupil, in such a school, eminent advantages for promotion and lucrative employment, and if such pupils were admissible at eighteen, or even seventeen years of age, it would be clearly such pursuits and evinced a capacity for them, all the advantages we could command for their thorough instruction in those branches of knowledge which would best fit them for their prospective profession. But, while the tastes and capacities of the pupils are but imperfectly developed; while even their physical powers are undetermined; while the question of indenture is rather what place we can get than what place we would choose, and while the obstructions and embarrassments occasioned by the provisions of the ordinance and terms of the indenture, are not likely to be diminished by having an older and more sensitive (as well as more sensible) class to bind--to say nothing of the restrictions which our limited appropriations impose--it seems to your Committee that our pupils, in the mass, will be more likely to secure eligible positions, under indentures, at fourteen, or soon after, than if retained to a later period of life and furnished with higher intellectual endowments. That there are exceptions to this principle we shall none of us deny.[73]

On the basis of the deliberations, the committee concluded their report with the observation that the "narrowness" of the means to support the institution meant ". . . that so far from extending an enlarging the basis of our operations, or elevating the standard of our instruction, we are rather in

---

[73] Ibid., pp. 13-14.

danger of being obliged to reduce both still further."[74]

On this account, unless an increase in appropriations would be realized, the committee sustained ". . . the course recently adopted by the Board of improving the earliest opportunity after the pupils arrive at the age of fourteen, to indenture him to some useful business.. . . ."[75] However, even beyond their expeditious reaction to fiscal realities, the committee noted in passing that while there would be benefits from a ". . . more extensive and liberal education of a select class of our pupils. . . it is, moreover, to be considered, that there are disadvantages connected with the retention of an older class of pupils, in the institution, which our inability to retain them helps us to escape."[76]

Significantly, the committee believed the lack of "a powerful home or parental influence" to be one such disadvantage which, they suggested, could be compensated by "the instruction and discipline of a proper master" through an early apprenticeship:

> The domestic arrangements of the Institution must always and necessarily partake largely of the nature of a family or boarding school. A part of the pupils will be chiefly under female instruction and discipline to which those of maturer age will reluctantly submit. Most of the motives and principles which are supposed to govern the students in an ordinary college, are but imperfectly felt (if felt at all) in an Institution so totally different as ours is in its whole design and organization. A powerful home or parental influence which follows the lad to a College proper, is a potent auxiliary to the discipline established there. And though all may not feel it in their own persons, they will still be subject to a public sentiment, of which it is a chief element. The parent's authority is generally in perfect unison with the authorities of the College. We have not a large share of this helpful influence here. In many cases there is nothing to derive it from, and in others a positive influence is exerted adverse to the wholesome discipline and economy of the Institution. Hence it is that other things being equal, we should rather desire that a large majority of our pupils having attained the age of fourteen, were put to a trade as soon as they can be well assured

---

[74]*Ibid.*, p. 19. [75]*Ibid.* [76]*Ibid.*

> of the instruction and discipline of a proper master. In many European establishments, of a character somewhat akin to this, provision is made in University scholarships for such beneficiaries of public or private charities, as promise to reap unusual advantages from it, thus avoiding the evils and embarrassments which are inseparable from mingling children of tender age with youth who are impatient of control and full of restless desires to escape from it. But there is no intermediate place for our pupils to occupy between our school-rooms and playgrounds, and the stern realities of an apprenticeship.
>
> To prepare them for those realities, nothing is more important than the strict yet kind and saluatary discipline--moral, intellectual and physical--which our boys are placed here to receive. Under this discipline they ought to be well fitted for the best indentures the country offers, and while our present inability to organize a department for a higher grade of instruction continues, it would seem to be most in harmony with the leading design of the Institution, to transfer them as early as practicable by the terms of the will, to the hands of those who are to train them for the occupations and responsibilities of manhood.[77]

With the formulation of basic principles to be followed in carrying out Girard's apprenticeship program thus established, the Directors sought to carry into effect the binding-out of the orphans. The first indenture had been signed on April 30, 1853;[78] however, shortly after, it evidently became apparent to the Directors that changes in the traditional apprenticeship arrangements would be necessary since there had been difficulty in obtaining masters who would provide board and lodging for apprentices in the master's own residence.[79] As a result of a bill forwarded to the City Councils by the Commissioners of the Girard Estate, the Councils passed on July 7, 1853, "A Supplement to the Ordinance passed December 2d, 1852," entitled "An Ordinance to provide for the binding out of Orphans in the Girard College."[80] This

---

[77] Ibid., pp. 19-20.

[78] Cheesman A. Herrick, op. cit., p. 353. Herrick notes: The first student of the College to be placed under indenture was Benjamin P. Wrigley whose indenture was signed April 30, 1853.

[79] Cf. the previous discussion of this point, pp. 103,104,110,111.

[80] Journal of the Common Council of the City of Philadelphia for 1852-1853: Beginning October 15, 1852, and Ending September 29, 1853, pp. 230-231.

supplement dealt with the boarding of apprentices and the alteration of indentures and provided:

> Section 1. Be it ordained and enacted by the Citizens of Philadelphia in Select and Common Councils assembled, That the Board of Directors of the Girard College may, in their discretion, omit in the indentures of apprenticeship provided that the master shall provide for boarding and lodging for his apprentice in his own place of residence, and allow the master to provide such other place for boarding and lodging his apprentice as shall, on investigation in every case by the Board of Directors, be approved by them: Provided the Board of Commissioners of the Girard Estate consent thereto, and that every subsequent change of residence shall also be approved as heretofore provided.[81]

Before the end of 1853, it had also become evident that serious problems were presenting themselves that made the continuing binding out of the students practicable only with flexibility and with recurring modifications of the criteria which had been accepted some months earlier. It would not be possible to attribute all these problems to the changing social context in which apprenticeship may have had a declining relevancy;[82] but already prophetic

---

[80] Journal of the Common Council of the City of Philadelphia for 1852-1853; Beginning October 15, 1852, and Ending September 29, 1853, pp. 230-231.

[81] Ordinances of the Corporation of the City of Philadelphia Passed Between January 1, 1850 and June 6, 1854, op. cit., p. 1354.

[82] See in this connection, Edward Meredith Fee, The Origin and Growth of Vocational Industrial Education in Philadelphia to 1917, p. 49, particularly Fee's observation: "The decline of apprenticeship is even more strikingly illustrated in a study of the apprenticing at Girard College which was set up under the provisions of Stephen Girard's will. Girard boys were to be bound out between the ages of fourteen and eighteen years to agriculture, navigation, arts and mechanical trades according to their capacities and inclinations. In 1852, before the Directors had bound the first boys, they reported that Girard's sole design in maintaining and educating orphan boys morally, physically and intellectually in boyhood was that they might become covetable apprentices and eventually useful and happy men. This plainly indicated duty imposed an insuperable task on the directors of Girard College with which they struggled for many years, in the face of the realization that even before Girard's death 'the practice of keeping apprentices with the master at his home had become nearly obsolete,' in Philadelphia. . . . In 1852, the directors deplored this condition with which they had to contend and attributed

assessments were being made about the necessity for significant changes. In a report to the Board of Directors on October 12th, 1853, President Allen indicated that there were obvious inconveniences at the college ". . . incident to our present unsystematic method of binding out the orphans, and can be remedied only by a radical change in that method."[83] To point up the inconvenience President Allen provided an extract from a report of the Principal Teacher of the Principal Department, Professor Stephens, which reads:

> I think it necessary to the usefulness of the Principal Department, that the time which the scholars will remain in the College, should be better defined than at present. A large majority of the pupils consider themselves as candidates, waiting for the first desirable situation that may offer. Although at last they may have waited years instead of months, their calculations are based on the shorter term, and accordingly, they consider their school days as virtually ended. In some instances, I am sorry to add, that I am of the same opinion. The future for each scholar is so utterly uncertain, that the most powerful and best of motives to exertion which a scholar can have, is taken away--the prospect of this, an impatient anxiety is substituted, which is most active in those who would otherwise be the best students. This state of feeling in school is calculated to destroy the spirit of application to study, and to some degree has done it. Also, as candidates for places are taken from all classes indiscriminately, the fragments of two classes will often have to be united, to the discouragement of the more advanced class. We cannot at present promise any class in school, more than one term of progress for the future, for however long members may remain at the College, they are liable

---

it to the selfishness of the masters, combinations among journeymen and to the attractiveness of weekly and monthly wages which induced parents to assent to such bargains through ignorance of the consequences to their children. The possibilities of the system of indenturing were by no means exhausted, however, and in the struggles of the directors to find and overcome the obstacles that had rendered traditional forms of apprenticeship obsolete, we have a number of clues that pointed to succeeding forms of vocational education." Although Fee's discussion of the declination of apprenticeship is perceptive, his discussion is misleading of a grand, evolutionary schema for the reformation of apprenticeship at Girard College by the Board of Directors. Actually, the Board of Directors laboriously and awkwardly adopted the apprenticeship concept against a whole host of pressures as the discussion in this chapter shows.

[83]Extract (From the Report of William H. Allen, President of the Girard College for Orphans, Made to the Board of Directors at its meeting, October 12th 1853, and ordered to be printed for the use of members.)

> at the end of each term, through no fault of theirs, to be joined with the class below them. The present method of binding out pupils, is equally destructive to the efforts of the teacher, as of the pupil. For it puts it out of his power to form any plan for his course of instruction, or pursue any method. The teachers in the Principal Department fully concur in the opinions here expressed.
>
> Mr. Holden was the first to call my attention to the subject last spring. Professor Becker informs me that he finds the continuous progress of classes already so far broken up, that each pupil requires separate instruction. Professor Gengembre says it is a common remark of the boys, that it is of no use to learn French, because they are going out pretty soon. It is at the request of these gentlemen, that I make known to you their opinions. I would not have the appearance of complaining of necessary evils. I can see that these evils may have been to some extent unavoidable at the outset of the business of binding out the boys; and it is because it seems to me that a system might now be established that will obviate them, that I would respectfully ask your attention to the subject.[84]

President Allen added that the experience of the previous six months in binding out the orphans had shown that the orphans would be in demand as apprentices and would be willing to work. Of fifty-six orphans who had been indentured or who were out on trial, only six had returned to the college after the trial period and that most of those boys who had gone out on a second trial had usually been successful. On this basis, he believed "It therefore appears that the argument in favor of binding out wherever a place may offer, lest another place equally desirable might not be found has lost much of its force."[85] In this connection, President Allen further noted that formerly he had advocated the binding out soon after the age of fourteen those orphans who had been known to exert an "unfavorable influence upon the morals and discipline of the College," but that since the removal of many of these boys, and although many of the better boys had been indentured, he had noticed "a more willing subordination and a more cheerful obedience" than before, obviating the motive to bind out older boys as soon as possible. To implement the needed changes,

---

[84] *Ibid.*, pp. 5-6.

[85] *Ibid.*, p. 1.

President Allen offered a plan for the Board's consideration, noting that if the plan were approved, a course of study would be submitted, ". . . sufficiently elementary to suit the age and capacity of the scholars, and at the same time sufficiently comprehensive to meet the requirements of the will of Mr. Girard."[86] The plan and the course of study were adopted by the Board.[87]

In spite of all the drawbacks that existed, apprenticeship became a very active program at Girard College. By the end of the year 1854, eighty-nine orphans had been apprenticed and thirteen other orphans who had been eligible to be bound out were allowed to cancel their indentures in order that they might accept situations in other states or to obtain places not eligible by indentures.[88] The goal of the Directors ". . . to make them [the orphans] good apprentices, and so to furnish them mentally and morally, so as to command the best places . . ."[89] appeared to have been achieved. In speaking of this success and in overview of the problems that had been expected, Henry W. Arey, Secretary of Girard College and Superintendent of Binding Out, reported the following in part in his first report:

---

[86] *Ibid*., pp. 3-4.

[87] *Sixth Annual Report of the Board of Directors of the Girard College for Orphans For The Year 1853*, pp. 5-8. For the complete text of the important modification see Appendix I, pp. . The following from the adopted plan has particular significance in light of the history of the college to this point: *Third*.--That the scholars who shall be admitted to the Principal Department, be placed on a course of study which shall occupy three years. . . . *Eighth*.--That during the time which shall intervene between graduation and binding or going out on trial, the graduates shall continue to reside in the College, and shall be employed in manual labor, or in pursuing such studies as may be assigned them.

[88] Henry W. Arey, "Report of Superintendent of Binding Out," *Seventh Annual Report of the Board of Directors of the Girard College for Orphans*, p. 15.

[89] *Seventh Annual Report of the Board of Directors of the Girard College for Orphans*, p. 7.

The important portion of Mr. Girard's scheme of benevolence, which requires that the orphan shall be taught an occupation in addition to receiving sustenance and education in his College, has been sufficiently tested during the past year, to justify and perhaps make interesting, a brief report of its results and came near for its experiment, the authorities of the Institution approached the subject with great anxiety, and perhaps, well founded doubts. The practical realization of all the hopes and wishes of the Founder, embracing as they probably did in his mind the elevation of labor, as well as individual charity, no portion of duty connected with the College could exceed it in responsibility, as certainly no one was so dependent on extraneous causes for its success or failure. Among these difficulties most prominent was the entire change, which, in the interval between Mr. Girard's death and the present time, has taken place in the relations between master and apprentice. Few mechanics of the present day in the city of Philadelphia receive apprentices, or admit into their homes and their families the lads who are acquiring from them a knowledge of their trade. Giving a weekly pension in recompense for their services, when the labor of the day is finished, the master considers that his duty is done and that no further moral or legal responsibility attaches to him; while the lad, relieved from all guardianship, is free to pass the rest of his time as he pleases: profitably, if his impulses are good, but disastrously, if the victim to evil inclinations or bad companions. And in perhaps a majority of cases, long before the period of legal age has arrived, eager for the practical freedom which appears to be the characteristic of the times, he throws off the slight restraint hitherto imposed upon him, and emerges into active life an unfinished and incompetent workman. While benevolent men, who have given the subject attention, are justly attributing much of the disorder and vice prevailing in our large cities to this unhappy change in the education of the laboring classes, it was manifest that the Directors of the College could not feel it consistent with the obligation imposed upon them by the confidence of Councils, to allow their orphans to go out into the world exposed to all the trials and temptations which the present system encourages. It was therefore an anxious experiment, whether places could be found for the pupils where a home as well as an Instructor would be furnished--where moral and personal restraint would be continued--and where the guardianship of the lad would be merely transferred from the Institution to the master

It is most gratifying to be able to report that the experiment has been tried and with greater success than the most sanguine anticipated. A much larger number of applications has been received than the College could possibly supply, and as experience makes more perfect our system, and the good conduct of many of our lads becomes better known, a gradual but decided improvement in the character and grades of the situations offered is apparent; giving reason to hope that we will hereafter be able to accomplish still more for society and these children.[90]

---

[90]Ibid., pp. 13-15. In April, 1854, by an Ordinance passed in Councils, it was enacted that in addition to the duties required of him, the Secretary

While this success continued, there were at the same time other changes that were impending. In his report for 1856, the President of the Board of Directors noted that changes were expected in the future but that none appeared to be immediately necessary.[91] However, a year later, in his report for 1857, he noted that there was an evident need for consideration of those orphans who, for various reasons might be returning to the college even after being indentured and of those who might be remaining after their course of study had been

---

of the College was to act as the Superintendent of Binding Out. Ibid., p. 7. For the first catalogue containing the names of the apprentices, and the names, residences and occupations of the masters, see Appendix J, pp.

[91] Ninth Annual Report of the Board of Directors of the Girard College for Orphans for the Year 1856, pp. 11-12. See particularly, the observations of the President of the Board on the possible changes that might be required: "While the comprehensive mind and clear intelligence of Stephen Girard established the general plan with perfect precision; while he has so marked the outlines of his system of enlightened benevolence as to prevent either misunderstanding or deviation; he has yet left to those to whom he has entrusted its practical management and supervision, the opportunity, as indeed he has imposed upon them the duty, of accommodating its subordinate provisions to such changes as may take place, from time to time, in the number of pupils, in the enlarged means of maintaining and instructing them, in the inclinations which they may severally exhibit, in the varying habits of trade and industrial occupations, and in the modifications that science and improvement may make in the different classes of pursuits into which he designs that the objects of his bounty shall be fitted to enter. Looking to the future, we cannot but expect such changes, and we may reasonably anticipate in them increased opportunities for extending, more widely and beneficially, the philanthropic provisions of which the foundations have been so excellently laid. As these shall aruse we sgakk be best guided in the future by the experience of the past. As the resources of the institution shall be gradually increased· as the number of the orphans received into it shall be gradually enlarged; as the regulations for their comfort and moral training continue to be successively tested by a careful and unprejudiced observation of their actual results; as we shall see, in practice, the effects of systems of intellectual instruction upon minds, differing in capacity and upon inclinations swaying to the exercise of different faculties; we shall be prepared to apply the lessons of experience to the emergencies that shall arise. Looking to the present situation of the institution, the amount of its annual resources, the ages and number of the pupils, and the existing opportunities for their favorable introduction into active life, there does not appear to be any material alteration which it is now expedient to suggest, or which may be immediately looked for or desired."

completed.[92] A reference to this subject issue was made at a meeting held by the Board of Directors on January 13, 1858. The subject was referred to a special committee and the committee reported to the Board on February 23rd.[93] The report of this committee and its bearing on future events has particular interest because it points up a salient feature of the growth and development of the college: At Girard College the course of study and apprenticeship continued to undergo an apparent gradual evolution with certain underlying conceptions always in evidence, but with necessary alterations, from time to time, indicative of changing viewpoints and suggestive of influences, not always apparent, upon the line of development. The underlying beliefs guiding the directors were based upon Girard's desire that the orphans should receive the branches of a sound education, suitable and rational exercise and recreation, and were to be inbued with the purest principles of morality. The report of the committee proceeded from these assumptions to what they thought the college was to be: "That is to be his [the orphan's] _home_, his _school_, his _church_: and (if he dies) there is to be his _grave_."[94]

The major problem seen by the committee seems to have gone beyond a concern for the orphans who might remain or return, but rather revolved on the possible years of residence that would apply to all orphans. Rather than

---

[92] _Tenth Annual Report of the Board of Directors of the Girard College for Orphans For The Year 1857_, p. 19.

[93] _Report_, _. . ._, (Board of Directors of the Girard College for Orphans, [February 23d,] 1858, [This report notes that the report was adopted by the committee on February 23, 1858].) On January 13, the subject has been referred to the Committee of Discipline and Discharge. By amendment, other members of the Board were added thereby creating a special committee. On February 10, the special committee requested of the Board that the Committee on Instruction be added to the special committee. The request was granted, constituting a joint committee on the subject.

[94] _Ibid._, p. 2.

responding primarily to the problem of the orphans who would spend the most time at the college, the committee noted that owing to the "obvious inequalities" in the possible years of orphan's attendance, they believed that it was their duty ". . . to administer the system so that (if, in any wise, possible) the orphan who has the least time to stay shall enjoy such advantages as shall compensate for the neglect (not his own) to secure an earlier admission."[95] To offset these inequalities, the committee suggested:

> To this end it may be needful to increase the corps of instructors, to subdivide classes, and to give the various departments facilities for adapting the teaching to these subdivisions, so that the exigencies of each individual case may be duly regarded. If this is true of the department of letters, it is still more obviously true of the department of morals, inasmuch as the proper inculcation of "the purest principles of morality," seems to have been quite as prominent an object of the Founder's concern as the advancement of his beneficiaries in useful knowledge--but especially as moral idiosyncracies in children require a much more discriminating treatment than is needful for mere intellectual culture. The physical and domestic training of the pupils, also, constitutes a distinct subject of our care, and deserves a not less specific and systematic process of education than the intellectual and moral. Indeed, they are so intimately and inseparably connected, that it is difficult to conceive on what principle their disjunction, as exhibited in our present arrangements, can be justified or even explained.[96]

The report dealt at length with the daily routine of the orphans at the college, describing in depth the domestic associations at the college, the moral character and habits of the orphan, and the influence of the teacher, prefects, and governesses on the general development of the individual orphan with each point leading up to the committee's desire to bring about the influence that a "good home" would have on the character of a child. In their approach to attain this, they intended "to make every department--the chapel, the schoolroom, the refectory, the dormitory, and the playground--directly tributory to the combined and simultaneous improvement of the minds and hearts,

---

[95] Ibid.

[96] Ibid., pp. 2-3.

the morals and manners of our [the] pupils."[97]

---

[97] *Ibid.*, pp. 14-15. This touches fundamentally a recurrent theme in the history of education at Girard College, *e.g.*, the moral element and its place in the instruction of its students. Girard had desired ". . . that all the instructors and teachers in the college shall take pains to instil into the minds of the scholars the *purest principles of morality* . . ." Throughout the history of the college, this has remained one of the (if not, at times, *the* major) efforts of the administrators. Moreover, soon after Girard's death, his heirs sought to have the will set aside, using as one of their arguments the contention that Girard's educational plan (particularly his exclusion of ecclesiastics) was un-Christian and in conflict with the Constitution and Laws of Pennsylvania. In 1836, the Circuit Court of the United States had decided on this issue in favor of the executors but on appeal the case was taken before the Supreme Court of the United States. The case was argued first in 1843 but the court ordered a new argument for the January 1844 term. This re-argument was conducted with Daniel Webster and Walter Jones representing the heirs and Horace Binney and John Sergeant representing the executors of the estate and the City of Philadelphia. Justice Story delivered the opinion of the court which, in part, reads ". . . we are satisfied that there is nothing in the devise establishing the College, or in the regulations and restrictions contained therein, which are inconsistent with the Christian religion or are opposed to any known policy of the State of Pennsylvania." [This famous case is reported as *Vidal* v. *Girard's Executors*, 2 How. 127 (1844)].

However, it is interesting to note that Webster's argument before the court against the exclusion of ecclesiastics became as widely known as the decision delivered by the court. Soon after Webster's presentation, a committee composed of interested citizens representing several Christian denominations secured Webster's permission to have his argument "published and extensively disseminated." They noted: ". . . the powerful and eloquent argument of Mr. Webster. . . demonstrated the vital importance of Christianity to the success of our free institutions, and its necessity as the basis of all useful modern education; and that the general diffusion of that argument among the people of the United States is a matter of deep public interest." (See in this connection letter from H. L. Ellsworth to Hon. Daniel Webster. Washington, February 13, 1844, *infra*, p. 4. The correspondence between the committee and Webster and citations from Plato, Cicero, and Burke appeared as prefatory material to Webster's argument to which was also added a critical essay on Girard's will by Bishop White of Pennsylvania and an "Extract from the judgment of the Supreme Court of Pennsylvania, in the case of Updegraffe vs. the Commonwealth" in which the court maintained that Christianity was part of the common law of the State. The item was published as *Webster's Speech. A Defense of the Christian Religion, and the Religious Instruction of the Young. Delivered in the Supreme Court of the United States February 10, 1844, in the case of Stephen Girard's Will by Hon. Daniel Webster*. It is also interesting to note that after Webster's death on October 24, 1852, President William H. Allen had been invited and had accepted to deliver a eulogy on Daniel Webster which had been requested by the City Council of Philadelphia. In an overview of Webster's career, President Allen noted: "In the Girard College case he [Webster] labored under the disadvantage of not having the law on his side, but his argument is valuable as a defense of

One further aspect of this document is worthy of note--the brief but significant section dealing with orphans who might remain in the college after completion of their studies or who might return after being indentured, the prime purpose in convening the special committee:

> If our House of Reformation, erected and used for the purpose of reforming viciously disposed children, regard the voluntary return of an inmate to their custody as a hopeful indication, and are glad to extend to such an one protection and relief, we cannot persuade ourselves that an institution pre-eminently designed and fitted to be the ORPHAN'S HOME, must shut its gates against any one of its former inmates, who without any fault of his own, is turned adrift and seeks a temporary shelter and support at our hands.
>
> We may safely regard a provision for such cases as among the "details in relation to the organization of the College and its appendages," which the testator necessarily left to be arranged by the guardians of his charity, and we cannot doubt they

---

Christian education, and as a testimony of a great mind in favor of the benefits and blessings of our holy religion. Had he known at the time, that the noble sentiments he was pronouncing, were the very sentiments which would animate the Trustees and Directors of the College, he would have been spared the utterance of those gloomy forebodings, the greater part of which proved imaginary within his own life-time." (See in this connection, William H. Allen, _Eulogy on the Character and Services of the Late Daniel Webster, Pronounced at the Request of the Select and Common Councils of the City of Philadelphia, January 13, 1853_, p. 28).

Consequently, individuals who have had official connections with the college appear to have shown a predilection to provide measures that not only would tend to sustain the opinion of the Supreme Court but rather even to underscore it. Typical of this was the resolution passed by the City Councils of Philadelphia in the Fall of 1853 to authorize the Commissioners of the Girard Estates to print 500 copies of the arguments of Horace Binney and John Sergeant together with the judgment of the court in the Vidal case. (See _Arguments of the Defendant's Counsel, and Judgment of the Supreme Court U.S. in the case of Vidal et al Versus the Mayor etc. January Term 1844_. [Printed by Order of the Commissioners of the Girard Estate] 1854). Herrick in the same connection has noted in his _History of Girard College_: "So widespread was the effect of the Webster speech, and so damaging, that the Commissioner of the Girard Estates sought in 1854 to correct in some measure the false impression thus created [that the College was to be a school for propagating atheism] by having printed the arguments of Horace Binney and John Sergeant on the other side of the case, and the unanimous decision of the United States Supreme Court, handed down by Mr. Justice Story," (p. 181). For an extended discussion of the will controversy, see Cheesman A. Herrick, _Stephen Girard, Founder_, pp. 141-158.

> will see it to be in accordance with the whole spirit of the endowment, to receive back temporarily such of our deserving youth as have been by some unforseen event deprived of a home as apprentices . . . .
>
> . . . .
>
> Besides, the occasional return of an apprentice, we are likely always to have with us a few orphans, who for some cause, fail to secure places when their course of study terminates. At this time, some half dozen of this class are residents at the college. They are quite as much of a burden to themselves as to us. Without a systematical exercise for mind and body, they are very likely to contract habits most unpropitious to a useful or agreeable apprenticeship. It can hardly be questioned we think, that some provision should be made for such cases, not only for the maintenance of such residents, but for their further improvement. To this end, and for other and more permanent uses, we submit to the consideration of the Board the propriety of erecting a plain, movable, iron workshop, large enough to allow fifty boys to be employed at a time, in such useful manual occupations as may be found practicable, and a knowledge of which will prove of advantage to them, whatever business they may follow. There are many resident orphans of the older classes, who would greatly prefer some employment of this kind to the amusements of the play-ground, and it would be easy, by judicious alternations, to give all who wish for it an opportunity to practise some handicraft. The expense of such a building with a roof projecting sufficiently to keep dry a considerable area of ground for out-of-door exercise in wet weather, need not exceed two thousand dollars. For the few who might occasionally return to the college as their only home, and the few who fail to obtain a place at the close of their course, it might be needful to devise some combined system of labor and study; and also suitable provision for the board and lodging of all such temporary residents, such as would correspond with a spare bed and a seat at the table of a respectable home.[98]

The report closed with seven resolutions offered for the judgment of the Board.[99] On March 24 following, the resolutions were adopted by the Board.[100] At the same meeting a resolution was passed which referred the resolutions passed back to the joint committee ". . . to report to this Board as early as possible, a plan, in detail, in accordance therewith, and making the altera-

---

[98] Ibid., pp. 17-20.

[99] Ibid., pp. 30-32. These resolutions are found in Appendix K, pp.

[100] Ibid., p. 32.

tions necessary therefore in the present system of instruction, training, discipline, household arrangements and binding out, together with the requisite changes in the number, duties and salaries of the officers and teachers, and in the existing by-laws and regulations, and together also with such modifications of the ordinances as it may be necessary to propose to councils."[101]

The subsequent report was made the following year on April 28th.[102] From an examination of the membership of the Board of Directors for the years 1858 and 1859, there was apparently a change in the membership of the joint committee of 1858 to that of 1859.[103] The tone of the report indicates this

---

[101] Ibid.

[102] See in this connection, Report of the Special Committee on Homes, . . ., Made to the Board of Directors of the Girard College, April 28th, 1859; Proposing Certain Changes in the Instruction and Household of the College.

[103] See in this connection, Catalogue of the Girard College for Orphans for the years 1858 and 1859. These catalogues are usually found appended to the Annual Reports of the Board of Directors of the Girard College for Orphans. Significantly, four members of the 1858 committee, Frederick A. Packard, William Martin, Henry D. Gilpin, and William J. Duane were no longer members of the Board of Directors for 1859. A later President of the Board of Directors of the College has noted: "Very soon after the organization of the College the great importance of more instruction for the boys in the use of tools became apparent. In 1848, a committee of the then Board of Directors, of which Mr. William J. Duane, who prepared Mr. Girard's will, and the accomplished Henry D. Gilpin, were members recommended in the strongest language, some mechanical instruction but from some cause, no satisfactory teaching was then introduced." See in this connection, Fifteenth Annual Report of the Board of Directors of City Trusts. Report for the Year 1884, p. 14. William J. Duane, it is to be recalled, had been Girard's confidante, his solicitor, had drafted the final will, and had been an executor of the estate. It is not known if his interest in mechanical instruction was derived from his discourses with Girard or from what he believed necessary to the education of the orphans. In this connection, the historian James Parton notes that "with him alone" Girard discussed the projected institution and that Duane "without revealing his purpose, made inquiries among his travelled friends respecting the endowed establishments of foreign countries." See James Parton, Famous Americans of Recent Times, p. 242. See also in this connection Wilfred B. Wolcott, "Background of the Educational Provisions of the Will of Stephen Girard" (Unpublished Ph.D. dissertation, University of Pennsylvania, 1948.) Walcott

as well.

In the 1858 report much stress was placed on the need for the instructors prefects and governesses to be of "tried skill" if there was to be the proper development of the moral and intellectual character of the orphans.[104] In the Report of 1859, the committee appeared to take a defensive view of this:

> The want of an anxious, reflecting, earnest desire heretofore to impart knowledge on the part of some of the instructors, seems to have been reciprocated by an inattentive listlessness on that of the pupils. A spiritless, formal discharge of mere duties seems to have been too much the prevailing spirit of the household, subject, it is true, to most praiseworthy exceptions, but none the less evident on that account. To throw the blame on these things on the respectable and intelligent instructors employed in the educational department of the College, and to make them alone responsible for the existing state of things, would be most unjust, as your Committee believe it has in some degree been produced by the want of a more strict supervision and enlightened interest heretofore exercised by ourselves and our predecessors. To expect isolated teachers, unencouraged by commendation and unchecked by observation, to continue from year to year to instruct with vogor and energy classes of unambitious, objectless pupils, is to look for that which has never been seen any educational institution, and which ought not to be expected.[105]

---

attempted ". . . to discover what it was in the life of Stephen Girard that made him provide through his will for an institution for 'poor male, white, orphan children' . . ." (p. 8). His investigation revealed in part the following: "We have no right to state as a fact, nor indirectly to imply that Stephen Girard was fully aware of the developments of educational theory and practice during his long lifetime. . . . It is obvious that Girard was interested in education. There is no doubt that he developed a theory of education which found final expression in his will. . . . There has been a temptation to assume a causal relationship between certain co-existent facts in searching for the basis of Girard's educational ideas. . . . [Girard's library contained works of Rousseau and Voltaire; he had named a ship for Rousseau and one for Montesquieu; he had used words resembling the words used in _Émile_ which resembled words used by John Locke; and some statements of Girard bear resemblance to Franklin, Jefferson, Rousseau, and Locke.] To draw a clear line of descent for these ideas, implying causal relationship, requires a boldness of imagination that scorns the banalities of scientific method and mocks merrily the prose of facts." (p. 43.)

[104] _Report_. (February 23, 1858), _op_. _cit_., p. 7.

[105] _Report of the Special Committee on "Homes," . . ., op. cit._, p. 4.

Beyond this defense, however, the committee saw fit to suggest that the absence of instruction devoted to facts and things perhaps provided a better reason for the existing state of things. They explained:

> Mr. Girard laid down the basis of the education to be given to the pupils. They ought to be taught facts and things--navigation, astronomy and geography.
>
> This mariner and merchant knew the value of an every day education. He knew that a mariner and merchant required instruction in the branches he designated in his will should be taught in his College. He felt no doubt that some one of his beneficiaries might be induced to follow his way in life, and seek to be a mariner, qualified as such from the education received in his Institution, endowed by the munificent Founder, who, in his last legacy, styled himself mariner and merchant.
>
> Yet, in the fact of these facts and plain deduction from the life and legacy of Girard, there is not at this moment, after eleven years of effort to systematize a plan of leading facts and things, two sticks of wood in or about or connected with this Mariners' College to show even to the pupils what is the form of a ship or vessel. Navigation taught on black-boards, without even the rudest idea of what is the form of the structure to be navigated, is a formal, spiritless effort at instruction. This fact speaks more than pages of criticism. It is a disgrace that such an omission should so long have existed.[106]

In order to compensate for this, they suggested alterations in the plans of instruction and household government which included:

> To stimulate the pupils to improvement by preferments to higher classes, and by opportunities for obtaining practical knowledge of facts and things, in classes which are specially devoted to imparting such knowledge; thus making physical education a part of the course of instruction, and at the same time a recreation. . . .
>
> The Prefects, or at least two of them, if possible, ought to be competent mechanics, carpenters, locksmiths, or workers in metals, or mariners, &c., at the discretion of the President and Board of Directors.
>
> The Mechanical Prefects shall have charge of selected pupils, and instruct those who for merit are assigned to this class in facts and things, and a practical knowledge of those branches, the use of tools, &c. No pupil shall be in the classes of these Pre-

---

[106]*Ibid.*, p. 5.

> fects unless he has earned that position and its advantages, by merit as pupil in department, and attention to his studies, or either. These Prefects shall be required one hour in the evening to instruct by oral teaching their classes, in the branches of which they have charge. . . .
>
> The physical education shall be regulated and adapted to the age of the pupil. The higher classes shall as before stated be under the teaching of Prefects. A ship, such as now exists in similar institutions in Europe, ought to be constructed for the purpose of giving such pupils a knowledge of and acquaintance with seamanship, and thus as a gymnastic exercise, unite useful instruction with physical improvement. Mere play without any other object than play should be encouraged among the younger pupils. With the elder pupils physical education should be one result of the practical knowledge of facts and things taught as has been indicated.[107]

On April 28, 1859, the date of the report's submission, the recommendations of the Committee were adopted and the President of the College was instructed to carry out the plans and suggestions as indicated.[108]

It is interesting to note that the report fails to make any mention of orphans who might be remaining in the college or of those who might be returning after being indentured. An explanation for this might be derived from a report of the Committee of Visitation which was made in the interim between the two committee reports. On November 11, 1858, George F. Gordon, Chairman of the Committee of Visitation on Girard College for October presented the committee's report to the City Councils.[109] In the report, Chairman Gordon saw fit to make known his views on the proposed changes (recommended in the 1858 report) in the management of the college and are as follows:

> My attention has just been called to this report, issued by Messrs. Packard, Perkins, Flood, Martin, Gilpin, Fox, Duane, Watson. This report is exceedingly well written, and contains important suggestions which should meet with prompt considera-

---

[107] Ibid., pp. 8-12, passim.   [108] Ibid., p. 12.

[109] Journal of the Common Council of the City of Philadelphia, Beginning November 11, 1858, Ending May 5, 1859, p. 19.

> tion and action on the part of the present Directors. It contains one suggestion, however, which should receive prompt and continued disapproval, namely: the receiving back into the College such orphans as have been bound out and for reasons returned. Every orphan should be impressed with the unalterable fact, that, when he leaves the College, he must, through thick and thin, carve his way to fortune. The idea of erecting a separate building, for such as may be too lazy or too proud to work is monstrous. A palace for orphan loungers would, indeed, be a novelty. No American boy, 14 or 18 years of age, with a good education, should be considered an orphan. Let the great lesson of independence and self-reliance be fully taught:--Every orphan bound out from the College should carve his own way through life, and on no account be received back into the College.[110]

Equally significant are the committee' suggestions for an extension of the studies which in themselves reflect the general contemporary development of the art movement within the framework of a practical arts education.

> In looking over the trades to which the orphans are bound out, it is observable that very few are bound to artistic professions. Would it not be well to make an effort to direct the minds of the orphans to the higher branches of art? They are taken into the College at an age when they could be formed into almost any shape, or given the impulse to any tendency.
>
> Might not practical art--designing to be taught?--wood engraving, steel engraving, painting, statue, modeling, and such other kindred arts as would lead the minds of such orphans in the higher walks of artistic profession? Such a course of culture would be productive of varied and important results. It would teach the orphans, to some extent, the use of tools, a thing very much needed in the College. It would fit them, on leaving the College, at once to enter into profitable employment, in the arts named; as well as make them better fitted for any profession or trade, which they may adopt. It would be a credit to the College--for if the courses here intimated be

---

[110] "Report of the Committee on Girard College For the Month of October, 1858," Journal of the Common Council of the City of Philadelphia Beginning November 11, 1858, Ending May 5, 1859, Appendix pp. 36-37. This report is atypical among the reports of the Committee of Visitation. While not explicitly indicated, it evidently meant to point up the progress made during the first decade of the college's operation. The report discusses at length and with vigor (rather than briefly and perfunctorily) many facets of the institution and includes a useful appendix noting the annual cost of maintaining the college from 1848 to 1858, general notes on the total cost of the buildings, the orphan's fund, addresses at the college, and ordinances passed relating to the college.

adopted, some one, or more orphans would go forth from the College to astonish and charm the world with new attainments and new degrees of perfection in art and science.[111]

---

[111] Ibid., p. 33. This report also provides an interesting background to the operation of the Committee of Visitation. The original Ordinance of November 9, 1848, which provided for a standing Committee of Visitation, (see in this connection fn. 10, supra) had been followed by an Ordinance approved July 3, 1854. The ordinance provided: "The members of the Select and Common Council shall constitute a Standing Committee of Visitation to the Girard College for Orphans; and the President of each Council shall immediately after passing of this bill, and annual hereafter, on the organization of Councils, divide the members of their respective Councils into twelve sub-committees of twelve members each; six of whom shall be of Select and six of the Common Council, and who shall serve for one month in the order in which they are constituted as aforesaid. The said sub-committees to visit the Girard College for Orphans at least once in each month, and examine the condition thereof, and report the same to the Standing Committee of Visitation, or to Councils at their discretion, at such times as they shall deem expedient." (See in this connection, Journal of the Common Council of the Consolidated City of Philadelphia, Beginning June 12 and Ending December 2, 1854, p. 97. Appendix p. 28). The Report of the Committee of Visitation noted: "This ordinance which is still in force, imposes on each member of councils, the duty of visiting and attending to the interests of so much of the Girard Trusts, as may relate to the well-being of the College. During the years of 1854 and 1855, and part of 1856, (being since Consolidation,) Joint Visitation Committees were regularly appointed, and performed their duties by monthly visits. Report of these committees may be found in the Appendix to Select and Common Councils. Since that time until the appointment of this committee, for some reason* [The asterisk referred to a footnote which reads: "The reasons assigned are, the disagreement between Select and Common Councils in regard to Joint Committees. And, also, the law required that the Visiting Committees should be composed of equal members of both Councils, which on account of the increase of members of Common Council, could not be easily done. Neither of these reasons, however, are [sic] sufficient for the neglect of the duty of Visiting the College. The spirit and letter of the law is--that the Committees shall be appointed; the trifling question of the number of the committee should not have prevented their appointment for a moment."] neither Council have appointed Visiting Committees to the Girard College for Orphans. On the 30th of October [1858], Mr. Gordon presented the following resolution, which was unanimously adopted, and the committees appointed. Whereas, By an Ordinance approved July 3, 1854, the Presidents of each council are authorized to 'divide the members of their respective councils, into sub-committees, for the purpose of visiting monthly the college. And, Whereas, The Presidents of these councils, as well as the Councils of 1856 and 1857, have failed to appoint such Committees. Therefore, be it Resolved, That immediately on the passage of this Resolution by Common Council, the President of the Council shall appoint Committees to consist of eleven members for each of the months of October, November, December, January, February, March, April, and thirteen in the month of May; to visit the Girard College monthly. Said committees to co-operate as Joint Visiting Committees with similar Committees of Select Council, if such should be appointed. Provi-

As a result of the reports of the special committees of 1858 and 1859, the Board of Directors of Girard College noted in their report for the year 1859, a series of improvements which they believed desirable and for which they requested appropriations from the City Councils. Of particular interest, the Councils requested a workshop; but, perhaps even more significant, is the view in which the request was made as is evident from the following:

> Other improvements are very desirable, and will be made as soon as means shall be placed at the disposal of the Board for that purpose. Among these may be enumerated gas lights along the north front of the buildings; a gavel road along the north front of the buildings designated as Nos. 1 and 2, and along the west side of No. 2, to meet the road running eastward from the gate; the grading and draining of the play-ground; the substitution of gravel or sand for the clay surface of the ground north of the

---

ded, Nevertheless, that, if the Select Council shall fail to elect, the committees appointed by Common Council shall proceed with their duties according to the Ordinance and previous custom. Under this Resolution for October, visited the College on the 19th of said month, being the first Visiting Committee of Councils since 1856." (Report, supra, pp. 24-25).

It is also worthy of mention to note that on May 26, 1856, a bill was offered in the Select Council entitled "An Ordinance to dispense with the monthly Visiting Committees of Councils to Girard College." No action apparently was ever taken. (See Journal of the Select Council of the City of Philadelphia, Beginning May 12 and Ending November 6, 1856, p. 59, Appendix, p. 30). Moreover, subsequent to Gordon's resolution, on June 9, 1859, "An Ordinance relating to the appointment of Monthly Visiting Committees to the Girard College" was passed in Common Council. It provided, "That so much of an Ordinance, passed July 3, 1854, as requires the appointment of six members of the Select Council and six members of the Common Council, on each monthly visiting Committee to the Girard College, be, and is hereby repealed, and, that hereafter each of the said monthly committees shall be composed of four members of the Select, and eight members of the Common Council." (See Journal of the Common Council of the City of Philadelphia Beginning May 9, 1859, Ending November 3, 1859, p. 125, Appendix pp. 85-86). On June 30, 1859, the bill was passed by the Select Council. (See Journal of the Select Council of the City of Philadelphia, Beginning May 9 and Ending November 3, 1859, p. 124). However, even the following year, the Visiting Committee for the month of January, 1860, saw cause to note to the Councils, the following: "Your Committee think that inasmuch as the law makes every member of councils a Trustee of the College, that a greater interest on the part of Councils should be manifested, by a prompt and full attendance, of the Visiting Committees, on the days appointed for that purpose. The Girard College is justly the pride of our City and all the interests of its management should be cherished with increasing care, and constant attention by Councils." (See Journal of the Common Council of the City of Philadelphia Beginning November 10, 1859, Ending May 3, 1860, p. 143, Appendix p. 458.

main building, where the pupils take their recreation during recess from school; a swimming pond or pool; a gymnasium; and a workshop. The Directors earnestly solicit from Councils such appropriations as will enable them to make these improvements, especially the five last mentioned which are designed to promote the health, comfort and physical development of the pupils. The condition of the play ground is such as to render it useless during about one third of each year, except at the risk of the health of the orphans. The appliances and facilities for exercise and recreation are too limited, both in number and extent. While ample provision has been made for the mental culture and moral instruction of the orphans, adequate appropriations have not hitherto been made for their physical education and training. The Directors are of opinion that while a well-furnished and properly conducted gymnasium unites exercise with recreation, it tends to develop the muscles symmetrically, to improve the health, to strengthen the constitution, and give elasticity and grace to the movements of the body. It is known that several of the leading educational institutions in this country are providing apparatus for gymnastic exercises, and instruction in its use; and it is the wish of the Directors that Girard College may equal the best of them in the completeness and efficiency of its means and methods of forming "sound minds in sound bodies."

A workshop, in which the orphans might learn to use their hands while they are learning to use their heads, is almost as necessary as a gymnasium. The greater part of the pupils skills in the handling of tools acquired before they leave the college, would make them more desirable and efficient as apprentices, and consequently increase the demand for them. It is believed that many of the older pupils would prefer the shop to the play ground as a place of recreation, and that the practical knowledge which they would there acquire, would be such as Mr. Girard intended when he said that they should learn "facts and things."[112]

---

[112] _Twelfth Annual Report of the Board of Directors of the Girard College for Orphans for the Year 1859_, pp. 11-12. Another event in 1859 was full of significance for Girard College; the Supreme Court of Pennsylvania had ruled on who was an "orphan" within the meaning of the will. To explain the situation fully and bring out the important facts, it is necessary to look back to the years soon after Girard's death. Girard had not provided a definition of what he believed to be an orphan. Evidently Nicholas Biddle had discussed that at his table with John Quincy Adams and with Judge Joseph Hopkinson of the United Stated District Court for the eastern district of Pennsylvania. This conversation led to correspondence between the men which was published in the _National Gazette_ in June 1833. Both Judge Hopkinson and Adams had believed that an orphan was a child without living parents, but after thought had changed their views. It appears that Judge Hopkinson had begun the correspondence to Adams, noting that after he had consulted various authorities, he believed that the loss of a father made a child an orphan. Adams, on the other hand, responded

Another attempt to provide mechanical instruction was made the following year. It is significant, however, that the evident purpose in requesting

---

that on the basis of his own investigation he had arrived at the conclusion that the death of any parent constituted an orphan ". . . for every purpose that can entitle the individual so designated to receive any benefit or advantage." Hopkinson answered this by noting that while Adams had provided valued classical arguments and logical conclusions, he believed that the legal definition--a fatherless child--would be used if a question should occur on this point. (See in this connection Letter from Joseph Hopkinson to John Quincy Adams, Philadelphia, April 20, 1833; Letter from John Quincy Adams to Joseph Hopkinson, Quincy, May 8, 1833; Letter from Joseph Hopkinson to John Quincy Adams, Philadelphia, May 14, 1833. All items in Hazard's Register of Pennsylvania, XLV, No. 12 (September 20, 1834, pp. 188-191). Hopkinson's view was similarly held by Lieber in his Constitution and Plan of Education for Girard College for Orphans in 1833 but proposed that a child would be considered fatherless: "(1) That has lost its father by death; (2) Whose father has not been heard of for the successive years, through proper authorities, satisfactory to the Board of Admission have been made; (3) Whose fathers labor under an incurable disease or informity, such as blindness, deafness, insanity, epilepsy, informity of old age, or any other physical or mental deficiency, that renders him incapable of earning his livelihood." (pp. 151-152).

Later in 1838, a special committee had been appointed to consider the word orphan along with other measures that should be taken preliminary to the opening of the College. The committee, chaired by Nicholas Biddle, reported that they were of the unanimous opinion that an orphan was a fatherless child, noting that it was a limited sense of the term but more in keeping with the accepted practice in the United States and in Europe. This view, they added, was also acceptable to President Bache and William J. Duane. (See in this connection, "Report of Special Committee, December 5, 1838;" letter from N. Biddle, Esq. to A. D. Bache, Philadelphia, November 17, 1838; and letter from A. D. Bache to N. Biddle, Esq., Philadelphia, November 22, 1838. All items are in Reports of Committees, Resolutions, &c., Relative to the Organization of the Girard College for Orphans. [Printed for the use of the Board of Trustees], 1839, pp. 29-39). The practice of the Board had been to accept the definition of a "fatherless child;" but in June, 1858, the Board of Directors had directed the Committee on Admission to give preference ". . . to children who have [had] lost both parents, provided their condition renders them special objects of consideration." When this practice became known, the Board was prevented from filling existing vacancies by a process from the Supreme Court of Pennsylvania on behalf of a mother ". . . on the ground that an orphan is a fatherless" and not solely a "parentless child." (See Eleventh Annual Report of the Board of Directors of the Girard College for Orphans, For the Year 1858, pp. 14-15). In 1859, the Supreme Court of Pennsylvania held: "That a fatherless child was an orphan within the meaning of the will; and that a preference was to be given to orphans born within the original limits of Philadelphia, as laid out by William Penn, and existing at the death of the testator." (See in this connection, Souhan v. City of Philadelphia, 33 Pa. St., p. 9, as found in Will of Stephen Girard. With Acts of Assembly and Decisions Relating Thereto, p. 42.

this instruction indicates a further change in the thinking of the directors of the college. The recreational provisions appear to have been seriously circumscribed and the idea that this instruction would make the orphans better apprentices seems to have derived its own merit. The President of the Board of Directors noted:

> The Board have for several years had their attention turned to the subject of providing within the walls some mechanical employment for the older and larger pupils, before they leave the institution. It will be seen how important to their future welfare it is that they should be accustomed, at least in some degree, to the use of tools and machinery, and to the habits which are needed in the workshop, before they go out to active participation in the affairs of the world, and how much more desirable they would be as apprentices, if this preliminary instruction could be had. The subject is attended with some practical difficulties, but the Board have asked this year for a small appropriation to make the experiment, and as a nucleus around which to build up the more thorough and complete system which experience may dictate. This matter is earnestly recommended to the favorable consideration of Councils.[113]

The year 1860 also saw an alteration in the organization of the departments of instruction. The tripartite division suggested by Lieber had been essentially continued without modification until this time except for a change in the relationship of the schools which occurred in 1858. At that time, the Board explained:

> The system hitherto in use in the Institution, was based upon the division of the schools into the Principal Department and Primary Schools, Nos. 1 and 2, analagous in their relations and rank to the Primary, Grammar, and High Schools now existing in the public system of education.
>
> The pupils admitted to the College were placed according to the amount of their previous education, in the different classes of the lowest school, or Primary, No. 2; and as they completed the course of instruction in that school, were promoted to Primary, No. 1, and from thence ultimately to the still higher course of the Principal Department. The new plan which,

---

[113] Thirteenth Annual Report of the Board of Directors of the Girard College for Orphans, For the Year 1860, pp. 8-9.

> has recently gone into operation, contemplates first, the equalizing of the two primary schools, both as to relative rank, and the extent and character of the instruction imparted in each; and, secondly, the establishment of a new or infant department, for such orphans as enter the Institution entirely uninstructed, or who, from deficient mental powers, lag behind their better constituted companions. For it will be remembered, that the qualifications for admission into the College are, by the terms of the will, orphanage and destitution,--not mental activity or education.[114]

In 1860, the division of the pupils into principal and primary schools had been set aside, and the pupils were divided "according to their advancement in knowledge." This arrangement provided for the use of six Forms, numbering from one, the lowest, through six, the highest. Under this plan the course of study was arranged so that a student of fair capacity would be promoted from class to class and from form to form and be able to complete the entire course of study in eight years. Among its noted benefits, the new arrangement would enable those orphans who would be bound out before they had reached the sixth form the opportunity to acquire some knowledge of the higher branches before leaving the college.[115]

The attempts to provide mechanical instruction met with success in 1861. In his report for the year, the President of the Board of Directors noted that the subject had been attended by some "practical difficulties" but a manual labor department had been organized, affording twenty pupils employment for part of the day in mechanical and horticultural industry. The accomplishments of this experiment, the President believed, gave promise of even greater

---

[114] Eleventh Annual Report of the Board of Directors of the Girard College for Orphans, For the Year 1858, p. 7. The report also noted that the president of the college believed that this change would benefit the orphans in two ways: ". . . first, by removing what has hitherto been a bar to their progress, and, secondly, by establishing a healthy competition between the primary schools, which will be mutually advantageous to each." (Ibid., p. 8).

[115] Thirteenth Annual Report, op. cit., pp. 4-5.

results and indicated that the plan should be made an integral part of the college. Since the idea had already accepted in principle, he added that the Board would exert their efforts to widen the branches of industry involved with the hope that the plan would eventually become self-sustaining [116]

Attendant practical difficulties had not been limited to the subject of providing mechanical instruction; the year 1861 marked a year of disturbing influences within and without the college clearly outlined in the report of the President of its Board of Directors. Of major concern was the Civil War which it was believed would affect the estimated income for the college which was derived from the Girard estates. A general redirection of expenditure was necessary and this necessitated not filling vacancies that occurred in binding out or in dismissing pupils for a part of the year. To curtail expenditures even further at the end of the year, the Board of Directors had reduced the salaries of all the officers and some employees and abolished some positions which were considered not indispensible and where the duties could be performed by others.[117] The report also noted that the number of dismissed pupils was larger than usual, a fact which the Board attributed largely to the "disturbed state of the public mind" which added to the "restlessness and unquiet spirit" of the orphans. The war, it was believed, also affected the number of applications by masters for apprentices from the college[118] and as well induced many masters to allow their apprentices to enter military service, which in some cases, was done without the permission of the master.[119]

Also noted in the report was a difference of opinion between the Board of Directors and the Mayor of the City on certain admission policies. The

---

[116] _Fourteenth Annual Report of the Board of Directors of the Girard College for Orphans, For the Year 1861_, p. 7.

[117] _Ibid._, pp. 4-5. [118] _Ibid._, pp. 3-4. [119] _Ibid._, pp. 8.

Board, in their view, in order to extend as widely as possible the advantages of the Institution, had limited admission to one child in a family. The Mayor, on the other hand, thought this to be in violation of the will and had brought this to the attention of the City Councils.[120] The Board defended their position by noting in part the opinion of the law officer of the city who was of the opinion that the Board had been invested ". . . with the exercise of a sound discretion as to the shades of difference in the comparative merits of the applicants"[121] as allowed them by the clause "all other things concurring" in Girard's directions for admission to the college. Evidently, the Board continued this admission practice.[122]

It would be difficult to attribute the changes that took place in the college the following year directly to the economy begun in 1861; but there is no doubt that the desire for economy measures accompanied by the accession of new ideas epitomized in the person of Richard Vaux as President of the Board of Directors clearly imposed a new chapter in the history of the college In his first annual report, Vaux immediately proceeded to matters of continuing contention by reviewing the "short but interesting history" of Girard College. In speaking of the aims of the college, he noted that the college had gone into operation with a ". . . diversity of opinion that was natural. The will itself had created it. The institution was without precedent. There was no standard anywhere by which to settle or determine the initial question

---

[120] _Ibid._, p.9.

[121] _Ibid._, p. 10.

[122] See in this connection, Article XXI; para. 6, Holograph will, which reads, "These Orphans, for whose admission application shall first be made, shall be first introduced, all other things concurring--and at future times priority of application shall entitle the applicant to preference in admission all other things concurring. . . ." Later, under the administration of the Board of City Trusts, there were no restrictions on the number of children from a family.

involved. . . . These divergent views, if carried out to their conclusions, would on the one hand have terminated in a university; on the other, an orphan home."[123] As to the Bache report, he believed, "By reference to the elaborate report made by Professor Bache on his return, it can be seen how laboriously he performed the duty assigned him;"[124] however, as to the usefulness of the report, he added, "It does not appear to have occurred to those who relied on trans-Atlantic investigations, by which to interpret the intentions of the testator, that the difficulty was augmented rather than elucidated."[125] In this sense, he explained:

> . . . the social, economical, conventional, political and industrial condition of the peoples of Europe and America are wholly dissimilar. It is therefore easily to be perceived how unsatisfactory any effort must be to harmonize the proposed, with the practical results contemplated by Mr. Girard, if the letter and the spirit of his testament are thus to be reconciled. The deduction must be, that experience is the true test of the relations which must be created between the intention of the testator and its practical development.[126]

Having established an "experience" motif, Vaux moved on to point up what experience had shown to be the relative merits of the divergent views by noting:

> If, to support the pupils of the College in luxury, giving them not only a liberal but a collegiate education; exciting and cultivating tastes and habits which are their concomitants, and then, by legal indentures, apprentice them to the trials and deprivations which belong to the novitiate of either trades or handicrafts, was the unyielding purpose of the plan of the testator, experience has hardly sustained it as practicable. But if "a better education" with plain food, clothing, and admitted comforts, or, in the words of the will, a comfortable maintenance which belongs to a home, thus by economy and disretion dispensing the advantages to the largest number of bene-

---

[123] Fifteenth Annual Report of the Board of Directors of the Girard College For Orphans, For the Year 1862, pp. 5-6.

[124] Ibid., p. 5.

[125] Ibid., p. 7.

[126] Ibid., pp. 7-8.

> ficiaries, while for those of decided talents opportunity is afforded to eliminate them, was his aim, then that experience which the history of the College has given, not only approves this latter system of administration, but sanctions it by the force of a construction decreed by utility and success. During the last few years this system has gained on the favorable opinions of the Directors. It is not yet a demonstration.[127]

Vaux then suggested a reason for the failure of the Board of Directors to fix a conclusive direction for the college.

> To change every year a portion of the constituents of the Board, is to render any system of administration unstable. It is not, therefore, surprising that as yet no determined and settled policy as between the extremes here noticed was agreed upon, when the record shows that seventy-two gentlemen have, during the fifteen years of the life of the Girard College, been appointed as directors.[128]

Vaux believed that a middle course between the extreme views was an absolute necessity, also noting that the Board had been making a practical effort to equalize the conflicting views during the previous eighteen months. He saw the middle course as ". . . the solution of difficulties, if not obstacles, which must be obviated or removed, else the College will degenerate into a splendid failure. Such a result will be the consequence of intention without purpose, action without aim."[129]

To underscore the results of what he called "this undetermined course of administrative policy," Vaux provided tables and figures indicating the yearly enrollments; the number of students who had died; been dismissed, or who had their indentures cancelled; and the number of pupils who had absconded. He concluded that under this policy, in the fifteen years of the college's efforts only one hundred and twenty pupils had been educated, apprenticed, and of age (attainment of legal majority); and, while one-fifth of the entire expenditure for the college was for the Collegiate Department, only an

---

[127] *Ibid.*, pp.9-10. [128] *Ibid.*, p. 10. [129] *Ibid.*

average of seventy-five out of three hundred and twenty-three pupils had received any collegiate instruction.[130]

If experience had shown anything, Vaux believed, ". . . it is the propriety and legality under the will, of reconciling the extreme interpretations which its text may suggest,"[131] an opinion he also believed was held by the directors for the previous two years. He saw the propriety as "perspicuous" because it enlarged the capacity of the institution and increased the number of beneficiaries. He tested this propriety by providing the following table:

In the Year	The average number of pupils was	Sum Appropriated	Sum Expended
1851,	300,	$62,900.00	$61,794.14
1852,	295,	61,250.00	60,512.37
1853,	295,	63,800.00	63,309.76
1854,	300,	73,225.00	71,402.37
1855,	300,	83,330.00	81,754.84
1856,	305,	85,380.00	82,963.33
1857,	295,	92,340.00	88,173.42
1858,	350,	87,280.00	81,949.38
1859,	325,	88,430.00	85,762.25
1860,	340,	87,080.00	80,943.53
1861,	375,	93,930.00	81,547.49
1862,	400,	77,375.00	73,247.72 [132]

He pointed out that the figures showed the economic efforts in disbursing the annual rppropriation; that there were sufficient means to have increased the number of pupils; and that due to the unsettled and undetermined administrative policy there was a ". . . great disparity between the expenses and the yearly average of pupils."[133]

In overview, Vaux stated some conclusions that would follow from deductive reasoning based on the experience of the previous fifteen years and which reads as follows:

> Directing attention singly to the conclusions which are here attempted to be deduced, though not claimed to be oracular, it will not be unwarrantable to assume that the former

---

[130] Ibid., pp. 11-14.

[131] Ibid., p. 16.

[132] Ibid., p. 17.

[133] Ibid., pp. 17-18.

> policy of the administration of the College, has not realized results which were attainable. As an institution of learning, having a University character to establish, it has not been successful. As an "orphan establishment," with the distinctive features of an educational institution, it has failed of its largest usefulness. This want of success is attributable to the fact, that the concurrence of all its means to this object was impossible of reconciliation. So from their character, so by reason of divergence of the theory and practice which the will permits to exist. Thus, so, necessarily. The failure of largest usefulness, has resulted because of the conflict of opinion as to what the College ought to be.[134]

To these conclusions, Vaux added that "most gratifying results" had been produced by the recent system of economy which also testified to the recent action of the Board. Beyond even this, he noted: "It has done more, it has proved beyond cavil or controversy, that there existed a stern necessity for the economical reform which has been so successfully secured."[135]

This report also makes it clear that other changes were intended. Vaux took particular notice of Girard's will and his use of the term "orphan establishment" to point up the cooperative purpose of the Board of Directors which as well indicated a new direction of policy and only required the cooperation of the City Council.

> To train the yough to be useful citizens, is the present purpose of the Directors. It is the plain purpose of the will. It is worthy of the respect of intelligent and conscientious minds. It should be sanctioned by official earnest co-operation. This purpose is but giving a "better education," and a more "comfortable maintenance" to as "many orphans as may apply for admission" for the benefits of this "College," "institution," or "orphan establishment." To carry out this purpose requires no radical change in the present system in operation in the College. On the contrary, This system needs only to be so modified as to <u>increase the number of pupils</u>. To absorb every dollar which by right belongs to the objects of this trust, is the only requirement which may be regarded as a novelty. To devote the "College, out-buildings, and grounds" for the purposes of the maintenance and education of as many orphans as may apply for

---

134 <u>Ibid</u>., p. 19.

135 <u>Ibid</u>., pp. 20-21.

> admission; and so economically disburse the funds appropriated, as to meet this demand, is the present policy, desire and design of the Board.[136]

The idea of change was also implied in the resignation of William Allen as President of the College on December 31, 1962.[137] Although no explanation was given for his retirement from office, it was noted that "a change in the office of Matron was deemed proper, in order that the Board might introduce at the same time [as the election of a new president] increased vigor and economy in the domestic administration of the establishment."[138]

As to the place of industrial instruction, Richard Vaux reiterated the idea that a knowledge in the use of tools would make the orphans better apprentices. He saw distinct benefits for two groups of orphans: those who showed a lack of mental ability that was necessary for acquiring instruction in the higher branches of the college course who were too young to be apprenticed or for whom places could not be found; and those who had finished the college course and whose age was near to the maximum time allowed by the will and were idle. For both groups he believed it advisable ". . . to learn useful knowledge in handicraft labor."[139] He found justification for this couched in the progress already made by some of the orphans which he pointed up in a condensed statement from a report of their teachers as follows:

---

[136] Ibid., pp. 28-29. The report also notes that on December 10, 1862, the following preamble had been adopted: "Resolved, That in the opinion of this Board, Girard College was not intended to be solely an institution for the mental instruction of youth, but one which will give to its inmates "a better education than they usually receive by an application of the public funds," one that will fit them to become good, useful, and practical men, and train them for agricultural, mechanical, and such other pursuits as may be suitable to their individual capacities." (Ibid., p. 27).

[137] Ibid., p. 35.

[138] Ibid., p. 37. See also in this connection, Cheesman A. Herrick, History of Girard College, p. 149. Herrick notes that President Allen interpreted the reduction of his salary as a vote of lack of appreciation and thereby resigned.

[139] Ibid., p. 40.

> The gardener has an average of eight boys in his class: their labor is equal to, if paid for, about $500 a year. Instructed in this useful branch of agriculture they are made valuable to those who select them as farmers. In the shoemaking class there is an average of four boys daily engaged. They learn in this branch of labor the use of tools, and habits of careful attention to their work. The work performed by them is equal to about $500 for the year.
>
> The average of pupils employed by the carpenter is yet but one per day. The advantage of instruction in this branch needs no comment. To acquire any knowledge in it is desirable [140]

In summary of this success Vaux noted: "The effect of this instruction has been to render the pupils more willing to be apprenticed to tradebranches of industry. . . . As an experiment, it has been successful, not only on those within its immediate influences, but also on the pupils generally."[141]

Yet, even beyond this success, theproblem of placing boys as apprentices remained. In speaking of the importance of handicraft manipulations, Vaux suggested, "A boy with such knowledge is more readily apprenticed than one educated in 'words and signs' and not 'facts and things.' In this connection, and most properly here, it is well to remark, that the demand for places is greater than the demand for apprentices." And later in speaking of the tasks of the directors, he noted:

> The apprentice-fact, in the requirement of legal transition from College, to trade-life, cannot be avoided, and is an increasing obstacle in our future. To render this administration successful, with the difficulties which attend it, demands, that the directing authority should be permitted uninterruptedly to attempt its practical solution in success.[142]

Vaux's report for 1862 augured the modifications that were to be found in the internal administration of the college in 1863. In speaking of the cooperation of the Board of Directors in making these modifications, he noted: "Those who were not fully prepared to adopt them, impressed with their value, and trusting that experience would justify the experiment, willingly consented

---

[140] *Ibid.*, pp. 40-41. [141] *Ibid.*, p. 41. [142] *Ibid.*, p. 44.

to their submission to the test of a fair trial."[143] Paramount among the changes found in the system of administration was the new policy that allowed for the appointment and removal of all officers in the household and academic departments of the college by the President of the college.[144] Vaux believed that it would follow ". . . that unity and harmony in the administration must be eventually secured."[145] Among the advantages of such an adoption, Vaux listed some of the "striking results" which he held were attained: "the saving of money in the departments, the wise and liberal economy, the uniformity of action in regard to the discipline and regulations, orderly, and official industry, the regulated supervisor [and] the earnest anxiety of the heads of departments to harmonize in the discharge of their duties, in order to secure success. . ."[146] All these results, he believed, added in eradicating the "systemless inertia" which had been about to settle over the destiny of the institution. In contrast to this, he maintained:

> If no other benefit to the College and its future character has been secured, the fact is that henceforth, under the present arrangement, its direction must be uninfluenced by every and all considerations, but those which rest on the most highly approved principles for regulating educational establishments, which partake of the nature of a home and a college united. Under such a principle in its government, the happiness of the pupils; the increase in their number yearly, as the will requires; home influences, and the Christian care of their morals; the best education; the training for usefulness in life; the adaptation of the institution to the aims of the founder, including instruction in "facts and things" theory and practice, mental and manual, and industrial or handicraft education; features made prominent, and those which are new, thus engrafted in the now unfolding character of the institution.[147]

---

[143] Sixteenth Annual Report of the Board of Directors of the Girard College for Orphans, For the Year 1863, p. 4.

[144] Ibid., p. 5.

[145] Ibid., p. 6.

[146] Ibid., p. 7.

[147] Ibid., pp. 8-9.

As part of the new arrangements Vaux explained that the single idea of a college had been eclipsed by the unity of a college education and a practical education with an increase in the number of pupils and ". . . comprehensiveness of purpose in the spirit of the administration of the institution. . ."[148] as its coincidents. Expanding on this, he noted that during 1863 the number of pupils had been increased from four hundred to five hundred. He also pointed out that the success of the instruction in manual labor, although limited, had led the Board of Directors to believe it desirable to create a department of instruction along with a professorship devoted to polytechnic instruction and which might be designated "Industrial Science." However, Vaux added that since at that time the office of the President of the College had still been only temporarily filled, no time limit had been set for the needed planning.[149]

President Allen had terminated his presidency on December 31, 1862. From January 1, 1863, until July 1st of the same year, the office had been temporarily held by Henry W. Arey, Secretary of the Board of Directors. On July 1, 1863, the newly appointed president, Major Richard Somers Smith, took charge of the college. Vaux noted that it was Smith's ". . . record of qualifications from experience and practical learning, which seemed to indicate him as the most suitable for the position."[150] It would be difficult to adduce who had prompted the idea that polytechnic instruction should be organized in the college; whether the Board of Directors had arrived at it previous to the selection of Smith, or that it had been a result of Smith's

---

[148] Ibid., p. 11.

[149] Ibid., pp. 9-12, passim.

[150] Ibid., p. 13.

own deliberations with the Board of Directors.[151] In any event, Smith's own background would suggest that he would have been keen to broaden the scope of practical studies in the school. A graduate of the United States Military Academy in 1834, Smith resigned from the Army in 1836 to take up engineering in civilian life. In 1840, he was reappointed in the army and served at West Point as an instructor and assistant professor of drawing

---

[151]It is interesting to note that Gustavus Remak, a director of the college and the chairman of the committee on instruction, saw fit, during the inaugural ceremonies of Smith as President of the College, to speak at length on polytechnic schools in Europe and the Polytechnic College of Philadelphia. He also expressed the hope that a polytechnic school should be engrafted upon the Girard College System. He evidently believed that such instruction would be more in line with what Girard had intended since he saw the course of studies as then provided as nearly that of what was found in the public schools to which he added ". . . that is, for the lower classes." (Ibid., p. 73) For Girard College he had higher hopes: "And the Girard College may yet become the alma mater of men as great as Fulton, Franklin, or Morse. Why should it not? Give to this talent the opportunity to develop itself. Let those fit only for shoemakers or tailors become so. We will honor them as much as others, if they are good men; but let those who are made for higher education receive it." (Ibid., p. 74). See also in this connection, Thorstein Sellin's account of Richard Vaux (1816-1895) in the Dictionary of American Biography. Vaux is credited with being instrumental in introducing vocational and technological training into the college curriculum. In An Eulogium On The Honorable Richard Vaux delivered at Girard College, Philadelphia, by the Hon. Michael Arnold on May 17, 1895, Arnold believes that Vaux's first public utterance on the subject of manual instruction was made in Vaux's first message to the City Councils of Philadelphia on January 5, 1857, at which time Vaux was Mayor of the city. Vaux, in recommending a liberal appropriation for the support of the Central High School of Philadelphia made the following statement: "If to its present plan of education could be added a mode of instruction permitting pupils to undertake mechanical employments, the greatest good would result. Young men who have finished their course in the higher branches and are ready for life's context, which then begins, seem to look with disfavor on industrial vocations for a livelihood. It must not be forgotten that labor is disnified when it is educated and intelligence in all its branches is as important as in any merely intellectual pursuits." (pp. 4-5). In speaking of Vaux's influence at Girard College, Arnold maintains that Vaux planted the seeds of manual instruction twenty years before a successful department was established (p. 18).

It is of interest to note that Richard Vaux was the son of the philanthropist Roberts Vaux (1786-1836) who was one of the directors of the Girard Trust in 1832 who had been selected to form a plan for the establishment and management of the College and that considerable correspondence had been carried on between the senior Vaux and Francis Lieber. See in this connection, Joseph J. McCadden, Education in Pennsylvania, 1801-1835, And Its Debt to Roberts Vaux, pp. 138-139.

from 1840 to 1855; as quartermaster, 1846-1851; and as treasurer, 1852-1855. Resigning from the army in 1856, he became professor of mathematics, engineering, and drawing in the Brooklyn Collegiate and Polytechnic Institute. In 1859, he joined the staff of Cooper Union as a teacher of mechanical drawing and then its director until 1861 when he was recalled into military service. On May 30, 1863, Smith resigned from the army to accept the presidency at Girard College.[152]

Extracts from the monthly reports of the president of the college to the Board of Directors which Vaux appended to his Annual Report indicate Smith's part in the early development of the polytechnic idea at the college. In his report to the Board of Directors on September 22, 1863, he pointed out that any plan that contemplated the introduction of instruction manual labor at the college should be considered as a department of instruction and, as such, should be maintained as any other department and not necessarily be self-supporting.[153] As to the merits of such a plan, he noted:

> As to its bearing upon the mental cultivation of the pupils, it must, in order that its benefits may be efficiently applied, interfere in some degree with the time given to school studies. Its importance and value would, however, fully justify the retardation in the speed with which the studies might otherwise have been gone over; while another advantage of the system might be looked for in the good effect upon the studies which would be produced by the alternation of intellectual and manual culture. . . .
>
> I think it is admitted that the absence of any well organized system of manual instruction is a want in our teaching. The "poor white male orphans," dwelling for eight or ten years in comfort

---

[152]See in this connection, Thomas M. Spaulding's account of Richard Somers Smith (1813-1877) in the Dictionary of American Biography. See also the First Annual Report of the Trustees of the Cooper Union For the Advancement of Science and Art, January 1, 1860, p. 4, which lists Smith as an instructor in mechanical drawing, and the Second Annual Report of the Trustees of the Cooper Union For the Advancement of Science and Art, January 1, 1861, p. 3, which lists Smith as Director of the School.

[153]Sixteenth Annual Report, op. cit., p. 37.

> almost amounting to luxury, waited upon by servants and machinery in nearly all his domestic requirements; unused to labor, or laboring only occasionally, with some reward in view in the form of extra privileges, finds it hard to descend from his fancied elevation to the lot of a simple apprentice, and his disappointment is not soothed by the discovery that with all his learning, he has not learned wherewithal to give ready satisfaction to his master.[154]

On this basis, he recommended as soon as possible the organization of a Department of Manual Instruction.[155]

Smith's plan for polytechnic instruction came a month later on October 24, 1863. Now, apparently, the idea for a polytechnic system became more entrenched, as is evident from the following:

> After much reflection, I propose the organization of a new department of instruction, to be called "The Department of Industrial Science." I am more than ever convinced of the great advantage to the College's reputation and usefulness, to be derived from the introduction of such a practical course of study as could be brought into operation by a well arranged and conducted system of class-rooms, (shops), where instruction in many branches of industrial art could be given to a large number of pupils; instruction that would stay by them forever, because impressed by them by actual manual practice. For example: the making of models of bridges, roof-trusses, and of joiners' work in general; models of castings, machines &c.; and the use of the wood-lathe. Moulding and casting in plaster of Paris. Working in iron, at the forge and the lathe. Type founding and stereotyping; type-setting and printing. Electroplating; photography; dyeing; soap-making; the manufacture of pigments; and many applications of Chemistry to common life, needless now to mention. The polytechnic idea also includes the development of Graphic Geometry, and the making of its appropriate models; also the formation of a School of Design, for the cultivation of original ideas of form and color, as applied to domestic wares, of metal or pottery, to gas-fixtures, furniture, patterns, for calicoes, wall papers, &c., &c., &c.
>
> Under such a system, moreover, the higher branches of mathematics and physics would be pursued with a zest that must always accompany that healthy digestion of book-knowledge, consequent upon the application of school learning to practice.[156]

Other suggestions were made by Smith. In his October 24th report he had also suggested that a chair of Moral Science, Rhetoric, History, and the

---

[154] *Ibid.*, pp. 37-38. [155] *Ibid.*, p. 38. [156] *Ibid.*, pp. 39-40.

Constitution be established.[157] In a report on December 7, 1863, he suggested a system of honors and rewards for students who showed "fidelity to duty" or were distinguished in "talent and success."[158] His plans and suggestions were well-received with promise for trial the following year. Vaux's own optimism is evident from the following:

> It was apparent to those who made a critical examination into the relation of each of the pupils to the College, and its obligations to them, individually or classified on the basis of mental capacity and physical fitness, that a college education, as it is called, was impossible to be imparted or acquired by a percentage of those pupils. They were inmates of the "Orphan Establishment," so, for a certain period of time, and could only be returned to out-door life as apprentices to learn a handicraft. Those who in five years could not be taught more than the simplest rules of arithmetic, would reach a ripe old age before they would be proficient in a college course of study, and then to learn a trade, would educate them, probably for decaying examples of a mis-spent life. Those who had received a good education, and wished a practical education added to it, thus to fit them for their future, were left half way between instruction and knowledge.
>
> Co-mingling such diversity of individualities in one institution, governed, as this is, by the letter and spirit of the will of the founder, could not fail to make its condition far from satisfactory. The boys were in an abnormal educational existence. Without ambition, impulse, motive, they were all on a level of mind and aim--to be, ended their effort. The quick, intelligent, active-minded, were on the same plane as the dull, slow, sluggish. The future of the one class was darkened by the shadows thrown over it by that of the others. Life, activity, energy, ambition, motive, were existing, but undeveloped.
>
> To correct this condition, it seemed necessary to adopt the polytechnic system as far as possible. Thus, with a plan of honorary rewards for scholarship and conduct; education in industrial sciences and arts; a college course of study and a polytechnic course of education, it was believed, would begin a new era in the history of Girard College.[159]

This philosophy represented a significant departure from existing practice but was to prove shortlived.

---

[157] Ibid., p. 40.

[158] Ibid., pp. 142-144.

[159] Ibid., pp. 16-18.

III

> It may be stated then, that Girard College for Orphans is a home where the pupils are taught and trained as far as their capacities admit, for their duties and destiny in life. They receive such intellectual education as they are mentally qualified to acquire, and such instruction in practical handicraft as is best suited to their usefulness, and benefit to themselves. It enhances the Home, the College, and the Workshop, in which these essential qualities, as well as cultivated capacities of mind, morals and muscles are developed and educated. This, Stephen Girard intended to be the true meaning of his bequest, when its purpose and intention are carefully investigated.[160]

As is manifest from this quotation, Richard Vaux's Annual Report for 1864 pointed up his belief that the abstract question of the true meaning of Girard's bequest had finally been settled. Vaux was a man of pronounced views and strong in his expression of them as is evident from the following:

> The meaning, the true idea, the broad interpretation, the testator supposed were to be reached, by the same process, which created them in his mind. They have been discerned after years of a vacillancy of administration, which, like the action of a pendulum of a clock, courses the real progress of time to be marked, after reaching the extremes of interpretation.[161]

---

[160]Seventeenth Annual Report of the Board of Directors of the Girard College For Orphans For the Year 1864, pp. 11-12. Cf. the views of a special committee of the Board of Directors noted on p. 128 which capsuled what the committee thought what the college was to be: "That is to be his [the orphans] home, his school, his church. . . ."

[161]Ibid., p. 8. The extreme interpretations were epitomized in another of Vaux's references to the intent of Stephen Girard which reads in part: "Girard College is unlike educational establishments which exclusively devote themselves to the teaching of knowledge in its higher or highest outreachings; or, a foundation dedicated to instruction in a collection for gathering of studies or sciences; or, a universal school, in which are taught all the branches of learning, and all the faculties of science and art, separate and distinct from any other duty. It has none of these exclusive characteristics. The intention of the founder falls far short of such an ambitious aim. He regarded the needs and wants of a class of society, neglected, and subjected, by its surroundings. This class, if left to itself, would yield nothingness as its negative contribution to the community, but require in return donations which stern benevolence must pay by the force of self-protection. Thus the delicate and difficult questions of social science were united with those less abstruse, of a moral and educational character. Less abstruse, because they belonged to the familiar example of a Home and a School, united in an "Orphan Establishment," as Girard has designated this Institution." (Ibid., pp. 6-7).

In speaking of the present administration, Vaux noted that "So much had been gained by an enlightened and harmonious direction"[162] which Vaux credited to the policy which delegated the president of the college as the responsible head of the institution, and the Board of Directors to the responsibility and higher duty of legislation. This position of the Board of Directors, he believed, freed its members to devote themselves ". . . to the duty of fostering and extending the usefulness, elevating the character, adding well considered improvements, enlarging the benefits and maintaining the character of this noble bequest."[163]

Obviously, Vaux considered the establishment of a department of Industrial Science as a forward looking improvement. As a rationale for this department Vaux noted that since the time when Girard had drafted his will, a change had taken place in the industrial social organization due, in the main, to the discontinuance of the indentured apprentice system. Vaux delineated these changes as follows:

> Master mechanics are disinclined to undertake the responsibility of the domestic governance and trade education of apprentices, which the indenture requires. The custom now prevailing, is to give the boy a stipulated sum as wages, to pay for his food, lodging and clothing, and leave him to his own control, except while at his daily mechanical labor as a learner. Many of the trade organizations have seriously injured the character of skillful workmen, depreciated acquirement, and levelled down proficiency in practical as well as theoretic mechanical knowledge, by the views they have taken on this apprentice question, in its relation to handicraft teaching.[164]

Vaux added that this had made it apparent that the pupils should attain capacities that would induce the employers to enter into indentures but that the education provided did not include all the requisites: The answer lay in industrial science. Significantly, Vaux recognized this as the intent of

---

[162] *Ibid.*, p. 16. [163] *Ibid.*, p. 15. [164] *Ibid.*, p. 17.

Stephen Girard. He asserted:

> To educate the pupils in industrial science, theoretic and practical, was the true intention of Mr. Girard; it was the spirit of his devise; it was a marked feature of the college; it was the teaching of necessity; it was to be the objective point of the practical training which the will so distinctly demanded.[165]

Vaux admitted that the new department of industrial science was only a half year young, but he was confident that the pupils would be better-fitted apprentices since they were educated not only mentally, but manually--a fact which would make them doubly qualified for employment.

The new department was under the charge of Professor Vanderwyde. He conducted two classes, junior and senior, of thirty pupils each. In the junior class, the students were taught physics, chemistry, and anatomy; and in the senior class, mathematics applied to mechanics and analytical chemistry. Out of six daily recitations and lectures, two were held in a work room which provided: (1) Applied Mechanics--Type-setting, printing, book-binding, type-casting, stereotyping, turning, carpentering, &c., (2) Applied Chemistry--Analytical and manufacturing chemistry, daguerreotyping, photography, electrotyping, electroplating and practical instruction in the electric telegraph. Apart from this remained the teaching of shoemaking which had been the first experiment in manual labor at the college and had proved to be self-supporting.[166] In overview of what the evidence had suggested, Vaux argued for a continuation of the program:

> It is difficult to see how a system better adapted to the intention of the testator could be inaugurated in the Institution which his will has founded. Equally difficult is it to believe, that such a system of administration and policy, having such aims and ends in view as this now in operation under the present direction, could be ignored or subverted by the spirit of mere opposition, Broad, comprehensive, practical, on the ground that it is progressive,

---

[165] Ibid., p. 18.

[166] Ibid., pp. 19-21.

> over one stationary or reactionary. The public mind of the people, on questions of true practical progress, never favor retrogression. It prefers development and improvement, rather than unyielding belief in the virtue of immobility [167]

However, even with these apparent successful aspects of the report, some time worn problems were still in evidence. Vaux again voiced the necessity for stability in administration: "It cannot be stated too broadly or plainly stated, that changing one-third yearly of the whole member of directors,--six out of eighteen--is a serious detriment to the institution."[168] He

---

[167] _Ibid._, p. 23. Vaux cited further evidence to support his point quoting extensively from a written review of the college of which the following excerpts are representative: "We can scarcely overstate the bad effect of this first mistake [style of the buildings]. It has constantly tended to obscure Mr. Girard's real purpose, which was to afford a plain comfortable home and a plain substantial education to poor orphans destined to gain their livelihood by labor. * * * That huge and dazzling edifice seems always to have been exerting a powerful influence against the stricter constructionists of the will. It is only within the past two years that this silent but ponderous argument has been partially overcome by the resolute good sense of a majority of the Board of Directors. * * * These Directors appointed by the City Councils are eighteen in number, of whom six go out of office every year, while the Councils themselves are annually elected. Hence the difficulty of settling upon a plan, and the greater difficulty of adhering to one. Sometimes a majority has favored the introduction of Latin and Greek; again the manual-labor system has had advocates. Some have desired a liberal scale of living for the pupils; others have thought it best to give them Spartan fare. Four times the President has been changed, and there have been two periods of considerable length when there was no President. There have been dissensions without, and trouble within. * * * _There are indications, too, that the period of experiment draws to an end, and that the final plan of the College, on the basis of common sense, is about to be settled._" (_Ibid._, pp. 24, 25, 26, 27). Although not explicitly noted, the review is undoubtedly James Parton's paper, Girard College and Its Founder," in _The North American Review_, Vol. 100 (January, 1865). In this full text, Parton writes the following of Vaux: "Mr. Richard Vaux, the present head of the Board of Directors, writes reports in a style most eccentric, and not always intelligible to remote readers: but it is evident that his heart is in the work, and that he belongs to the party who desire the College to be the useful unambitious institution that Girard wishes it to be. His reports are not written with rose-water. They say _something_. They confess some failures, as well as vaunt some successes. We would earnestly advise the Directors never to shrink from taking the public into their confidence. The public is wiser and better than any man or any board. A plain statement every year of the real condition of the College, the real difficulties in the way of its organization, would have been far better than the carefully uttered nothings of which the Annual Reports have generally consisted," (pp. 97-98). (This item has been republished in James Parton, _Famous Americans of Recent Times_).

[168] _Ibid._, p. 9.

suggested that the City Councils continue their re-appointment course which they had partially adopted. Vaux also expressed concern over the appropriations allocated for the college. In speaking of the department of industrial science he noted that the entire 1865 appropriation for the department had been small, fearing that little progress could be made on such an inadequate sum. To point up the inadequacy he commented that Professor Vanderwyde had brought $8,000 worth of private property consisting of apparatus and tools which was being used to instruct the pupils and that an application submitted for the cost of transportation of the material to the college had been refused. Nevertheless, Vaux remained optimistic: "Yet with these discouragements the department is growing and gaining. When enlarged views unite with just conception of the true objects and interests of Girard College, this will be corrected."[169] However, his remarks were more candid in speaking of overall appropriations. Vaux reminded the members of the City Councils that it was generally accepted that Stephen Girard had intended the college as the primary object of his benevolence. This he believed was underscored by a legal opinion submitted by the City Solicitor to the City Councils on January 3,

---

169 Ibid., pp. 20-21. However, in a Report to the Committee on Instruction dated January 27, 1865, and appended to Vaux's Annual Report, President Smith was not disposed to any such optimism. He rather suggested that the disallowance of Vanderwyde's transportation charges [$225] ". . . may show what would probably be the fate of any application for funds in the present state of information as to the importance of value of the kind of education to be derived from the new department, and the apparatus gratuitously supplied." (pp. 53-54). Accordingly, he recounted how, while comparative professors received $1500 per annum and a dwelling, rent free, Professor Vanderwyde received $1600 and no dwelling. Unlike others who had the use of college property, the college had use of the property of Vanderwyde, without compensation. As to the departmental budget of $400 Smith opined that the industrial department would not be able to obtain what had been hoped and expected of it. This experiment he believed would soon meet with a temporary check since the allocation was not sufficient for proper instruction in both the classroom and laboratory.

1833, that "The completion and maintenance of the college was the first duty presented by the will for which the income was primarily to be used "[170] Rather, Vaux had found it regrettable that some years had shown the appropriations for the college to be less than the sum estimated by the Board of Directors and that while the sum required for salaries at the college had been reduced, the salaries of others not connected with the college but in other positions under the Trust Estate, had been increased. While Vaux was sure that those expenditures were in conformity with the appropriations, he asked if more revenue could be appropriated for the college especially since 143 applicants awaited admission.

Little change took place in advancing the work of the industrial science department during the next few years. Richard Vaux had stepped down as president of the Board of Directors in 1865 and passed out of the directory of the college in 1866. The reports of the new president of the board and his successors shed little light on any efforts to extend the program which Vaux had spoken of so optimistically if not desirably. Rather, it appears that the industrial science department was maintained as a theoretic discipline rather than a practically-oriented one. This is not to suggest that the maintenance of the industrial science department as a theoretic discipline allowed Girard College and its management a confrontation of the greater problems which Vaux, no matter how inadroitly had addressed himself to, but rather that the problem of responding to a declining apprenticeship with all its curricular implications still had to be resolved. The prevailing conditions of apprenticeship were outlined by the president of the Board of Directors in his Annual Report for 1865 as follows:

---

[170] Ibid., pp. 42-43.

> The difficulty of finding suitable places for our pupils as apprentices seems to increase, instead of being diminished. Since the time at which Mr. Girard's Will was framed, the whole system of apprenticeship, as it then existed, has practically been broken up. As a necessary result, masters are unwilling to take the responsibilities which, in years gone by, were expected of them; and the position of an apprentice being rendered derogatory in popular estimation, neither side are prepared to enter into the relation. The contaminating influences of such sentiments are speedily felt, and however a boy may be inclined at first to submit to the dictates and authority of a master disposed to do his duty, he soon is tempted to regard himself as bound by a restraint from which he should be free, and to consider the terms of his indenture as those of an unmeaning contract, and one from which every effort should be made on his part to be liberated. Notwithstanding these hindrances, however, the directions of the Will are being carried out as far, and with as good an effect, as can be reasonably expected.[171]

In an encouraging note, the president added that five orphans had been selected to attend a newly opened United States school for naval apprentices with only one orphan "proving himself unworthy of the position." This arrangement, the president believed, allowed the board to carry out the views of the founder of the college in desiring that navigation be taught.[172]

Significantly, the president of the Board of Directors noted in his report for 1866 that the subjects being taught at the college formed more than what had been usually termed as an ordinary English education. "The studies embrace not merely reading, writing, grammar, arithmetic and geography, but navigation surveying, practical mathematics, astronomy, natural, chemical and experimental philosophy, drawing, book-keeping, and the French and Spanish languages. To these are to be added such other learning and science as the capacities of the several scholars may merit or warrant."[173] As a

---

[171] _Eighteenth Annual Report of the Board of Directors of the Girard College for Orphans for the Year 1865_, p. 13.

[172] _Ibid._, p. 14.

[173] _Nineteenth Annual Report of the Girard College for Orphans For the Year 1866_, p. 6.

rationale for such subjects, the president provided the following commentary on Girard's educational intentions for the college:

> It must be apparent to every one that Mr. Girard had higher views than rendering all of the pupils of this Institution mere ordinary scholars, fitted to be put apprentices to a handicraft, and to be toiling as unremunerated operatives all their lives. For whilst it is true he has made apprenticeship a necessary part of the course to which every inmate of the College is to be subjected, he had the correct view of labor as honorable in itself, and in this free country so to be united with intelligence and education, as should enable its possessor to rise from the condition of a mere journeyman into the position of a merchant, a sea captain, a manufacturer or a tradesman, one carrying on business for himself, and making his way in the world by thrift, and knowledge, and industry. And his views were correct in theory, although found not to be entirely so when carried into practice. For in this land of liberty the idea of having any one as a master is repugnant to the immature ideas of those just launched into the busy world, and such ideas seem to be proportionably increased by the amount of education previously received. Nevertheless, in many instances both theory and practice are productive of good results, and the pathway of toil is seen to be the one best fitted to secure for those subjected to it, ultimate success.[174]

As has already been said in an earlier connection: At Girard College the course of study and apprenticeship continued to undergo an apparent gradual evolution with certain underlying conceptions always in evidence, but with necessary alterations, from time to time, indicative of changing viewpoints and suggestive of influences, not always apparent upon the line of development. Significantly, the previous prominence of the industrial science department in the earlier reports of Vaux was no longer in evidence in the Annual Report for 1865 and that one perceives an increased emphasis upon manual labor activities as is evident from the sole reference to practical studies in the 1866 Annual Report in the following: "The working class has faithfully performed its duties during the period which has elapsed since

---

[174] Ibid., p. 7.

our last report, and it is contemplated to render it more efficient in the future by the introduction of machinery."[175] Perhaps in this one finds reason for the reference in the same report of the resignation of Professor Vanderweyde as Professor of Physics and Industrial Sciences at the college.[176]

The need for a defined solution to the problem of apprenticeship became even more pronounced in the *Twentieth and Twenty-first Annual Reports* of the Board of Directors. In the *Twentieth Annual Report*, the president's concern was clearly evident in the following:

> Difficulty has been experienced in binding out our pupils in accordance with the terms of Mr. Girard's Will, and this difficulty appears to increase in consequence of the breaking up of the old system of apprenticeship, and the introduction of machinery into trades which were formerly carried on by the labor of the hands. This difficulty has been met hitherto by the efforts put forth to find proper positions for our graduating pupils, but we cannot fail to see that in the future these difficulties will be increased until, possibly, permanent situations can only be found for a few of those desiring them, upon their reaching the age suggested as a proper one for entering upon the course of apprenticeship. When this point is reaches, it will be necessary to devise some means for harmonizing the directions of the Will with the existing order of affairs.[177]

And, in the *Twenty-first Annual Report*, the president noted:

> Orphans are discharged from the College by binding them out, by cancelling their indentures, or by dismission for vicious conduct. By the Will of Mr. Girard, they are to be bound out between fourteen and eighteen years of age. It is rare, however, to bind a boy before the age of fifteen, and the greatest number are bound between sixteen and seventeen. After a boy passes the age of seventeen, it is difficult

---

[175] *Ibid.*, p. 16.

[176] *Ibid.*, p. 15. Vanderweyde's pessimism or dissatisfaction on this same point was not unqualified. See in this connection Letter from P. H. Vanderweyde to Richard Vaux, New York, March 31, 1868.

[177] *Twentieth Annual Report of the Board of Directors of the Girard College for Orphans For the Year 1867*, pp. 8-9.

to place him, on account of the limited time he will have to serve after his labor shall have become profitable to his master. . . .

Although forty-two boys have been bound during the past year, the number who are waiting for places is constantly increasing. This does not arise from any deficiency in the demand for boys, but from an unwillingness on the part of employers to take them under indentures. We have now on hand forty boys who are ready and anxious to go out to trades, some of whom are eighteen years of age, and many over seventeen.

The question, what shall be done with these boys, is one of great importance, and its solution cannot be postponed much longer. The apprenticeship system, as it existed in Mr. Girard's time, is almost obsolete; and the execution of that part of his Will which requires that the orphan shall be bound out to trades, between the ages of fourteen and eighteen, has become somewhat difficult. If legislation is necessary to enable the Board to dispose of those who are old enough to learn trades, by some other method than indentures, or if the Courts of Law or Equity have jurisdiction in the case, it is our opinion that the interposition of the Legislature or the Courts should be invoked without delay.

Ten of those who are waiting for situations, are pursuing special studies, and thirty are employed in manual labor. However diligently they may study or work, we submit that their time would be occupied more profitably to themselves, in learning occupations by which they may hereafter earn a livelihood. We may also add, that those who are eighteen years old and upwards, are occupying the places and receiving the maintenance to which applicants for admission are of right entitled.[178]

In order to appreciate the curriculum problem as it involved apprenticeship, it is necessary to understand the grouping of classes during this time. Instruction at this time at the college consisted of classes which were grouped into larger divisions, called Forms. In the first Form or primary department, the branches taught included reading, spelling, and the rudiments of geography and arithmetic. Students were placed into classes depending upon qualifications, but regularly the course occupied two years. The second

---

[178] Twenty-First Annual Report of the Board of Directors of the Girard College for Orphans For the Year 1868, pp. 17-19.

Form was considered in parity with the grammar schools of the public city schools. The branches taught included reading, writing, spelling by dictation, defining, arithmetic, grammar, geography and history. The length of time in this course ranged from two to three or more years depending upon individual accomplishments. The third Form or Academical Department was considered to correspond to the High School of Philadelphia. The departments of study included English branches, continued; mathematics, including algebra, geometry, plane and spherical trigonometry, surveying and navigation; Latin, French and Spanish languages; history, moral philosophy and the Constitution of the United States; chemistry and natural philosophy; drawing, penmanship and book-keeping. The usual length of the course occupied three and one-half years. These Forms allowed the average student to complete the prescribed curriculum in eight years.

The highest class was considered the graduating class and consisted of those students who had completed their final examinations and while waiting for apprentice situations were required to either pursue studies for which they exhibited a special aptitude or to engage in some manual labor activity as might be assigned to them.[179]

Under these conditions, the description of manual labor or the working class supplied in the Twenty-First Annual Report and the recommendation for a widening of the work experiences available are both significant and relevant and are quoted *in extenso*:

> MANUAL LABOR
>
> Boys who from incapacity or indisposition to study, are not deriving benefit from instruction in the schools, are transferred to the working class, at the age of fifteen years.
>
> After the completion of the prescribed course of study, the members of the graduating classes, may continue

---

[179] *Ibid.*, pp. 11-13.

the study of those branches in which they have previously excelled, until they go out to trades, or they may be placed in the working class, to learn something of tools and handicraft.

The working class, at the present time, numbers thirty boys, part of whom work with the carpenter, part with the gardener, and the remainder, when they are not employed as monitors or in other special duties, are engaged in the manufacture and repair of schoes. The working boys take recreation with the others after the close of the schools, and remain with their sections in the evening, where they have facilities for reading and writing.

In consequence of the increasing difficulty of finding employers who will take boys under indentures, the working class has become too large for our existing facilities for manual labor, and it will soon become necessary to enlarge them, by introducing a greater variety of handicrafts.

It is indeed worthy of consideration, whether all the pupils who are over fifteen years of age, should not be required to work at some manual labor during a part of every day. The hands need to be educated as well as the head, and if a boy is permitted to reach the age of eighteen, without training his limbs to work, he becomes unwilling to engage in mechanical occupation, and seeks employments which, as he erroneously believes, are more respectable, because the labor in them is easier and more cleanly. But he soon discovers that these occupations are over-crowded and poorly paid.

To carry out this plan, a large sum of money will be required for shops, tools, superintendents and materials; and it cannot be expected that the department will ever be self-supporting. But the outlay will be amply repaid if our pupils are made more valuable as apprentices, and the demand for them thereby increased. _The College is for the benefit of the orphans_; not the orphans for the benefit of the College.[180]

---

[180] _Ibid._, pp. 16-17. It is interesting to note the remarks of the president of the Board on apprenticeship in the _Twenty-Second Annual Report of the Girard College for Orphans For the Year 1869_, p. 7, which reads in part: ". . . many of our graduates have risen to stations of eminence and usefulness as well in the learned professions as in business and the mechanic arts, upon the educational foundations here well and substantially laid. And in this connection it may be observed as a slight indication of the general good character of our graduates, that although the system of apprenticeship has almost become obsolete, yet we have thus far found no lack of employers willing to take our pupils, as soon as it becomes necessary under the Will of Mr. Girard to bind them out."

However appealing the recommendations might have appeared, the _Twenty-Second Annual Report of the Board of Directors_ does not suggest that any immediate follow-up was made in this direction. However, the need outlined in the report for 1868 was fully realized by the Board of City Trusts who assumed the management of the college by an Act of the Legislature of the State of Pennsylvania which amended the charter of the City of Philadelphia and which was passed on June 30, 1869. In order to understand the situation more fully, it is necessary to go back a few years to the time, interestingly enough, when Vaux had passed out from the management of the college in 1866.

The early crosscurrents of educational aims and objection which had affected the early history of the college had been exacerbated by this type of control. Herrick, in commenting on this entire early period, cogently notes: "Throughout the period of councilmanic control the Directors of Girard College were at the mercy of the City Councils in financial matters;"[181] and in another ". . . there were growing differences between the Board of Directors and the Councils which had appointed them. The feeling at times was intense."[182]

Many events have already been noted that would suggest the intensity of the situation between the Board of Directors and the City Councils: but from 1866 to 1869 circumstances arose which aggravated even further the existing conditions. In 1866, the President of the Board of Directors noted in the _Annual Report_ for 1865 the following:

> During the past year, whilst there has been no lack of kindness exercised towards the pupils, and every effort has been made to win obedience by gentle and not by harsh methods,

---

[181]Cheesman A. Herrick, _op_. _cit_., p. 50.

[182]_Ibid_., p. 54.

> every flagrant violation of discipline has been sternly and promptly rebuked. In two or three cases of gross delinquency, when crime was actually perpetrated, calculated to endanger the lives of others, even the severest measures have been resorted to, and the guilty parties have been promptly handed over to the House of Refuge. These examples have been productive of a most salutary influence, and, as the result, it may be truthfully said, that the discipline of the household is as perfect as could be expected. The pupils seem contented and happy. Efforts have been made, as far as practicable, to add as much as possible, a home influence to the necessary mental and moral training bestowed. And although it is difficult to secure such an influence in its largest and fullest extent, yet what has been done has tended to render less burdensome the restraint which a seclusion from the world necessarily engenders.[183]

Apparently, this provided a bssis for the Board of Directors to present a bill to the Legislature asking authority to commit pupils of the college to the House of Refuge for improper conduct; for on April 5, 1866, a joint resolution was passed by the Select and Common Councils which protested against the passage of the act. Their resolution reads in part:

> WHEREAS, a bill has been presented to the Legislature, which is said to have originated in the present Board of Directors of the Girard College, asking authority to commit pupils of the College to the House of Refuge and for improper conduct.
>
> AND WHEREAS, the passage of this bill would be a stretch of power not exercised in any College or Academy in the land, and nothing could be presented for legislative action more calculated to affect the popularity and utility of that noble Institution, than for the mothers of children to realize that their sons, if admitted to the benefits of the College, may, through the caprice or incapacity of those having charge of the Institution to properly discipline them, be transferred to and incarcerated in the House of Refuge. Therefore
>
> _Resolved, By the Select and Common Councils of the City of Philadelphia_, That these Councils do most earnestly protest against the passage of such an Act, and respectfully request the Legislature of the State of Pennsylvania not to inflict such a vital injury upon Girard College, at present an ornament

---

[183] _Eighteenth Annual Report_, _op. cit._, p. 6-7.

> to both Metropolis and Commonwealth, by the enactment of such an unjust and unnecessary law.[184]

The following year, another event occurred that would tend to point up the growing dissatisfaction between the two groups. On September 11, 1867,

---

[184] Journal of the Select Council of the City of Philadelphia: From January 1 to July 1, 1866, p. 185. Also evident in this period were the difficulties encountered by the Board of Directors in maintaining the enrollment which had been increased in 1863 and which had approximately remained at 500 pupils. This reflected the overall financial intricacies in obtaining requested appropriations for the College and is pointed up by a resolution passed by the City Councils on May 11, 1865, which reads "That the Directors of the Girard College be and are hereby requested not to admit any more pupils into the institution until the Committee on the Girard Estates shall have been able to examine and report to councils upon the sufficiency of the appropriations to pay the additional expense that may be incurred by further admissions." See in this connection, Journal of the Select Council of the City of Philadelphia: From January 1 to July 1, 1865, p. 255. Subsequent to this, the President of the Board of Directors sent a communication to the City Councils on July 13th, 1865, explaining the financial condition of the college with particular note of the fact that there were a few years whereby the surplus from previous appropriations had been used and had prevented any financial difficulties, but that the increased number of pupils brought about by previous members of the Board had begun a deficit which had been carried from year to year, culminating in a total deficit of $16,000 as of July 1, 1865. He approved of the Council's policy of limiting the further admission of pupils until the Committee on the Girard Estates would be able to investigate the revenue to support any new admissions. See in this connection, Journal of the Select Council of the City of Philadelphia: From July 1 to December 31, 1865, p. 28, Appendix pp. 36-37. On November 23, 1865, the City Councils passed a supplementary appropriation of $12,000 for the year 1865 based upon a report and bill forwarded by the Committee on the Girard Estate who had felt themselves able to grant only a part of the amount applied for. (Ibid., p. 210, Appendix pp. 162-163). On December 14, the Board of Directors requested the City Councils to repeal the May 11, 1865, resolution which prevented the admission of additional pupils in the college. The request was referred to the Committee on Girard Estates with no apparent action taken (Ibid., p. 253). On March 15, 1866, another request was sent by the Board of Directors to the City Councils and was similarly referred to the Committee on Girard Estates with no apparent action. See in this connection, Journal of the Select Council of the City of Philadelphia: From January 1 to July 1, 1866, p. 134. However, on December 20, 1866, the City Councils passed a series of resolutions submitted by the Committee on Girard Estates which allowed for appropriations for the college for the year 1867; appropriations to cover the deficiencies of preceding years; and another resolution which enabled the Directors to admit additional pupils to make the whole number five hundred. See in this connection, Journal of the Select Council of the City of Philadelphia: From July 1 to December 31, 1866, p. 220, 221; 231-232; Appendix pp. 627-629. Two years later on December 16, 1868, the City Councils passed a resolution forwarded by the Committee on Girard Estates which authorized the Directors of the College to admit additional pupils to make the whole number five hundred and twenty. See in this connection, Journal of the Select Council of the City of Philadelphia: From July 2, 1868 to January 1, 1869, p. 275, Appendix p. 236.

the Board of Directors of the College voted President Somers Smith out of office and nominated and elected William H. Allen, the former president of the college, to fill the vacancy occasioned by the removal of Smith which was to take place on November 1, 1867. The Board's reasons for the decision were based upon the belief that the college had been for some time not conducted to their satisfaction or in accord with principles they believed that should have been followed. The preamble, which expressed the dissatisfaction, reads as follows:

> WHEREAS, In order to attain a full success for the purposes of this charity, it is indispensably necessary, in the opinion of this Board, that the administration of the College should be marked by a broad, vigorous, and comprehensive policy; that it should be so conducted as to constantly evince a hearty sympathy for its orphan children, and a reasonable respect for the interest and feelings of their relatives and friends, in order that the Institution may have the strong and sustaining influence of a favorable public opinion; that its discipline, while firm, should never be harsh or tyrannical, so as to make the obedience of its inmates the result of love rather than fear; that at all times and under all circumstances should the injunction of the founder be held especially sacred, to "form and foster a pure attachment to the republican institutions;" that, by a reasonable regard for the feelings and interests of its officers, a cordial and kindly relation should be encouraged and kept up towards the Institution, the President and each other; and, that finally, it should be so managed as to exhibit a more thorough and willing obedience to the wishes and intentions of the Directors, as expressed by their resolutions, adopted from time to time, or by the Code of Rules made for the government of the College.
>
> AND WHEREAS, In the opinion of the members of this Board, the College has not for some time been conducted to their satisfaction, or in consonance with the principles enumerated above; therefore,
>
> RESOLVED, That the office of President is hereby declared vacant from and after the first day of November next.[185]

On this basis, a "Joint Special Committee of Inquiring Relative to the

---

[185] Journal of the Select Council of the City of Philadelphia: From July 1, 1867, to January 2, 1868, Appendix pp. 50-51.

Management of Girard College" was appointed by the City Councils and charged ". . . to examine into all the circumstances connected with the removal of the late president, Major R. S. Smith, with power to send for persons and papers, and to report the result of the investigation to councils at as early a date as practicable, and consistent with a faithful discharge of its obligation to the community."[186] The report of the committee was submitted on February 20, 1868, and provided an Appendix to the _Journals of Councils_ amounting to 586 pages made up largely of testimonies received by the committee which were prefaced by a majority and a minority report, neither of which suggested the reinstatement of Major Smith.

As Herrick indicates: "This report gave aid and comfort to both sides in the controversy; it also probably satisfied neither side."[187] The majority report sustained Smith's removal but added that it ". . . was effected in a harsh and unnecessarily summary manner."[188] In contrast, the minority report held that "the manner of Smith's dismissal is deserving of severe censure, but the effort since made to destroy his reputation by charging him with disloyalty and other serious offences, we regard as entirely inexcusable and entitled to the strongest condemnation."[189]

The entire investigation with its concomitant allegations from all sides of the City Councils and the Board of Directors no doubt prompted unfavorable opinion of the administration of the college. Moreover, even as the investi-

---

[186] _Ibid._, p. 52.

[187] Cheesman A. Herrick, _op. cit._, pp. 57-58.

[188] _Journal of the Select Council of the City of Philadelphia: From January 1 to July 1, 1868_, Appendix p. i.

[189] _Ibid._, pp. vi-vii.

gation was being conducted, there was a motion in the City Councils to reduce the number of Directors of the College[190] and another to direct the "Joint Committee of Inquiry Relative to the Management of the Girard College . . . to inquire and report upon the propriety of repealing the Ordinance providing for monthly visitations by the members of the two chambers, and introducing in place thereof, if necessary, some other plan of inspection by which some more useful results can be accomplished; and also whether any abuses exist in the management of the said college."[191]

The best description of this early period and the transfer of control is provided in the Seventh Annual Report of the Board of Directors of City Trusts and reads as follows:

> In the year 1854 the City Charter was made to embrace the whole County of Philadelphia, placing the Councilmen representing the old City in a minority. Frequent and violent political changes in the City government induced partisans to use sacred trusts to a greater or less extent for party patronage. The tried officers who had become familiar with their duties were removed and replaced by professional politicians, who were compelled to pay a percentage on their salaries to the dominant political organization, and to employ mechanics who were influential with the party. The most rigid party rules were also applied by Councils to Girard College, by removing every director who did not belong to the dominant political party. As no nation, nor state, nor city government could long survive under such a rule, so the usefulness of the College was being curtailed and imperiled by it. An attempt to reduce the preference in admitting orphans to the College, given in the Will to the old City, was defeated by the Supreme Court. The only surviving executor of Mr. Girard united with other citizens in a successful effort to have the Trust placed beyond the reach of those who were likely to use it increasingly for party patronage. On the thirtieth of June, 1869, the Legislature of the State, with the greatest unanimity, amended the Act incorporating the City of Philadelphia, by "creating a board called Directors of City Trusts, to be the agents or officers of said City," charged with all the "rights and powers of the

---

[190] Journal of the Select Council of the City of Philadelphia from July 1, 1867, to January 2, 1868, Appendix pp. 52-54.

[191] Ibid., p. 98.

> City concerning all property and estate whatsoever, dedicated to charitable uses or trusts, the charge or administration of which are now, or shall hereafter become, vested in, or confided to, the City of Philadelphia."[192]

After the passage of the law, the City Councils sought to contest the validity of the law. On February 18, 1870, Justice Sharswood of the Supreme Court of Pennsylvania, delivered the unanimous opinion of the court affirming the validity of the law.[193] Upon this decision, the Board proceeded to the execution of its powers and duties. On February 25, 1870, the Board took possession of all the property and appointed committees to determine the condition of the various trusts (twenty-nine in number) and to plan for their conduct. Eight standing committees were appointed: Committee on Finance and Accounts; Committee on Property of the Girard Estates within the City of Philadelphia; Committee on Property of the Girard Estates without the City of Philadelphia; Committee on Household of Girard College; Committee on Instruction and Library of Girard College; Committee on Admission and Discipline and Discharge of Girard College; Committee on the Property and Administration of the Wills Hospital and Other Trusts; and an Executive Committee which consisted of the Chairman of the seven standing committees with the President of the Board as Chairman.[194]

---

[192] Seventh Annual Report of the Board of Directors of the City Trusts. Report for the Year 1876, pp. 7-8. An early joint reaction of the City Councils to the transfer of control took the form of a "Resolution of Request to the State Legislature," protesting against the passage of the law establishing Directors of City Trusts, on January 21, 1968. See in this connection, Journal of the Select Council of the City of Philadelphia: From January 1 to July 1, 1869, p. 50.

[193] First Annual Report of the Directors of City Trusts, For the Year 1870, p. 6.

[194] By the act creating the Board of City Trusts, the Board was to be composed of fifteen persons, including the Mayor of the City, the presidents of the Select and Common Councils and twelve other citizens who were to be appointed by the Judges of the Supreme Court of Pennsylvania, together with the Judges of the District Court and the Court of Common Pleas of the City

IV

> The Executive Committee is composed of the Chairman of the seven Standing Committees, the President of the Board being the Chairman. The Board referred to this committee the following important Preamble and Resolution:
>
> Whereas it is specially enjoined in the will of Mr. Stephen Girard, that the orphans of his college shall be thoroughly trained in moral and industrial habits, therefore,
>
> Resolved: That the Executive Committee, comprising the Chairmen of all Standing Committees, consider and report plans and estimates for instructing and training each pupil in some department of handicraft, and also such changes from the community to the family system, as the Committee may after investigation deem desirable, and likely to promote a higher type of moral virtue in the pupils.
>
> Much time will be given to the consideration of subjects of such vital importance as those contained in the resolution. Dignifying labor and giving the pupils habits of industry with the ability to manipulate actively, can hardly be over estimated, although these advantages are likely to be overlooked in a school where mental instruction is to be prominent.[195]

The problem presented to the Executive Committee, although formidable, did not seem incapable of solution. The following year, in 1871, the President of the Board provided the Executive Committee with a rationale for handicraft instruction.

> The Executive Committee was also directed by the Board, "to consider and report plans and estimates for instructing and training each pupil in some department of handicraft."
>
> It may be well, first, to consider the importance and practicability of introducing a general system of manual labor into Girard College before much time is spent on the details. At present, with few exceptions, the time of each boy in the College is divided between mental culture and amusement. This dignifies mental culture, but not labor; habits of industry

---

and County of Philadelphia. (See in this connection, First Annual Report of the Directors of City Trusts, For the Year 1870, pp. 29-30). Under the Pennsylvania Constitution of 1874, the appointing power was restricted to the Judges of the Courts of Common Pleas. See in this connection, Fifth Annual Report of the Directors of City Trusts, Report for the Year 1874, pp. 5-6.

[195] First Annual Report of the Directors of City Trusts for the Year 1870, pp. 26-27.

> cannot be formed under the existing system, and, owing to the community life, the pupils of the College have less skill in manipulating, and in the use of tools, than home trained boys. Money, earned by a lad's own productive industry, aids him in rightly estimating its value, and it often stimulates and encourages boys, who, though disheartened in school, manifest good mechanical skill. Surely some time can be gleaned from school and play to acquire handicraft and habits of industry, although mental culture must ever be paramount in Girard College. It will be impossible to give even rudimentary instruction in the various branches of industrial pursuits, to which the pupils of the College are indentured. A fair measure of skill in manipulating, can no doubt be acquired, if every boy who enters the College is obliged to work in wood, or paper, or straw, or in some other department of handicraft.
>
> Manual labor as an aid in moral training, and in acquiring habits of industry, and also, the family system, have been tested in schools and reformatory institutions, both in Europe and in this country. The members of the Committee will naturally strive to obtain reliable information from those who have witnessed the working of these principles.[196]

However, while there seemed to be an urgency in developing a system which would provide an adequate training in handicrafts without detracting from the mental culture aspect of the college, the only evident effort in this direction appeared in the Annual Reports of the Directors of City Trusts beginning with the year 1874.[197] In 1874, an additional teacher was retained in order to introduce the system of Drawing and Penmanship into the lower classes which would complement the system already in practice in the higher classes.[198] One

---

[196] Second Annual Report of the Directors of City Trusts, For the Year 1871, p. 24.

[197] It is of interest to note a reference found in the Fifteenth Annual Report of the Board of Directors of City Trusts. Report for the Year 1884, p. 14, which explains that in April 1873, a recommendation was made by the Executive Committee through its chairman that the trade of manufacturing paper boxes and tinware be introduced, but that this was not adopted.

[198] Fifth Annual Report of the Board of Directors of City Trusts. Report for the Year 1874, p. 17. See also Appendix M, p. , for the "Course of Study for Eight Years and Six months" dated January 1875.

year later, the President of the Board admitted, in somewhat apologetic terms, "The only progress made in the introduction of manual labor has been the extension of the shoe manufactory, in which boys are regularly employed in the interval between leaving school and being indentured as apprentices.[199] Yet, his following report for the year 1876 appeared to take on a different direction, testifying to the general stimulus given industrial education by the International Centennial Exhibition at Philadelphia in 1876. His statement serves as a terminus and a beginning in manual and industrial education for a school which ironically found itself with a continuing uncertain and unresolved direction for its practical education commitment:

> Strict attention is paid to the mental training of the orphans that are indentured to the City; thus far, however, the _hand_ has only been educated in penmanship and drawing. The introduction of handicraft is receiving attention, and suggestions from citizens who have practically considered this subject will be thankfully received by the Directors of City Trusts.[200]

---

[199] _Sixth Annual Report of the Board of Directors of City Trusts. Report for the Year 1875_, pp. 8-9.

[200] _Seventh Annual Report of the Directors of City Trusts. Report for the Year 1876_, pp. 14-15.

CHAPTER IV

INDUSTRIAL EXPANSION AND NEW CHALLENGES

I

> From time to time some of the directors recognized the importance of mechanical instruction, but after one or two attempts further efforts in this direction were abandoned, as those proved utter failures. It was not until Dr. Runkle, of the Massachusetts Institute of Technology, at the instance of the late Mr. William Welsh, then president of the Board of Directors of City Trusts, delivered a short address on the subject in the lecture-room of the Franklin Institute in this city, that any practical mode of introducing this branch of study into the college was presented.[1]

The conditions at Girard College in 1876 were very favorable for the development of a mechanical course of instruction. It is to be remembered that in the first year (1870), the Board of Directors of City Trusts had assumed control, the Board had referred a preamble and resolution to the executive committee which provided a continuing charge to the executive committee to ". . . consider and report plans and estimates for instructing and training each pupil in some department of handicraft. . . ."[2] The Board had believed such training to be of vital importance since it would dignify labor and would give the pupils habits of industry especially enjoined in the will of Stephen Girard.[3] However, at the close of the year 1876, the extent of

---

[1]Extract of Letter from W. Heyward Drayton to Charles H. Ham. Philadelphi [September, 1884] in Charles H. Ham, Manual Training: The Solution of Social and Industrial Problems, pp. 346-347. Mr. Drayton was then President of the Board of Directors of City Trusts.

[2]First Annual Report of the Directors of City Trusts, For the Year 1870, p. 27.

[3]Ibid.

practical instruction at the college remained essentially unchanged with guidelines for any new type of instruction or training in a speculative stage. The need for such a plan was underscored by the no less pressing problem of the persisting declination of apprenticeship which had made it increasingly manifest that a method should be found which would offset the unwillingness of many employers to take indentured apprentices. In his Annual Report for the Year 1876, Mr. William Welsh, President of the Board of Directors, noted: "So many of the most desirable workshops being virtually closed against all apprentices, the Directors have under consideration some arrangement by which the graduates of the College may have access to such positions, their education and training giving them special fitness for them."[4] In his Annual Report for the Year 1877, he outlined several areas under consideration:

> Owing to the increase in the number of pupils, and the unwillingness of very many employers to take indentured apprentices, this department of their duty gives the Directors of City Trusts increasing solicitude, and led to the appointment of a special committee to consider the subject. As boys are received into the College when from six to ten years old, and bound out between fourteen and eighteen, there is a prevailing belief that there is ample time for industrial training, as well as for mental culture. Mr. Girard, in his Will, plainly indicated his desire that the pupils should be so fitted in the College for productive industrial pursuits that habits of industry would become a moral principle. He indicated suitable occupations, and named agriculture first. The special committee has under consideration the feasibility of leasing to some skillful agriculturist and teacher, part of the farm lands belonging to the Girard Estate, in Schuylkill or Columbia County, with a view of securing for such of the graduates as are fitted for it, a scientific and practical education in all the departments of agriculture, and thus increase the interest of lads in this productive occupation. Navigation is named second, and although there is theoretical instruction in navigation given in the College, yet thus far there have been few opportunities found for indenturing boys to those who would give them practical instruction. The Will next designates arts, mechanical trades, and manufactures, and the Directors may find that some trades

---

[4] Seventh Annual Report of the Board of Directors of City Trusts. Report for the Year 1876. p. 19.

> can be advantageously taught in the College, and that to prepare for other trades, the eyes and hands of boys who have taste and an aptitude for it, may be instructed in mechanic arts by skillful teachers, as they now are in drawing and penmanship. Shoemaking is now taught to boys who have finished their studies, and are waiting for suitable situations; but skill and industrious habits are rarely if ever acquired when there is no aptitude for, or a dislike to, the trade or occupation.
>
> The whole subject will receive the consideration its importance demands, and the success of special instruction in the department of drawing, affords an incentive to arrange for special instruction in other departments, suited to well trained and educated boys.[5]

No less propitious was the coincident general impulse for practical training in the use of tools and machinery as a result of the Centennial Exposition of 1876. In this connection, a future president of the College, Cheesman A. Herrick, noted, "Girard College was well abreast of the movement for manual training which swept over the country immediately after the Centennial Exposition of '76. . . .[6]

---

[5]Eighth Annual Report of the Board of Directors of City Trusts. Report for the Year 1877. pp. 10-11. The year 1877 was the first instance in which any boy born outside of Pennsylvania was admitted into the college. Previously, the applicants from the State of Pennsylvania had exceeded the capacity of the college; but due to an expansion of facilities, the college was able to increase its former approximate capacity of 550 places for students to a new capacity of 870 places. The directors of the college had been long anxious to increase the number of pupils as a result of a decision of the Supreme Court of the United States made in 1868 which ". . . recognized that the entire income from the residuary estate of Stephen Girard's bequest may be used exclusively for the maintenance and education of orphans in Girard College, and for providing increased accommodations, until the whole of the College property is fully occupied for this purpose." (Ibid., pp. 5-6). [The case is reported as Girard v. Philadelphia, 74 U.S. 1 (1869).] The directors had been delayed in erecting additional buildings due to attempts to open streets through the college grounds. These attempts apparently began in 1871 (See Second Annual Report of the Board of Directors of City Trusts, For the Year 1871, pp. 8-9) and continued through 1876, finally resulting in a decision that was adverse to opening streets through the college grounds. (See Seventh Annual Report of the Board of Directors of City Trusts. Report for the Year 1876, pp. 13-14.)

[6]Cheesman A. Herrick, "Girard College President's Report for 1913," in Fifty-Fourth Annual Report of the Board of Directors of City Trusts of the City of Philadelphia for 1913. p. 136.

This is evident from the following report:

> In 1876 the Centennial Exhibition gathered into its brilliant focus many of the results reached by the best thinkers and most practical men of the civilized world; among them, a simple method of teaching the rudiments of practical mechanics to boys, which seems to have been thought out by Russian instructors, and has become popularly known as the "Russian plan." One of the first to appreciate and utilize this system was the President of the Institute of Technology in Boston, Mr. John D. Runkle. He introduced it into that institution, and on the invitation of Mr. Welsh, the President of our Board, in the Fall of 1877, in a lecture at the Franklin Institute, demonstrated its simplicity and practicability to an audience, among whom were some of our members.[7]

In anticipation of what type of instruction might be given, the Board of Directors saw fit to include space in five newly erected buildings of the college for such instruction, but admittedly required further deliberation on the subject before any definite plan would be followed. In their _Annual Report for 1877_, it was noted: "Sixteen rooms have been finished in the

---

[7]_Fifteenth Annual Report of the Board of Directors of City Trusts. Report for the Year 1884_, pp. 14-15. As president of the Massachusetts Institute of Technology, John D. Runkle had been aware of a problem faced by many technical schools: How to provide meaningful shop instruction for mechanical engineering students? In the Russian exhibit at the Centennial Exhibition he saw a solution to this problem and the practicability of providing shop instruction as a part of general education. See in this connection, Letter from John D. Runkle to Charles H. Ham, May 22, 1884, quoted in Charles H. Ham, _op. cit._, pp. 331-332, particularly the following extract: "From the first the course in Mechanical Engineering has been an important one in the Institute of Technology. A few students come with a knowledge of shop-work, and had a clear field open to them on graduation, but the larger number found it difficult to enter upon their professional work without taking one or two years of apprenticeship. This always seemed to me a fault in the education, and yet I did not see the way to remedy it without building up manufacturing works in connection with the school--a step which I knew to be an inversion of the true educational method. At Philadelphia, in 1876, almost the first thing I saw was a small case containing three series of models--one of chipping and filing, one of forging, and one of machine-tool work. I saw at once that they were not parts of machines, but simply graded models for teaching the manipulations in those arts. In an instant theproblem I had been seeking to solve was clear in my mind; a plain distinction between a mechanic art and its application in some special trade became apparent. My first work was to build up at the institute a series of Mechanic Art shops, or laboratories, to teach these arts just as we teach chemistry and physics by the same means. At the same time, I believed that this discipline could be made a part of general education, just as we make the sciences available for the same end through laboratory instruction."

basements of these buildings for playrooms, or for mechanical instruction, if the committee that is now considering the subject of industrial education becomes convinced that it can be advantageously introduced into the College."[8]

Although the Annual Report for the following year noted that a "shop for instruction in handicraft"[9] had been included among the renovations made during the year on the college buildings, little change took place during the next few years in extending shop instruction. However, in the same report, the Board pointed out, "The Board have under consideration the question of technical education, and for the purpose of determining the advisability of introducing into the College some instruction in the mechanic arts and useful trades, they are obtaining information on that subject, which is now being considered by a special committee, appointed for the purpose."[10]

In the Annual Report for the Year 1880, the Board again noted that the subject of "Technical Education" was still undergoing consideration and that there had been considerable correspondence on the subject from schools in the United States as well as in Europe. However, the Board apparently found it necessary to explain the reasons for the obvious delay. They observed: "The great importance of this question [technical education], the expediency of its

---

[8]Eighth Annual Report of the Board of Directors of City Trusts, op. cit., p. 8.

[9]Ninth Annual Report of the Board of Directors of City Trusts. Report for the year 1878, p. 11.

[10]Ibid., p. 12. It is significant to note that phonography was introduced in the year 1880. As a rationale for this branch of study, the Board noted: "It is confidently expected that a knowledge of this branch of education will be of great advantage to the pupils, and will make it easier for them to find suitable places when they leave college. The condition of apprenticeships existing at the time Mr. Girard made his Will, and which was in his view, has greatly changed. They have become very few and comparatively scarce, and while his directions are followed, yet this is done with very great difficulty. Whatever improves the capacity of the orphan, will be an additional recommendation for the apprentice." See in this connection, Eleventh Annual Report of the Board of Directors of City Trusts. Report for the Year 1880, p. 11.

addition to the course of study, the expense involved, and its conformity with the provisions of the Will, make the Directors cautious and deliberate in coming to a fixed resolution on the subject."[11] In 1881, a plan of instruction was agreed upon. Significantly, W. Heyward Drayton who had been Chairman of the Committee on Mechanical Instruction at the time provided a description of the plan in 1884 at which time he was President of the Board of Directors.[12] His Annual Report for the Year 1884 is invaluable since it contains a brief summary of the general efforts to introduce mechanical instruction into the college. Of the plan chosen in 1881, he writes the following:

> It was not, however, until the year 1881, after great deliberation and an elaborate report from a special committee, that the Board carefully considering three plans suggested

---

[11]Eleventh Annual Report of the Board of Directors of City Trusts. Report for the Year 1880, p. 10. Beyond correspondence with other schools, the Annual Report for the following year noted: "The schools of Paris have been thrice visited by members of the Board, to observe the practical working of the system. . . ." See in this connection, Twelfth Annual Report of the Directors of City Trusts. Report for the Year 1881, p. 8.

[12]William H. Drayton was appointed a Director of City Trusts on February 14, 1872. He was elected President of the Board on December 10, 1884, and remained as president until his death on October 9, 1892. After his death, the following minute of a Board meeting held on October 11, 1892, unanimously adopted and ordered to be printed in the Twenty-Third Annual Report of the Board of Directors of City Trusts of the City of Philadelphia For the Year 1892, "To him as Chairman of the Committee on Mechanical Instruction particularly belonged the cultivation of that branch of useful study. Selected by President Welsh for his especial fitness for that purpose, he gave years of persistent labor and careful thought to the subject of its introduction in the Girard College. At his instance, practical, personal and theoretical knowledge was obtained from the schools of Russia, Paris and Boston, and by means of public lectures the subject pressed upon the observation and thought of his associates and the community; his faithful and intelligent work was finally crowned by its introduction into the College in its present Mechanical Hall, which was first opened to the Girard College pupils about the time of his election to the Presidency of the Board in December, 1884." (p. 6). See also in this connection, Alexander Biddle, In Memoriam: William Heyward Drayton. An Address to the Pupils of the Girard College, Read January 24, 1893. [This address is appended to the Twenty-Third Annual Report, supra.]

> to them--First, establishing machine shops in connection with the school; Second, a large establishment with various tools and appliances suitable to many trades, with competent instructors in each branch; Third, elementary instructions only; not to teach a trade nor secure a product, but to train the pupils in the use of tools--instruction, not construction,--in fact the Russian system;--adopted to introduction into the College; the first two plans, being not only expensive, but in the opinion of some members of the Board, not in accordance with the scheme of instruction prescribed by Mr. Girard for the education of his beneficiaries.[13]

The significance of the action taken in regard to technical education was pointed up by the directors in their Annual Report for the Year 1881. The report noted: "The Directors find themselves much embarrassed in carrying

---

[13]Fifteenth Annual Report of the Board of Directors of City Trusts, op. cit., p. 15. For a detailed account of the Russian system, its origin, principles, equipment used, courses of instruction, and methods of teaching, see Charles A. Bennett, History of Manual and Industrial Education 1870-1917, Ch. I. Briefly, the Russian system was the result of the efforts of Victor Della Vos, director of the Imperial Technical School of Moscow, and his shop instructors. The purpose of the school was to train civil and mechanical engineers, draftsmen, foremen, and chemists. To supplement the theoretical instruction with practical application, the school provided extensive construction workshops in which the students as well as hired workmen produced work under contract to private individuals. In 1868, Della Vos found the "no-teaching," imitative, or apprenticeship method then used unsatisfactory, and thereby set up individual instruction shops, (e.g., joinery, wood turning, blacksmithing, locksmithing, etc.) separate from the construction shops, allowing students to work in the latter shops only after completing the require course of instruction. It was in the separation of the shops that allowed Dell Vos the opportunity to provide a method whereby the necessary skills of a trade could be abstracted and systematized into a series of graded exercises which employed the use of drawings, models and tools. Della Vos' own description in devising his system deserves note: "By the separation alone of the school workshops from the mechanical works, the principal aim was, however, far from being attained; it was found necessary to work out such a method of teaching the elementary principles of mechanical arts as, firstly, should demand the least possible length of time for their acquirement; secondly, should increase the facility of the supervision of the graduationary employment of the pupils; thirdly, should impart to the study itself of practical work the character of a sound, systematical acquirement of knowledge; and fourthly, and lastly, as should facilitate the demonstration of the progress of every pupil at every stated time. Everybody is well aware that the successful study of any art whatsoever, freehand or linear drawing, music, singing, painting, etc., is only attainable when the first attempts at any of them are strictly subject to the laws of gradation and successiveness, when every student adheres to a definite method or school, surmounting, little by little, and by certain degrees, the difficulties to be encountered." (Victor Della Vos, "Description of the Collections of Scientific Appliances Instituted for the Study of Mechanical Art in the Workshops of the Imperial Technical School of Moscow," as quoted in Charles A. Bennett, supra, pp. 48-49).

out Mr. Girard's instructions as to apprenticeship."[14] They explained that there were few persons to be found who would assume the responsibility with but little control over the apprentice and other obstacles that were in the way of the apprentice learning the mechanic arts. "The only remedy seems to be to give the pupils mechanical knowledge and skill within the College as part of their daily routine."[15] The directors believed that the European plan of Technical Education was one that might be introduced with great advantage and that since the solicitor had given his opinion that such an experiment was permissible, the "test of experience" would justify the usefulness of the plan during the following year.[16]

II

> The year just passed has been one of experiment and severe trial to all branches of the College, every department of which has undergone changes, with enlargement and improvement in view of the great increase in the number of orphans to be accommodated within its limits.[17]

In January 1882, an appropriation was made for the purposes of mechanical instruction; and workshops were fitted up in the basement of one of the build-

---

[14] Twelfth Annual Report of the Board of Directors of City Trusts. Report for the Year 1881, p. 8.

[15] Ibid., p. 9.

[16] Ibid.

[17] Thirteenth Annual Report of the Board of Directors of City Trusts. Report for the Year 1882, p. 5. The number of boys in attendance at the college on the first day of January, 1882, was 878; an additional 300 were added during the year; 71 left the college between 14 and 18 years of age to enter suitable occupations; and 3 boys died. At the close of the year, there remained, 1,104 boys in attendance. (Ibid., p. 7). Undoubtedly, President Allen's death on August 29, 1882, added to the difficulties which presented themselves with the care of 300 additional students. In December 1882, Adam H. Fetteroff was elected the fifth president of Girard College. (Ibid., p. 8). The year 1882 also brought a change in the grouping of classes in the college. The classes, formerly grouped to three schools, were now grouped into four. See Appendix N, p. , for the "Course of Study for Eight Years, dated January 1882.

ings. Mason T. Mitchell was employed as superintendent of the workshops; and, at the suggestion of the Board, visited the School of Technology in Boston, the Stevens Institute in Hoboken, the Cooper Institute in New York; and the Spring Garden Institute in Philadelphia.[18] In April of the same year, mechanical instruction on a small scale began at the college.[19] From 150 to 200 boys divided into five classes received daily instruction for about six hours a week.[20] The success of the instruction was made eminently clear in the Annual Report for the following year. The directors noted: "The gratifying experiment in mechanical teaching last year has induced the Board, when compelled by the condition of the steam boilers after the use of many years, to provide new boilers and a boiler house . . . and to connect therewith as a matter of advantage and economy, a building for the purposes of mechanical instruction in metals and woods."[21] The condensed extracts from a report to the Board which outlined the need for expanded facilities are significant for the description they contain of the first efforts and success of mechanical instruction at the college, and are quoted *in extenso*, with the direct quotations so indicated with which the Board justified their recommendations:

---

[18] *Ibid.*, p. 8. Cheesman A. Herrick, *History of Girard College*, p. 236, notes that Mitchell had formerly been employed by the Baldwin Locomotive Works and had served as superintendent of instruction in the manual trades at the Spring Garden Institute and was familiar with the industrial training system of England and other European countries including the schools of Russia and Copenhagen.

[19] *Fourteenth Annual Report of the Board of Directors of City Trusts. Report for the Year 1883.* p. 13.

[20] *Thirteenth Annual Report of the Board of Directors of City Trusts. loc. cit.*

[21] *Fourteenth Annual Report of the Board of Directors of City Trusts. loc. cit.*

"Heretofore, the boys have only been instructed in metal working. This, an experiment undertaken with great caution and on a small scale, in deference to the misgivings of some members of the Board, and with the experience of one or two failures in the same direction has, we are happy to report, from its inception, in April, 1882, to this time, continued to give such entire satisfaction, has proved so useful and attractive to the pupils, and has helped us so materially in securing occupation for no less than thirty of our boys in first-class mechanical establishments, where, instead of having to learn the most rudimentary branches, they are at once recognized as useful workmen and paid accordingly, that we feel encouraged to recommend to the Board that the instruction now confined to metal work, such as filing to line, sawing and filing, known as template work, fitting, dovetailing, chamfering, chipping and sawing, free hand filing with hand vise, etc., be extended to wood work in its various branches."

We have before referred to the importance of extending mechanical instruction to be given to boys, to wood work. Heretofore, the work has been confined to iron and steel alone, and in seeking employment our lads are restricted to this kind of work. We think it advisable and strenuously recommend to the Board to extend the teaching to the using of tools in wood. We see no reason why this character of instruction should not be equally successfully taught and the demand for wood workers is almost as great as for workers in metals. While free hand drawing is admirably taught in the College, there is little time or opportunity for mechanical drawing which is so important to the skilled mechanic. We advise that this be made part of mechanical instruction, etc.

No attempt has been made to teach the pupils any distinct trade, except perhaps a few boys of remarkable natural ability for mechanics; in view of the early age at which they are compelled to leave the college this would be impossible.

They are taught the use of tools, and how to handle them in the workshop, as they are taught to read, write and cipher in the school rooms; the one course enabling them to become clerks, bookkeepers, conveyancers, the other, machinists, furniture-makers, blacksmiths, cabinet-makers, locksmiths, and to obtain employment in kindred trades.

The Instructor also reports, "that he has in view the adoption of plans whereby illuminated objects of machinery, embracing a much wider scope of explanation, may be introduced with much advantage, which will familiarize the boys with what they will meet with in mechanical business. A pause is frequently made, when the attention of classes is called to the elucidation of points bearing upon particular stages of their work, and whilst general attention is given there have come back to us expressions of thanks from those who are testing the knowledge thus obtained in their daily work of life."[22]

In December, 1884, the Technical School building was completed and formally opened on December 9th. The commodius building which allowed for a greater variety of technical teaching was considered by the Board comparable ". . . with the best models of workshops of this character."[23] The Board added that while the school was being built, some members of the Committee on mechanical instruction, accompanied by the Mayor of the City, the president of the Common Council, and Mr. James H. Windrim, the architect of the Trust, had visited the workshops at Stevens Institute in Hoboken, the Adler Institute in New York, and the Institute of Technology in Boston. Of all the schools visited, however, it was found that ". . . the machinery, the arrangement of the workshops and workbenches of the Institute of Technology in Boston most nearly what they were seeking, drawings and measurements of many of these were made by Mr. Windrim, aided in every way by Professor Runkle, who gave up his whole time to the committee while in Boston."[24]

---

[22] Ibid., pp. 13-14. It is interesting to note in the same report in light of the success of mechanical instruction that a new committee, The Committee on Mechanical Instruction, was added to the standing committees of the Board of Directors of City Trusts for the following year, 1883. William Heyward Drayton is listed as its chairman. In the Fourteenth Annual Report the Board noted that the Board had now been divided into eleven standing committees, an increase of four over the original seven. A comparison of the different listings of committees indicate that the four new committees included a Committee on Mechanical Instruction; a Committee on The Infirmary, a Committee on Shield's Almshouse Fund; and a Committee on Appropriations.

[23] Fifteenth Annual Report of the Board of Directors of City Trusts, op. cit., pp. 15-16.

[24] Ibid., p. 16. No detailed description of the first workshops constructed at Girard College exists; however, the shops evidently were modelled after those of the Institute of Technology of Boston. In describing the shop for vise work in cold metalwork at Boston, Runkle noted that the shop contained ". . . four heavy benches, each eighteen feet long, three feet wide, and two and one-half feet high. To each bench, eight vises were attached. It was supposed that one teacher could instruct thirty-two students at a

By the end of the year 1884 about 250 boys were under instruction in the use of tools dealing with metal and wood. Elementary instruction in wood work had been introduced at the college even before the new building had been completed and although only taught for a few months, the students had shown a preference for this branch of study over the other.[25] With the erection of a suitable building, the Board was able to add smith shop and foundry instruction the following year. Likewise mechanical and geometrical drawing were also added to the curriculum. With apparent pride the Board noted: "We believe that all of these are necessary to equip a lad to go out from the College and take his place among the young mechanics of our country."[26] On this note, the Board set forth the plan of shopwork instruction for students at the college:

> While each study is taught to every pupil old enough to handle tools, careful supervision by the master soon discovers the particular branch in which each seems to display most capacity; to which after he has gone through the whole

---

time, and this has been found to be about the right number. At the beginning of the course, it is quite enough; but later, when students have acquired skill and independence, this number can be successfully taught." (See in this connection, John D. Runkle, "The Manual Element in Education," p. 196, in _Forty-First Annual Report of the Board of Education, State of Massachusetts, 1876-77_, as quoted in Charles A. Bennett, _op. cit._, p. 324.) In the _Fifteenth Annual Report of the Board of Directors of City Trusts_, it was also noted in passing: "It is only a tribute to the Spring Garden Institute of Philadelphia, to say that the intelligent manufacturers and practical mechanics who manage it, and from whom we have had much help, adopted this Russian system, or one quite similar several years before it was introduced into the College, incorporating it, however, with more advanced teaching than our Board has felt to this time warranted to undertake." (p. 17)

[25] _Ibid._, pp. 16-17. This report also noted that phonography continued to be successfully taught and added: "Typewriting is also taught to such boys who display an aptitude for it. Its introduction is so recent that nothing can be said of it, experimentally, but the increasing demand for experts in this art seems to promise another opening for the employment of our orphans who leave the College to struggle for a living." (_Ibid._, p. 17)

[26] _Sixteenth Annual Report of the Board of Directors of City Trusts. Report for the Year 1885_. p. 13.

> curriculum, he will be permitted to devote most of his attention during the residue of his stay in the College.
>
> The plan of instruction proposed to accomplish this end, is to commence with the draughting room, where the beginner will be required to make a drawing of some simple article, or piece of machinery, which he will then take to the wood working and turning department and work out as a model for the foundry, where he will be taught to cast it in metal. From the foundry he will take his casting to the metal bench, and there complete it for the purpose of its design. This finished, he will begin again with some more complicated piece of work in the draughting room, going through the same routine again and again until, draughtesman, wood worker, turner, forger and skilled worker in metal, he either goes out into the world competent to earn his living at least, in some one of these employments; or if, in the judgment of the Superintendent, the lad, still under eighteen years of age, is sufficiently instructed in each branch, and shows a preference for one, and has not found a suitable place, he may be permitted to make himself more perfect in that one which he prefers.[27]

The introduction of mechanical instruction at the college seemed providential to the directors when viewed in light of the scarcity of apprenticeships available. It was observed that in 1884 when metal work alone was taught, only about one-third of the boys who left the college entered mechanical trades; but with the introduction of wood work and turning in 1885, it was found that by the end of 1885 that two-thirds were able to obtain work in mechanical occupations.[28] The following year, the results of the plan of shop work instruction continued not only to be gratifying but appeared to provide an answer to the problem of finding places for apprentices, and, no less significant, helped in providing a better learning atmosphere. They explained:

> Hence, while the boy learns no special trade, he becomes proficient in drawing plans and handling the tools used in carpentering, forging, foundry work, and metal working, and is unwearied by the monotony of repetition. This method has produced good results, having not only rendered our boys able to earn a support often before completing the College course, but has relieved us, to a great extent, from having to seek

---

[27] _Ibid._, pp. 13-14.

[28] _Ibid._, p. 14.

> places for them as apprentices. Formerly such situations being often unattainable, we were obliged, under the Will, to send them out of the College at the end of their term, to struggle for a support for which they were imperfectly prepared. But now we have more applications for boys than we can supply, and a lad must be very dull or negligent, for whom a good place cannot be found, at living wages, before he reaches the end of his term, and this, notwithstanding, the number of boys who have left the College this year is greater than ever before, exceeding that of last year by more than fifty per cent, yet of the 163 boys who have gone out, only one was 18 years old. Before this branch of instruction was introduced, not more than one-third of those who left entered into mechanical pursuits, last year 57 per cent did so, while this year the percentage was 65. The President of the College speaking in his report, of the marked improvement in the conduct of the boys during their recitations, largely attributes it to the influence of our Manual Training Department, where, he says, "in addition to the education of the hand and eye, which a lad receives in this department, he has the benefit of a certain amount of physical exercise which improves his health, clears his brain, and puts him in a better frame of mind for all the school tasks and school restrictions."[29]

Notwithstanding the obvious intent of the text, the detailed explanation of shopwork instruction and the placement of pupils makes clear the evident modification in the policy of the "binding out" of students. Previously, students were discharged from the college by being bound out to suitable trades and occupations; because they had reached the limit of age (eighteen years) fixed by the will, without accepting situations; and, by expulsion. In describing these discharge procedures in 1870, the Board of Directors also noted:

> The Board have occasionally cancelled the indentures of a pupil, and allowed his mother or next friend to remove him from the College when a combination of circumstances seems to render it for the advantage of the pupil. Applications for this favor are frequent, but the Directors watching over the interests of their charge, usually reject these applications,

---

[29] _Seventeenth Annual Report of the Board of Directors of City Trusts. Report for the Year 1886._ pp. 15-16.

> that the lad may perfect himself in some trade or occupation, by which he may become self-supporting and a productive citizen.[30]

Apparently, during the 1880's, this latter policy of cancelling indentures became an acceptable practice.[31] The extent of this practice and its effect on the conditions and circumstances of apprenticeship were epitomized in the Annual Report for the Year 1888 in which the Board observed:

> No more striking illustration of the change in the apprentice system can well be afforded than is shown by a comparison between the number of boys bound out this year and in 1870, when our first report was made. Of the one hundred and twenty-one boys who left the College in 1888, desiring occupations, we were able to obtain indentures for but six, while one hundred and fiften found ready employment. In the year 1870, out of seventy boys who left the College, fifty-three were indentured. Fortunately, however, the training now given in the use of tools, in free hand, mechanical and geometrical drawing, in short-hand and type-writing, and in telegraphy, enables us to find places for them with comparative ease. This is best shown by the fact that while formerly at least ten percent of the pupils were unable to obtain positions before reaching the age of eighteen, last year there were none, and this year but. two, on an average less than one per cent, who remained in the College until compelled to leave on age.[32]

---

[30] First Annual Report of the Director of City Trusts, op. cit., p. 24.

[31] It is interesting to note that in 1885, a Superintendent of Admission and Indenture was employed by the college. (See in this connection, Sixteenth Annual Report of the Board of Directors of City Trusts, op. cit., p. 15). Included among his duties was the following: ". . . he shall receive applications for apprentices, and seek places for those ready to be indentured, make all needed investigations as to the standing of parties wishing boys, and make out indentures of binding out; he shall visit all pupils under indentures, or out on trial, and those who have secured places without their being indentured until they become of age, at least quarterly, see that they are properly cared for and instructed, and make a written report of such visits to the Committee on Admission, Discipline and Discharge." See in this connection, Acts of Assembly Creating the Board of City Trusts, By-Laws for the Government of the Board of Directors of City Trusts Adopted June 10, 1885, to take Effect September 1, 1885, p. 10. Previously the duties of placing and supervising boys just out of college was under the charge of the secretary of the Board. Cheesman A. Herrick, op. cit., p. 347, notes that due to the increase in the number of pupils, the duties of the secretary had to be divided.

[32] Nineteenth Annual Report of the Board of Directors of City Trusts. For the Year 1888, p. 11.

There seemed to be little doubt that mechanical instruction held the key to enable the students leaving the college to obtain "renumerative employment."[33] This type of education and its relation to industry was equally a subject of earnest consideration to the public.[34] Significantly, the arguments and demands of the general advocates of manual training also in fact mirrored the evolving character of Girard College which the Directors believed to be was in keeping with Girard's intent that the scholars of his college should be taught "facts and things, rather than words or signs."[35]

The next few years saw a continuing expansion and evident success.[36] To advance the progress in mechanical instruction, the directors sought to

---

[33]Eighteenth Annual Report of the Board of Directors of City Trusts. For the Year 1887. p. 11.

[34]See in this connection, U. S. Bureau of Education, Industrial Education in the United States: A Special Report, 1883, p. 75, particularly: "The entrance to industrial occupations has been beset by difficulties and discouragements. The apprenticeship system first degenerated and then died. Scarcely any one but a father will direct a novice in mechanical labor and he rarely has ability and opportunity. Now the defect is being remedied. Boys are going from our manual training schools and departments of mechanical engineering to honorable and responsible positions in mills, foundries, and factories. Three or four years of study and practice have given them a broad intelligence and more training than the customary seven years' of apprenticeship ordinarily given to boys of the olden time."

[35]An excellent illustration is provided by Edward A. Krug, The Shaping of the American High School, who in discussing the demands of educators and public leaders in the 1880's for the introduction of manual training and business subjects noted the following argument from the inaugural address of the governor of Pennsylvania: "The main fault of our present system is, that it leads directly and inevitably to that which is abstract, and away from that which is practical. It deals in words and signs, and not with facts and things. The graduate of our average high school, as all experience proves, is educated away from all industrial pursuits, and into a fitness for those employments which involve only mental training." (p. 14)

[36]Additional numbers of boys were admitted to the college in 1886 and 1890. In 1886, the enrollment was increased to 1371, and in 1890 to 1574. See in this connection, the Seventeenth Annual Report of the Board of Directors of City Trusts, op. cit., p. 97; and the Twenty-First Annual Report of the Board of Directors of City Trusts, For the Year 1890, p. 10.

extend the areas of instruction and as well to admit additional boys to the School of Mechanical instruction. In 1887 at a joint meeting of the Committee on Instruction and Library and the Committee on Mechanical Instruction it was resolved: "That hereafter all boys in the Mechanical School who have reached the age of fifteen years, and who show a marked aptitude for manual training; shall receive eight hours instruction in said department, the selection of such boys to be made by the Chairman of the Committee on Instruction, the Chairman of the Committee on Mechanical Instruction, and the president of the College."[37] On February 1, 1888, the joint committee met ". . . to consider the subject of additional hours for study in the Mechanical School and the admission of more boys from the lower classes."[38] At this meeting, President Fetterolf was present by invitation and submitted the following plan and reasons intended as a substitute for one referred to the joint Committee by the Board:

> Resolved, That hereafter the boys shall receive Mechanical Instruction from the time they enter the second grade of the Third School, in accordance with the present regulations as to the length of time for instruction.
>
> Among the reasons which I offer for it, are--
>
> 1st It will accomplish all that is intended in the eight hour resolutions, and more.
>
> 2d. It will send to the Mechanical School 160 additional boys.
>
> 3d. It will meet the wants of boys who are more in need of

---

[37]Board of Directors of City Trusts, Minutes, Committee on Instruction, Vol. I, February 3, 1871 to June 6, 1902, Minutes of July 8, 1887, p. 277. Evidently, this was a general increase in the hours of instruction provided since in a reply to questions proposed to the Superintendent of Mechanical Instruction by the Committee on Mechanical Instruction, Mason Mitchel, indicated that "More hours per week can be advantageously occupied in instructing the advanced classes; but not to all classes . . .; [and] the most favored class actually receives five and a quarter hours per week instruction." See in this connection, Board of Directors of City Trusts, Minutes, Committee on Mechanical Instruction, Vol. II, June 8, 1882 to May 3, 1895, particularly Minutes of February 27, 1885, pp. 31-32, and March 9, 1885, pp. 35-37.

[38]Minutes, Committee on Instruction, Vol. I, op. cit., p. 287.

Manual Training than many of those to whom the eight hour resolution contemplates giving additional time.

4th. It will enable us to send boys to the Mechanical School at an age when they are more eager, more apt, and more tractable than they are when they reach the upper classes of the Fourth form.

5th. It has been found that the boys who left the College from the Fourth form during 1887, less than one half went to Manual occupations, while those who went out from the lower forms more than three fourths are making their living with their hands.

6th. The eight hour resolution would take valuable time from the fourth school course--the substitute will not interfere whatever."[39]

Fetterolf's plan was adopted,[40] thereby allowing 160 additional boys to be admitted to the School of Mechanical instruction by the end of the year 1888, totalling upwards of 450 boys in this department.[41]

In their efforts to extend the courses available in mechanical instruction, on September 9, 1887, the Committee on Mechanical Instruction passed a resolution that printing and telegraphy be added to the curriculum of department of Mechanical Instruction.[42] While the Annual Report for the Year 1888 lists telegraphy among the course offerings, there is no further evidence that the course was continued.[43] In fact, a comparison of the courses in

---

[39]Ibid., pp. 287-288. In explanation of the division of the schools: The Primary School took one and one half years for completion; the Second School, one year; the Third School, two years; and the Fourth School, three and one-half years. The second grade of the Third school to which Fetterolf referred would be the last year of that school. See in this connection, Appendix O, pp. , for the "Course of Study for Eight Years," dated January 1882, as already noted supra.

[40]Ibid.

[41]Nineteenth Annual Report of the Board of Directors of City Trusts, loc. cit.

[42]Board of Directors of City Trusts, Minutes, Committee on Mechanical Instruction, Vol. II, June 8, 1882 to May 3, 1895. p. 103.

[43]Nineteenth Annual Report of the Board of Directors of City Trusts, loc. cit.

mechanical instruction for the years 1889 and 1890 indicates that printing was instituted in the year 1890 and that by 1893 this course had also been discontinued.[44] No apparent reason for the discontinuance of these courses is available.[45]

There were also other attempts to enlarge the course offerings and these met with mixed results. On April 4, 1890, Richard Vaux, Chairman of the Committee on Mechanical Instruction had been requested to submit a plan by which other branches of mechanical instruction might be introduced.[46] On May 9th following, he submitted a plan in which he recommended the introduction of plumbing and electrical engineering. The recommendation was approved

---

[44]See the _Twentieth Annual Report of the Board of Directors of City Trusts For the Year 1889_, pp. 11-13. _The Twenty-First Annual Report of the Board of Directors of City Trusts for the Year 1890_, p. 75; and the _Twenty-Fourth Annual Report of the Board of Directors of City Trusts for the Year 1893_, pp. 142-147. In the _Twenty-Fifth Annual Report of the Board of Directors of City Trusts of the City of Philadelphia for the Year 1894_; it is cursorily mentioned that included among the course of study of the Manual Training School was instruction ". . . to a limited extent in type-setting and printing." (p. 7) Actually there is no evidence that printing was continued until it was added as a department of instruction in 1914, subsequent to efforts began in 1913.

[45]Ernest Cunningham, a student at Girard College 1884-1892, and an employee of the college from 1892-1942 indicates: "They tried to introduce a little printing or type-setting for a term or so, but it didn't go over somehow and was dropped." See Ernest Cunningham, _Memories of Girard College_, p. 162.

[46]_Minutes, Committee on Mechanical Instruction, Vol. II, op. cit._, pp. 152-153. It is interesting to note that Richard Vaux returned to the administration of Girard College as a Director of City Trusts in 1884 and remained as a Director until his death on March 22, 1895. Of his participation on the _Board of Directors of City Trusts_, it was noted, "He was especially interested in Mechanical Instruction and the great success of this branch of the administration of Girard College is to be attributed chiefly to his enthusiastic supervision as Chairman of the Committee." See in this connection, _Twenty-Sixth Annual Report of the Board of Directors of City Trusts of the City of Philadelphia for the Year 1895_, pp. 5, 7, 8, _passim_. Significantly, the same report does not list the Committee on Mechanical Instruction among its committees for the following year. Evidently, the work of this committee was placed under the charge of the Committee on Instruction and Library for the college.

and referred to the Board.[47] In 1891, instruction in the practical branches of electrical mechanics was added to the School of Mechanical Instruction.[48] Concurrent with these efforts to extend the course of study in mechanical instruction there was a question in 1890 as to whether the "shoe shop," which had come to be known as the Department of Leather should be made one of the branches taught in the Manual Training School. The question was referred to President Fetterolf,[49] and his reply reads as follows:

> Girard College, October 3, 1890
>
> To the Committee on Mechanical Instruction:
>
> Gentlemen:
>
> At the September meeting of your Committee, a communication was received from Mr. Chairman Vaux, suggesting some changes, and a re-organization of the department of leather; and, it was on motion, resolved that the communication be referred to the President of the College to report at a subsequent meeting of the Committee, whether it is desirable to have shoemaking made one of the branches taught in the Manual Training School. In

---

[47] Minutes, Committee on Mechanical Instruction, Vol. II, op. cit., pp. 154-155.

[48] Twenty-Second Annual Report of the Board of Directors of City Trusts for the Year 1891, p. 11.

[49] Minutes, Committee on Mechanical Instruction, Vol. II, op. cit., September 5, 1890, pp. 160-161. It is interesting to note that on October 8, 1886, the following resolution had been adopted and sent to the Board of Directors "Resolved, That all boys having completed the prescribed curriculum, and not taking the post graduate course, by reason of excellence in their studies; shall be assigned in the Industrial Department to the class of Mr. I.E. Shimer [Superintendent of the Shoe Department] until they find employment outside the College; and that whenever such boys return from situations held on trial, they shall at once go into the said class and be put to work until other places are found for them; and in addition thereto all such other boys as shall be selected by the Committees on Instruction and Mechanical Instruction." (Ibid., p. 83) Later, on January 4, 1889, the Committee on Mechanical Instruction passed the following resolution: "Resolved that the Sec. of the Board see Mr. Shimer, Supt. of the Leather Department and ascertain if he cannot increase the quantity of shoes made in his department, so as to meet all the demands of the College." (Ibid., pp: 129-130) The question of extending the course of instruction apparently grew out of the increasing demands imposed on the shoe department by the additional boys being enrolled in the college; obviously instruction in this subject would serve a dual purpose.

compliance with this resolution, I beg to respond as follows:

The department of leather, formerly known in the College as the Shoe Department, was organized about the year 1872. Its purpose has been two fold: 1st, to serve as a place where idle and incorrigible boys could be put to manual labor: and, 2d, as a shop for repairing and making shoes for the boys. It has never been considered a department of instruction, although boys have constantly been taught shoemaking. It differs from the Mechanical School, as well as from other departments of the College in the following respects:--

1st The men employed in it are not rated as instructors, but as workmen.

2d The hours of work are from 7 A.M. to 6 P.M. each day, while in the regular school, boys are employed but six hours each day, and on Saturday, but two.

3d It is considered principally in the interest of the College; while the regular schools have only the good of the boys in view.

4th As only the idle incorrigible boys are sent to it, the better class of pupils look upon it as a place of punishment, and correction.

It is, however, a part of the institution that is still serving a good purpose, and if abolished would cause inconveniences. If it should be decided by your Committee to have boys systematically taught to work on leather, I recommend that the present Shoe Department be transferred to the care of the Committee on Household and that a new Leather Department be organized under the control of the Committee on Mechanical Instruction and that boys be sent to it by turns, as they are now sent to the other departments of the Mechanical School. I do not, however, consider it desirable to have shoemaking taught as one of the branches in our Manual Training School, inasmuch as it is not a trade requiring any degree of manual skill. A few days since, I took occasion to visit the shoe factory of John Mandell of this city.

In conversation, Mr. Mandell said: "Shoemaking by machinery is no longer a trade. A man of average ability can become an efficient operator in two weeks. For a man who has learned to make shoes by hand, we should have us use: it would take too long to unlearn him."

On general principles, I do not favor putting the boys of the college to work on machinery, for the reason that it does not give them manual skill; and, also because it is attended with more or less danger. Neither do I favor our undertaking to teach trades of any kind.

The average age at which our boys leave the College is sixteen and one half years, an age at which a lad has barely sufficient maturity of mind to enable him to choose for himself what trade is best suited to his strength and natural capacity; and at which no boy can be expected to have learned any of the standard trades. Furthermore, to give any boy the idea that he has learned a trade, or that he has skill which he does not possess, is to give him a concept of himself, which will be more likely to injure than to improve his chances of success in life.

> The principal of the New York Trade Schools, in a paper read before the American Social Science Association at Saratoga Springs, September 2d, says: "The plan which seems best suited to American needs is to let the lad remain at school until eighteen, develop him mentally, morally and physically, and by the latter, I mean to develop his body by gymnastics, and his mind and hand by manual training. Then, when he is old enough to know for what sort of work he is suited, let him go, if he wants to be a mechanic, to a trade school to learn his trade, precisely as young men go to the professional, the agricultural, and the business school."
>
> Respectfully submitted,
> (Signed) A. H. Fetterolf, President[50]

Further action on Fetterolf's report was postponed for the time,[51] but on April 3, 1891, the Department of Leather was transferred to the Committee on Household and Informary.[52]

What is sensed in all of these efforts is the very clear concern with

---

[50] Ibid., October 3, 1890, pp. 162-165. In contrast to this report, President Fetterolf was a proponent of the concept of "self-help." In the President's Report for 1890, he included under the caption "Improvements Suggested": Our boys should be taught more self-help. Their life here is in a measure unnatural, being so different from that in the family, where children learn to do many things that come to them in their daily home life. We cannot expect, under any circumstances, to accomplish all that can be done for the child in the family, but we can do more than has as yet been done. The boys might be taught to do, at least, some things that are now done for them. The more they are taught to do for themselves, the more useful and self-reliant they will be when they enter active life." See in this connection, Twenty-First Annual Report of the Board of Directors of City Trusts, op. cit., pp. 71-72. He addressed himself to the same point again in his Report for 1891 in which he argued: "The boys of the mechanical school could turn their manual skill to practical and profitable use, if, at stated and regular times, they were taken by their instructors to assist in the numerous repairs that are constantly needed in and around the buildings. It would also teach them to do just such work with hammer and chisel, saw and plane, as they will find to do in their own homes after they leave the institution. Screw driving and nail driving, the repairing of floors, reviewing a broken sash cord,putting a new lock on a door in place of an old one, are some of the lessons in practical carpentry which are not easily taught in the class-rooms. A few hours a week of such industrial training would serve as an excellent supplement to the teaching given in the shops." See in this connection, Twenty-Second Annual Report of the Board of Directors of City Trusts for the Year 1891, p. 84.

[51] Minutes, Committee on Mechanical Instruction, Vol. II, op. cit., p. 162.

[52] Ibid., pp. 176-177.

a newly fashioned curriculum which would give the students of Girard College more training in practical and mechanical instruction. However, nowhere is the almost ambiguous philosophy which characterized the college at this time and which continued through the early 1890's more apparent than in the following extract taken from the "President's Report For 1890" somewhat awkwardly an explanation not of a functional curriculum but of the problems which were being encountered as the society became more complex and industrialized.

> It is our object to prepare boys to earn their livelihood as soon as they leave us. This fact must be constantly kept in mind, as, in this respect, Girard College differs from most other schools, public or private. From the latter, many boys and young men go to higher institutions of learning, or enter upon professional studies. The Girard boy, being generally without means to enable him to continue his studies, must, on leaving school, at once think of bread-winning. Practical studies must, therefore, be our first consideration. Having finished these, we may give attention to those branches in the course of study which give knowledge which is to be valued for its own sake. We lay, therefore, much stress on thorough and systematic drill in the rudiments, believing that, to make a boy proficient in a few studies, is better than to leat him have a superficial knowledge of many branches.[53]

In view of the desired goals, Fetterolf's position on manual training in the same Annual Report provides an interesting contrast:

> MANUAL TRAINING
>
> In the department of Manual Training, the interest is well kept up, and good results are evident on every hand.
>
> It is most gratifying to note the interest which the boys take in this department, and the eagerness with which they enter upon their work. The lessons are considered a provilege rather than a task. To boys entering upon mechanical pursuits, the skill which they here acquire will be of great benefit, while to those taking up other occupations, the training of the eye and hand will be of educational value.
>
> In all Manual Training Schools, it is well to guard against too much machinery, and too much specializing.

---

[53]Adam H. Fetterolf, "Girard College President's Report for 1890," in _Twenty-First Annual Report of the Board of Directors of City Trusts, For the Year 1890_, p. 67.

> Usually, when the lad once begins to work with machinery he loses his interest in hand tools, and, in consequence, makes thereafter but little progress in manual skill. The result will be much the same as it is in the large manufactories, where, owing to the extensive application of machinery, the workmen, with few exceptions, are without manual skill. Neither is it the province of the Manual Training School to give training in any one special branch. This should be left to the Trade School, to which boys are admitted who are supposed to have acquired general manual training, and who are of sufficient age and maturity of mind to choose their specialties with discretion. Manual training prepares boys for the learning of a trade, just as academic training prepares young men for professional study.[54]

The reiteration of "Neither is it the province of the Manual Training School to give training in any one special branch" appeared in the Annual Report for the Year 1893 in the description of the Mechanical Department in the "Course of Study for Eight Years" dated January, 1894, which was appended thereto.[55] "It is not the purpose of this Department," stated the preface, "to teach special trades, but rather the essential principles and processes underlying all trades."[56] The course of study for the Mechanical Department which covered five years was intended to enable the student ". . . to discover

---

[54]Ibid., p. 68. Fetterolf's interest in the value of manual training in the general education of students points up his alliance with the advocates of manual training, e.g., Calvin M. Woodward, Manual Training in Education, particularly, "In a manual training school the aim is not the narrow one of 'learning a trade.' Neither is dexterity sought in special operations which may be only small parts of even a trade. Neither is there any thought of manufacture with a view to selling something that will yield an income. The object of every feature is education in a broad and high sense." (p. 61) See also in this connection the Eighth Annual Report of the Commissioner of Labor (1892) which was devoted to Industrial Education in which the following comment was made of Fetterolf's remarks on manual training: "This remark defines the use and limitations of manual training, in its relation to skilled labor, with clearness and, apparently, with absolute justice. Manual training is merely preparatory discipline of the eye and hand, not trade teaching." (p. 68)

[55]See in this connection, Twenty-Fourth Annual Report of the Board of Directors of the City Trusts of the City of Philadelphia for the Year 1893, pp. 83-147.

[56]Ibid., p. 142.

any special aptitude he may possess; andwhatever industrial occupation he may choose to take up in after life, he will [would] be better fitted to enter upon it intelligently and with ready adoption."[57] In describing the scheduling of the classes it was explained that approximately six hundred students were assigned to this department; each pupil averaging five hours of instruction per week with each class or section assigned to one of the departments for one week passing through all departments on a rotation basis; and the students of the three upper classes of the Fourth School permitted to elect a department for specialization for any given term.[58]

It is also interesting to note in the Annual Report for the Year 1893 Fetterolf's endorsement of the introduction of plumbing which had been recommended by Richard Vaux in 1890, and apparently Fetterolf's own suggestion that blacksmithing be extended as another department of instruction in the Mechanical School. He opined: "To my mind it would be better to devote less time to the foundry, and put in its place plumbing and blacksmithing. During the nine years that our foundry has been in operation, nineteen boys have

---

[57] Ibid.

[58] Ibid. In his "President's Report for 1893," Fetterolf described this new course of study as ". . . being well adapted to the needs of such institutions as ours. While there are no radical changes it is nevertheless an improvement on the curriculum formerly in use, in that it outlines and defines clearly the work in each grade and contains for the teachers many valuable suggestions and direction. There are two features to which we would call special attention, viz.: The Character Lessons and the Observation Lessons. Character is the foundation on which the structure of life rests. In order to make the foundation firm, secure and safe, the virtues must be instilled with the same care and skill that are exercised in teaching the ordinary branches of the school course. By Observation Lessons it is intended to teach boys to observe and to think, to take notice of and interest in the facts and phenomena of nature." (Ibid., pp. 39-40) Cf. the "Course of Study for Eight Years," dated January, 1882, included as Appendix P, p. , which featured Object Lessons for the First or Primary School. Object teaching in the younger classes had been introduced in the year 1870 and had evidently been successfully continued until the curriculum was revised in 1893. See in this connection, First Annual Report of the Director of City Trusts, op. cit., p. 20.

gone out to plumbing and seventeen to blacksmithing. In plumbing there has been no instruction and in blacksmithing but little."[59] In 1894 these courses were also added to the Mechanical Department.[60]

Yet, while the course offerings had been expanded, the year 1894 pointed up the need for "additional time" in manual training in light of the continuously changing manpower demands of industry which in turn made the matter of the type of education to be given a complex one. The directors noted:

> Whilst Mr. Girard in his will specifically states that many of the details of the organization of the College are necessarily left to those selected to administer its affairs, he yet names, in Paragraph 7, Item XXI, so many branches of a sound education which the orphans admitted into the College are to receive, that less time is left for manual training than seems desirable under the changed condition of the occupations in which our graduates are to find their future support.
>
> It is, however, the settled policy of the Board to increase generally the hours of instruction in this Department of the College to all the pupils, and still more to those showing talent for mechanical pursuits.[61]

But it was in Fetterolf's examination of manual training in 1895 which undertook to consider the basic question which underpinned or provided an underlying ethic for the college, that one perceives in a sense an attempt to find the education necessarily required for the Girard College student. He suggested for consideration the following question: "In what way and by what means can we best develop the special capacities and aptitudes of each boy, so that he may most easily find his proper place in life and become a self-dependent and self-governed man?"[62] Fetterolf saw the new curriculum

---

[59]Twenty-Fourth Annual Report of the Board of Directors of City Trusts for the Year 1893, p. 41.

[60]Twenty-Fifth Annual Report of the Board of Directors of City Trusts of the City of Philadelphia for the Year 1894, pp. 6-7.

[61]Ibid., p. 7.

[62]Twenty-Sixth Annual Report of the Board of Directors of the City of Philadelphia for the Year 1895, p. 110.

which enlarged the work of each department as giving a greater variety and more practical worth which would generally add to teaching effectiveness. As to the contemporary conditions of manual training he recognized, "Some friends of manual training are now advocating trade teaching. Whether this is better than to give mere skill of hand and knowledge of the use of tools is a question. In Girard College, in which the boys are all very young, I believe that the best results are obtained by giving the all-round training which will enable the lad to employ his time to the best advantage when he leaves the College to earn his livelihood."[63] In defense of this position Fetterolf noted that statistics had seemed to indicate that specializing had not brought a better return than the results of general teaching in a five-year period that ended in 1894. During this period, boys entering mechanical pursuits had been forty per cent less than when little or no trade teaching had been attempted. While Fetterolf admitted that this was not conclusive proof, he did believe that the boys generally enjoyed the idea of being taught the general use of carpenters' tool, but that their interest was lost as soon as they became aware that they were being taught the carpenter's trade. However, although Fetterolf was assiduous in his efforts in behalf of manual training as a handicraft ideal, he did concede that there was a link between manual training and trade training:

> While we would thus emphasize the fact that manual training is not trade teaching, we hold that it brings pupils a long way on towards the learning of the trades. This is because the instruction is based on the principles underlying the trades, not in the details of the trades themselves. It is the result of applying the science of education to the learning of trades. As a trained mind is the best preparation for the study of a profession, so are the trained hand and the trained eye the best preparation for the successful acquisition of a trade.

---

[63] Ibid.

> We believe that the problem is now being satisfactorily solved under the wise action of your Board, recently taken, first in restoring class teaching in place of the elective system, and second, in giving to graduate pupils the privilege of taking a special course in any one of the departments of the Mechanical School. This will give manual training to all and trade instruction to such as shall desire and merit it.[64]

However, although the new curriculum and the efforts to provide special courses in mechanical instruction provided a seemingly stable outlook, Fetterolf's remarks on instruction the following year pointed up the complexity of the college's overall curriculum changes.

> The last two decades have been full of educational progress and of educational fads. Many new ideas have been advanced, new systems have been adopted, and new methods have been introduced. The changes have been mostly along the line of enlarging the scope of the child's studies and in making the lessons easier and more entertaining, and school life more pleasant. Much attention has been given to varying the daily and weekly programme, lest the child should tire of sameness. As a consequence, old theory of giving a thorough drill in the essentials has been, of necessity, abandoned. So many new subjects have been put into the school curriculum that it has become over-crowded, and thoroughness has been well-nigh impossible. Teachers are confronted with a problem which embarrasses, perplexes, and confuses, and the children are taken over so much ground in a very limited time that they can have at best only a smattering of any subject. There may be, under this new condition, more superficial knowledge, but there is less mental training; more intelligence, but less power of concentrated thought. A period of reaction appears to be at hand. A demand is made for a simpler curriculum with

---

[64] _Ibid._, p. 11. It is interesting to note that Fetterolf's statement appears to be a direct result of the observations of the Massachusetts Manual Training and Industrial Education Commission which in describing the effectiveness of the mechanics instruction at Girard College saw fit to add: "Many of the promoters of manual training for boys have been at pains to emphasize the fact that their schools do not teach trades. While this is true, it is also true that their schools do bring their pupils a long way on towards the learning of many trades. And this is because the instruction is based on the principles underlying the trades, not on the details of the trades themselves. It is the result of applying the science of education to the learning of trades." See in this connection, _Report of the Commission to Investigate the Existing Systems of Manual Training and Industrial Education_, (1893), p. 19.

> fewer branches, in order that there may be time for better and more thorough work. If habits of observation are to be inculcated there must be given time for observation, and if habits of thinking are to be formed there must be sufficient time allowed for thinking.[65]

In summarizing these remarks, the Directors evidently were understanding of the problem but saw fit to note: "The provisions of Mr. Girard's will requiring instruction in many branches not ordinarily taught to scholars so young as ours, make it impossible to give sufficient time for the proper instruction in many things enjoying the present attention of teachers, and the President's appeal for a 'simpler curriculum' deserves consideration."[66]

III

> The last fifty years cover a period of great educational awakening. There have been so many changes, that we have come to speak of the education of the present day as the new education. Yet these changes have not, in every instance, meant improvements. Many experiments have proved failures. In speaking of this subject, our learned Commissioner of Education, Dr. William T. Harris, says, "Experiments are so costly that one must be cautious in undertaking them. Ninety-nine fail and one succeeds." Our policy has been to keep well abreast of the times, and to take up with a new idea, not because it is new, but because it is good; and to give up old methods and old systems, not because they are old, but because they are no longer the best.[67]

As Girard College entered its second half century, it was at a point in its history where three forces became graphically clear: (1) apprenticeship, and the variant forms of indenture associated with it had

---

[65]Adam H. Fetterolf, "President's Report for 1896," in _Twenty-Seventh Annual Report of Board of Directors of City Trusts of Philadelphia for the Year 1896_, pp. 113-114.

[66]_Twenty-Seventh Annual Report of the Board of Directors of City Trusts for the City of Philadelphia for the Year 1896_, p. 10.

[67]Adam H. Fetterolf, "Historical Address," _Semi-Centennial of Girard College_, January 3, 1898, p. 74.

atrophied and in reality had died; (2) a heavy frenetic pursuit now had been undertaken in manual and practical instruction; and (3) trade-oriented educational concepts had begun to emerge.

As has already been noted, during the 1880's it had become an acceptable practice to cancel the indenture binding a boy to the college to enable him to accept suitable employment. By 1898, the profound social and technological changes had removed all but a few of the surviving remnants of the traditional apprenticeship system at the college.[68] In describing the contemporary conditions of apprenticeship, Fetterolf explained:

> Under the will of the Founder, the boys on leaving the College are to be "bound out" to suitable occupations, as those of agriculture, navigation and mechanical trades, arts and manufactures." While the old apprentice system which obtained in Mr. Girard's time was a help and a convenience in the early history of the College, it gradually became a serious hinderance. Employers refused to enter into the obligation of master, and the average boy disliked the idea of being an indentured apprentice bound to an employer for a definite number of years; so that binding out grew more and more into disfavor, until it finally became a question of whether we should give up business offering the best opportunities for bright and energetic lads. The Board of Directors wisely chose the former alternative. Under our present system, when a boy has found suitable employment, or has reached the age when the authorities think he should no longer remain in the Institution, his college indenture is cancelled, and he is returned to his mother or next friend. While we consider ourselves thus legally relieved from all responsibility, we still keep an oversight over the boy until he becomes twenty-one years of age. Our Superintendent of

---

[68]The "Catalogue of Apprentices," dated December 31, 1897, lists eight existing indentures. The annual reports of the Superintendent of Admission and Indentures indicate that there were only seven bindings beyond that date scattered over the next eight years, the last occurring in 1905. See in this connection _Twenty-Eighth Annual Report of the Board of Directors of the City of Philadelphia for the Year 1897, et seq_. See also in this connection, pp. , _supra_.

Admission and Indentures visits, as far as he is able, all boys under twenty-one years of age at least once a year.[69]

On the note that "The beginning of the second half-century suggests a suitable time for the introduction of needed improvements,"[70] Fetterolf placed in foremost position a recommendation for the extension of manual training. He explained that barely one-third of the total enrollment, approximately five hundred and fifty boys, were receiving "hand teaching." He also noted that of the boys who had gone out from the college during 1897, sixty-three had gone out from the Fourth Form having received from three to five years of manual training; one hundred and seven from the Third Form having received from one to three years; and nineteen from the Second Form having received no manual training at all. Fetterolf believed that of all the boys leaving the college, those from the Second and Third Forms were most likely to earn their living from manual occupations and yet these boys received the least instruction in manual skill.[71] However, in summarizing Fetterolf's report, the Directors, almost in reiteration of their report for the previous year, detailed the curricular problems which were proving enduring:

---

[69]Adam H. Fetterolf, *op. cit.*, p. 76. Lack of progress in the school room or malconduct also allowed for the cancelling of a boy's indenture to the college. See, *e.g.*, the *Twenty-Fourth Annual Report of the Board of Directors of City Trusts*, *op. cit.*, p. 16, particularly the following resolutions which had been adopted: "*Resolved*, That under the direction of the Committee on Admission, Discipline, and Discharge, the Superintendent of Admission and Indentures shall find places for all pupils who have become fifteen years of age, and who have failed to reach the Fourth School"; and "*Resolved*, That the College Indentures of all such pupils, and of those who may become fifteen years of age without reaching the Fourth School, shall be cancelled with the usual outfit by March 31, 1894, and thereafter within thirty days after they become fifteen years of age, unless places be found for them."

[70]"Girard College President's Report for 1897" in *Twenty-Eighth Annual Report of the Board of Directors of City Trusts of the City of Philadelphia for the Year 1897*, p. 300.

[71]*Ibid.*

> It is difficult to comply with the will of Mr. Girard and at the same time introduce into the curriculum of the Institution the studies deemed proper for these later days.
>
> Many matters vital for college students cannot be taught in Girard College because of the comparative youth of its pupils, and also by reason of the already overcrowded course of study.
>
> It is perhaps possible to admit into the Manual Training School a greater number of the boys than are taught there at present, but the low average age of the pupils (twelve years and seven months) makes any large additions impracticable.
>
> The fact that some of our pupils are as young as six years, and none are over eighteen years of age, dominates here as well as in many other matters in Girard College. In wishing to add this, or in deploring the absence of that, desirable thing, it must be remembered that our boys are compelled to leave College at an average age several years less than that at which young men enter other colleges.[72]

None the less, the following year Fetterolf indicated: "The need of some simple and light form of manual training for the younger boys had long been recognized; and accordingly the Sloyd system, useful both for its immediate results and as a preparation for the course in the Mechanical Department, was introduced in the early autumn."[73]

---

[72]<u>Twenty-Eighth Annual Report of the Board of Directors of City Trusts of the City of Philadelphia for the Year 1897</u>, pp. 8-9.

[73]Adam H. Fetterolf, "Girard College President's Report for 1898," in <u>Twenty-Ninth Annual Report of the Board of Directors of City Trusts of the City of Philadelphia for the Year 1898</u>, p. 125. The Sloyd system originated in the Scandinavian countries as part of the custom of the people to engage in some useful form of handwork or home industry during the long, dark evenings of winter. In time, many of the products were sold; but, changing industrial and social conditions eventually saw a breakdown in home Sloyd. However, many saw distinct benefits in this type of training and by the mid-nineteenth century several Scandinavian countries established schools which allowed for the development of Sloyd skills which they believed had economic and character building merits. In the main, American Sloyd instruction was introduced in the United States through the efforts of Lars Erikson and Gustaf Larsson, both of Sweden. Sloyd in the United States was considered for the purposes of general education and its general education theory is usually ascribed to the work of Otto Salomon, the proponent of "Educational Sloyd." For a detailed account of the development of the Sloyd system see generally Charles Alpheus Bennett, <u>History of Manual and Industrial Education 1870-1917</u>, Ch. II, XI.

In overview he explained that work in the Mechanical Department had been limited to pupils of the Third and Fourth Forms only because the work was too heavy and largely too difficult for the younger boys; but that a general provision for hand-work was needed. As to the usefulness of such instruction, he observed, "The value of hand training even for the younger boys requires at this day no demonstration, not only because of its general moral influence in inspiring a respect for, and a love of, physical labor and in cultivating habits of neatness, order, and exactness; but also because of its direct advantage in training the eye and the sense of form and touch, and in imparting dexterity of hand in the use of tools."[74]

With the introduction of the Sloyd system, approximately 300 pupils who comprised the two upper grades of the Second Form received instruction for one period a week which was two hours in length.[75] By the following year, Fetterolf was pleased to report that the Sloyd school was achieving the highest expectations that the pupils had shown a marked development of skill in the use of tools. His description of the work in Sloyd characterizes the traditional features of this plan of instruction:

---

[74]Adam H. Fetterolf, "Girard College President's Report for 1898," loc. cit. Fetterolf's description of the value of Sloyd appears to be generally taken from the aims of educational Sloyd in Otto Salomon, "Theory of Educational Sloyd," as quoted in Charles A. Bennett, op. cit., pp. 67-68, particularly, "To instill a taste for, and a love of, labor in general. . . . To instill respect for rough, honest, bodily labor. . . . To develop independence and self-reliance. . . . To train in habits of order, exactness, cleanliness, and neatness. . . . To train the eye and sense of form. . . . To cultivate habits of attention, industry, perseverance, and patience. . . . To promote the development of the physical powers."

[75]Adam H. Fetterolf, "Girard College President's Report for 1898," loc. cit.

> The work is conducted along the lines of general education rather than as a means of special development of technical skill. To this end the instructor has followed pretty closely the course of models as developed by years of study in the best Sloyd training schools. The characteristic feature of this course is the progressive series of exercises continuing through the entire course. Each model depends upon the one preceding, and is in turn a preparation for the succeeding one. The models are useful, serviceable, and in most cases familiar objects, calculated to arouse the lively interest of the pupil. The exercises, as well as the tools employed, are arranged with reference to the worker's growing power, calling for a gradual increase of effort, step by step, while the first exercise with each tool is calculated to give a correct effective impression of its typical use.
>
> During the year the boys have made 46 different models. The largest number made by any one boy is 26, while the average is about 12. In the making of these models there are 26 different exercises, involving the use of 20 different tools. While it is not to be expected that every boy has become thoroughly skillful in the use of these twenty tools, he has learned their names and the general and special use of each, and not a few have evinced marked skill. In addition to the regular class work, many of the boys have shown a strong desire to work during the intervals of school, gladly giving up the recreation hours for the privilege of working in the Sloyd room. This privilege is frequently granted to such pupils as show the most skill and diligence in their regular work. Some of the models made during the extra hours show a high degree of efficiency. All the work in this department is done from working drawings, which the pupils are taught to understand and read.[76]

The experimentation with the Sloyd system, however, proved tendentious; social forces were dictating changes which were largely inescapable and were not unlike those changes which, no matter how unintentional, had largely come in the wake of the decline of apprenticeship and the variant forms of indenture. The socially imposed need for "practical" trade-oriented educational programs soon became apparent at Girard College, in keeping with the generally discerned changes that were occurring in

---

[76]Adam H. Fetterolf, "Girard College President's Report for 1899," in <u>Thirtieth Annual Report of the Board of Directors of City Trusts of the City of Philadelphia for the Year 1899</u>, p. 112.

the life of the nation.[77] In this respect, it is interesting to note Fetterolf's comments on manual training at the college at the turn of the century:

> Our school of manual training is keeping well abreast of the times. . . . The fact that the junior classes take the most interest in the school, shows the wisdom of the policy adopted some ten years ago, when the question was raised as to whether the work in this department should be extended by sending more boys or by giving more time to the boys already in attendance. It has been evident from the first that, with rare exceptions, boys who are looking forward to graduation do not take up with mechanical pursuits.[78]

And even the following year, Fetterolf cursorily mentioned, "The Manual Training Department is holding its own, and the boys continue to be interested in shop work. This is especially true of the Sloyd School."[79] However, the directors reported: "Important changes in the course of the studies in the Mechanical School have been made, to go into effect with the school term on February 1st next. This will admit a larger number of pupils, with more hours of instruction, into this important

---

[77]See generally R. Freeman Butts and Lawrence A. Cremin, A History of Education in American Culture, Ch. IX, "The Emergence of Industrial America."

[78]Adam H. Fetterolf, "Girard College President's Report for 1900," in Thirty-First Annual Report of the Board of Directors of City Trusts of the City of Philadelphia for the Year 1900, p. 117. In this connection it is interesting to note Fetterolf's analysis of the positions obtained by boys who completed the course of study and which is representative of the placement of such boys in the late nineteenth century: "The Departments of Mathematics, Book-Keeping and Commercial Arithmetic, and Phonography and Typewriting, continue to be of the greatest practical value, as our boys so generally go out to counting-house and office work. Of those who have graduated during the present year, fully seventy-five per cent have gone to business and clerical pursuits." See in this connection Adam H. Fetterolf, "Girard College President's Report for 1897," in Twenty-Eighth Annual Report of the Board of Directors, op. cit., p. 297.

[79]Adam H. Fetterolf, "Girard College President's Report for 1901," in Thirty-Second Annual Report of the Board of Directors of City Trusts of the City of Philadelphia for the Year 1901, p. 136.

branch of the College. It is believed that these changes will much benefit our young men when seeking employment after graduation."[80]

The reason for such changes is perhaps best found in the elaborate report of the Superintendent of Admission and Indentures for the same year which points up the complexity of providing a functional practical curriculum. The following paragraphs are presented here to show the apparent concern for the prevailing conditions of industry which were increasingly becoming more complex:

> Seventy years have gone since the will of Stephen Girard was written, and each one as it passes more fully confirms the wisdom of his expression therein, "I would have them [the orphans] [sic] taught facts and things rather than words or signs."
>
> Whereas it was the custom, twenty or thirty years ago, to pursue the prescribed four years "classical" course in the universities and colleges of the country, we find, at the opening of a new century, that the former curriculum has been greatly modified, and that the student may now choose one of many lines of study which tend toward the practical rather than the literary.
>
> A young man who is closely in touch with business firms requiring clerks in their counting houses, has just informed me that in almost every instance the stipulation is that shorthand shall be one of the candidate's qualifications; and he added, "It is advisable to have a knowledge of book-keeping also."
>
> While the graduates of Girard College, by reason of proficiency, have no difficulty in securing positions as clerks or stenographers, the lower grades of pupils who desire to learn trades or draughting, having to compete with those taught in the schools for manual training exclusively, are, necessarily, at a disadvantage.
>
> A lad of fifteen years, who applied for a position to learn draughting, was answered, a few weeks ago, in writing, as follows: "Recently we have adopted the plan of taking boys from the Manual Training School or from the Williamson School, who have had considerable training in mechanical drawing."

---

[80] *Thirty-Second Annual Report of the Board of Directors of City Trusts of the City of Philadelphia for the Year 1901*, p. 9.

> The new system of more extended instructions in the mechanical school, about being adopted, will be watched with much interest, and ought to result eventually in enabling pupils to command satisfactory wages immediately upon leaving the College, instead of their being a burden for a considerable time upon self-sacrificing mothers or friends.[81]

The new system began at the opening of the year 1902 and was formally acknowledged as the introduction of trade teaching. Under this system, ". . . a course was arranged by which such boys as elected to do so, could spend four hours a day during their last two years in one department of the Mechanical School."[82] Their curriculum consisted of spending their mornings [8 to 12] in their regular classes and attending their trade work in the afternoon [1 to 5] and on Saturday morning for an additional four hours which enabled the boys to receive twenty-four hours of trade instruction each week for their last two years of college course. The initial course began with twenty-five boys in the following chosen departments: electrical mechanics, 8; wood work, 7; metal work, 6; and foundry, 4.[83]

On January 31st, 1904, the first pupils graduated from the experimental course in trade instruction. They included 5 boys in electrical

---

[81]John S. Boyd, "Girard College Report of the Superintendent of Admission and Indentures (1901)," in Thirty-Second Annual Report of the Board of Directors of City Trusts of the City of Philadelphia for the Year 1901, pp. 186-187.

[82]Adam H. Fetterolf, "Girard College President's Report for the Year 1902," in Thirty-Third Annual Report of the Board of Directors of City Trusts of the City of Philadelphia for the Year 1902, p. 136.

[83]Ibid.

mechanics; 6 in wood working; and 3 in metal working. Of the course's anticipated success it was observed that a gentleman from one of the largest industrial establishments had visited the college and noted: "I have visited the Mechanical Instruction Department of the Girard College and examined the boys' work in the pattern shop, machine shop, foundry, and blacksmith shop, and was surprised at its excellence, particularly that of the boys in what is known as the Trade School."[84]

It is interesting to note that it had been made equally evident that work in Stenography and Typewriting should be extended. This was done with the extension of both equipment and time; and it was found that the demand for graduates who were expert in these fields exceeded the supply.[85] The Board of Directors, in commenting on this demand for stenographers and typewriters, saw fit to add: "It is hoped that there may be a like demand for the graduates who have creditably passed the additional course of two years' training in the Mechanical School."[86]

---

[84]Adam H. Fetterolf, "Girard College President's Report for 1903," in Thirty-Fourth Annual Report of the Board of Directors of City Trusts of the City of Philadelphia for the Year 1903, p. 129. See also the "Girard College Report of the Superintendent of Admission and Indentures (1903), in the Thirty-Fourth Annual Report of the Board of Directors of City Trusts of the City of Philadelphia for the Year 1903, p. 203: "Of the twenty-six members of the class just leaving the College, twelve have chosen the mechanical instead of the regular literary course, and although it is too soon to report definitely as to the results, the record of several of them, as furnished by the Superintendent of one of the largest manufacturing establishments in the city, is particularly satisfactory."

[85]Adam H. Fetterolf, "Girard College President's Report for 1903," op. cit., p. 130.

[86]Thirty-Fourth Annual Report of the Board of Directors of City Trusts of the City of Philadelphia for the Year 1903, p. 17. The evident changes in the curriculum necessarily required a complete revision of the course of study for the college which was implemented during the year 1904. In overview of the changes involved Fetterolf examined the problems of such an undertaking: "In the field of education there are many problems yet to

However, in commenting on the success of manual training and trade instruction at the end of 1905, Fetterolf presented an interesting aspect in the follow-up of the trade school graduates. In overview of the general attitude toward manual training, he observed that the number and influence of the detractors of this type of education was constantly decreasing, a fact pointed up by the general increase in the number of such schools and the accompanying enlarged enrollments. Yet, he noted that the question was often asked: "Why do so few graduates of manual training schools become and remain mechanics?"[87] He had discerned that one-third of the graduates of the Manual Training School of Washington University in St. Louis go on to higher education immediately upon graduation or after working a year or two and nearly thirty per cent of the graduates of the Manual Training School of Philadelphia had entered college.

---

be solved, and in making out a course of study for any school certain questions will arise--for instance: What studies shall be included? What excluded? What are the relative educational values of the different studies? How much time should be devoted to each? &c. It is not to be presumed that in the course submitted herewith, or in any course that has yet been devised, these questions have been fully or finally answered. Suffice it to say that in preparing this course they have been borne in mind and carefully considered. It is believed that this production embodies a broad, generous conception of education, is in harmony with generally accepted and verified principles of education, and is well adapted to the peculiar conditions and requirements of this institution. With earnest, faithful, and progressive teachers to carry it into execution, it will, we believe, prove to be a marked advance upon preceding revisions." See in this connection Adam H. Fetterolf, "Girard College President's Report for 1903, *op. cit.*, pp. 138-139. For the "Curriculum of the Department of Mechanical Instruction" see Appendix , pp. . See also Appendix , pp. for the "Course in Sloyd." Both items are in Girard College, *Course of Study for Eight Years, 1904*.

[87]Adam H. Fetterolf, "Girard College President's Report for 1905," in *Thirty-Sixth Annual Report of the Board of Directors of City Trusts of the City of Philadelphia for the Year 1905*, p. 160.

At Girard College, he noted:

> With Girard College it is found that not more than fifty per cent of our trade school pupils take up and continue in mechanical pursuits. This may be accounted for in two ways: First, bright and capable boys who may begin work in shops are soon found worthy of promotion to other departments where salaries are higher and work more congenial. Second, the pupils being generally the sons of laboring people are disposed to shun manual labor. The children of artisans are as a class averse to manual pursuits. They have in their minds only the darker side of the workingman's lot, since their fathers and in some instances also their mothers have had to struggle hard to make a living in the sphere of common labor. It will be found everywhere that the children of the working classes prefer the so-called genteeler occupations of the countinghouse or salesroom. In the manual training school of Philadelphia less than ten per cent of the students are sons of artisans. While these schools are popular and the attendance large the patrons are mostly merchants and professional men.[88]

Nevertheless, the remainder of President Fetterolf's long tenure was spent in a continuing attempt to bring into clear focus those forces which were dictating a curriculum of preeminently trade orientation. It appears clear that Fetterolf understood that the trade orientation mold that had begun to take form at Girard College was to set a vocational pattern that was to continue for some decades to come. His own commitment to this was made eminently clear in his reports for 1907 and 1908. In 1907, he delineated the curricular problem which faced secondary schools in a general exposition on the subject:

---

[88] Ibid., p. 161. It is interesting to note that on May 1st following, an "Employment Department" was added to the administration. As part of its duties a register was kept of all the applications received for the employment of boys. Out of 150 applications received, there were 115 applications for clerks and bookkeepers; office and errand boys; stenographers and typewriters; and stock and storeboys. See in this connection Adam H. Fetterolf, "Girard College President's Report for 1906," in Thirty-Seventh Annual Report of the Board of Directors of City Trusts of the City of Philadelphia for the Year 1906, pp. 163-164.

> It is a serious question as to what should be the course of instruction in what is known as secondary schools,--how far the course should be cultural and to what extent vocational. When we get beyond what is known as the fundamentals we are confronted by a diversity of interests. Some would make the vocational course exclusively commercial, claiming that the lad should be trained for business, others would give prominence to the manual arts in order that the boy might be prepared to take up advanced work when he enters the shop or the factory. In other words they claim that the accountants should be taught not only the science, but the art, of keeping accounts; that the mechanic should be taught not merely the proper use of tools, but a trade. In short, they want the school not only to lay the foundation, but also to rear the superstructure.[89]

Then in his discussion of manual training he spoke at length of the type of education needed to prepare boys for their life's vocation--namely, vocational education and its applicability at Girard College.

> With the addition during the year of another teacher of Sloyd, we have added 320 boys to the number receiving manual training. With this extension in hand training a boy who completes the full course of eight years will have at least seven years of manual teaching. This we believe to be progress in the right direction. There is a growing conviction that modern education as given by our public and private schools fails to fit boys for properly entering upon their life vocation, and that there is needed a vocational training. It is found that the opportunities for a young boy who enters a shop or other industrial establishment immediately on leaving school has but a meagre chance of learning thoroughly the business or employment to which he has engaged himself. This is owing not to any fault of his own, or to the disposition of his employers or overseers. It is owing to conditions. His work is hap-hazard at best. If it is to the interest of his employers to change his position every three months it is changed, and if it is to their interest to keep him at one thing for a long while, he may spend years at one kind of work, however simple or unimportant it may be; and as a result the lad grows to manhood with a very inadequate equipment in the vocation which he has chosen. . . .
>
> This raises the question whether vocational training can be given at any other than vocational schools. In European

---

[89]Adam H. Fetterolf, "Girard College President's Report for 1907," in _Thirty-Eighth Annual Report of the Board of Directors of City Trusts of the City of Philadelphia for the Year 1907_, p. 159.

> countries this problem has already been solved or is in a fair way of being solved, especially in Germany, where most progress has been made. This is notably the case in the Kingdom of Wurtenberg. In the town of Stuttgart there are taught no less than 85 separate trades or industries, ranging from architects and electrical engineers to servants and errand boys. In other countries, such as France, Austria, Hungary, Belgium, England, Switzerland, and Italy, these schools find greater favor year after year, and action establishing them is looked upon as a national duty. The time is no doubt near at hand, when the States, and more especially the cities of this country will take action.
>
> Whether more can be done at Girard College than we are now doing is of course a problem. We are restricted by the Founder's Will. Had the Founder been able to foresee that in time the apprentice system would be so completely abandoned he might have given different directions as to what the pupils of his College should be taught. It may be argued that new conditions require a new adjustment. This is a question for the Directors to determine.
>
> That Mr. Girard did not have in mind a vocational training for the boys of his College is evident from the fact that he directed that they should be bound out to *learn* trades when they leave the institution. We should, however, give all that is in our power to prepare the boys to avail themselves properly of the opportunities which come to them when they enter active life. There should be manual training for those who may take up manual occupations, commercial training for those who may enter counting houses or mercantile pursuits. In general, we should prepare them for the ever-increasing complexity and specialization of industrial life.[90]

In his report for 1908, he addressed himself to the same problem. The significance of his statement lies in establishing a point of reference in time when many forces were united in an effort on the behalf of vocational education, and which in itself provides an interesting background for the developments at Girard College:

> What kind of education is of most worth is still one of the problems pressing for solution. The interest in this question seems to tend to bring manual training, industrial training, and more especially trade teaching, more and more to the fore. In November, 1906, the National Society

---

[90] *Ibid.*, pp. 161-163.

> for the Promotion of Manual Education was organized. This Society has been busy at work, and at the end of its first year of existence it had established committees in thirty-eight different States. Some of these committees have already aroused and crystallized public interest in favor of the movement, while others not going quite as far as trade teaching, are, nevertheless, much interested in what they call practical teaching.
>
> It must be admitted that boys going to employment who have not been educated in some special trade or business are likely to drift for the first two or three years. A recent well-known report of the Industrial Commission of the State of Massachusetts states that 25,000 children were found to be in the vocational field between the ages of fourteen and sixteen. This report further declares that: "For the great majority of children who leave school to enter employments at fourteen and fifteen, the first three or four years are practically wasted years, so far as the productive value of the child and so far as increasing his efficiency and productive industry are concerned. The employments upon which they enter demand so little individual skill that they are not educated in any sense."
>
> Having referred to this question somewhat at length in my report for 1907 I should not perhaps bring it up again. It is well, however, that we should carefully consider the present-day conditions of the business and industrial world, in order, if possible, to meet them by putting into operation the proper agencies. In industrial and trade teaching Germany is far in advance of all other countries with the result that she is rapidly forging ahead in manufacturing skill. Take this illustration as one of many: the single item of machinery and tools. Germany's sales to the United States have doubled in five years from 1900 to 1905. Meanwhile, America's sales to Germany in this line are now about one-third of the totals of five years ago.[91]

However, on December 8th, 1909, due to impaired health, President Fetterolf presented his resignation to the Board of Directors of City Trusts. His official connection with the college ceased on January 31st, 1910. On February 25th following, Professor Cheesman A. Herrick, Principal of the William Penn High School for Girls, Philadelphia, was appointed to fill

---

[91] Adam H. Fetterolf, "Girard College President's Report for 1908," in <u>Thirty-Ninth Annual Report of the Board of Directors of City Trusts of the City of Philadelphia for the Year 1908</u>, pp. 159-160.

the vacancy. Herrick assumed his duties on April 1, 1910.[92]

Herrick's assumption of the presidency, in view of his own training and professional career, allowed for a grand evolution schema which continued those commitments begun by Fetterolf.[93] In his first annual report to the Board of Directors, Herrick underscored the need outlined in a report by Girard College's Vice-President Winthrop D. Sheldon that ". . . the first need of Girard College in the direction of its educational organization is [was] for a new high school building."[94] Herrick believed that the facilities as found were not adapted to school purposes with insufficient room for the development of a complete high school. This recommendation reflected in part a need for the total reorganization of the high school which had been suggested by the Vice-President and in which Herrick concurred.[95]

---

[92]*Fortieth Annual Report of the Board of Directors of City Trusts of the City of Philadelphia for the Year 1909*, pp. 10-11.

[93]Cheesman A. Herrick (1866-1956) came to the presidency of Girard College after long service in public schools and after he had established the first business and commerce course at Central High School in Philadelphia. As an early advocate of vocationally-oriented education his appointment was propitious in view of the movement toward trade and vocationally-oriented education that had evolved in the last years of President Fetterolf's tenure. There is no life of Herrick in the DAB; see the brief note in the *National Cyclopedia of American Biography*. XLVII (1965), pp. 106-107.

[94]Cheesman A. Herrick, "Girard College President's Report for 1910," in *Forty-First Annual Report of the Board of Directors of City Trusts of the City of Philadelphia for the Year 1910*, p. 162.

[95]Sheldon had served during President Fetterolf's tenure; for an assessment of Sheldon's contributions to the curriculum at Girard College (which curriculum lay within the responsibility of the Vice-President) see Cheesman A. Herrick, *History of Girard College*, pp. 167-168.

As to the placement of the boys in employment, Herrick noted that since the reports of the Superintendent of Admission and Indentures pointed out that a larger number of boys obtained positions as clerks, stenographers, and the like, there would be a distinct advantage in establishing a specialized school or department for commercial instruction which would parallel the work done in the mechanical school's last two years since he believed that boys entering commercial pursuits were ill-prepared for the duties they were assuming. In overview of the present conditions, he observed:

> At present we are teaching a little stenography, typewriting, bookkeeping, and similarly a little of the five or six trades given in our Mechanical School. The result is a dissipation of the boy's effort and a failure to give him a point of view, to furnish him the fundamentals of an education, or to afford a facility by which he may go out and take his place in doing the work which the world demands of him. As a consequence our boys are compelled to take positions at very low salaries and try to make good their deficiency by attending night schools or perfecting themselves after they get into positions. As a matter of fact many of them drift from one thing to another.[96]

---

[96]*Ibid.*, pp. 163-164. Herrick also noted that the condition of employment had an influence on the age which boys were discharged from the college. He observed: "The tendency, with the decrease in the practice of apprenticeship and the putting on the schools the duty of preparation for life, has been to advance the age at which boys are sent from the College. Forty years ago a fourteen-year old boy could go out and begin employment with much better prospects than can a fourteen-year old boy similarly go out and begin work to-day. Heretofore a trade or commercial skill was secured very largely after the period of employment began. Under present conditions, however, the schools are asked to give considerable facility in the trade or commercial calling, so that if Girard College is fully to discharge its responsibilities to the boys who are committed to its care it must expect to keep them beyond the minimum time set by the Founder." (*Ibid.*, p. 181). This tendency to maintain boys at the college for a longer period of time tended to produce a large waiting list for places in the college. In order that the limited number of boys admitted were "truly worthy" under the terms of the will, in 1910, the Board of Directors engaged the services of a field agent to investigate the applicants for admission to determine: "First, whether they are poor, white male orphans; and second whether they are normal boys who can profit by the service that

In reference to trade instruction he believed the efficiency and fine results of the mechanical school was in all probability the best grade of work being done anywhere in America, but suggested the desirability of introducing the subjects of printing, gardening, the building trades, and painting. All of these trades, he believed, would allow the possibilities of utilizing the boys for work at the college which was presently being done by outside labor.[97] As a result of these efforts, September 1911, boys reaching the third year of the Fourth Form were assigned for a special branch of instruction either in the mechanical school or the commercial department. Herrick saw the following benefits from such specialization:

> This gives the possibility of two full years of specialized work with more time and less divided interest than heretofore. By the time a boy has reached the usual third year of a high school course he begins to have definite prospects as to his future career, and if he has shown aptitude for mechanical pursuits, he should be furnished the opportunity to specialize in the trade school and be given some efficiency in working with his hands. If, on the other hand, his inclinations seem to be for clerical work or some branch of commercial activity, he should be given sufficient time to perfect himself in these lines. Our new arrangement makes such a specialization possible.[98]

---

the college gives, and can render for this service a return to the community." (*Ibid.*, p. 183). It is also of interest to note that the following year (1911) the title Superintendent of Admission and Indenture was changed to Superintendent of Admission and Discharge. While no apparent reason was given, Herrick notes at a later date that the change of title came about ". . . when cancellation of indentures ceased to be the method by which boys were dismissed from the College." See, in this connection, Cheesman A. Herrick, *History of Girard College*, p. 348.

[97]Cheesman A. Herrick, "Girard College President's Report for 1910," *op. cit.*, p. 169.

[98]Cheesman A. Herrick, "Girard College President's Report for 1911," in *Forty-Second Annual Report of the Board of Directors of City Trusts of the City of Philadelphia for the Year 1911*, p. 161.

Also, in 1912, the organization of the schools was changed from four <u>Forms</u> and in its place was adopted a primary school consisting of four years; a grammar school of three years; and a high school of four years with each year divided into two terms as previously organized.[99] With the organization of a formal high school, the curriculum prescribed allowed for boys to train in fundamental high school studies for two years, and to provide the opportunity for specializing either in preparation for commercial life or industrial activity in mechanical trade in the last two years. This, it was believed, would make it possible ". . . to adapt

---

[99]The change in terminology was made in 1911 due to the recommendation of Herrick. See in this connection, <u>Board of Directors of City Trusts, Minutes, Committee on Instruction, Vol. III, July 2, 1902, to April 4, 1913</u>, Minutes of November 3, 1911, p. 300. However, the change in terminology began with the 1912 school year. As a rationale for such a change, Herrick explained: "We were constantly at a disadvantage in the comparison of our work with the work of institutions elsewhere. We are receiving boys from the public schools both of Philadelphia and Pennsylvania outside of Philadelphia, and boys so received are graded under the normal public school system of a grade for a year of school attendance. By the adoption of a similar method of classification and gradation it became possible for us to receive and assign boys with more certainty and with less loss to them. Beginning with February 1st, 1912, our terminology was changed to an elementary school and a high school, each under a separate plan of organization. As the matter was worked out the elementary school was sub-divided into a primary school of four years and a grammar school of three years; the high school was given a four-year curriculum. Each of the years here mentioned is divided into two terms with intermediate classes and semi-annual promotions, so that there is the flexibility of gradation and promotions which will have the largest regard for the progress of a boy. A boy, if he comes to us when six years of age and proceeds regularly through all the grades of the College will have, with normal progress, eleven years in which to complete the school course, or he will graduate at seventeen. Thus, on this arrangement, there is the allowance of one year for retardation. Similarly, if a boy comes to us older than six years, he will have had under conditions at present existing, a school progress that will enable him to begin higher up in the grades than the first, so that he will have less work to complete than would be required if he came at the earliest possible age.

"In the making of a curriculum both for the Elementary School and the High School, due regard has been had for the plans of studies existing in the schools of Philadelphia and more broadly, Pennsylvania, and on every

the school course to the life purposes and evident capacities of the boys."[100] In the same connection, it was also believed that the mechanical school could be utilized for relieving the difficulties and failures in the high school and, to some extent, the upper years of the elementary schools. After careful study a plan was recommended and adopted which established a form of an intermediate high school or pre-vocational class which would specialize in industrial activity. Under this plan, boys who were over-age and for whom graduation would be impossible and boys who had no aptitude for regular high school work would spend one-third of the day in the schoolroom studying the fundamental English branches and shop arithmetic or mathematics and two-thirds of the day in the shops or doing practical work around the college. This, it was believed, would suit requirements to capabilities and reduce the degree of failures formerly found in the High School Department.[101]

Apparently in line with Herrick's thinking that the boys should be trained to work and the suggestions made by Vice-President Sheldon,

---

count we are the gainers from having the close correspondence of our schools to schools elsewhere. We are receiving teachers who are used to a fixed system of grading, and can adapt themselves more easily to a similar system under our own organization. We have constantly before us the stimulus and the standards of the schools outside and have already received an impetus from the work which they are doing. We have made the transfer to a new system and passed the first year with gain rather than loss, and in the years to come we should gain to a larger degree." See in this connection Cheesman A. Herrick, "Girard College President's Report for 1912," in _Forty-Third Annual Report of the Board of Directors of City Trusts of the City of Philadelphia for 1912_, pp. 165-166.

[100]_Ibid._, p. 167. See Appendix , pp. for the High School Curriculum contained on p. 167 of the same report.

[101]_Ibid._, pp. 170-171.

Herrick reported in 1912, "The mechanical instruction work has been adapted and made more practical. . . ."[102] The departments of woodworking and electrical construction had been reorganized; the department of plumbing had been discontinued and the space formerly occupied by plumbing was placed at the disposal of the woodworking department which was ". . . doing much practical work in the framing of pictures, the building of furniture, the making of repairs and in similar lines."[103] Other improvements were also suggested and included curricular revisions in the mechanical school such as more emphasis in mechanical or trade drawing and additional space for the extension of work in printing.[104]

In 1914, the following changes were recorded:

> Changes have been introduced during the year in the Mechanical school in such directions as the centralizing of the early work in fewer shops, and the reduction of the amount of rotation of classes from department to department. This has made possible the utilization of the more specialized trades, such as printing and electrical work, for definite trade instruction either for those who are in the last two years of the regular High School course, or for those who have been assigned to the Intermediate High School Class.

---

[102] *Ibid.*, p. 172.

[103] *Ibid.* The concept of "training boys to work" was considered an integral part of each boy's education beyond even their work in mechanical instruction. "Work in Girard College," Herrick believed, "should be made in some measure a part of the life of the institution. A boy should be taught to work for himself and to have some reward for his labor." (*Ibid.*, p. 219). His plan for self-help ranged from having the boys making their own buttons to having the boys receiving a money reward for their labor around the college performed during their play time or holiday period. (*Ibid.*, pp. 219-220).

[104] Cheesman A. Herrick, "Girard College President's Report for 1913," in *Forty-Fourth Annual Report of the Board of Directors of City Trusts of the City of Philadelphia for 1913*, pp. 134-135.

> The space on the second floor of the Mechanical School building has been more equitably divided between the Electrical Department and Carpentry on one side and Printing on the other. The print shop has been transferred from the first floor to the latter being transferred to the north side of the Machine Shop. The Printing Department has been equipped with a goodly supply of new type and new presses, including a small cylinder press of the Michle pattern. Beginning with September, this work was put in charge of a competent instructor who has had a large experience as a practical printer.[105]

The year 1914 also saw the introduction of an elementary industrial class for grammar school boys who were between fourteen and sixteen years of age and exhibited little gratitude for regular school work. The class was intended as practical training for the Intermediate High School or for an apprenticeship in a trade and consisted of a two-year curriculum as follows:

First Year		
English	5	periods per week
Arithmetic	5	" " "
History, Geography, Civics	5	" " "
Drawing	5	" " "
Shop (Wood)	10	" " "
Total	30	

Second Year		
English	5	periods per week
Arithmetic, and simple equations	5	" " "
History, Geography, Civics	5	" " "
Drawing	5	" " "
Shop (Metal)	10	" " "
Total	30	[106]

Another adaptive response which President Herrick employed was a modification of the Gary Platoon System. In March, 1913, Vice-President Sheldon

---

[105] Cheesman A. Herrick, "Girard College President's Report for 1914," in _Forty-Fifth Annual Report of the Board of Directors of City Trusts of the City of Philadelphia for 1914_, pp. 136-137.

[106] _Ibid._, pp. 138-139.

retired.[107] In December, 1913, his successor, Joseph M. Jameson, recommended a time arrangement that would provide different playground hours for older and younger boys, thereby eliminating overcrowding and would permit the academic work of the Junior and Senior to be scheduled in the morning, leaving the entire afternoon for commercial or trade instruction. He reasoned, "Such a continuous period at which all boys are in attendance, thus giving complete freedom for the assignment of work in accordance with the aptitude and progress of the boy is necessary in my judgment to the highest efficiency of such instruction."[108] This suggestion was underscored in his report for the following year but was now based upon the philosophy of William Wirt, Superintendent of Schools of Gary, Indiana. He urged that a careful study be made of the plan of the Gary system with a view to a reorganization of the educational work of the college.[109] In his report for 1915, Herrick noted that with the consent of the Committee on Instruction he had visited schools in Cleveland, Ohio; Gary, Indiana; Chicago, Illinois; and St. Louis, Missouri. Herrick admitted that while the Gary idea was not applicable in its entirety to Girard College, there was a wealth of suggestions for the needs of the college.

---

[107] Forty-Third Annual Report of the Board of Directors of City Trusts of the City of Philadelphia for 1912, p. 149.

[108] Joseph M. Jameson, "Girard College Report of the Vice-President, December 31, 1913," in Forty-Fourth Annual Report of the Board of Directors of City Trusts of the City of Philadelphia for 1913, p. 193.

[109] Joseph M. Jameson, "Girard College Report of the Vice-President, December 31, 1914," in Forty-Fifth Annual Report of the Board of Directors of City Trusts of the City of Philadelphia for 1914, pp. 179-180.

He explained that in brief, the Gary plan lengthened the school day and divided it into the following parts: "1. Recitation in a conventional classroom; 2. More formal instruction presented by means of lantern slides, moving picture films, and general lectures; 3. Shop instruction and industrial activity; 4. Playground and recreation activity."[110] Herrick further explained that groups of boys were assigned to each of the functions at different hours. By interchanging groups, all activities were carried on at the same time. As to the applicability of such a plan for Girard College, he observed:

> The wisdom of this plan for Girard College should be obvious. Instead of our limited playground space being occupied for brief intervals in the morning, at noon time, and in the late afternoon, and then so congested that satisfactory participation in games is next to impossible, the playgrounds would be occupied by smaller groups throughout the day; also the gymnasium and swimming pool could be, by the divided group plan, kept in operation continuously; similarly the lecture hall, the moving-picture machine, lantern, etc., could be worked to their limit of usefulness. But, perhaps, the most important gain from the suggested change of organization would be in the opportunities it would give for vocational instruction, and for the employment of boys in smaller groups in various forms of industrial activity about the Institution. In the attempt to treat all boys alike, there is an unavoidable vacuity in the daily life of those resident in Girard College. It has been impossible to carry on the industrial operations satisfactorily without taking boys in half classes from school. This we have been doing, but always with apologies to the regular teachers and to ourselves. When the organization of the College recognizes work as an essential element in the daily routine, and provides a time on the schedule when it is to be done, the idea of work will be impressed upon the boys' minds as an element in their education.[111]

---

[110] President's Report and Catalogue of Pupils Girard College, The City of Philadelphia, Trustee, for the Year 1915, p. 33.

[111] Ibid., pp. 33-34.

Significantly, Herrick's recommendation that a "divided group" plan be implemented the following September [1916][112] paralleled the establishment of a six-year Elementary School Course, followed by a five-year High School Course which was to become effective upon assuming possession of a new high school building which was now nearing completion.[113] In October, 1916, the "divided group" plan was put into effect.[114] In 1916, it was also noted that the transfer of boys from the college to employment had been found to be relatively easy. Aside from the industrial prosperity of the period, it was believed that this was due to the better training the boys received in preparation for both industrial occupations and commercial life; the effort of the organized and individual alumni; and the cultivation of possible employment by the department of Admission and Discharge.[115] These conditions lent themselves to enable older boys of the Intermediate High School to obtain summer work which provided encouraging results. In addition, other boys were guided to employment in stores on Saturdays especially during busy holiday seasons.[116]

---

[112] _Ibid._, p. 47.

[113] _Ibid._, p. 12. Admittedly, this was an attempt to achieve the "six and six" division which formed the basis of the theory in behalf of the Junior High School. At Girard College, the maximum prescribed age limit of eighteen necessitated a "six and five" combination. (_Ibid._, p. 13).

[114] _President's Report and Catalogue of Pupils Girard College, The City of Philadelphia, Trustee, for the Year 1916_, p. 20.

[115] _Ibid._, pp. 67-68.

[116] _President's Report and Catalogue of Pupils Girard College, The City of Philadelphia, Trustee, for the Year 1917_, p. 68.

Of singular importance in 1917 was the introduction of a part-time system of instruction for boys of the Intermediate High School classes in conjunction with the Chester shipbuilding company in Philadelphia. Whether in response to the pressing labor demands dictated by the conditions of World War I or as Herrick has suggested, "This plan [part-time system of education] was instituted in the hope of rendering a patriotic service to the Government in war time, but the successs of the undertaking was so immediate and obvious that the same idea was extended to other branches of industry in and around Philadelphia."[117]

The Cooperative education concept was particularly fruitful and should be underscored as a major effort during this period. In many ways, the experience at Girard College presaged the main tenets of the Smith-Hughes Act whose enactment by the Congress in 1917 was a belated affirmation of the need to bring into a clear focus and into a meaningful _rapport_ the schools and that sector of the society which was industrial.

---

[117]Cheesman A. Herrick, _History of Girard College_, p. 244.

CHAPTER V

THE PRONAOS OF SOCIAL CHANGE

I

> Perhaps the most interesting single educational development of the year has been the introduction of a part-time system of instruction for boys of the Intermediate High School classes. Boys above sixteen years of age who have made considerable progress in their trade are permitted by the authority of the Committee on Instruction to work in two week shifts. The boys are in pairs, one being at employment, while the other is at school. When the time for the shift comes, the boy who has been in school spends a Saturday with the boy who is at employment in order to get connected up with the work and to make the transfer without embarrassing the work.[1]

At the conclusion of the year 1916, President Herrick advised in the _President's Report for the Year 1916_ that the year had been fraught with many changes in equipment and administration and that he could not foresee another year with as many fundamental changes as had taken place. He observed: "Of necessity, changes come in cycles. Constant and too frequent disturbances are not healthful. It would appear that what Girard College can now do to best advantage is to settle down and work out carefully and thoroughly many of the new plans on which we have recently entered."[2]

However, the year 1917 saw Girard College in a period of marked educational and social change: the cooperative part-time venture was

---

[1] _President's Report and Catalogue of Pupils Girard College, the City of Philadelphia, Trustee, for the Year 1917_, p. 49.

[2] _President's Report and Catalogue of Pupils Girard College, the City of Philadelphia, Trustee, for the Year 1916_, p. 72.

certainly one with an experiential model; the college exhibited an emerging strong private school philosophy; and, there was a vigorously continued experimentation and adaptation at the College in keeping with the needs of its students, as the needs of the students reflected changing societal contexts.

Dictating a unique development was the fact that Girard College, while a private school, was well in the mainstream of public education, if not in the forefront of contemporary educational theory and innovation. Visitors from all over the world visited the College, and the list of general lecturers and chapel speakers included many pedagogical pioneers, who, to be sure, helped to provide Girard College with a singularly contemporary educational awareness.[3] The Girard presence was everywhere. The _Minutes of The Committee on Instruction_ has copious entries requesting, and, in most instances the granting, the necessary permission for the school administrators to attend the various conventions and associational meetings frequently scheduled during the World War I period,[4] a

---

[3]See, for example, the following annual report which is representative: _President's Report and Catalogue of Pupils Girard College, the City of Philadelphia, Trustee, for the Year 1919_ (p. 32) which notes that the educational lectures of the year were given by Professors Frank M. McMurray and William H. Kilpatrick, both of Teachers College, Columbia University. See also, Herrick's observation in the _President's Report and Catalogue of Pupils Girard College, the City of Philadelphia, Trustee, for the Year 1918_, that "numerous countries, even from far-away Japan, have spent considerable time here, and in general the responses have been helpful and interesting." (p. 87). Herrick also noted in the same report that "Repeatedly during the past year has the College been called upon to give counsel to the managers of other institutions, near and far. . . . During the past year we have had ample evidence that the influence of Girard College reached even to the uttermost parts of the earth. . . ." (p. 89).

[4]See in this connection, _Board of Directors of City Trusts, Minutes, Committee on Instruction, Vol. IV, May 9, 1913 to September 8, 1922_, Minutes of February 6, 1920 (p. 241) which requested permission for the Vice-President of the College to attend a meeting of the National Society for Vocational Education in Chicago on February 19th to 21st [1920] and permission for the

time which the educational historian Lawrence Cremin has referred to as "a great divide in the history of progressive education."[5]

As noted above, cooperative education was particularly fruitful during this period. Although the part-time arrangement with the Chester Shipbuilding Plant was discontinued in January 1919 "after fourteen months of experiment" due to the required traveling distance, plants nearer to the College were used in this continuing practice. At Girard College, this part-time arrangement was used as well for Saturday employment, and had generally been found to work satisfactorily, prompting the trial implementation of part-time work in commercial as well as industrial fields. Writing in 1919, Herrick saw an employment "advantage" in cooperative education, in that it was, in a measure, an apprenticeship. Hopefully, he saw great promise in the extension of the cooperative program that was to be implemented on February 1, 1920 to include boys in the "Senior-2 Division" of the regular high school (actually those who were in the College for their last five months).[6] However, in his report for 1920, President Herrick noted that the changing conditions of employment had imposed difficult problems for this group and necessitated that the

---

Supervisor of Elementary Schools to attend the Department of Superintendence of the National Educational Association in Cleveland on February 23rd to 28th [1920]. These requests were approved with "all the expenses in connection therewith to be paid by the college."

[5]Lawrence A. Cremin, The Transformation of the School, p. 179.

[6]President's Report . . . for the Year 1919, op. cit., pp. 50-51. See also in this connection, Letter from Joseph Jameson, Vice-President to Dr. Cheesman A. Herrick, President. Philadelphia, April 3, 1919 in Board of Directors of City Trusts, Letters and Reports, Vol. II, 1919, pp. 889-892. This letter recounted the obvious promising results of the cooperative program and suggested a possible extension of the program to the Senior class at the College.

cooperative arrangement be discontinued for the regular high school "temporarily, at least."[7] Nevertheless, the following year, 1921, saw Herrick noting that "Unsettled industrial conditions and the scarcity of places for apprentices, have led to an almost complete discontinuance of the cooperative plan even for the Intermediate High School." Hopefully, Herrick expressed the idea that there would be a resumption of the program when business conditions became more favorable.[8]

Parallel with the developments of cooperative education were the continuing attempts to maintain a high standard of trade instruction in keeping with the demands of industry and congruent with the needs of Girard College graduates. In an effort to provide practical experience for students trained in handwork, Herrick noted in his report for 1918, that the departments of the mechanical school were increasingly more expected than ever to supply the needs of the College. Beyond this, there were also attempts made to extend and coordinate the work in trade drafting by a fundamental change: by establishing the drafting room as the central department of the mechanical school; and further by extending the instruction of the machine shop in having those students receive instruction in heat treatment in the forge shop in order to extend their machinist skills. Herrick also cited the fact that the printing department was now called upon to an increasing degree to do work for the College.[9]

---

[7]President's Report and Catalogue of Pupils Girard College, the City of Philadelphia, Trustee, for the Year 1920, pp. 34-35.

[8]President's Report and Catalogue of Pupils Girard College, the City of Philadelphia, Trustee, for the Year 1921, pp. 40-41.

[9]President's Report . . . for the Year 1918, op. cit., pp. 26-27.

The apparent success in having boys of the mechanical school produce practical things was pointed up in the following years in the Annual Reports for 1919 and 1920. Typical of these reports was the prideful account for the year 1920, with great valuation placed on the repair and construction jobs performed by the students as follows:

Carpentry Department	$1,500
Drafting Department	360
Electrical Department	1,550
Forge Department	560
Foundry Department	1,450
Machine Shop	800
Pattern Shop	530
Printing Department	1,250
	$8,000 [10]

With a rationale thus supplied, Herrick quoted the Report of the Superintendent of the Mechanical School that "This increasing production program has made the need for additional floor space more apparent each year."[11] The report further explained that the lack of space made it not possible to properly develop present trades or to offer instruction in other trades. Apart from a general lack of space in all shop areas, the Superintendent noted that a new course of instruction should be offered in the automobile, the motor truck and the tractor.[12]

What is apparent in this appeal is an adaptive response to the educational needs of the students. In the past, the governing body of Girard College had found it necessary frequently to explain the function of the College. President Herrick was no exception and his statement on vocational education at Girard College deserves attention:

---

[10] President's Report . . . for the Year 1920, p. 32.

[11] Loc. cit.

[12] Ibid., pp. 32-33.

> Girard College is primarily a vocational school. The Founder provided that when boys were to leave the Institution, they should be placed at practical employments. No doubt, according to the custom of the time, the Founder had in mind the assignment of boys under the old apprenticeship system, by which they were in part to be taught trades and trained in business after they went to work. The change that has been going on in industry and commercial life during the past forty years has placed upon schools an increasing necessity for equipping young people to make themselves useful at once when they commence employment, rather than for them to undergo training after they begin work.[13]

Other adaptive responses suggested by President Herrick find fuller meaning when seen against the aforementioned statement on Girard's employment intentions for his student wards. In this light, Herrick's recommendation that boys should be taught seamanship[14] is made clearer when _vis à vis_ the continuing reference to Stephen Girard's wishes. Following this expressed policy, in December 1920, nine boys were transferred from the College to the "Schoolship Annapolis" under the charge of the Commissioners of Navigation of the Delaware River.[15]

---

[13]_Ibid._, pp. 30-31.

[14]_President's Report . . . for the Year 1918_, _op. cit._, p. 92.

[15]_President's Report . . . for the Year 1920_, _op. cit._, p. 53. The navigation program at Girard College had a continuing history. Herrick's account of the events leading up to the placing of boys on the "Schoolship Annapolis" deserves noting:

"When Stephen Girard described the educational plan for his Institution, he provided, first, for training in the fundamental English subjects, including reading, writing, grammar, arithmetic and geography, following which he gave directions for various practical studies and more advanced branches. In the list of practical studies, navigation was placed first. Similarly, when the Founder mentioned the 'suitable occupations' to which those educated in the College should be apprenticed, he placed navigation second in the list, being preceded only by agriculture. These facts indicate the regard in which Mr. Girard held the occupation to which he gave his early life.

Seventeen years after the College was opened, the then Board of Control, in an annual report, drew attention to the difficulties which had been encountered in carrying out the express desire of the Founder that the boys should be taught navigation. Attention was drawn to a plan then entered upon by which five pupils from the College were handed over to a school for naval apprentices, which had been started by the United States. The arrangement, it was stated, was undertaken with the consent of the nearest relatives of the boys concerned, and in compliance with the eager desire of the boys themselves to undergo the training offered. Report was made that the results from this experiment had been encouraging.

In 1873 the Board of Directors of City Trusts received a communication from the Council of the Board of Trade urging that the pupils of the College be taught practical navigation. This communication was referred to the Executive Committee, which a month later made report that while theoretical instruction was then given in the Institution, there was no means available to teach practical seamanship. This report was then communicated to the Board of Trade, and at the same time the question of teaching practical seamanship by the use of a 'model ship' was referred to the Committee on Instruction for consideration as to 'practicability and cost.' The matter next appeared before the Board in the annual report in 1877, in a statement that there were few boys leaving the College under apprenticeship for instruction in practical seamanship.

In 1885, in accordance with a motion duly passed, the Board of Directors appointed a Committee of Five to consider the question of having a schoolship located in Philadelphia, for the education of boys in practical navigation. This Committee made repeated reports of progress and in November of the year in question, presented a series of preambles and resolutions approving a plan of the City Councils of Philadelphia to secure a schoolship to be operated from a port of Philadelphia. The provisions of the Girard will with regard to teaching navigation at the College seem from this time to have been merged into the city plan for a schoolship. In 1888 an opinion of the Solicitor of the Girard Estate was submitted, questioning the legal right to appropriate funds for the support of a schoolship. Further consideration of this interesting matter was given by the Board in the early nineties, after which there seems to have been no further action. In 1905 the annual report of the President of the College drew attention to the method of teaching the theory of navigation then in vogue and showed the relations of navigation to the mathematics instruction at the College.

The same matter was considered in the President's report for 1912, the attention being again drawn to the possibility of using a schoolship for practical instruction, but no action was taken on this suggestion. So the matter continued until the year under review, when by action of the Board of Directors, the President was instructed to stimulate the interest of the boys in navigation, through inviting former students of the College or others who are engaged in this occupation to speak here, and in other ways that seemed practicable.

In pursuance of this plan an invitation was extended to Captain Dempwolf, of the 'Schoolship Annapolis,' to speak to the boys of the High School in the past autumn, following which an opportunity was given boys, with the consent of their mothers, to enlist for a two years' course of training on this schoolship. Approval was given to an arrangement by which the outfits necessary for the boys on the schoolship were furnished in lieu of the outfits which they would ordinarily receive, and with the consent of the Committee on Admission and Discharge, nine boys were, in the month of December, transferred from Girard College to the schoolship. Four more are being similarly transferred as this report is prepared.

The unique character of Girard College was no less obvious during this period. In a measure, it was functioning as a vocational school. Yet, in President Herrick's Annual Report for 1918, in speaking of discipline at the College, a particular observation on the foundation status that the College enjoyed is noted. Herrick observed:

> We need to re-emphasize that Girard College is not aiming to be an orphanage, but that it is a school - home, a public institution, richly endowed, under the care of the Mayor and citizens of the City of Philadelphia for the sole purpose of receiving and educating deserving boys. The College is not a "home" in the sense in which that term is usually employed; on the other hand it is not a "school" in the sense in which the term is applied to the private boarding schools. It is an endowed foundation which occupies a middle ground between these two institutions.[16]

President Herrick's observations, again, underscore the unique character of Girard College as an educational institution. Although it was privately endowed, it was clearly influenced by the ubiquitous developments in public education; as an urban institution it remained sensitively

---

In brief, the plan is that these boys shall receive in their first year a general training in the fundamentals of navigation, and in the second year they will receive specialized training in preparation for either deck officers or engineer officers. Deserving boys, it is held, will be equipped by a two-year course of theoretical and practical instruction on the schoolship, so that they will receive commissions in the American Merchant Marine, either as assistant engineers or as third deck officers.

With the entrance of the United States into a new period as a seafaring nation, there seems to be unusual opportunities for our boys in the directions indicated, and so far as we can see, no other calling promises so immediate and certain a return to a deserving boy as does the completion of a course on the schoolship.

Unquestionably, training for the sea in America has been neglected in favor of training for land occupations. When the United States entered upon the building of a fleet of merchant ships, as one of the results of the World War, we were without sufficient officers to navigate these ships. There is, at present, an unmistakable vocational need for training in seamanship. As Stephen Girard was, before all else, a mariner, and as in seamanship he laid the foundation for his notable career, so the Institution which his business success made possible would seem to have a special commission to promote a training for the sea. In doing this, we will only be following the expressed direction of the Founder." (pp. 51-54)

[16] President's Report . . . for the Year 1918, op. cit., p. 45.

responsive to social needs; and its independent endowment allowed it to reflect advanced theoretic and practical educational experimentation. Each of these diverse themes is pursued in continuing reflections and animadversions in President Herrick's reports for 1919 and 1921.

In commending the urban environment in which Girard College had known its genesis (and inveighing against any plan to move out of the city) President Herrick observed:

> With the passing of time and the working out of the problem of a part-time employment we get a new point of view on the question of the rural or urban location of the College. Some persons who have given only a cursory examination to our problem have jumped to the conclusion that it would be greatly to the advantage of Girard College if it could be located in the country. While there would be special gains in some directions from a rural location many of the lines of activity mentioned above would then be quite impossible. Rural location for an institution has obvious disadvantages as well as some advantages. While there are gains from isolation and inaccessibility, there are corresponding and even greater losses. The two great vocational aims of Girard College are commercial life and industrial service. Both of these are largely represented in a great metropolitan district like that in which the College is located. The spirit of the commercial and industrial world which is important in a system of training like ours can be brought into the College more largely in the city than it could be in the country. The boys, even while they are undergoing training, may be placed at employment for longer or shorter intervals. The part-time arrangement would be quite impossible if the College were located in the country. A very considerable number of boys who find employment on Saturdays, and during the shorter as well as longer vacations, would be largely denied the privilege if the College were located in the country. These employment opportunities are part of the education of the boys and to be prevented from enjoying them would mean serious loss.
>
> In the placement of boys when they are prepared to leave the Institution there are similarly obvious gains from the urban location of the College. A prospective employer can reach promptly the source of supply of labor, and can have his needs met immediately; under present conditions there can be a vital contact between the placing in positions from the College and the boy at employment which is greatly to be desired. In case of a boy being promoted in a position or transferred from one position to another, the Department of Admission and Discharge can use the opening thus made for the placing of an additional boy. Boys may be visited at

> their employment and altogether there is a closeness of contact and a vital relation under the present arrangement which would be largely lost should the work of the College be done even a short distance from the city.
>
> In the matter of keeping up the necessary relationships between the homes from which the boys come and their life at the College we should be at a great disadvantage in the country. The degree privileges, the contact with the home due to visits of members of the staff in case the boy is in need of having such contacts established, the calling of the mothers to the College for interviews, the receiving of mothers in large numbers on special days, the visits home in case of the illness of a member of the family or of an important event in the family history, all keep up the boy's interest in the family circle which means much in his education, and is a better guarantee for his identification with the family life when he leaves the Institution.
>
> The mothers of the boys at Girard College have come to accept as an invariable rule of the Institution the arrangement that in case of the illness of a boy, or of his suffering from an accident or being in need of surgical attention, the mother will be at once summoned to the Institution so that she may be consulted, and have a personal contact and full knowledge of all that is going on. In certain cases we have deemed it necessary to send a taxicab for a mother, even in the middle of the night, so that she might come to the bedside of a sick boy. All this is greatly to be desired if we are to make the College what we have set before it as an ideal: namely, that it shall be a supplement to not a supplanter of the home. These services could not be so well rendered under a rural establishment.[17]

Girard College's obvious reaction to, and incorporation of, experimental constructs which were largely characteristic of the public sector (*e.g.*, themselves illustrative of the evolving Progressive Movement) are suggested by the following:

> A well-recognized principle of finance may properly be applied to Girard College in the statement that schools cost money and good schools cost more money than poor schools. The General Education Board of New York City which established the Lincoln School for experimental and demonstration purposes saw at the outset that the school would prove more expensive than an ordinary school. This Board justified a large expenditure on the Lincoln School from the indirect service which the school would render in making demonstrations of work along

---

[17]*President's Report . . . for the Year 1919*, *op. cit.*, pp. 52-54.

> special lines. In many ways the commission to Girard College from the Founder and the educational opportunity which is here offered are along the lines of the plans for the Lincoln School, and the aims which the General Education Board set for the Lincoln School are substantially the aims which we should recognize for Girard College. In this connection we may well remind ourselves again of the concluding sentence in the very illuminating report on "Education in Europe," prepared by Alexander Dallas Bache, the first President-elect of Girard College, and submitted to the Trustees of the College in 1839. "Our founder has furnished them the means of establishing a series of model schools for moral, intellectual, and physical education, embracing the period of life from early youth almost to manhood, the importance of which to our city, and even to the country at large, can hardly be estimated."[18]

In speaking of Girard College's independence, President Herrick spoke glowingly of the great private school tradition. He observed:

> The purposes of Girard College, broadly stated, are to serve the common weal through giving a preparation for efficient and useful living. The purposes of Stephen Girard in the founding of the College are not dissimilar to the original purpose of the founder of the Harrow School in England, or to that of Judge Phillips in establishing the famous Andover School in Massachusetts. After setting forth that youths were to be instructed in the fundamentals of an education, Phillips said that his school was more especially to teach "the great end and the business of living."[19]

In essence, this multi-faceted Girard College experience (as conceptualized by its senior officer) brought it to the threshold of its seventy-fifth anniversary which was observed in 1923.

---

[18] _Ibid_., p. 83. For an overview of the Lincoln School (New York City) see Lawrence A. Cremin, _The Transformation of the School_, pp. 280-291.

[19] _President's Report . . . for the Year 1921_, _op_. _cit_., p. 13.

II

> When the College was opened, January 1, 1848, the Residuary Fund of the Estate of Stephen Girard, the income from which, he directed in his Will, should be used primarily for the maintenance and further improvement of the College, and then was to be applied to the purpose of carrying out the provisions of his secondary trust, was about $3,000,000 and the number of pupils 95. The expenditures for maintenance the first year were $31,821.83. In 1873, at the end of the first twenty-five years, the Residuary Fund was $4,962,735.22, while the number of pupils had increased to 546, and the annual cost of maintenance to $188,000.00. In 1898, when the College had been opened fifty years, the Residuary Fund had increased to $11,700,000, the number of pupils to 1,536 and the annual cost of maintenance to $480,000.00. To-day, after an existence of seventy-five years, the Residuary Fund is $51,000,000, the number of pupils 1,545 and the annual expenditure for maintenance $1,300,000.00. In addition to the $51,000,000, which is all income producing, there is carried on the books as the nominal value of the College grounds and buildings--$4,500,000.00, making the total Capital $55,500,000.00.
>
> . . . .
>
> This is a wonderful showing. But wonderful as it is, it will be surpassed in the future. I am going to make a prediction that twenty-five years hence, on the first day of January, 1948, when the One Hundredth Anniversary of the inauguration of this College will be celebrated, if nothing unforeseen happens, and in the meantime the Estate has been managed in a wise, conservative, and business-like manner, and the present financial policy as adopted by the Board of Directors of City Trusts in 1897 is not changed, but strictly adhered to, the Residuary Fund providing income for the maintenance and improvement of Girard College first, the primary object of the testator, and for the secondary trust, as directed in his will, to wit: "to enable the corporation of the City of Philadelphia to maintain a competent police force, to improve the city property and in effect to diminish the burden of taxation," will be at least One Hundred Millions of Dollars.[20]

Girard College celebrated its seventy-fifth anniversary in 1923 with a clear awareness of both accomplishment and still evolving needs. Reflecting on the most recent accomplishments of the College, President Herrick proudly singled out the benefits the College derived from the implementation of the "platoon plan" which he described as follows: "Perhaps no

---

[20]Edwin S. Stuart, "Address." At the Celebration of the 75th Anniversary of the Opening of Girard College, January 1, 1923. Fifty-Third Annual Report of the Board of Directors of City Trusts of the City of Philadelphia for 1922, pp. 23-24.

single feature introduced into the schools of the College in the past dozen years has contributed more to progress in our educational activities than has the adoption of what was earlier called the divided group plan, but has in other places been termed 'the Gary System,' 'the work-study-play plan,' and the 'platoon plan.'"[21]

Yet while the prevailing educational situation was a source of satisfaction to the College, the administration knew the College was struggling with an already deteriorating plan of cooperative education and was faced with the need for additional space in the Mechanical School building which would give room for new departments of instruction.

What is certainly obvious during this period is that Girard College was not without the desire to provide many individualized training schemes (e.g., apprenticeship and cooperative education) notwithstanding continuous, organized group instruction. The noted educational historian, Lewis Flint Anderson, has said of this period that beyond the efforts of the pioneer trade schools, ". . . four [types of schools] have risen into prominence as institutions for vocational education in the industries: the apprenticeship or corporation school, the cooperative school, the continuation school, and the evening school."[22] In speaking of Girard College as a pioneer trade school, he saw fit to note that Girard College was one of the instances where ". . . the Gordian knot of the problem of maintenance was solved by the munificence of the endowment, which provided board, lodging, clothing, school books, and utensils as well as tuition."[23]

---

[21]President's Report and Catalogue of Pupils Girard College, the City of Philadelphia, Trustee, for the Year 1922, p. 24.

[22]Lewis Flint Anderson, History of Manual and Industrial School Education, p. 228.

[23]Ibid.

However, the particular significance of his assessment assumes a singular importance when it is realized that at Girard College these types of schools (*i.e.*, industrial schools) became congruent concepts (with attempts at implementation) in the school's evolution.

As an apprenticeship school, Girard College's early history had attested to its general efforts to place all its students as apprentices and had, as late as 1920, transferred boys to the "Schoolship Annapolis" to be taught seamanship.[24] This same concept had also been applied in the school's "production program" which, as in the case of the corporation schools, was primarily designed to fit the employees, in this sense the students, for the more efficient performance of their duties.[25]

The practicability of the cooperative school or part-time school was equally an established feature of the Girard College curriculum and was regarded as a successful facet of the school's trade courses.[26] However, it was noted in 1924 that unfavorable employment conditions had a deleterious effect on the placement of boys into this program. President Herrick observed:

> The number of boys working under the cooperative plan of employment has been smaller than for any year since this plan was put into operation. Industrial depression has no doubt lessened the opportunities for boys to carry on practical work in connection with their education. It seems desirable to continue a part time system so that with changed conditions an additional number of boys may be assigned to this useful branch of work.[27]

---

[24]See *supra*, p.   for a discussion of the "Schoolship Annapolis."

[25]See *supra*, p.   for a discussion of the school's "production program."

[26]See *supra*, p.   for a discussion of cooperative education at Girard College.

[27]*President's Report and Catalogue of Pupils Girard College, the City of Philadelphia, Trustee, for the Year 1924*, p. 81.

The lessened demand for boys was further noted in President Herrick's Annual Reports for 1926 and for 1928.[28] Later, it was noted: "This system of cooperative work was maintained after the War [I] and did not cease until about 1929, when a general slacking in the labor market deprived the boys of this opportunity for part-time work."[29]

The continuation school program at Girard College formed an abiding major precept in the school's formulation of basic procedural guidelines. However, the tendency of boys to continue longer at the College took on a new meaning and relevancy in 1919 when President Herrick pointed to the effect of compulsory schooling on the general leaving age of the students. He observed:

> There are still a considerable number of boys, however, who become restless and dissatisfied before they are sixteen years of age, and the placement of these to advantage presents a real problem. We have, however, the satisfaction of feeling that while a few years ago a considerable number of boys left us under what was known as the fifteen-year-old rule, that number has been greatly diminished and we now look to sixteen as the lowest age at which boys should leave the Institution. The present compulsory continuation school law in Pennsylvania, which places upon employers the necessity of providing for the attendance of boys on continuation schools if they are employed under sixteen years of age, has had the tendency of keeping boys in school for a longer period.[30]

---

[28]See in this connection, President's Report and Catalogue of Pupils Girard College, the City of Philadelphia, Trustee, for the Year 1926, p. 75; President's Report and Catalogue of Pupils Girard College, the City of Philadelphia, Trustee, for the Year 1928, p. 89.

[29]Report of the President, Girard College, the City of Philadelphia, Trustee, for the Year 1942, p. 37.

[30]President's Report . . . for the Year 1919, op. cit., pp. 78-79. Lack of cognitive progress or disciplinary infractions allowed for the cancelling of a boy's indenture to the College. See in this connection, for a more detailed discussion of the cancellation of indenture, p. 208, supra. For an extended discussion of the discharge of students, see Cheesman A. Herrick, History of Girard College, pp. 339-364. The best examination of the types of Continuation Schools is found in William P. Sears,

This same theme, that the boys exhibited a tendency to continue longer at the College, was reiterated in the Annual Report for 1923.[31]

The Girard College experience, however, incorporated two seemingly incongruous developments: on one hand, emphasis was on the practical phase of education; and, on the other hand, the College was paying greater attention to boys going on to colleges and other institutions of higher learning as is evidenced by quotations from the Annual Report for 1923 which states the concern thusly:

> A mandate from the Girard Will that the boys attending Girard College are to be taught "facts and things" rather than "words and signs" has resulted in our placing emphasis on the practical phases of education; the further fact that boys are expected to go to employment immediately on leaving the College has pointed to the necessity for vocational education. While a few boys have gone to college, we have always regarded preparation for College admission as an incident in the training given at Girard College.[32]

* * *

The Roots of Vocational Education, pp. 114-115. Basically, Sears points out that there were two types of continuation school: one to assist individuals between the ages of sixteen and eighteen, and commonly known as the 'part-time trade extension school: and the other, to assist those between the ages of fourteen and sixteen and commonly known as the general continuation school." Necessarily, Girard College students can be regarded as falling into both groups. A clear philosophy for continuation school referral was enunciated by President Herrick: "Increasingly in recent years we have sought to eliminate boys who do not make good use of their privileges. The provision in the Girard Will, that boys shall be sent from the College at between fourteen and eighteen years of age, indicates clearly that the Founder had in mind that boys, when fourteen and above, should be continued only when they made good use of the opportunities which the College gives them. A compulsory attendance of all boys until they are eighteen would work badly. Many boys ought to meet the responsibilities of employment at sixteen years of age. Some can profitably go to work at an earlier age than sixteen, under the plan by which they may keep on with their education in a continuation school." President's Report . . . for the Year 1925 . . . pp. 20-21.

[31] President's Report and Catalogue of Pupils Girard College, the City of Philadelphia, Trustee, for the Year 1923, p. 74.

[32] Ibid., p. 26.

> An increasing number of our boys are going to college; the total who are in attendance on higher institutions this year includes thirty-seven who are giving their full time to college attendance and twenty-one who are taking evening school courses. The record of Girard College boys in higher institutions is creditable, and the desire to go to college grows steadily.[33]

It is of importance to note that endowments of the sort providing for the maintenance of Girard College students were generally rare in other educational contexts. The necessity for Girard students to work during the day and obtain vocational instruction in the evening in keeping with the generally encountered practice of evening schools was necessarily obviated; however, references to the schedule of the high school building at Girard College occasioned by the implementation of the "divided group" plan which rotated the use of the various facilities of the College noted that the ". . . building has been called into use for study and recitation from seven o'clock in the morning until nine o'clock at night."[34] Similar references are also made to other buildings of the College. This adaptation of resources to the needs of the students and the curricula which were being implemented at the College are yet further examples of the necessary flexibility which the Girard College administration had to observe to allow the College's continued functionality within the parameters of what Stephen Girard's intentions affirmed.

These developments must be understood in the context of a wide range of problems which Girard College encountered in attempting the implementation of defined educational objectives. The request for additional shop areas was repeated by President Herrick in 1922 and 1923 and was couched in the recommendation that an addition to the Mechanical School would allow

---

[33]*Ibid.*, p. 74.

[34]*President's Report . . . for the Year 1916*, *op. cit.*, p. 21.

for better instruction in trade subjects already given, provide room for new areas of instruction, and allow for additional instructional space at the high school building itself.[35] In apparent contrast to President Herrick's somewhat plaintive plea that the College "settle down" in his 1916 Annual Report[36], his prefatory remarks to his Annual Report for 1924 set a more vigorously progressive tone in keeping with the constantly changing demands imposed on Girard College. He observed:

> Obviously, an individual or an institution which has reached the point of complete satisfaction with results is completely and hopelessly tied to the past. A form of "mental scleiosis" has set in, and under such conditions progress or betterment is beyond hope. If any principle of educational philosophy seems to be clearly established, it is that a progressive system of training is necessary in a progressive society.[37]

The completion of an addition to the Mechanical School building was fully realized in 1925. President Herrick hailed the addition and noted: "The most important single change for the year at Girard College has been the completion of the rebuilt Mechanical School and the furnishing of new equipment and the beginning of a new attack on the educational problem to which this school devotes itself. The re-constructed Mechanical School is more than double the size of the original building.[38] The addition allowed for two new departments of instruction to be included, namely, painting and finishing, and auto mechanics.[39]

---

[35] President's Report . . . for the Year 1922, op. cit., pp. 79-80; President's Report . . . for the Year 1923, op. cit., p. 77.

[36] President's Report . . . for the Year 1916, op. cit., p. 72.

[37] President's Report . . . for the Year 1924, op. cit., p. 9.

[38] President's Report . . . for the Year 1925, op. cit., p. 40.

[39] Ibid.

The year 1925 also saw a change in the high school curriculum which was to be implemented the following February. The curriculum for the last two years of the High School Department was revised, creating three groups of students to allow more recreation time for the older boys: a grouping of instruction in the Junior and Senior years into three divisions, intended for those seeking college admission; and the inclusion of elective courses for those boys with particular course preferences. The revised curriculum is as follows:

A. FOR COLLEGE PREPARATION--LIBERAL ARTS

JUNIOR YEAR

English and Public Speaking	U. S. History
Plane Geometry	Spanish

SENIOR YEAR

English and Public Speaking	Spanish
Social Problems	Physics

B. FOR COLLEGE PREPARATION--ENGINEERING COURSES

JUNIOR YEAR

English and Public Speaking	U. S. History
Plane Geometry	Physics

SENIOR YEAR

English and Public Speaking	Advanced Algebra and Solid Geometry
Social Problems	French, Review

C. GENERAL COURSE

PREPARES FOR ENTRANCE TO WHARTON SCHOOL

JUNIOR YEAR

English and Public Speaking	U. S. History
Plane Geometry	Physics or Spanish

SENIOR YEAR

English and Public Speaking	Trigonometry and Surveying, or Advanced Algebra and Solid Geometry, or Spanish, or Free-hand Drawing and Art History[40]
Social Problems	
Physics, or Chemistry, or French Review	

---

[40] *Ibid.*, pp. 37-38.

For succeeding decades, the over-arching concerns at Girard College (in keeping with the constant attempt to refine and implement a viable vocationally-oriented curriculum) was the development of the Mechanical School concept. And yet, as this very development was pursued, Girard College simultaneously attempted a variety of other educational curricula impinging on (1) a private school philosophy not unlike the elitism of the British public school; (2) a strongly articulated high school program essentially congruent with developments in the American public sector; and (3) a post-secondary school instruction and junior college philosophy.

III

> Education in America has been designed primarily for the book-minded boy. Many boys have failed in Girard College owing to their inability to meet the demands of an academic curriculum. These same boys, when given an opportunity to express themselves through handwork, are both successful and happy. The various activities of the College in recent years in the direction of mechanical instruction have given an outlet to native abilities and have made possible a preparation for life which never could have been secured through books alone. Mechanical instruction has itself gone through an evolution in Girard College, as it has elsewhere. The earlier form of training of "hand and eye" became almost as dull and lifeless as the formal training from textbooks. A better method has gradually been worked out, which makes shops into practical workrooms and gives boys the stimulus of creative production in actual work. Boys who are asked to turn out real, finished products do not lack in interest, as is proved by the encouraging response of our boys during the past year; we moreover believe that such training gives boys a high conception of the vocations which they will follow through life.[41]

In reality, the Mechanical School had developed as an educational concept as far as was to be brought by the Girard College administration, and it remained, in essence, the model which was to be maintained over

---

[41] President's Report . . . for the Year 1926, op. cit., pp. 36-37.

the course of the following generation. The Mechanical School concept (largely catalyzed into being by the Centennial Exposition in Philadelphia in 1876) had evolved from the early 1880's to the form which it was to maintain.[42] The salient features of the Mechanical School (essentially to remain unchanged) included the following three phases:

> The first consists of elementary manual arts [or Sloyd] pursued by every boy from the second term of the fourth grade to the end of second grade. The second phase consists of prevocational courses from the seventh grade through the second year of high school. . . . The third phase, for the boy who chooses a mechanical trade, consists of two years of intensive trade training . . .[43]

This Mechanical School (or handwork instructional as sometimes referred to) theory and practice proved abiding and has reflected a blending of the uniformity of vocational programs prescribed by the vocationalists who brought about the uniform nature of federally-supported vocational programs and in addition the Girard College individuality since Girard College had been independent of federal support and has been allowed the not too often found luxury of possible experimentation with new programs

---

[42]See in this connection, supra, pp. 178-206.

[43]Girard College. Course of Study VII [Mechanical School Instruction], 1933, p. 8. See, generally, Appendix N. Elementary manual arts at Girard College was a term used interchangeably with Sloyd. In the President's Report for the Year 1938, p. 45, it was noted that the shop work introduced into many schools as a result of the Philadelphia Centennial Exposition in 1876 was called "Sloyd Work" and that since 1898 Girard College had a "Sloyd Department." However, it was obvious that while the nature of the work expanded and changed, yet the old name remained. In 1938 the name was changed to "Manual Arts." The problem of terminology in relating the historical background of industrial arts has been developed at length by Melvin L. Barlow, History of Industrial Education in the United States, pp. 239-291. See also in this connection, L. F. Ashley, "Chronological Development of the Industrial Arts Concept," Industrial Arts and Vocational Education, Vol. 26 (October, 1937), pp. 309-312. At Girard College, there is continuing reference to prevocational courses; however, in the President's Report for the Year 1945, p. 28, it is noted that the Principal of the High School reported, "The Industrial Arts course has taken on form and purposefulness."

or innovations that was indicative of contemporary federally-funded ones.[44] President Herrick was moved to note in his Annual Report the following:

> In 1927 as in no preceding year of the administration of Girard College we have been conforming to the rule, "Send the whole boy to school." Educators in every field of interest concur in the conclusion that a fundamental lesson which all education should teach is power of concentration and a capacity to get down to hard work. This lesson can be taught much more definitely and much more easily in handwork instruction than in instruction based upon text-books.
>
> The enlarged, remodeled building for mechanical instruction and related book work has made possible a highly satisfactory year in 1927. In the main, the progress has been along the lines earlier attempted and in fulfillment of the ideals already established. One unusual feature of trade-school instruction at Girard College is the outlet which the institution furnishes for the productive work of the shops. In the school year from September 1926 to June 1927, the school turned out materials which, on a conservative estimate aggregated in value, $19,150.37.[45]

And yet, unlike the terminal program structure usually found in the contemporary vocational programs, the Girard College schema occupied the unique position of allowing for both practical and academic preparation. President Herrick re-emphasized this point quite eloquently in 1928 when he wrote the following:

> Girard College occupies an intermediate place between practical education, which seeks to get boys ready for living in the work-a-day world, and academic education the purpose of which is to prepare them for professional study and continued higher education. We must, therefore, maintain practical education, which has a liberal element, and an academic training, which is directed to practical ends. It follows from our problem that we shall be saved from having the educational process degenerate into merely disciplinary education on one side, or a bread and butter training on the other.[46]

---

[44]For a discussion of the uniformity found in vocational courses since the passage of the Smith-Hughes Act (1917), see in this connection, Melvin L. Barlow, _op. cit._, pp. 292-338.

[45]_President's Report and Catalogue of Pupils Girard College, the City of Philadelphia, Trustee, for the Year 1927_, p. 48.

[46]_President's Report and Catalogue of Pupils Girard College, the City of Philadelphia, Trustee, for the Year 1928_, p. 41.

In his Annual Report for the Year 1925, President Herrick had forcefully suggested that the completion of the Mechanical School addition had marked the ". . . beginning of a new attack on the educational problem to which the school addresses itself."[47] This same "attack" motif was equally applied to the High School in 1928 when an addition to the High School building had been completed.[48] However, it is interesting to observe that President Herrick's rationale to improve the High School was prefaced by a recognition of the criticisms made by President Lowell of Harvard of secondary education in America. President Herrick explained:

> Education which is vital must in some way be related to the life which boys are to lead after they go out from school, and constantly those shaping the educational policies of Girard College are holding before their mind's eye the future life which our boys will lead, and there is a conscious attempt to adapt education to serve them in the meeting of the responsibilities of their own futures. This approach and attitude make the business of education a serious matter, and one which saves our boys from becoming the victims of any system of coddling or rendering "soft" the educational process.
>
> Shortly after the beginning of 1928 the faculty of the High School met for an attack on the problem of betterment in various departments of instruction.[48]

As may be the case, the immediate result of the "attack" was the distribution of a series of guidance suggestions to the various departments of instruction by the Vice-President. However, the basic problems which the High School addition was apparently intended to mmet were those caused by the increased number of boys who would be receiving secondary school instruction at the College. In 1925, the College had entered into a program of enlargement (of which obviously the High School was a part)

---

[47]See supra, p.

[48]President's Report . . . for the Year 1928, op. cit., p. 42.

to increase the student population.[49] In discussing the increased use of the High School by a greater number of boys, President Herrick pointed up the followed added dimensions:

> The unprecedented increase in secondary education in the years immediately following the World War has added enormously to the expenditures for education, and has given this branch of the field a much larger place in the general scheme than it had ever before occupied. This movement has been evidenced in Girard College as it has been in the country at large. In 1910, not more than twenty-five per cent of the boys in attendance on the College were receiving secondary school instruction; in 1928 fully fifty per cent of the boys were in that department of training.
>
> The above changes are due to several cooperating causes. First, high school education is now begun earlier in the Girard boy's life than it was eighteen years ago; secondly, our boys at admission are received into more advanced grades, and there is less necessity for elementary school instruction; and, third, by means of more rapid and regular promotion, incidental promotions in term time, and the making up of grades through summer study, boys are pulled along so that an increased proportion of the school is in the upper division.[50]

The significance of more boys being in attendance at the High School took on an even greater relevancy in 1930 when President Herrick explained in his Annual Report that "The child labor laws of Pennsylvania properly discriminate against boys going to employment under sixteen years of age, and in some instances we have been forced to provide post-graduate instruction for those who have been graduated in advance of a suitable age for them to find positions."[51] With this rationale, President Herrick developed the following argument:

---

[49] President's Report and Catalogue of Pupils Girard College, the City of Philadelphia, Trustee, for the Year 1931, p. 73.

[50] President's Report . . . for the Year 1928, op. cit., p. 40.

[51] President's Report and Catalogue of Pupils Girard College, the City of Philadelphia, for the Year 1930, p. 44.

A hundred years ago, when Girard planned for his College, he directed that boys should be kept here until they were between fourteen and eighteen years of age, implying at the same time that the length of time which they should be kept after they were fourteen should be dependent on their deserving. In the hundred years that have elapsed since the Girard Will was drawn, there has been an unmistakable lengthening of the period of education. In the last fifty years the apprenticeship system which was common in Girard's day, has largely gone into disuse, and employers now expect boys to come to them prepared to render a useful service from the first. Were Girard making his Will at the present time, we may well believe that he would provide more rather than less school training to prepare boys for employment.

The carrying forward of the program of enlargement affords an opportunity to provide for post-graduate instruction for a group of deserving boys, the like of which the College has never before had, and perhaps may never have again. . . . The time, therefore, has seemed opportune to bring forward the suggestion that post-graduate study be offered to boys who complete the present requirements of the College at sixteen or seventeen years of age. This will, in effect, establish a junior college in our scheme of education.

The Girard Will laid down a rigorous and advanced plan of studies which the College has never fully carried out and probably never can carry out for the majority of boys who are required to leave the College at eighteen years of age or under. A select group, however, can be brought nearer to meeting the requirements of the Will than has been true heretofore. It is the feeling of the officers of the College that this plan of post-high school instruction for a limited number of boys will render an enlarged service to them and will stimulate and develop instruction in the College all along the line. Such an advanced course will raise the educational level of the College, and will prove helpful to the morale and *esprit de corps* of the institution as a whole.

When the present President of the College was invited to appear before a committee which was appointed to select and nominate a President for Girard College early in 1910, he was asked what he conceived to be the ideal for the institution. The answer he made was that Girard College should serve as a series of model schools which would point the way for the most approved educational methods. Later, when an opportunity was afforded him to study the history of the College, he was interested to find that this same ideal had been expressed by the first President-elect, Dr. Alexander Dallas Bache.

. . . .

> A further possible advantage of this junior college plan will be that boys who enter a higher institution may secure credit for one or perhaps two years' work. As was pointed out by the late President Harper of the University of Chicago, the first two years of college instruction can be given quite as advantageously in a smaller institution where there are fewer disconcerting influences than are found in a larger college or university. The admirable results secured in the English public schools, the French lycée, and the German gymnasia come from the carrying forward of the methods of disciplinary education of the secondary school through what is in effect two years of American college work. In American education there is an unmistakable trend toward broadening the period of the secondary school to include the junior high school on the one side and the junior college on the other. One of the limitations of the American school system is lack of continuity of educational effort. The primary school, grammar school, high school, and college are so disjointed that one who goes through these several steps in educational progress suffers repeated dislocations and maladjustments. Educationally the products of our secondary schools are at a disadvantage when compared with the products of the secondary schools in Great Britain, France and Germany.[52]

"The year 1931," wrote President Herrick, "saw the beginning of a new plan which we trust in time will make Girard College an institution the educational scope of which, will more nearly conform to the name the institution bears." He further explained: "No activity in the past year is more notable, or is likely to have a larger influence in the future educational scope of the College than was the beginning of what is in effect junior college work, through the establishment of a two-year post-high school course for boys who graduate at sixteen or under, and a one year course for those who graduate at seventeen."[53] The program of studies for this instructional group of the first students (12) to be admitted to post-high school instruction was outlined by President Herrick as follows:

---

[52] President's Report . . . for the Year 1930, op. cit., pp. 44-49.

[53] President's Report . . . for the Year 1931, op. cit., p. 48

> To make sure that this instruction should be of real collegiate grade, the part time services was secured of three college teachers,--a teacher of mathematics from the University of Pennsylvania, who is giving courses in Advanced Algebra and Analytics, a teacher of economics from the Wharton School of the University of Pennsylvania, who is giving instruction in General and Applied Economics, and a teacher of accounting, from Temple University. In addition, other courses in English, foreign languages, social sciences, chemistry, music, and in printing are being carried forward. The aim is to require at least three academic courses of college grade of each boy in this course, and to give an opportunity for the election of other academic subjects, and instruction looking to a better vocational equipment.[54]

The matter was again alluded to when President Herrick reviewed the primary orientation of his twenty-three year tenure; the Girard experience had evolved into a conventionally (if flexibly structured) high school, but with a solicitous regard for vocational and occupational components:

---

[54] Ibid., pp. 49-50. It is of significance that the College celebrated the hundredth anniversary of Girard's death, noticing the munificence of the endowment in a time of depression, as is evident in the following: "The hundredth anniversary of the death of Girard turned the thought of the community again to the increase in the Girard Estate, due to the conservation and judicious handling of the principal. With the exceptions of Harvard and Yale Universities, which are now credited with endowments of over ninety millions of dollars each, Girard College has a more munificent endowment than any other educational institution in America. The last report of the Board of Directors of City Trusts shows that the residuary estate aggregates eighty-nine millions of dollars, though it should be said that not all of this endowment is income producing. The size of this endowment has been a God-send during the past year, making it possible for the Board in control of Girard College to carry forward and improve the high order of service established for the boys already in the college, to increase the number in attendance, and out of income to continue the plans of enlargement and betterment without interruption. To have accomplished these results in any year would be notable, but to have accomplished them in a year of depression is, we believe, unprecedented." (Ibid., pp. 91-92.)

> First, there has been the recognition of Girard College as an accredited secondary school from which the certificate of the graduates is now widely accepted by institutions of higher learning. An increasing number of our boys have been going to college in late years, and practically all who have gone have made a success of their college work. Several have won distinction in the higher institutions which they have attended. In addition the training is for vocations, through which boys are sent out prepared to meet the demands of practical life.
>
> The primary aim of the College is to give first a fundamental general education, efforts being directed to this end throughout the Elementary School and for the first two years of the High School. During the last two years of the High School, specialization is introduced, with every encouragement to a boy to prepare himself along the line of what is likely to be his future interest. If there could be one criticism of secondary education in general in America, and perhaps also the same criticism could be applied to higher education, it is that our young people study loosely and carelessly too many subjects. A focusing of effort along a narrow line in which a student is interested is likely to develop more power, and to lead to more useful results. Twenty-four years ago the boys in our High School studied both trade school and commercial subjects. Of late in the last two years they are asked under guidance to choose between the commercial and the trade school divisions, and to devote their afternoons to the special branch of the division to which they go. Not only this, but after choosing one or the other of these divisions, they are still further narrowed in their effort to a particular trade or line of study in which they have shown special interests and aptitudes.[55]

What trades should be taught along with efforts to reproduce the conditions of industrial work have long remained perennial problems in the teaching of trades. Even before the opening of the new "re-constructed" Mechanical School, it was suggested that telegraphy, wireless operation, engraving, and watch and clock repairs be considered as new courses of instruction.[56] Evidently, the suggested courses were never pursued. As

---

[55] President's Report and Catalogue of Pupils Girard College, the City of Philadelphia, Trustee, for the Year 1933, p. 49.

[56] Board of Directors of City Trusts, Minutes, Committee on Instruction, Vol. V, October 6, 1922 to June 3, 1932, Minutes of May 9, 1924 (p. 63).

noted earlier, however, instruction in painting and finishing and in auto mechanics were added to the curriculum, and in 1939 the sheetmetal shop was expanded to a full trade course.[57]

At Girard College, apprenticeship and cooperative education had both been attempts to correlate or combine school instruction with shop or factory training. With the apparent failure of these work-apprenticeship exchanges to provide for the transmission of skills, Girard College, not unlike its public school counterpart, had attempted to simulate work conditions by performing the work of industry within the school shop.[58]

In 1927, the Committee on Instruction approved a plan by which the College would be empowered to enter into an agreement which would provide for the following:

---

[57]President's Report and Catalogue of Pupils Girard College, the City of Philadelphia, Trustee, for the Year 1939, p. 23. In 1923 a special committee of the Board of Directors of City Trusts had been formed to consider the purchase of a tract of land close to Philadelphia which students could use for their vacations and agricultural pursuits. While Stephen Girard made no specific provisions for agriculture to be taught, he did list it as one of "the suitable occupations" to which boys should be bound out. The proposal in 1923 was typical of the proposals made from time to time in this direction. See in this connection, President's Report . . . for the Year 1923, op. cit., pp. 79-81. The only outcome from these proposals was apparently the purchase of a camp site in the Poconos (Pennsylvania) in 1929. See in this connection, President's Report and Catalogue of Pupils Girard College, City of Philadelphia, Trustee, for the Year 1929, p. 52. President Herrick observed in this report: "Not only does the Summer camp furnish the opportunity for recreation and relief from the tedium of living in the same place and under the same conditions the year round, but it affords also an unusual opportunity for training. . . . In other words, a Summer camp affords an opportunity to teach the basals of life." (pp. 57-58)

[58]The last unsuccessful effort to provide for the transmission of skills through a work-apprenticeship arrangement was attempted in 1922 when the Committee on Instruction requested President Herrick ". . . to make inquiries as to whether it is feasible and expedient to have a larger number of boys accommodated on the School Ship Annapolis by reason of a contribution by the College to the cost of their maintenance." See in

> Resolved - in order to provide the proper instruction in heavy machine work for the pupils in the Mechanical School Machine Shop of Girard College, that the Committee on Instruction be authorized and empowered to enter into an arrangement with one or more manufacturing concerns, whereby said concern or concerns will supply and deliver to the College the necessary materials, upon which the pupils of the Machine Shop will perform the required work at such time and in such manner as is most desirable for purposes of instruction, the College to receive no compensation for the work done, and the said concern or concerns to allow for reasonable spoilage or materials and to remove from the College the finished products.[59]

An agreement with the Link Belt Company had been arranged to carry out the plan for this work, but this was not carried out. Later, in 1941, when renewed attempts at such a program were prompted by a desire to cooperate in the National Defense Program, it was explained that "Preliminary arrangements with two or more companies were made in 1927 but were never carried out because business began to fall off and the companies felt that it was unfair to their employees to farm out work in this way when the employees themselves were on a part-time schedule.[60] As a rationale

---

this connection, Committee on Instruction, Vol. V, op. cit., Minutes of October 6, 1922 (p. 2). In a subsequent report, President Herrick reported that arrangements to such an end were possible and that ". . . there appears no difficulty other than a possible legal one." (Ibid., p. 5). Minutes of December 8, 1922 record the opinion of Francis E. Brewster, Solicitor for the Estate, as follows: ". . . it is my opinion that the Board of Directors of City Trusts may place on a school ship (provided, of course, that such placing is for the purpose of instruction in navigation) such pupils of Girard College as are desirous of taking such training and who shall have remained in said college until they have arrived at an age of not less than fourteen years, the enrollment upon the school ship to expire at a date not later than the date of the twenty-first birthday of such pupil. However, the Board, in my opinion, has no right to pay for any of the expenses incurred for the maintenance and education of any minor so indentured." (Ibid., Minutes of December 8, 1922, p. 11). In 1941, Francis E. Brewster reiterated his stand when again asked for an opinion. Brewster's "adverse opinion" concerning the right of the Board of Directors to provide training outside the College, prompted the conclusion that the matter should be dropped. See in this connection, Committee on Instruction, Vol. VI, op. cit., Minutes of January 3, 1941 (pp. 206-207) and Minutes of February 7, 1941 (p. 210).

[59]Committee on Instruction, Vol. V, op. cit., Minutes of February 4, 1927 (pp. 157-158).

[60]Board of Directors of City Trusts, Minutes, Committee on Instruction, Vol. VI, June 30, 1932 to June 16, 1944, Minutes of December 19, 1941 (p. 235).

to implement such an agreement, President Herrick observed: ". . . that the work was to be engaged in only for instructional purposes." It was further noted that under a "Gentlemen's Agreement," the company should make a gift or donation after calculating spoilage to the Girard College Alumni Fund or to use the amount to set up a scholarship at a local university for a Girard College alumnus.[61]

The pervasive influence of World War II was apparent in the Girard College experience. Girard College President Merle M. Odgers[62] outlined the possible changes that might directly occur in his Annual Report for the Year 1940.

> Not many decades ago American secondary schools had as their main objective the preparation for college admission of a small number of students who were to enter the professions, the arts, and the sciences. The subsequent change in the number and the objectives of secondary school students has emphasized the importance of vocational education and has presented to educators, especially those in public schools, many difficult problems. In our century the enrollment in American high schools has doubled every decade; the Twenties saw it increase seven times faster than our population.
>
> . . . .
>
> It is desirable to say something concerning the relation of the Mechanical School to the National Defense Program, in which almost all Americans have joined either in activity or in spirit. Vocational schools throughout the nation are becoming increasingly involved in this program, chiefly by organizing afternoon and evening classes of adults to make full use of existing equipment. By the terms of the Girard Will we cannot join in such activities without special permission from the courts. Whether, as time goes on, the production of specified articles may be assigned to us, remains to be seen. However, this does not mean that we are not doing our part in training for National Defense.
>
> It is no indication of complacency to say that our school shops have for many years been doing the very things which the government now urges all schools to do. During the years when industry

---

[61] Ibid.

[62] On April 2, 1940, Merle M. Odgers was inducted as President of Girard College. (President Herrick had completed twenty-five years as President of the College.) There is no life of Odgers in the DAB.

> almost ceased to train young men for the skilled trades, and large numbers of so-called vocational classes in schools were little more than classes in industrial arts, our Mechanical School has maintained its fine equipment of factory-type machines, has trained our boys in practical production work, and has satisfactorily prepared them to take whatever jobs in industrial production were avilable. That upwards of seventy graduates of recent years are now employed in the Glenn Martin airplane factory in Baltimore, and that our graduates are quickly absorbed in other expanding industries, indicate that our present responsibility is to keep on doing what we have been doing.
>
> Girard College does not need to make drastic modification in order to take its part in a National Defense program. We do believe, however, that the immediate employability and skill of our boys in connection with the Defense Program will be improved by providing more opportunities to use light portable machine tools such as electric hammers, electric drills, and welding equipment. We are therefore planning to add early in 1941 several relatively inexpensive pieces of such equipment, so that a larger number of our boys may receive training in the use of these tools. A few hours of training will be enough for boys already well taught in fundamental machine work.[63]

However, the extent to which Girard College was to be allowed to participate became clear in President Odgers' Annual Report for the Year 1941. He explained:

> Under the terms of the Girard Will (the first paragraph of Section XXI and the codicil dated June 20, 1831) our work must be restricted to Girard boys. We cannot offer our equipment for use in evening classes of WPA or NYA youth, or for the part-time training of workers in industry. These privileges are being granted on a splendid scale by the public vocational schools of the nation. Nor does the government, as yet, expect any school to produce specific items for use in the army or navy. That is the job of industry. However, as part of the instructional procedure in the machine shop and foundry our boys make parts of defense machinery produced by a neighboring industrial plant which supplies the material. The instructors see in this not only a fine educational experience for our boys but also a sense of satisfaction to both

---

[63] Report of the President Girard College, the City of Philadelphia, Trustee, for the Year 1940, pp. 25-27.

> boys and instructors that Girard College can do something specific and very helpful in the cause of National Defense.[64]

The immediate effects of the war on Girard College life were given by President Odgers in a capsule review in his Annual Report for the Year 1943. He concluded:

> For 1943 no marked progress can be noted of the sort that in the past we could point to with pride. We have experienced the wartime difficulties of all boarding schools. We have been troubled by shortages in domestic help, by the closing of the House Group and the Summer Camp, by a turnover in the staff of the Household Department, by scarcities, rationing, higher costs, and delays in the delivery of materials, and by two quarantines. Most departments, however, have given their usual high level of performance and even those most hampered by war conditions have done truly commendable work.
>
> No essential services have been curtailed There has been some increase in the emphasis laid on physical education, and changes have been made in other features of the older boys' training to meet the needs of the armed forces. But

---

[64]Report of the President Girard College, the City of Philadelphia, Trustee, for the Year 1941, pp. 44-45. President Odgers saw fit to note that "The outstanding event in the High School for the year was the survey conducted in the spring under the direction of the Cooperative Study of Secondary School Standards." (p. 38). Generally, the Evaluating Committee commented favorably on the High School program; however, the following comments were made: "The most serious problem which disturbed the visiting committees was in relation to the Intermediate High School. The feeling of segregation from the rest of the group which this group has, seems to be unnecessary. The visiting committees recommend a general curriculum in the High School, with emphasis upon general functional education. . . . When such curriculum is developed, the boys with abilities similar to those of the boys in the Intermediate High School might select this curriculum. This work could be provided under the administration of the High School as one of the choices in the High School program. . . . As far as the visiting committees could determine, these boys are capable of doing a kind of work which in other schools is recognized as satisfactory." (p. 39). President Odgers acknowledged these criticisms as being on the "right track" and that the usefulness of this unit had been outlived. (Ibid.) In President Odgers' Annual Report for the Year 1942, he noted the following: "The recommended abolition of the Intermediate High School and the substitution of a general course were referred to [in the 1941 Annual Report]." This change was made in September, 1942. See in this connection, Report of the President Girard College, the City of Philadelphia, Trustee, for the Year 1942, p. 26.

> there has been no great change made in our basic educational offering, since we are still preparing our boys primarily to live in a world at peace. A considerable extension of the Student Work Program has been necessary. Boys and staff have both had additional burdens placed upon them because of the war, but the relatively high level of student morale is very gratifying to the staff.[65]

However, the war experience at Girard College was a clearly differentiated experience from that which prevailed generally in the nation. The restrictive criteria for outside participation imposed by the terms of Stephen Girard's Will were further exacerbated by the ineligibility of the College to serve in a multiplicity of training and other educational programs which, generally, proved a boon to other educational institutions.

> Congress has enacted legislation providing payment to schools for the rehabilitation training of men who leave the armed services. Both public and privately endowed schools may enroll for this work. The terms of payment of tuition, however, are so restricted that few, if any, endowed schools can undertake this work without facing a serious financial loss. Girard College is completely debarred from giving such training under the terms of the Will. Even for our own alumni, the best we can do is to advise them concerning opportunities for retraining in other institutions.[66]

---

[65] President's Report and Catalogue of Pupils Girard College, the City of Philadelphia, Trustee, for the Year 1943, pp. 66-67. The Student Work Program had been instituted at Girard College in 1933 when the effects of the depression upon the College's revenue had compelled an economy program. The program had begun as one of "self-help" and has continued in varying form. See in this connection, President's Report . . . for the Year 1933, op. cit., p.   The "self-help" idea had a continuing history at Girard College. Many of its administrators believed that the boys would benefit from such a program. See in this connection, supra, pp. 199 and 223.

[66] Report of the President Girard College, the City of Philadelphia, Trustee, for the Year 1944, p. 25.

Nevertheless, Girard College emerged from its war experiences, obviously affected, but apparently unshaken. For the Mechanical School, President Odgers made note of its underlying philosophy while suggesting that its rationale was of proven value and would remain. He noted:

> Post-war reconversion in the Mechanical School means preparing our boys for peace-time industry. This reconversion calls for a change of emphasis rather than a substitution of content. Our philosophy of vocational education is based on the proved value of our three years of prevocational training designed to give our boys opportunity for self-discovery through exposure to the fundamentals of a considerable number of industrial and commercial occupations. This is followed by two years of intensive experience in one line of work selected under conditions of continuing guidance.
>
> Even during the war years your Board has been sympathetic and generous in making allotments for new equipment. Our hopes that satisfactory equipment for the Mechanical School might be secured from government surplus material have not been realized. Investigation has shown that, so far, government surplus material has either been unsuited to our use, badly worn, inaccessible, or so involved in procedures for buying ("as is" and "where is") by a method of competitive bidding and in unit lots, that we could not make satisfactory purchases. Better fortune may be ours in the future; we feel certain that we shall find available items in other areas.[67]

This same theme, *i.e.*, that any expected changes in the Mechanical School (which by now had administratively become the Mechanical Department of the High School) would reflect ". . . no changes in the basic program . . . but such would be mainly in the form of emphasis rather than eliminations or additions" was set forth in 1946.[68] These changes were implemented the following year and were outlined by President Odgers as follows:

---

[67] *Report of the President Girard College, the City of Philadelphia, Trustee, for the Year 1945*, p. 28.

[68] *Report of the President Girard College, the City of Philadelphia, Trustee, for the Year 1946*, p. 33. This report also notes that the Head of the Mechanical Department recommended a full trade course in plumbing and welding. (*Ibid.*) These recommendations were apparently not followed.

> The most significant and important change in the Mechanical Department has been the reduction of time devoted to prevocational and exploratory courses, which will be carried on in the future under the supervision of the trade teachers. Much more individual attention is now given to the younger boys. No exploratory work, however, is given below the seventh grade; thus is shortened the gap between the prevocational work and trade instruction. The entire staff of the Mechanical Department has centered its efforts on economy measures [italics added], and pupil hour cost has been appreciably reduced. Wherever possible, equipment and supplies have been obtained from Government war-surplus sources. Unlike much of this material given to schools, the great bulk of what we have obtained has been profitably distributed and used in the Mechanical Department, the Department of Buildings and Grounds, and in other departments.[69]

The necessity for economy was cogently outlined by President Odgers in the following year (1948) which unceremoniously brought Girard College

---

[69]*Report of the President Girard College, the City of Philadelphia, Trustee, for the Year 1947*, p. 29. In this *Report*, President Odgers reviewed, if somewhat circumspectly, the history of the Post High School which had in a half generation run its course: "The Post High School was started in 1931, largely because of our inability to place the youngest graduates of that period in positions or in college. Since that time it has provided for such boys a year of freshman college work. The University of Pennsylvania granted sufficient credit for this Post High School work to enable a Girardian to complete the College of Liberal Arts or the Wharton School course in three years and a summer session. Other colleges followed this example. Following the war it became difficult to place students in any college of first rank with advanced credit. Moreover, we have much more income from the Minor Trusts for helping boys go to colleges and universities than heretofore, and the Alumni Loan Fund has also grown to very considerable proportions. And then too we have never been able to provide a real college freshman situation, for the class has always been small and has had nowhere to live but the Junior School Building, where the observance of the usual rules concerning smoking and freedom of movement must be observed. It is generally recognized that both as a matter of educational and social adjustment it is better for a student upon leaving his preparatory school to enter at once upon a full four-year course instead of breaking the program by attending two different institutions of higher education. The Post High School appeared to have outlived the usefulness which it certainly had in the past. The work of the Post High School will be concluded early in 1948. This will permit a considerable saving, particularly in the recovery of part of the service of a few of our best teachers who have given time to the Post High School. It should be understood, however, that we shall keep our eyes open to the possibility that with changes in the world about us a Post High School may again become a desirable feature of our work." (*Ibid.*, pp. 32-33.)

to the centennial of its founding.

> Inflation has severely affected the work of Girard College. Unlike many other educational institutions and educational systems, we are unable to resort to increased tuition fees, increased tax rates, or increased state appropriations to meet higher costs. Our income has increased despite the limitations imposed upon trusts funds, but the increase in income is far outstripped by the increase in the costs of services and supplies.
>
> As a result, we have been under the necessity of eliminating or curtailing many of the useful services which we consider desirable in order to lower the budget for 1949 under that of the year just passed by approximately one quarter of a million dollars. Boarding schools everywhere, of course, have had to meet this problem of inflated costs. Schools charging tuition fees have adjusted their fees to the change in the purchasing power of money. Such tuition increases have been unavoidable because of the widening gap, in dollars, between what the student pays for his education and maintenance, and what it costs to provide them. Girard, however, has no present alternative but to cut its pattern to fit the cloth and, while recognizing that almost all economies in a contracted program are harmful, make such curtailment or elimination of services as will cause the least harm. Further decrease in income or the value of the dollar would lead to a reduction in the number of boys carried on the rolls.[70]

IV

> The Centennial made 1948 an unforgettable year at Girard College. And now the first year of its second century closes with the institution in enviable condition except in the matter of income necessary to meet current costs. We hope, but there is no assurance, that the next few years will find Girard College not too adversely affected by budgetary problems. Of one thing the writer is sure--the loyalty and devotion of those who are carrying on the work of Girard College, for they have a deep conviction of the importance and worthwhile nature of their task. As he goes to various phases of his work, from Board meetings to kitchens, from office interviews to Chapel, from classes to soccer practice, from dormitory visits to battalion drill, from student meetings to staff conferences, the writer is impressed by the character of the men, women, and boys, old and young, who make Girard what it is, from the President of the Board to the "newbies" in the House Group, and he is proud to be associated with them.[71]

---

[70] *Report of the President Girard College, the City of Philadelphia, Trustee, for the Year 1948*, p. 33.

[71] *Ibid.*, p. 35.

The Centennial at Girard College in 1948 was the occasion of a broad spectrum of praise and commendation of the College's efforts in behalf of orphaned youth. How widely known Girard College had become nationally is affirmed by President Harry S. Truman's ceremonious function as one of the celebrants at the occasion.[72] Other individuals spoke on a variety of themes: the financial resources of the College; the fatherly benefactions of Stephen Girard; Stephen Girard as an individualist; the meaning of Founder's Day; the fruits of perseverance and work; the freedom of man; Stephen Girard as a Franco-American, banker, mariner and merchant, and educational pioneer; the animus and intent of Stephen Girard's will; the significance of Girard College among educational institutions; reflections of former students; and valedictory orations.[73]

---

[72]President Truman's visit to Girard College was appropriately made on Founder's Day, May 20, 1948, and he was presented with a statuette of Stephen Girard in memory of his visit which occurred during the Centennial celebration of the College and on the 198th anniversary of Stephen Girard's birth. The address by President Truman is found in _Proceedings of the Girard College Centennial_, pp. 167-172. The volume notes that President Truman was the seventh President of the United States to have visited the College. The other Presidents included: James K. Polk, Franklin Pierce, Benjamin Harrison, James Buchanan, Ulysses S. Grant, and Rutherford B. Hayes. (_Ibid._, p. 16.)

[73]See generally, _Proceedings_ . . . _Centennial_. It is noted in the _Proceedings of the Girard College Centennial_, ". . . the chief purpose of this Centennial Celebration was to show the development of Girard College as an educational institution. The very core of the proceedings, therefore, consisted of a series of carefully planned addresses on educational topics presented by men of national prominence." The Educational Symposium took place on May 19th, 20th, and 21st of May 1948. The participants included Dean Ernest O. Melby of New York University; Dr. Claude M. Fuess, Headmaster of Phillips Andover; Dr. George F. Zook, President of the American Council on Education; Dean William F. Russell, Teachers College, Columbia University; and Dean Harold Benjamin, College of Education, University of Maryland.

No one of these discourses dealt with the realities of program implementation at Girard College; and, perhaps, objective critical assessments would have been considered inappropriate. However, E. Duncan Grizzell, Dean of the School of Education of the University of Pennsylvania, did deal, if somewhat cautiously, with Girard College as an institution, evolving as a result of three important influences, which Grizzell notes as ". . . the traditional patterns of the institutions of the land of their origin, the social, economic, and other influences of their present environment, and the ideals to which they are dedicated."[74]

Grizzell boldly sketches out the uniqueness of the College at the time of its origin, pointing up that unlike its public school counterpart, the College was free from public tax support but yet retained under public control (*i.e.*, its Board of Directors of City Trusts). Girard College, Grizzell notes, was born at a time of the well-known American academies and high schools and had withstood the struggle for survival, a claim only a few of the early schools could make. Of equal relevancy was Grizzell's reference to the early design of Girard College being an outgrowth of European models due to the efforts of Francis Lieber and Alexander Dallas Bache;[75] and Grizzell's own opinion that the often suggested English Public School influence on Girard College was more dominant in the more recent years, largely due to President Herrick's study of English Public School practice, than in the early years as had often

---

[74]E. Duncan Grizzell, "The Place of Girard College Among Educational Institutions," *Proceedings of the Girard College Centennial*, p. 222.

[75]See *supra*, pp. 46-69.

been suggested.[76]

Grizzell's reference that the pioneer achievement of the school to provide an education in an independent boarding school for economically disadvantaged youth was not outside early pioneer educational contributions to the education of boys who were in the mainstream of social and economic distress. However, Grizzell is somewhat far-reaching in ascribing a contemporary uniqueness to Girard College based on ". . . reference to the objectives expressed or implied [italics added] in Girard's will."[77] Grizzell observes: "He [Girard] believed in a foundational education to a certain point for all, and formal education beyond that point should be provided by those who could profit by it."[78] Rather, Grizzell comes closer to hitting the mark in a subsequent paragraph where he notes:

---

[76]E. Duncan Grizzell, *op. cit.*, p. 223. President Herrick in his *Annual Report for 1927* had acknowledged the influence of the English Public Schools, but this remained essentially unconvincing and perhaps tendentious: "The early records of Girard College indicate the influence of the English public schools. In the first twenty-five years of Girard College's existence the example of Rugby was of large influence throughout the world. The changes introduced during the past year have brought new elements of the English public schools into the administration of the College. In a large measure the English schools are self-governing. One of their interpreters has well said that their character is determined quite as much by the boys themselves as by their masters. The observation has frequently been made that the regulations which boys make for each other and which they enforce one upon another are likely to be more strict and drastic than are rules made by their teachers or housemasters." See in this connection, *President's Report and Catalogue of Pupils Girard College, the City of Philadelphia, Trustee, for the Year 1927*, p. 18. Grizzell noted that the development of "smaller living units" was based on the English "house." Grizzell also noted that "The emphasis upon the development of character as a major function of the school is a generally recognized English practice and quite contrary to standard continental practice." (E. Duncan Grizzell, *op. cit.*, p. 223.)

[77]*Ibid.*, p. 224.

[78]*Ibid.* *Cf.* *Stephen Girard's Will*, Article XX, para. 7,9.

"Although Girard probably did not visualize his new institution as being concerned with preparation for further education, his curricular plans were so flexible that boys with intellectual aptitudes and interests have had no difficulty in meeting the requirements of higher institutions with the most rigorous standards. . . ."[79] For Grizzell, it is apparent that the importance he attributes to Girard College is based on the school's socializing function rather than its programatic constructs; in fact, the "fitting words" of President Herrick he chooses to close his discourse make this eminently clear:

> In the last analysis, Girard College is a little world. Boys are living their lives here in the formative periods. They are getting their equipment for the life to which they will later go, and they are fitted for the real world just so far as the elements and features of this world are brought into their training. In this newer conception of education, the school is more than a preparation for life, it is life.[80]

The Centennial was an auspicious occasion, but in many ways it marked an end to much of the search for viable programs which address themselves to a practical fulfillment for Stephen Girard's plan for meaningful, functional education for deprived youth. In a period of post-war uncertainty, and rapidly changing urban contexts, the administration at Girard College accommodated itself to a variety of influences no one of which it was able to completely control. Mounting fiscal problems preoccupied the Girard administration.

President Odgers had indicated in his Annual Report for 1948 that ". . . we have been under the necessity of curtailing many of the useful

---

[79] E. Duncan Grizzell, loc. cit.

[80] Ibid., p. 228. See also, E. Duncan Grizzell, "The Place of Girard College Among Educational Institutions," Educational Outlook, vol. XXIII (November 1948), pp. 32-38. This issue of Educational Outlook had as its theme, "A Century of Girard College."

services . . . in order to lower the budget for 1949. . . ."[81] For the most part, this attempt at general economy apparently formed the basis for an administrative reorganization which was begun in the Fall of 1949. The program was designed to provide the following:

---

[81] Report of the President . . . for the Year 1948, op. cit., p. 33. The fiscal problems are dealt with in considerable detail by the President of the Girard Board of Directors of City Trusts: "In 1898, and for some twelve or fourteen years later, we graduated 25 out of every 100 boys admitted to the College. From Dr. Herrick's incumbency down to the present we have graduated about 75 out of each 100 boys admitted. This was brought about by better selection of boys and greater attention to the boys as individuals in both educational and physical welfare. Larger expenditures per boy per year consequently became necessary. Of the 9400 boys admitted from 1898 to 1948, a greater percentage graduated than was the case with the 5900 boys admitted from 1848 to 1898.

In 1898 the average expenditure for maintenance and education was about $300. The budget for Girard College for the year 1948 contemplates an average expenditure per boy of $1750.

This means that for every boy in Girard College there must be invested capital amounting to $75,000 to provide an income of $1750 necessary to his maintenance and education. This is figured on the current interest rates of 2-1/2%.

The largest number of boys we ever had in the College was about 1800--by crowding we could probably accommodate 2000.

To maintain and educate 1800 boys on the basis of today's inflated costs would require an income of $3,150,000. This is approximately 2-1/2% on $135,000,000 invested capital--which we do not have.

An interesting comparison is that of our assets in 1897 as compared with those of 1947:

	December 31 1897	December 31 1947
Girard College Grounds & Bldgs.	$5,000,000.	$13,000,000.
Real Estate in Philadelphia	9,000,000.	19,973,000.
Real Estate Outside of Philadelphia . .	8,000,000.	3,661,896.
Personal Estate, Bonds, Mortgages . . .	4,900,000.	51,670,727.
Cash	25,000.	587,138.
	$26,925,000.	$88,893,629.

Note that $13,000,000 is not income producing. The real estate outside of Philadelphia provides addition to capital amount only. We, therefore, have $71,500,000 to produce income for Girard College." (Proceedings . . . Centennial, pp. 34-35.)

> (1) the better co-ordination of the entire life of the Girard boy, (2) an improved schedule of the day, week, and year to fit the needs of our boys at mid-century and the present-day geographical distribution of their homes, and (3) more economical operations and organization.[82]

Of particular note, was the feature of the new program dealing with vocational specialization:

> The replacement of the former sixteen-period-a-week assignment of vocational specialization for juniors and seniors with twelve periods a week in the first curriculum, fifteen periods a week in the second curriculum, and nineteen periods a week in the third curriculum. Thus, the boys of the first curriculum who progress faster, or are more academic-minded, have less vocational work than heretofore; those of the second curriculum have approximately the same amount as heretofore; those of the third curriculum have more vocational work.[83]

At this point in time, there is also a very clear diminution of programs and services and the evidence of continuing diminution in efforts along these lines. This is evident from President Odger's note:

> The budget for the year under review reflects many savings through the curtailment of services and the discontinuance of some positions and services. Among the positions discontinued as a matter of economy, rather than as part of the reorganization previously described, were those of two teachers, three part-time teachers, two industrial supervisors, one dentist, one shoe repairman, one watchman, three office employees, one science laboratory assistant, one postal clerk, and one assistant laundry foreman. Among others there were curtailments in painting and wall-washing, and elimination of summer school tutoring and some trips for large groups.[84]

In 1950, it was observed: "It is regrettable to note the inroads made on the work of the College by inflation, which forces the professional staff of the College to do its utmost not to sacrifice much progress

---

[82] _Report of the President Girard College, the City of Philadelphia, Trustee, for the Year 1949_, p. 14.

[83] _Ibid._, p. 15.

[84] _Ibid._, p. 51.

that has been made."[85] And in 1951 it was further explained:

> Unfortunately, there are several compulsions or forces that have Girard College at their mercy. First, there is the shrunken and shrinking value of the dollar: the inescapable effects of a national inflation, about which the Board and the administration can do nothing. Second, there is the relatively fixed income available. Third, there is the natural desire to compensate employees as well as possible, as is evidenced by the almost general increase in salaries and wages effected earlier this year and the general increase in wages planned for 1952. Fourth, there is the natural desire to avoid a reduction in enrollment in order to reduce expenditures. Fifth, there is a natural pride in the standards of excellence maintained by the College, a natural pride in its educational offerings and in the product that gives the College its enviable reputation. If it is assumed that one or more of these forces must give way before the rest, it can be easily understood how some intellectual blood, sweat, and tears are the portion of your Board and the administration of the College. Since we charge no fees at all, we cannot resort to an increase in fees, as most educational institutions have done.
>
> . . . .
>
> Yet even some alumni and other friends of Girard are surprised when they learn that for five years, from 1947 to 1951, both inclusive, Girard College has operated at a deficit. The effects of inflation are severe upon an institution which cannot resort to an increase in tuition fees, income from tax sources, or state appropriations, none of which Girard College receives. Since the expenditures for payrolls and supplies have exceeded the net income for five years, they have eaten into the modestly small surplus income to just that extent, as the following table shows:

Year	Net Income Available	Total Expenses	Deficit
1947	$2,351,242.11	$2,429,023.56	$77,781.45
1948	2,349,666.73	2,549,604.46	199,937.73
1949	2,081,885.51	2,341,543.35	259,657.84
1950	2,236,108.69	2,256,183.29	20,074.60
1951	2,236,030.80	2,295,688.10	59,657.30
Total	$11,254,933.84	$11,872,042.76	$617,108.92

> The highest average enrollment was equalled in 1939, when Girard College had 1735 boys and operated with total expenditures of $1,750,314.77. The following figures, which are separated in time by only twelve years, are interesting as revealing the effects of inflation:

---

[85] *Eighty-first Annual Report of the Board of Directors of City Trusts, Philadelphia, for the Year 1950*, p. 9.

Year	Average Number of Boys	Total Expenses
1939	1735	$1,750,314.77
1951	1303	2,295,688.10 [86]

Against these data, the expense of providing vocational education and the implicit consequences for this type of education become clear when seen against President Odgers' reflections on vocational training. He explained:

> Mr. Girard provided in his Will for a considerable list of academic subjects that the Girard student must pursue. Though he made no provision for vocational training, this has been added during the history of the College. Thus there has developed the unique double curriculum. We make no apology for vocational education, even though a legalistic person might raise his eyebrows at our offering it.
>
> At Girard College our purpose in offering vocational education is to prepare the boy to earn his living. But, because of the academic requirements of the Girard Will, *we are not in a position, even if we wished, to provide exclusively vocational curricula comparable to those offered by the so-called vocational high schools or trade schools*. [italics added]
>
> We are proud of our unique double curriculum, but our pride is tempered, in a period of financial pressure, by the fact that it is also uniquely expensive. For our upper years it demands virtually a double faculty. In the list of teachers that appeared in the last Annual Report one may count sixteen vocational teachers (twelve in mechanical instruction and four in business education), several times the number that one would find in another academic secondary school, public or private, of our size.
>
> Business education in itself, though somewhat comparable to classroom academic work, is expensive enough on the secondary level, but vocational education in the shops is unquestionably the most expensive type of secondary education, except tutoring. The student-teacher ratio is less favorable because of the necessity of keeping classes small, the plant is usually more expensive to maintain because of floor space required, and the equipment is costly to replace or repair. Thus, even under the most favorable conditions, training in the machine shop or the print shop of a department of mechanical instruction is considerably more expensive than classes in history or mathematics, for example.[87]

---

[86] *Report of the President Girard College, the City of Philadelphia, Trustee, for the Year 1951*, pp. 5-6, 24.

[87] *Ibid.*, pp. 16-17.

In 1952, the effects of post-war inflation were seen in a general reduction in the College staff, which reflected significant changes in vocational training. The changes encompassed a number of essential facets of the vocational program which in essence allowed for ". . . less freedom for the boys in the choice of vocational curricula."[88] The specific changes were as follows:

> The reduction in staff and in the variety of curriculum affected all departments of the upper school, but it might be well to summarize at this point the changes brought to vocational training by the economy program.
>
> . . . .
>
> The services of the instructor in machine shop practice and the assistant instructor in printing were discontinued on August 31. At this time the Department of Mechanical Instruction has the following eight shops: Automotive, Carpentry, Electrical, Machine, Pattern Making, Printing, Sheet Metal, and Trade Drafting. The staff consists of nine men: the department head and one instructor in each of the eight shops. The teaching of blue print reading has been restored and is being taught by the Machine Shop and Electrical Shop instructors. The instructor in sheet metal work was transferred to the machine shop, and the print shop was continued under one instructor. The small building adjoining the main building of the Department of Mechanical Instruction houses both the sheet metal shop and the foundry. Depending upon the needs of the boys it lends itself ideally to the operation of either, under the direction of the former instructor in foundry. The foundry will not be operated in the year 1952-53.
>
> The vocational trade shops for juniors and senior students are open five days a week during the three afternoon periods, a total of fifteen periods a week. Pre-vocational courses, sometimes called exploratory or "try-out" courses, are held during the mornings with eighth-grade students receiving instruction in carpentry, pattern making, and sheet metal work, ninth-grade students receiving instruction in auto mechanics, printing, and mechanical drawing, and tenth-grade students receiving instruction in machine shop practice, the electrical shop, blue-print reading, and in other vocational offerings. In the eighth and ninth grades boys spend two double periods each week for twelve weeks in each of the three shops. In the tenth grade, boys spend two double periods each week for nine weeks in each of two shops, and

---

[88] _Report of the President Girard College, the City of Philadelphia, Trustee, for the Year 1952_, p. 19.

during the same eighteen weeks they divide two additional double periods between blue-print reading and the study of vocational opportunities, the last mentioned being taught by the department head. During the remaining eighteen weeks of the tenth grade, boys attend eight periods each week in business-education exploratory courses, five periods of which are in junior business training and three in typewriting.

In the tenth grade, two sections of approximately thirty boys each attend shop courses the first half of the year, while the other two sections pursue business education; in the second half of the year the sections reverse their activities. In the pre-vocational shop courses for eighth and ninth-grade boys, each section of approximately thirty boys is divided into three groups of ten boys each. Although this increases the number of morning periods a week in each teacher's roster, it is deemed advisable in order to make more intensive work possible. It also reduces the group size from fifteen to ten boys, and this is an improvement, especially for beginners, both in the instruction and in the important item of safety control.

The foregoing plans have been worked out with an eye to economy and the most effective use of the abilities of the remaining teachers in the two vocational-educational areas. The year 1952-53 will be more or less of a transition year. Even though there will be less vocational choice in the future, vocational shop classes will always be expensive for the reasons stated in my report for 1951. It will not be possible, for sound educational and for safety reasons, to expand their size to the requirements of the rest of the Board's economy program.[89]

---

[89] _Ibid_., pp. 20-22. See also in this connection, _Board of Directors of City Trusts, Minutes, Committee on Instruction_, Vol. VIII, April 1949 to December 12, 1961, Minutes of June 20, 1952 (pp. 94-95). The restoration of blue-print reading was evidently due to the continued request of the head of the Department of Mechanical Instruction, who, in an earlier _Annual Report_, had called attention again to ". . . the serious loss to boys in not having any instruction in blue-print reading. . . ." See in this connection, _Report of the President Girard College, the City of Philadelphia, Trustee, for the Year 1950_, p. 15. As an economy measure, it was also decided in 1952 to increase the size of the instructional groups. President Odgers explained: "In the spring of 1952 it was decided that, beginning in September, 'wherever feasible, and without depriving boys of any specific prerequisite for future training,' instructional groups in the standard branches of instruction should be increased in size to thirty or more. At the same time, your Board noted that this would involve the elimination of the third curriculum designed for boys of low ability and that when such boys were scheduled in the second curriculum of the class, the 'change, in spite of the best efforts of both faculty and boys, may result in the separation of some boys,' who, while able to keep up with the third curriculum, may be unable to cope

What is apparent during the late 1950's was an attempt by the College administration to maintain the vocational facet of the College while at the same time meeting fiscal responsibility.[90] Joined with this was the evident concurrent reality that more and more, the Girard College program was arduously developing into a college preparation sequence with the broad general curriculum which supported such a program. Vice-President E. Newbold Cooper[91] explained this in the President's Report for the Year 1954:

> The present Girard College secondary school program in part emphasizes preparation for college. It is strongly influenced in this direction by the fact that a steadily rising number of our graduates are attending institutions of higher learning. Increasingly higher education seems to be regarded as a national requisite. Our experience in this respect is the reflection of a national trend, which finds more students of all levels each fall seeking and obtaining opportunities

---

with the work of the second curriculum. The Board also decided that, beginning in the autumn, classes of fewer than fifteen should not be rostered, except with the specific approval of the Committee on Instruction." See in this connection, Report of the President . . . for the Year 1952, op. cit., p. 5. As noted, the size of vocational shop classes was not affected by this rule. However, as a further economy measure, the Board of Directors of City Trusts approved the sale of the Summer camp which would allow for a small increase in the College's income. See in this connection, Ibid., p. 10.

[90]The Minutes of the Committee on Instruction during this period include numerous entries allowing for the scheduling of shop classes with less than 15 students. See, e.g., Committee on Instruction, Vol. VIII, op. cit.; Minutes of June 20, 1952, p. 96; Minutes of September 18, 1953, pp. 137-138; Minutes of September 17, 1954, p. 179; Minutes of June 17, 1955, p. 206; Minutes of July 20, 1956, pp. 245-246; Minutes of June 21, 1957, p. 274; Minutes of September 20, 1957, p. 278; Minutes of June 20, 1958, pp. 297-298; Minutes of September 19, 1958, p. 304; Minutes of June 19, 1959, pp. 328-329. However, the Minutes of March 17, 1961 (pp. 379-380) and October 20, 1961 (pp. 392-393) record that due to a decreasing student enrollment, the Sheet Metal Shop and the Auto Shop would be discontinued in the fall of 1961.

[91]President Merle M. Odgers resigned the presidency of Girard College on December 1, 1954 to become President of Bucknell University. Vice-President E. Newbold Cooper assumed the duties and responsibilities of the presidency until the Board of Directors of City Trusts elected him president effective May 1, 1955. See in this connection, Eighty-fifth Annual Report of the Board of Directors of City Trusts, Philadelphia, for the Year 1954, p. 7.

> for advanced study. Social Security and Veterans' Administration payments enable a majority of our students to build up funds to finance from one to four years of further education. Alumni are making much use of the so-called "G.I. Bill," which provides money for post-high-school training in many branches of learning. We also have many other sources available for scholarships, so that a Girardian who has the ability can almost invariably obtain necessary aid. Our distinct responsibility is to maintain a curriculum preparatory for institutions of post-high-school grade and representative of high standards of academic achievement.[92]

In 1958, the reconsideration of a dual curriculum became more pressing in light of a general national concern with the national structure of education due in part to the groundswell for educational excellence exemplified by the efforts of Dr. James B. Conant. On this point, Vice-President Karl R. Friedmann[93] noted:

> Perhaps the most encouraging feature in national education is the finding reported by Dr. James B. Conant, former President of Harvard University and more recently United States

---

[92]President's Report and Catalogue of Staff and Students Girard College, the City of Philadelphia, Trustee, for the Year 1954, p. 20. The difficulty in managing a dual program of studies was pointed up by President Cooper in his Annual Report for the Year 1956. He noted: "The decision, therefore, made in 1949, under Dr. Merle M. Odgers' leadership, that provision should be made for a rising proportion of students who would require college preparation, has seemed ever more wise. More poor boys (and girls) are going to college in the future than was ever imagined in the past. . . . If the tendency for so many seniors to enter college directly after graduating here should continue, we may have to reconsider our total program, particularly with reference to the relative emphasis placed upon the academic and the vocational programs of study. It seems true that for a significant group of our students college preparation is becoming vocational preparation and cannot be ignored. In such a case, there may be need to provide more time for an increased academic program, smaller-sized classes, and a shorter period of vocational training. It should not be overlooked that the seeds of inspiration, ambition, and hope for advanced training are sown in the minds of the boys by the excellent staff." See in this connection, Report of the President . . . for the Year 1956, op. cit., p. 37.

[93]President E. Newbold Cooper died on August 4, 1957. Pending the selection of a President, Vice-President Karl Friedmann assumed the duties of the presidency. See in this connection, Eighty-eighth Annual Report of the Board of Directors of City Trusts, Philadelphia, for the Year 1957, p. 9.

> Ambassador to the Federal Republic of Germany, in his study, "The American High School Today," that the program on the secondary level is, in general, fundamentally sound. Changes in emphasis on some courses to develop better the capacities of the pupils, with special attention given to the academically talented, is a major theme of his report. In any school, the most effective operation of a good basic program becomes the prime responsibility of administration and staff.
>
> . . . .
>
> For Girard there are implications which point to curricular changes extensive enough to warrant reconsideration of the philosophy of a dual curriculum and the possibility of maintaining it for all students. Dr. Conant's proposals, particularly for the abler students, will result in stricter requirements for the more traditional academic subjects--English, foreign languages, social studies, mathematics, and science--and in more demanding course content.
>
> Admirable and desirable as the revisions in program may be, the effect at Girard would be to place further pressure and strain upon our curricular offerings. With the present limitation to a five-year course in secondary education, instead of the usual six years common to other school systems, and with the requirement of both an academic and vocational course for every pupil, the schedule does not permit additions to the program. It is inevitable that a serious reconsideration of our dual curriculum must be faced and a new program developed which will reflect both a basic philosophy as to the kind of school Girard ought to be and the quality of students needed to populate it.[94]

These developments must be understood in the context of a wide range of problems which Girard College encountered in attempting the implementation of defined educational objectives. In 1959, President Friedmann referred to other educational uncertainties influencing the administration of the College in his Annual Report:

> More than a century ago Stephen Girard laid upon those charged with the operation of his school the responsibility for providing "a better education, as well as a more comfortable maintenance, than they usually receive from the application of the public funds." In the early period of the school's history, an era when public education, especially on the secondary level, was almost non-existent in Pennsylvania and when orphan institutions were frequently

---

[94] Annual Report and Catalogue of Staff and Students Girard College, the City of Philadelphia, Trustee, for the Year 1958, pp. 13-14, 16.

> a disgrace to our communities, the achieving of the Founder's goal required only mediocre standards. But the great strides of the past two or three decades in the philosophy and practice affecting dependent children's care and in improved educational provision for all the children of all the people [italics in the original] make it very much more difficult to achieve the Founder's objective today.[95]

---

[95] Report of the President and Catalogue of Staff and Students, Girard College, Philadelphia, Pa., for the Year 1959, p. 35. Although the efforts to integrate Girard College (in keeping with the Civil Rights Movement whose genesis lay in the late 1950's) are outside the purview of this dissertation, it is important to call them to attention since these efforts directly intruded into (and in a sense further exacerbated) the educational problems which the College was experiencing along with those difficulties which had been evident for some period of time in articulating viable programs. For an overview of the litigation which surrounded the admission of non-whites to Girard College see Charles MacNamara, "Stephen Girard: The Will," Greater Philadelphia, LVII (January, 1966), pp. 62-64, 128-136; Bernard McCormick, "Girard College: The Way," Greater Philadelphia, LVII (January, 1966), pp. 65-66, 118-127; William G. Weart, "Five Injured in Clash Over Girard College," The New York Times, July 13, 1965, pp. 1, 22; Edward C. Burks, "N.A.A.C.P. Is Waging a 'War of Attrition' at Girard College," The New York Times, May 14, 1965; William G. Weart, "A Private School is N.A.A.C.P. Target," The New York Times, January 17, 1965; Peter A. Janssen, "1830 Humanitarian Who's Out of Step With 1965," New York Herald Tribune, December 19, 1965, p. 19. See also the following publications of the Girard College Alumni Association: "Girard Will Case," Steel and Garnet, LXII (October, 1957), pp. 1, 7; "Chronological History of Current Girard Will Case," Steel and Garnet, LXII (October, 1957); "District Court Says Girard Subject to Public Accommodations Act," Steel and Garnet, LXX (October, 1966), p. 3; Girard College Alumni Association, In Defense of the Will of Stephen Girard (Philadelphia, October 5, 1966); E. Alfred Smith, Stephen Girard and His Will (Philadelphia: Girard College Alumni Association [1960].) It is important to note, concomitant with much of the integration litigation, that legal administrative restructuring of the governing board of the College had occurred on March 25, 1959. "By decree of the Orphan's Court of Philadelphia County, . . . the Board of Directors of City Trusts was discharged as Trustee of the Estate of Stephen Girard, Deceased." (Ninetieth Annual Report of the Board of City Trusts of the City of Philadelphia for the Year 1959, p. 2.) The responsibility for the operation of the foundation was placed under the charge of the Trustees of the Estate of Stephen Girard, Deceased, whose members were appointed by the Orphans Court of Philadelphia. (Report of the President . . . for the Year 1959, op. cit., p. 13.) At the time of the transfer of the assets from the Board of Directors of City Trusts to the Trustees for the Estate of Stephen Girard, Deceased, the estate's value was placed at more than $100,000,000. See in this connection, "Girard Estate Assets Transferred to New Trustees," Steel and Garnet, LXII (March, 1959), p. 1.

The College had reached a point of stasis, and further development in the 1960's was almost totally precluded. As the College entered the 1960's, its administrators described its program in considerable detail. President Friedmann observed: "An educational institution needs to make its name and program widely and favorably known."[96] Beyond the newspaper releases on students and graduates to increase the public's awareness, President Friedmann indicated that ". . . two pamphlets, Learning About Girard College and Introducing Girard College, will be supplemented early in 1961 with a new all-purpose catalogue."[97] The Secondary School Program of Studies is presented in these publications in considerable detail, and it was so to remain to the present:

SECONDARY SCHOOL PROGRAM OF STUDIES

Junior High School

Grade 8		Grade 9	
English	4	English.	4
Speech Training	1	Speech Training . . .	1
Developmental Reading	1	French I	5
Arithmetic	5	Algebra I	5
United States History (Inc. Current Events)	5	Science	5
Science	4	Pennsylvania History	3
Pre-Vocational Shop . .	4	Pre-Vocational Shop. .	4
Library	1	Health	1
Physical Education . .	2	Social Guidance . . .	1
General Music	1	Physical Education . .	2
		Library	1

Two periods of Art or one Period of Instrumental Music are optional in the Junior High School. Instrumental music is optional in the Senior High School.

---

96 Report of the President and Catalogue of Staff and Students Girard College, Philadelphia, Pa., for the Year 1960, p. 30.

97 Ibid.

Senior High School

ACADEMIC

Grade 10		Grade 11		Grade 12	
English	4	English	4	English	5
Speech Training	1	Speech Training	1	Speech Training	1
French II	5	Plane Geometry	5	Problems of Democracy	4
Algebra II	5	U. S. History	4	French IV*	4
World History / Biology	5	Physics*	5	Algebra II	4
General Business and Typing	8	French III*	4	Trigonometry and Advanced Algebra	5
Pre-Vocational Shop	8	Business Education, or Shop	12	Art	4
Health	1	Library	1	Life Problems	4
Physical Education	2	Physical Education	2	French III	4
				World History	4
				Biology	5
				Chemistry	5
				Business Education, or Shop**	12
				Library	1
				Physical Education	2

*Required of enriched program
**8 periods for boys taking the enriched program

GENERAL

Grade 10		Grade 11		Grade 12	
English	4	English	4	English	4
Speech Training	1	Speech Training	1	Speech Training	1
World History	5	Plane Geometry	4	Problems of Democracy	4
Algebra I	5	U. S. History	4	French IV	4
World History / Biology	5	Physical Science	5	Algebra II	4
General Business and Typing	8	Physics***	5	Life Problems	4
Pre-Vocational Shop	8	French III	4	French III	4
Health	1	Business Education, or Shop	15	World History	4
Library	1	Library	1	Basic Chemistry	5
Physical Education	2	Physical Education	2	Business Economics	5
				Biology	5
				Business Education, or Shop	15
				Library	1
				Physical Education	2

***With the approval of the Science Department [98]

98"Secondary School Program of Studies," Girard College, Philadelphia, Philadelphia [1961], p. 7. The Secondary Program of Studies has remained the same as is apparent in the latest catalog, Girard College [1967], et seq. The reduction of 12 to 8 periods of Business Education or Shop for boys taking the enriched program was due to a change in the high school curriculum to allow college-bound students additional preparation in academic areas. This change points up the difficulty imposed by the dual curriculum and the inherent time limitations. See in this connection Committee on Instruction, Vol. VIII, op. cit., Minutes of March 18, 1960, pp. 348-349.

However meaningful the program of studies might have seemed, it is evident that curricular problems remained to be solved. In his Annual Report for 1963-64, President Friedmann described the general difficulties surrounding the curriculum for which he hoped a satisfactory solution might be found. He explained:

> For many years Girard College has required of all secondary school pupils preparation in both the academic and vocational fields, a dual program which has been a source of strength and pride. Trends in secondary education, however, are placing increasing pressure upon this concept. Requirements in a number of the academic fields, increased both qualitatively and quantitatively, can be met for the average student only by an increase in time allotments for these subjects. When this takes place, the development of vocational skills is adversely affected.
>
> Conditions largely beyond our control, both within and without the College, raise the question as to whether the dual program can function as effectively in the future as it has in the past. In the attempt to find an answer, a Curriculum Committee has been at work throughout the year. It is hoped that program recommendations can be ready for consideration during the coming year.[99]

It was apparent that no solutions were forthcoming.[100] Instead of curriculum revision, the fiscal health of Girard College was solicitously guarded, and with continuingly successful management. However, curriculum

---

[99] Report of the President and Catalogue of Staff and Students Girard College, Philadelphia, Pa., for the Year April 1, 1963 to March 31, 1964, p. 17. The Report of the President for 1961 extended from January 1, 1961 to March 31, 1962 in keeping with a change of the College's fiscal year beginning April 1. Subsequent reports follow that change.

[100] In the Spring of 1960 President Friedmann appointed a Committee to draft a statement of the school's present philosophy and objectives. The Committee submitted its report in 1964; instead of looking at curriculum, the Committee defined its task in socio-philosophical terms: "From the outset of its deliberations the Committee was determined (1) to take a hard look at the present College program in light of problems created by the rapidly changing world, and (2) to set forth definitive objectives toward which to strive in providing intelligent answers to these problems." See in this connection, The Girard College Program: Philosophy and Objectives, 1964, p. 2.

and programmatic response in a world which was changing ineluctably presented insurmountable problems to the Girard College administration. These sentiments were echoed by President Friedmann in his Annual Report for 1964-65, and presaged the decade which lay ahead:

> With its dual requirement in the academic and vocational areas, Girard offers broad opportunities in secondary education not usually available elsewhere. To some staff observers it appears that this breadth is achieved at the expense of sufficient depth to meet the national demand for improved education on this level. Time is the controlling factor. To complete in five years at Girard a more extensive secondary education program than is required at other schools, public or private, in six years is admittedly a most difficult task. The comparison of hourly requirements per course at other schools with those at Girard and the insistence upon both increased quantity and improved quality of offerings present a challenge that must be closely examined. Eventually the answer to this challenge may be found only in significant revisions of the Girard College program.[101]

---

[101] Report of the President and Catalogue of Staff and Students Girard College, Philadelphia, Pa., for the Year April 1, 1964 to March 31, 1965, p. 27. The last decade has shown no significant change in the Girard history; perhaps, significant change could not occur until the problems of deteriorating urban contexts were resolved, and Girard College's relationship to new urban constituencies defined. It is of passing interest to note that on Founder's Day (Mary 20, 1968) ". . . the United States Supreme Court made public its refusal to review the decision of a Federal District judge--later upheld by the Federal Appeals Court--ordering a change in the Will's specified admissions requirements." See in this connection, "A letter from the College President," Steel and Garnet, LXXII (July, 1968), p. 1. In June, 1968, the Board of City Trusts of the City of Philadelphia resumed control of the foundation. In September, 1968 non-white students were admitted to the College. In January, 1969 Dr. Gayle K. Lawrence assumed the presidency of Girard College. Continuing unresolved difficulties are made graphically clear in recent news accounts: Donald Janson, "Girard College May Close as Enrollment Plummets," The New York Times, August 13, 1972, p. 52; and "Girard College in a New Battle," The New York Times, May 27, 1973, p. 39.

APPENDIX A

EXCERPTS FROM THE STEPHEN GIRARD WILL[1]

XX. And, whereas, I have been for a long time impressed with the importance of educating the poor, and of placing them, by the early cultivation of their minds and the development of their moral principles, above the many temptations to which, through poverty and ignorance, they are exposed; and I am particularly desirous to provide for such a number of poor male white orphan children, as can be trained in one institution, a better education, as well as a more comfortable maintenance, than they usually receive from the application of the public funds; and whereas, together with the object just adverted to, I have sincerely at heart the welfare of the City of Philadelphia, and, as a part of it, am desirous to improve the neighbourhood of the river Delaware, so that the health of the citizens may be promoted and preserved, and that the eastern part of the City may be made to correspond better with the interior: Now, I do give, devise and bequeath, all the residue and remainder of my real and personal estate of every sort and kind wheresoever situate, (the real estate in Pennsylvania charged as aforesaid) unto "the Mayor, Aldermen and Citizens of Philadelphia, their successors and assigns, in trust, to and for the several uses, intents and purposes hereinafter mentioned and declared of and concerning the same, that is to say; so far as regards my real estate in Pennsylvania, in trust, that no part thereof shall be ever sold or alienated by the said Mayor, Aldermen and Citizens of Philadelphia, or

---

[1] The excerpts are from the holograph will deposited at Girard College.

their successors, but the same shall forever thereafter be let from time to time, to good tenants, at yearly or other rents, and upon leases in possession not exceeding five years from the commencement thereof, and that the rents, issues and profits arising therefrom, shall be applied towards keeping that part of the said real estate situate in the City and Liberties of Philadelphia constantly in good repair, (parts elsewhere situate to be kept in repair by the tenants thereof respectively) and towards improving the same, whenever necessary, by erecting new buildings; and that the net residue (after paying the several annuities herein before provided for,) be applied to the same uses and purposes as are herein declared of and concerning the residue of my personal estate: and so far as regards my real estate in Kentucky, now under the care of Messrs. Triplett & Brumley, in trust, to sell and dispose of the same, whenever it may be expedient to do so, and to apply the proceeds of such sale to the same uses and purposes as are herein declared of and concerning the residue of my personal estate.

XXI. And so far as regards the residue of my personal estate, in trust, as to <u>two millions of dollars</u>, part thereof, to apply and expend as much of that sum as may be necessary, in erecting, as soon as practicably may be, in the centre of my square of ground between High and Chestnut streets, and Eleventh and Twelfth streets, in the City of Philadelphia, (which square of ground I hereby devote for the purposes hereinafter stated, and for no other, forever,) a permanent College with suitable out-buildings, sufficiently spacious for the residence and accommodation of at least three hundred scholars, and the requisite teachers and other persons necessary in such an institution as I direct to be established, and in supplying the said College and out-buildings with decent and suitable furniture, as well as books and all things needful to carry into effect my general design.

The said College shall be constructed with the most durable materials, and in the most permanent manner, avoiding needless ornament, and attending chiefly to the strength, convenience, and neatness of the whole: It shall be at least one hundred and ten feet east and west, and one hundred and sixty feet north and south, and shall be built on lines parallel with High and Chestnut streets, and Eleventh and Twelfth streets, provided those lines shall constitute at their junction right angles: It shall be three stories in height, each story at least fifteen feet high in the clear from the floor to the cornice: It shall be fire proof inside and outside. The floors and the roof to be formed of solid materials, on arches turned on proper centres, so that no wood may be used, except for doors, windows and shutters: Cellars shall be made under the whole building, solely for the purposes of the Institution; the doors to them from the outside shall be on the east and west of the building, and access to them from the inside shall be had by steps, descending to the cellar floor from each of the entries or halls hereinafter mentioned, and the inside cellar doors to open under the stairs on the north-east and north-west corners of the northern entry, and under the stairs on the south-east and south-west corners of the southern entry; there shall be a cellar window under and in a line with each window in the first story--they shall be built one half below, and the other half above the surface of the ground, and the ground outside each window shall be supported by stout walls; the sashes should open inside, on hinges, like doors, and there should be strong iron bars outside each window; the windows inside and outside should not be less than four feet wide in the clear: There shall be in each story four rooms, each room not less than fifty feet square in the clear; the four rooms on each floor to occupy the whole space east and west on such floor or story, and the middle of the building north and south; so that in the north of the building, and in the south thereof, there may remain a space of equal dimensions, for an entry or hall in each, for stairs and landings: In the north-east and in the north-west corners of the northern entry or hall on the first floor, stairs shall be made so as to form a double staircase, which shall be carried up through the several stories; and, in like manner, in the south-east and south-west corners of the southern entry or hall, stairs shall be made, on the first floor, so as to form a double staircase, to be carried up through the several stories; the steps of the stairs to be made of smooth white marble, with plain square edges, each step not to exceed nine inches in the rise, nor to be less than ten inches in the tread; the outside and inside foundation walls shall be at least ten feet high in the clear from the ground to the ceiling; the first floor shall be at least three feet above the level of the ground around the building, after that ground shall have been so regulated as that there shall be a gradual descent from the centre to the side of the square formed by High and Chestnut, Eleventh and Twelfth Streets: all the outside foundation walls, forming the cellars, shall be three feet six inches thick up to the first floor, or as high as may be necessary to fix the centres for the first floor; and the inside foundation wall, running north and south, and the three inside foundation walls running east and west (intended to receive the interior walls for the four rooms, each not less than fifty feet square in the clear, above mentioned,) shall be three feet thick up to the first floor, or as high as may be necessary to fix the centres for the first floor; when carried so far up, the outside walls shall be reduced to two feet in thickness, leaving a recess outside of one foot, and inside of six inches--and when carried so far up the inside foundation walls shall also be reduced six inches on each side, to the thickness of two feet; centres shall then be fixed on the various recesses, of six inches throughout, left for the purpose, the proper arches shall be turned, and the first floor laid; the outside and the inside walls shall then be carried up to the thickness of two feet throughout, as high as may be necessary to begin the recess intended to fix the centres of the second floor, that is, the floor of the four rooms, each not less than fifty feet square in the clear, and for the landing in the north, and the landing in the south of the building where the stairs are to go up--at this stage of the work, a chain, composed of bars of inch square iron, each bar about ten feet long, and linked together by hooks formed of the ends of the bars, shall be laid straightly and horizontally along the several walls, and shall be as tightly as possible worked into the center of them throughout, and shall be secured wherever necessary, especially at all the angles, by iron clamps solidly fastened, so as to prevent cracking or swerving in any part; centres shall then be laid, the proper arches turned for the second floor and landings, and the second floor and landings shall be laid; the outside and the inside walls shall then be carried up of the same thickness of two feet throughout as high as may be necessary to begin in the recess intended to fix the centers for the third floor and landings, and, when so far carried up, another chain, similar in all respects to that used at the second story, shall be in like manner worked into the walls throughout, as tightly as possible, and clamped in the same way with equal care; centres shall be formed, the proper arches turned, and the third floor and landings shall be laid: the outside and the inside walls shall then be carried up, of the same thickness of two feet throughout, as high as may be necessary to begin the recess intended to fix the centres for the roof; and when so carried up, a third chain, in all respects like those used at the second and third stories, shall in the manner before described, be worked as tightly as possible into the walls throughout, and shall be clamped with equal care; centres shall now be fixed in the manner best adapted for the roof, which is to form the ceiling for the third story, the proper arches shall be turned, and the roof shall be laid as nearly horizontally as may be, consistently with the easy passage of water to the eaves; the outside walls, still of the thickness of two feet throughout, shall then be carried up about two feet above the level of the platform, and shall have marble capping, with a strong and neat iron railing thereon. The outside walls shall be faced with slabs or blocks of marble or granite, not less than two feet thick, and fastened together with clamps securely sunk therein,--they shall be carried up flush from the recess of one foot formed at the first floor where the foundation outside wall is reduced to two feet. The floors and landings, as well as the roof, shall be covered with marble slabs, securely laid in mortar; the slabs on the roof to be twice as thick as those on the floors. In constructing the walls, as well as in turning the arches, and laying the floors, landings, and roof, good and strong mortar and grout shall be used, so that no cavity whatever may anywhere remain. A furnace or furnaces for the generation of heated air shall be placed in the cellar, and the heated air shall be introduced in adequate quantity, wherever wanted, by means of pipes and flues inserted and made for the purpose in the walls, and as those walls shall be constructed. In case it shall be found expedient for the purposes of a library, or otherwise, to increase the number of rooms, by dividing any of those directed to be not less than fifty feet square in the clear, into parts, the partition walls to be of solid materials. A room most suitable for the purpose shall be set apart for the reception, and preservation of my books and papers, and I direct that they shall be placed there by my executors, and carefully preserved therein. There shall be two principal doors of entrance into the College, one into the entry or hall on the first floor, in the north of the building, and in the centre between the east and west walls, the other into the entry or hall in the south of the building, and in the centre between the east and west walls; the dimensions to be determined by a due regard to the size of the entire building, to that of the entry, and to the purpose of the doors. The necessity for, as well as the position and size of other doors, internal or external, and also the position and size of the windows, to be, in like manner, decided on by a consideration of the uses to which the building is to be applied, the size of the building itself, and of the several rooms, and of the advantages of light and air: there should in each instance be double doors, those opening into the rooms to be what are termed glass doors, so as to increase the quantity of light for each room, and those opening outward to be of substantial wood work well lined and secured; the windows of the second and third stories I recommend to be made in the style of those in the first and second stories of my present dwelling house, North Water Street, on the eastern front thereof; and outside each window I recommend that a substantial and neat iron balcony be placed, sufficiently wide to admit the opening of the shutters against the walls; the windows of the lower story to be in the same style, except that they are not to descend to the floor, but so far as the surbase, up to which the wall is to be carried, as is the case in the lower story of my house at my place in Passyunk Township. In minute particulars, not here noticed, utility and good taste should determine. There should be at least four out-buildings, detached from the main edifice and from each other, and in such positions as shall at once answer the purposes of the Institution, and be consistent with the symmetry of the whole establishment: each building should be, as far as practicable, devoted to a distinct purpose; in that one or more of those buildings, in which they may be most useful, I direct my executors to place my plate and furniture of every sort.

The entire square, formed by High and Chestnut streets, and Eleventh and Twelfth streets, shall be enclosed with a solid wall, at least fourteen inches thick, and ten feet high, capped with marble and guarded with irons on the top, so as to prevent persons from getting over; there shall be two places of entrance into the square, one in the center of the wall facing High street, and the other in the centre of the wall facing Chestnut street, at each place of entrance there shall be two gates, one opening inward, and the other outward; those opening inward to be of iron, and in the style of the gates north and south of my Banking house; and those opening outward to be of substantial wood work, well lined and secured on the faces thereof with sheet iron. The messuages now erected on the south-east corner of High and Twelfth streets, and on Twelfth street, to be taken down and removed as soon as the College and out-buildings shall have been erected, so that the establishment may be rendered secure and private.

When the College and appurtenances shall have been constructed, and supplied with plain and suitable furniture and books, philosophical and experimental instruments and apparatus, and all other matters needful to carry my general design into execution; the income, issues and profits of so much of the said sum of two millions of dollars as shall remain unexpended, shall be applied to maintain the said College according to my directions.

1. The Institution shall be organized as soon as practicable, and to accomplish the purpose more effectually, due public notice of the intended opening of the College shall be given--so that there may be an opportunity to make selections of competent instructors, and other agents, and those who may have the charge of orphans, may be aware of the provisions intended for them.

2. A competent number of instructors, teachers, assistants, and other necessary agents shall be selected, and when needful, their places from time to time, supplied; they shall receive adequate compensation for their services: but no person shall be employed, who shall not be of tried skill in his or her proper department, of established moral character, and in all cases persons shall be chosen on account of their merit, and not through favour or intrigue.

3. As many poor male white orphans, between the age of six and ten years, as the said income shall be adequate to maintain, shall be introduced into the College as soon as possible; and from time to time, as there may be vacancies, or as increased ability from income may warrant, others shall be introduced.

4. On the application for admission, an accurate statement should be taken in a book, prepared for the purpose, of the name, birth-place, age, health, condition as to relatives, and other particulars useful to be known of each orphan.

5. No orphan should be admitted until the guardians or directors of the poor, or a proper guardian or other competent authority, shall have given by indenture, relinquishment or otherwise, adequate power to the Mayor, Aldermen and Citizens of Philadelphia, or to directors or others by them appointed, to enforce in relation to each orphan every proper restraint, and to prevent relatives or others from interfering with or withdrawing such orphan from the Institution.

6. Those orphans, for whose admission application shall first be made, shall be first introduced, all other things concurring--and at all future times priority of application shall entitle the applicant to preference in admission, all other things concurring; but if there shall be at any time, more applicants than vacancies, and the applying orphans shall have been born in different places, a preference shall be given--_first_ to orphans born in the City of Philadelphia; _secondly_, to those born in any other part of Pennsylvania; _thirdly_, to those born in the City of New York (that being the first port on the continent of North America at which I arrived:) and _lastly_, to those born in the City of New Orleans, being the first port on the said continent at which I first traded, in the first instance as first officer, and subsequently as master and part owner of a vessel and cargo.

7. The orphans admitted into the College, shall be there fed with plain but wholesome food, clothed with plain but decent apparel, (no distinctive dress ever to be worn) and lodged in a plain but safe manner; Due regard shall be paid to their health, and to this end their persons and clothes shall be kept clean, and they shall have suitable and rational exercise and recreation. They shall be instructed in the various branches of a sound education: comprehending Reading, Writing, Grammar, Arithmetic,

Geography, Navigation, Surveying, Practical Mathematics, Astronomy, Natural, Chemical, and Experimental Philosophy, the French and Spanish languages, (I do not forbid, but I do not recommend the Greek and Latin languages,) and such other learning and science as the capacities of the several scholars may merit or warrant. I would have them taught facts and things, rather than words or signs; and especially, I desire that by every proper means a pure attachment to our republican institutions, and to the sacred rights of conscience, as guaranteed by our happy constitutions shall be formed and fostered in the minds of the scholars.

8. Should it unfortunately happen, that any of the orphans admitted into the College, shall, from malconduct, have become unfit companions for the rest, and mild means of reformation prove abortive, they should no longer remain therein.

9. Those scholars, who shall merit it shall remain in the College until they shall respectively arrive at between fourteen and eighteen years of age; they shall then be bound out by the Mayor, Aldermen and Citizens of Philadelphia, or under their direction, to suitable occupations, as those of agriculture, navigation, arts, mechanical trades, and manufactures, according to the capacities and acquirements of the scholars respectively, consulting, as far as prudence shall justify it, the inclinations of the several scholars, as to the occupation, art or trade, to be learned.

In relation to the organization of the College and its appendages, I leave, necessarily, many details to the Mayor, Aldermen and Citizens of Philadelphia, and their successors; and I do so, with the more confidence, as from the nature of my bequests, and the benefit to result from them, I trust that my fellow-citizens of Philadelphia, will observe and evince especial care and anxiety in selecting members for their City Councils, and other agents.

There are, however, some restrictions, which I consider it my duty to prescribe, and to be, amongst others, conditions on which my bequest for the said College is made, and to be enjoyed, namely; First, I enjoin and require, that if, at the close of any year, the income of the fund devoted to the purposes of the said College shall be more than sufficient for the maintenance of the Institution during that year, then the balance of the said income, after defraying such maintenance, shall be forthwith invested in good securities, thereafter to be and remain a part of the capital; but, in no event, shall any part of the said capital be sold, disposed of, or pledged, to meet the current expenses of the said Institution, to which I devote the interest, income, and dividends thereof, exclusively: Secondly, I enjoin and require that no ecclesiastic, missionary, or minister of any sect whatsoever, shall ever hold or exercise any station or duty whatever in the said College; nor shall any such person ever be admitted for any purpose, or as a visitor, within the premises appropriated to the purposes of the said College. In making this restriction, I do not mean to cast any reflection upon any sect or person whatsoever; but, as there is such a multitude of sects, and such a diversity of opinion amongst them, I desire to keep the tender minds of the orphans, who are to derive advantage from this bequest, free from the excitement which clashing doctrines and sectarian controversy are so apt to produce; my desire is, that all the instructors and teachers in the College, shall take pains to instill into the minds of the scholars the purest principles of morality, so that, on their entrance into active life, they may, from inclination and habit, evince benevolence towards their fellow creatures, and a love of truth, sobriety, and industry, adopting at the same time such religious tenets as their matured reason may enable them to prefer. If the income, arising from that part of the said sum of two millions of dollars, remaining after the construction and furnishing of the College and out-buildings, shall, owing to the increase of the number of orphans applying for admission, or other cause, be inadequate to the construction of new buildings, or the maintenance and education of as many orphans as may apply for admission, then such further sum as may be necessary for the construction of new buildings and the maintenance and education of such further number of orphans, as can be maintained and instructed within such buildings as the said square of ground shall be adequate to, shall be taken from the final residuary fund hereinafter expressly referred to for the purpose, comprehending the income of my real estate in the City and County of Philadelphia, and the dividends of my stock in the Schuylkill Navigation Company--my design and desire being, that the benefits of said institution, shall be extended to as great a number of orphans, as the limits of the said square and buildings therein can accommodate.

APPENDIX B

TESTIMONY OF WILLIAM J. DUANE[1]

WM. J. DUANE being called, sworn by the Chairman, says:

Mr. Girard made more than one will before the one that I drew. The date of the one drawn before the one I drew in 1826, compared with the one I drew, was a miniature. The one I drew was in full length. The materials of the will of 1826 were, in part, used in preparing the will made in 1830. I drew the will of Mr. Girard of 1830. This is the will under which the trust originated. I was left out of the Select Council in October, 1832. I was in Council at the time of Mr. Girard's death. He died 26th December, 1831. In consequence of my relation to Mr. Girard, and position in Council, I took an active part in all matters preparatory to the execution of the trust. The offer of premiums was brought forward for models while I was in Council, against my consent. I believed it necessary to have the aid of some skilful gentleman in the erection of the College. I thought the will sufficiently explicit in the hands of some skilful gentleman. I should undoubtedly have consulted a skilful architect. My reasons for resorting to a skilful architect was, that I have not sufficient confidence in myself to consult about turning arches, and other particulars. If Mr. Girard had made me the sole trustee, I should have employed some skilful architect to aid me in carrying out the instructions of the will, the intention of the testator. Many conversations took place with Mr. Girard and myself, years before his death, in

---

[1] Reports of the Majority and Minority of the Select Committee Relative to the Estate of Stephen Girard . . . (Harrisburg: Henlock & Bratton, 1842), pp. 23-26.

relation to the College. At length, when we began to write the will, it occupied many weeks in preparing it. The outlines, the bones and muscles of the will, were all Mr. Girard's. The aid I rendered was in putting on flesh and color. As stated by Mr. Strickland, yesterday, Mr. Girard considered himself not merely a good merchant and banker, and farmer, but a good builder. Although, therefore, Mr. Girard was opposed to any interference with his views, his designs were carried out in the will, notwithstanding some doubts of my own were made known to him at the time. I made suggestions in relation to the College, which were invariably overruled. He said I did not understand building as well as he did. After the will had been made, conversations continued in relation to the contemplated College; and it was at my respectful suggestion that he changed the location. He took time to consider whether the alteration should be made. (I suggested the noise and tumult of the city, and the yellow fever, &c.) In consequence, Mr. Girard purchased the forty acres on the Ridge road, after making inquiries elsewhere. He visited Peel Hall twice before his death. On each occasion I was in his company. The grounds were examined, and under his direction an investigation was made to ascertain whether stone could be found to build a wall around, which was to have been done before anything else in relation to the College. He directed his mason to make a search for stone. I do not know that he ever stated to any one what his object was in relation to that purchase, or putting a wall around this. He employed as head mason, Mr. Ingram, to make inquiries in relation to the stone. It was found that the stone on the premises were not suitable. Mr. Girard continued to make inquiries. His mind was directed to the building of the College himself; and if he had lived, he would have built it. He also contemplated that his will should be redrawn from beginning to end, and additions and alterations made; and in that state of mind died. I remained four or five weeks in Mr. Girard's room, the door locked, making the will; upon which occasion all subjects were discussed--law, politics, religion and architecture--consequently, a great deal of conversation did take place between us in relation to the building. I took the most anxious pains to depict in writing what the College would be, if a painter had put it on canvas. The writing was read over two or three times, and drafts of several sections. Mr. Girard was a very good judge of language, excellent, no better. When a draft was submitted to him, he would alter, remodel, and then it would be written over. I have seen the College in progress of erection. When these pictures and models were exhibited in the Hall of Independence, I went there to look at them. The impression made by them upon me was of a painful character. I fancied what Mr. Girard would have thought, could he have risen from the grave and looked on. I do not think that he would have been pleased. If he had lived, I do not believe he would have built the College according to any of the plans, but according to his own. And to be satisfied of the correctness of my impressions, it seems to be only necessary to go in front of the College and open the will, and compare the one with the other. Several of my friends called on me, remonstrating with me against what was in progress. They thought there was about to be a departure from the will. One of them in particular, Mr. James Ronaldson, now dead, found much fault with me for not interfering to arrest what was going on. All that I could legally do was to speak to several influential persons, complaining about the building of a palace instead of a school for orphans. The complaint to me was this--I may be prolix--but as I have suffered much obliquy from my friends for several years for not interfering, this is the first opportunity I have had of explaining that I was powerless (legally.) I allude more in what I am saying, to my late friend, James Ronaldson. His complaint was founded upon that clause of the will, (the 26th clause.) He read it, and said you ought to step forward and see that a palace should not be built, to wit: "I recommend to them to close the concerns of my estate as expeditiously as possible, and to see that my intention in respect to the residue of my estate are, and shall be strictly complied with." I did not conceive that I had, legally, any right to interfere. I came to that opinion under the advice of counsel, not willing to trust my own judgment. As I could not interfere legally, I advised Mr. Ronaldson, and others who spoke to me on the subject, to address themselves to the Legislature of Pennsylvania. I believe that one or more memorials were sent to the General Assembly. In the spring of 1833, I gave that advice--whether it was done I cannot say. One was a memorial sent to the Legislature, signed by Thomas Hulme or Mr. Ronaldson, both opposed to the manner it was to be built. I believe that if the Legislature had done as they should, it would have prevented all the bad consequences that have followed; they would have checked Councils in their proceeding, and prevented the erection of the building. They did not discharge their duty to posterity in omitting to take hold of the matter. Their silence encouraged Councils to go on. I always thought the Legislature neglected their duty. Mr. Girard, in speaking of the will, always had the most beneficent view--he thought it would regenerate Pennsylvania, and the States around it. I have seen the tears roll down his cheeks in speaking upon the subject. I am led to make the last remark because Mr. Girard's memory has been badly treated--he was called an iron-hearted and iron-handed man. It is due to him, as my friend, to contradict this;--he was the very reverse. Accordingly, if I shall not be disrespectful to the Legislature, or this Committee, I think that at this late day legislative inteference may be injurious to the orphans and posterity. I think there is a disposition in the existing Councils to remedy, as far as they can, the evils which have been done. I speak as a member of the human family, not as a citizen of Philadelphia, and may myself have orphan children. Mr. Girard thought he could have completed the building in four years. He began it by making preparations for the wall. I have never gone to, or left the College, without sorrow. I have never compared the building minutely with the will. If I was about to go abroad, and make a contract with a builder to erect a house for me, and on my return found such a building as the College, I should say he had not complied with the contract. Have spoken with various members of Councils and Trustees, and never have heard a human being say the will had been complied with. The material variance in the construction of the College is in the columns. I can relate an anecdote of Mr. Girard, to show what he thought of columns. I heard Mr. Girard say he had a great mind to take down the columns in front of his Banking House--they ought never to have been there. This was in conformity to his settled principle. He was in favor of utilitarian measures. He had his own views of taste. I have no doubt he thought his plan in good taste. One reason he desired to change his will was, that he might go more into detail in the erection of the out-buildings. If by violation is meant departure from the views of the testator, I do think the will has been violated. In conversation, and by my pen, I did all that an honest man could do against the proceeding of Councils in building the College on their plan. I never memorialized Councils, as executor or citizen, upon the subject. I believe that out of the various plans submitted to Councils, there might have been a plan adopted which would have conformed as near as practicable with the intentions of the testator, and have prevented any complaint.

[The following question proposed by Mr. M'Cahen.] You have stated that the action of the present Legislature is likely to be injurious to the orphans.

I ask you again--in expressing your opinion, if you have in view the will and wishes of Mr. Girard, as to the education and future prospects of the orphan children to be educated in that College?

He answers and says:

I mean by saying the action of the present Legislature would be injurious, that I deprecate any annulment of the trust at present. That is, I hope the present Legislature will not annul the trust--any deprivation of the power of the City Councils or Trustees. Nearly all the mischief that can be done has been done, and because I think it wise and humane to make the most of the remainder of the fund, and carry out the intentions of the testator. That the College is rather a temple as it exists, than the building intended. That as a temple it is not suited for poor orphans, as the building intended would have been; but that it is in the power of those who shall have the care of the orphans, to prevent the unfavorable result apprehended by some from their being reared in such building as erected, rather than in the plain one contemplated by the testator.

W. J. DUANE.

Sworn and subscribed, February 25, 1842.

H. B. Wright, Chairman Committee.

APPENDIX C

COMMUNICATION FROM THE BOARD OF DIRECTORS OF THE GIRARD COLLEGE FOR ORPHANS TO THE SELECT AND COMMON COUNCILS [June 29, 1847]

TO THE SELECT AND COMMON COUNCILS.

The Directors of the Girard College for Orphans having learned that it is the desire of the Councils to be placed in possession of the views entertained by the Board for the organization of the College, and for the discipline and instruction to be administered therein; respectfully submit the following, as an outline of what is presently needed, and of that which may ultimately be the requirements of the institution. Their immediate object, however, is not to proceed farther than the election of the two principal Officers, viz: the President of the College, and the Matron; for the purpose of assisting them in the preparation of those minute details, that even the Primary department will demand.

The first of these officers they desire to elect as soon after Councils will authorize his appointment, as a compliance with the notice required to be given by Mr. Girard's Will, may permit; and thereafter, at some suitable time, to choose the Matron upon similar notice. When the appointment of these officers may have been approved by the Councils, and the President of the College elected, the efforts of the Board will be directed to the organization of the primary department as soon as practicable. It will be a school, in which shall be taught those branches of learning that receive attention in the Primary, Secondary, and Intermediate Schools, of what is familiarly known as the Public School system in the First District of Pennsylvania; and the instruction in which is given almost exclusively by female teachers. The complete success that has attended the labours of such teachers, both here and elsewhere, has induced the Board to adopt them for this department; and independently of the fitness of females to take charge of pupils of such tender age, their services can be commanded at more moderate salaries than those of men equally well qualified. The organization of such a department, and the proper selection of instructors for it, and of other agents, to take charge of the children when not actually engaged in study, are all, probably, that will be required for the first year, and all that this Board would now recommend.

This will be treading upon the safe and beaten path; and will afford sufficient time for the consideration of all those important and more expensive undertakings, that the plan of the liberal Founder contemplates. It must be recollected, that the Girard College has no prototype.

While liberal-minded men have heretofore provided for the establishment of Charity Schools, Orphan Houses, and endowed Professorships in Colleges, no one has ever offered so large a field, or so rich an endowment, for an institution, that shall commence its duties with the nursling, and only end them with the delivery to society of a highly educated man. Much that would seem to be applicable to schools and colleges, as ordinarily constructed, will no doubt be found inappropriate for us; and while modifications will be required, they must be the fruit of thought, and comparison. With these views, then, we submit, with great diffidence, and the consciousness of its imperfections, a plan for the organization of the Girard College for Orphans.

The report of a plan for a system of government and instruction for the Girard College for Orphans, necessarily involves the consideration of every provision that Mr. Girard has made in his Will, for the regulation of that establishment. We must turn, then, to that instrument, for the purpose of ascertaining, as well what is to be done in the preliminary stages of the existence of the College, as to what are to constitute its crowning features, when regularly in operation, as a literary institution of the highest grade.

Assuming, then, the College building, and its appurtenances, to be completed, the first duty devolving upon this Board would be, to cause plain and suitable furniture, and the needful books and apparatus to be provided; and the quantity and kind of these articles will of course depend on the age and number of the pupils to be first admitted, and the course of study they are to pursue.

The Will does not leave us in much doubt upon these points; because it expressly limits the age of the pupils when admitted, to a range of from six to ten years. The first arrangements must, therefore, be in regard to furniture, books and apparatus, only such as a large family of children, between those ages, would require in a well regulated family, of what is termed the middle class of society.

The furniture, books and apparatus, being provided, the next direction of the Will is, that a suitable number of instructors, and other agents, shall be selected, having reference to their competency in all respects; and that they shall be adequately compensated. The number and qualifications of these instructors and agents will be determined by the number of the pupils, and by their mental and physical condition when admitted. By their mental condition, we mean, whether they have ever received any regular instruction in the families of their parents, or in school; and by their physical condition, whether they have passed through the usual course of diseases affecting childhood, and thus been prepared for educational training, without resorting to medical treatment, or other means, for ensuring the requisite vigor of body, and protection from infectious or contagious maladies. The course of studies, and the careful bringing up of the children, in attachment to our American constitutional form of government, and in the knowledge of what constitutes true morality and virtue, are all laid down in the Will very clearly, and enforced by such recommendations, that no plan for the government of the College, not providing adequately for all of them, ought to be presented by this Board or receive the approbation of Councils.

We have then, in this brief summary of the requisitions of the Will of Mr. Girard, the main features of what our plan should contain, and individualizing these features, and attaching to each of them, independent, but still connected functions, we would divide our plan into three parts, viz: Government, Instruction, and Maintenance.

GOVERNMENT.

For insuring uniformity in the administration of such an establishment, and obtaining a complete supervision of every department, there must be a chief Executive Officer, who ought to be distinguished by some well known, and established title; and to whom all the other officers, agents and instructors, should be directly responsible for the performance of such duties as may, from time to time, be attached to their respective places, by the Directors. He should, we think, be styled the President of the College, and be the Governor and Father of the pupils. These two relations necessarily require that he must be a man of enlarged, and liberal education; of experience as a teacher, and that he should possess all those moral and social qualifications, that so complicated and important a trust demands. In a word, he must be qualified to direct all that is taught in the College, and to provide for the comfortable living of the inmates, by restraining the impetuous and wayward, and encouraging the timid and dull.

Requiring so much from such an officer, and limited as we are in the choice to those lay professions, which afford high compensation for the exercise of such talents, we think the salary of the President of the College ought to be Three Thousand Dollars per annum, in addition to a residence in one of the College out-buildings, already prepared for that purpose.

In the department of Government there should be, in addition to the President of the College, a Matron, who should be able, from her education and habits, to assist him in the scholastic and parental relations, that he must necessarily occupy.

Indeed, in the latter of these relations, there are few, we suppose, who would doubt the fitness of a woman of superior mind to discharge them fully. But the tendencies of our pupils will be constantly towards manhood; and while they ought to be placed in contact with the ever ready sensibilities of the female sex, the softening and humanizing effects of that contact must be invigorated, and framed for manliness, by the President of the College, and the male instructors and professors, who will be gradually brought into the service of the institution. While the Matron must be qualified to aid the President of the College in the supervision of the instruction to be given by the female teachers, she will be expected to examine and carefully regulate those matters that more especially concern the clothing, cleanliness, health, diet and lodging of the pupils.

It will not, of course, be expected, that in these she is to perform more than the wife and mother in a respectable and well-ordered household; but as the maternal head of the institution, her efforts will be felt in all that tends to make the pupils affectionate as brethren, and prepared to take their places, at no distant day, in the relations of husband and father. For such services, and to secure such influences, we have designated Eight Hundred Dollars per annum as her compensation, in addition to her boarding and lodging at the expense of the institution, in such one of the College out-buildings, and as part of the corps of female teachers, as this Board may hereafter designate.

INSTRUCTION.

The department of instruction naturally divides itself into three parts. First. That of primary education, which would embrace spelling, reading, writing, the ground rules of arithmetic, and some elementary portions of grammar, geography, history, and physical science.

Second. The Principal Course, which would probably commence with pupils of eleven, and continue until they reached fifteen years of age; and embrace Grammar, Geography, History, Arithmetic, Drawing, the principal branches of Geometry, and Mathematics, and their applications to Surveying and Navigation; Original Composition, the French, German, Spanish, and Latin languages, and full courses of Lectures on the Physical sciences, and Technology, and an elementary course on Moral science. In this department ought also to be taught, in connection with History, the political Constitutions of the several principal nations of Europe, and very much at large the Constitution and Laws of the United States, and of the several States of the Union.

Third. The Collegiate Department, in which the studies of the principal department should be extended; the Greek, Latin and Hebrew Languages, and the higher departments of the Mathematical, Physical and Moral Sciences, be prosecuted; and, indeed, all the branches of study pursued in a University, ought to be within the reach of those pupils that may be qualified for such advanced instruction.

As the ages of the pupils, when admitted, are to be between six and ten years, our first organization and arrangements must be made with reference to a body of children in that stage of life. For them, all that will be requisite is the instruction designated for the Primary department.

Upon the supposition, that during the first six months of the operations of the College, there will be admitted one hundred pupils, we would propose, that as nearly as practicable, all other things concurring, four divisions, as to age, should be first admitted, so as to form a regularly ascending classification, of nearly equal numbers; and that such rule should be observed in all subsequent admissions. For the instruction of such a number, there should be, in addition to the President and Matron of the College, one principal female teacher, and a first and second female assistant teacher.

The salary of the Principal female teacher should be Six Hundred Dollars per annum, that of the first assistant, Four Hundred Dollars per annum, and that of the second assistant Three Hundred Dollars per annum. They should all be boarded and lodged in the household of the Matron, at the expense of the institution. The division of the pupils into classes, and the particular division of the labours of the Principal, and her Assistants, must be made by the President of the College, after a careful examination of the mental condition of the pupils; and the branches to be first taught in the Primary department, and to whom they are to be taught, must also be confided to him.

In this department, there will be needed at least four Governesses, to take charge of the pupils during the hours of refection, recreation and sleep. These governesses ought to receive salaries of Two Hundred Dollars per annum each; they should board at the table of the Matron, but lodge in or near the dormitories of the pupils, so as to be ready to render them assistance in case of accident or illness. The advanced class in this department, would be ready, at the end of two years, to take their places in the principal department, and we would therefore designate the autumn of the year 1849, as the proper time for organizing that department.

We have already indicated the course of studies to be pursued in it, and it is only necessary to designate the corps of teachers for that department. There should be a Principal Male Teacher, and one male and two female assistant teachers. The Principal teacher should receive Twelve Hundred Dollars per annum, in addition to his residence in such one of the College out-buildings as may be designated by this Board for his use. The male assistant should receive Six Hundred Dollars per annum; one female assistant Five Hundred Dollars, and one Four Hundred Dollars per annum. The male assistant teacher should board at the table of the Matron, and lodge in or near the dormitories of the pupils; and the female assistants should board and lodge in the house of the Matron.

The arrangement of the studies in this department, and the division of labour among the teachers, must be made by the President of the College, according to the advanced standing of the pupils. In this department, at least three governors will be needed, to take charge of the pupils during the hours of refection, recreation and sleep. They should receive a compensation of Three Hundred Dollars per annum each, and board in the institution with the pupils, lodging in our near their dormitories, so as to be able to assist them in case of accident or illness. When the collegiate department is organized, the higher branches of education, and the instruction in the Physical Sciences, should be given by the Professors, but until then, proper courses should be instituted, and supplied with instructors drawn from the well established institutions of the City. Each of such courses would probably cost about Three Hundred Dollars.

At or about the age of fifteen, the most thoroughly trained students in this department would be prepared for the Collegiate department, and that of course, could not be regularly opened until the autumn of 1852. Although the consideration of what ought then to be taught, may involve considerable speculation, yet a strict compliance with the intention of the Councils in the Eighth Section of the Ordinance, requires that we shall attempt to indicate its appropriate courses of instruction. And here, the President of the College will probably first appear, as a regular scholastic functionary: in all the subordinate departments, he will be the Director, but not the actual teacher, except in regard to what will presently be mentioned. It is unnecessary to particularise otherwise than by the constitution of the Faculty, and by that which has already been mentioned above, what ought to form the course of study in this department. So far as a Collegiate course of the most extended character now goes, there should be

A Professor of Mental and Moral Philosophy.

A Professor of Chemistry and Mechanical Philosophy.

A Professor of Mathematics.

A Professor of Languages.

A Professor of Natural History, Anatomy, and Physiology.

A Professor of History and English Literature.

Assuming that the President of the College will fill one of these chairs, there will remain five Professors, whose salaries ought to be Two Thousand Dollars per annum each, in addition to their respective residences within the College walls. As the pupils admitted to the Collegiate department, may be supposed to be nearly, if not quite fitted for self control, in their hours of refection, recreation, and repose, but few, if any assistants to the Professors would be required, and we therefore do not deem it requisite to designate any: preferring to rely upon finding suitable tutors and monitors in a body of well educated young men, such as the students will undoubtedly be, who so far fulfil the conditions of Mr. Girard's Will as to entitle them to remain for instruction in this department of his College.

There are two departments of instruction that it will be found necessary to incorporate with, and form a part of all the foregoing, and these are Morals and Manners.

Mr. Girard has laid down, as one of the fundamental provisions for education in his College, that the pupils shall be taught the purest principles of morality and virtue. These golden principles, the pearls above all price, are now admitted by the whole civilized world, to be found in their greatest purity in the Holy Scriptures; and they can be fully taught from them without reference to the peculiar tenets of any religious sect. The instruction here must be regular and stated, and all the obligations which those scriptures teach for our duty towards God, and towards our neighbour, must be inculcated upon the pupils by the President of the

College, by the Matron, and by every teacher. It will be the special duty of the President of the College, and in case of his inability to attend, then of the Matron, either to give, or be present at the giving of such instruction, in order that a scrupulous regard may be paid to the prohibition of sectarianism; and yet at the same time, to secure the proper and full teaching of virtue and good morals.

While the President of the College shall give a general attention to the manners of the pupils; this branch of their education shall be specially cared for, by the Matron. By a prudent mingling among them, during their hours of study, and recreation, and at their meals, and by occasionally admitting them to her society as visitors; she may effect much by the influence of her example, and in case of need, by direct admonition or advice. The isolated, and conventual life of the pupils, without such advice and training, would lead to that unfitness for mingling with society, that is to be found too often in the graduates of our best Colleges.

MAINTENANCE.

The principal officer in this department will be a Steward: whose duty it shall be to provide plain and suitable food for the Matron, Teachers, and Officers, who are to be boarded in the establishment, and for the pupils; and who should be responsible for the cleanliness and good order of the apartments used by the pupils for refection and repose. His salary ought to be One Thousand Dollars per annum, in addition to his residence in a suitable building, to be provided for his use within the walls of the College. He should, under the direction of the Committee on the Household, make all needful purchases of food for the supply of the

Matron's table, and for the pupils commons; and have under his direction, such number of male and female domestics as may, from time to time, be deemed necessary by that Committee. He should also be responsible for the care and condition of the buildings and grounds of the institution, and give to the Janitor and Gardener such instructions, as will secure the observance of the rules that Committee may adopt in reference to them. The probable expenses of the department of maintenance, including the supplies of the Matron's and pupils' tables, and the wages of domestics, will be about One Dollar and Fifty Cents per head per week, for one hundred pupils.

The Clothing of the pupils, will, we suppose, be of the ordinary form worn by children of such ages; and it can perhaps be more economically obtained from respectable tradesmen, as it may be wanted, than by any attempt to make it in the establishment. In the primary department, it will cost about Fifteen Dollars per head per annum. The mending will be best attended to by employing regular tailoresses, to work either weekly, or oftener at the institution, who should receive wages by the day, and board and lodge at their own residences.

In connection with the department of maintenance, a medical department will be needed. In this, there should be at least two visiting Physicians, one of whom ought to attend at the institution daily, and oftener if required. They should receive salaries of Two Hundred Dollars per annum each: and in addition to their services in the household, as they may be required, one or both of them should examine into, and certify to the Committee of Admission and Discharge the state of health of all applicants for admission, and so far as they may be able to ascertain, whether the answers to the medical questions in the forms of admission, are verified by the appearance of the usual cicatrices, or other marks of past disease. A supply of the medicines in ordinary use should be provided, and be under the special care of the Matron.

CONCLUSION.

From the foregoing sketch of a plan for the government and instruction of the Girard College, it will be seen that the Directors recommend, in the first instance, the organization of a Primary department, to begin with about one hundred pupils; for whom the following Officers, Instructors and Agents, are, in their opinion needed.

1st.	A President of the College, ...	Salary,	$3000
2nd.	A Matron, ...	"	800
3d.	A Principal Female Teacher, ...	"	600
4th.	A first Assistant Female Teacher, . . .	"	400
5th.	A second Assistant Female Teacher, . .	"	300
6th.	Four Governesses, $200 each, ...	"	800
7th.	A Steward,.	"	1000
8th.	Two Visiting Physicians, $200 each, . .	"	400
9th.	Janitor, with board and lodging, . . .	"	300
10th.	Gardener, with board and lodging, . . .	"	300
			$7,900

The maintenance and clothing of that number of pupils, the wages of the house servants, and the supply of fuel, would probably cost Ten Thousand Dollars per annum, and the whole expenditure for Instruction and Maintenance for the first six months, with that number of pupils, be about Nine Thousand Dollars. It will be observed that this expenditure includes parental care as well as instruction and maintenance: and that the cost of these does not exceed what is allowed by the Commonwealth for the pupils in the Pennsylvania Institutions for the instruction of the Deaf and Dumb and Blind.

The supplies of Furniture, Books, and Apparatus for the same number of pupils, would cost about Five Thousand Dollars.

The foregoing estimates are made for one hundred pupils in the Primary, and the same number in the Principal department; but it ought to be observed, that while the expense of clothing the pupils will be increased as they advance in age, that increase will not be so materially felt in the annual outlay, as the salaries of the President and Matron of the College will remain constant, whatever may be the number of the pupils. And in the Collegiate department, although the expense of instruction will be greater per head than in the Primary and Principal departments; the services to be rendered by the Professors, in the advanced courses of the Principal department, will be to some extent fairly chargeable there. Such, then, is a brief outline of the plan that the Directors would recommend; it must hereafter be modified and enlarged, to meet fully the requisitions of the Will of Mr. Girard.

It must, like all other human designs, be subject to the changes which the progress of knowledge, in every department of life, necessarily brings. We trust that any plan will be so constituted, as to permit us to engraft upon it all that experience may prove to be good, and that, under the blessing of God, it may give to the world those who may be prepared, by its teachings, to be useful to mankind, and fitted for the enjoyment of his kingdom in Heaven.

By order of the Directors.

June 29th, 1847. JOSEPH R. CHANDLER, *President*.

APPENDIX D

PUBLIC LEDGER, Vol. 24 (No. 58), December 1, 1847 [Philadelphia]

The Board of Directors of the G.C. for Orphans, having taken charge of the premises and effects devised by Stephen Girard, and of the buildings erected by his trustees for a college for the maintenance and education of poor white male orphans between the ages of six and ten years; and having provided all things needful for carrying the general design into execution, now give notice:-

1st. That on the first day of January 1848 the College will be opened for the reception of orphans according to the provisions of Stephen Girard's Will, and according to any acts of the General Assembly of the Commonwealth of Pennsylvania, or ordinances of the Select and Common Councils of the City of Philadelphia which may be passed for the purpose of promoting the testator's objects.

2dly. That on and after the 15th day of December 1848, the directors will elect the following officers and agents: A President of the College, a Matron; a Steward, a Principal Female Teacher, a First Assistant Female Teacher, a Second Assistant Female Teacher, four governesses, and two Visiting Physicians; and that until the said day the Directors will receive applications from those who may desire to fill any of these stations.

3dly. That from and after the 1st day of December 1847, the Directors will receive applications from the admission of orphans into the college.

In order that those who may have the charge of Orphans, may act understandingly, the Directors prepared explanations and forms for their information, and they annex a copy of them to the present notice. They will besides, give such further advice and aid to applicants as may facilitate the early admission of Orphans into the College.

Those who have heretofore applied for the admission of Orphans, are requested to call on some one of the Committee on Admissions, in order to put their several applications in the shape described in the annexed forms.

By Order of the Board
Joseph R. Chandler
President of the Board of Directors
of the G.C. for Orphans

APPENDIX E

REPORT OF THE COMMITTEE ON ADMISSION AND DISCHARGE RELATIVE TO BINDING ORPHANS TO SUITABLE OCCUPATIONS

[February 27, 1852]

At the stated meeting of the Directors of the Girard College, on the 8th of October last, they authorized the Committee on Admission and Discharge, to "consider and report what measures ought to be adopted by the Directors, respecting the orphans who, from time to time, may arrive at between fourteen and eighteen years of age."

If, instead of simply authorizing the committee to consider and report, the Directors had desired prompt attention on the part of the committee, to the subject referred to them, they would so have expressed themselves, and the committee would have performed the duty at an early day. But, probably, the Directors conceived that the proposed inquiry was a grave one, and that ample time for reflection was necessary. Besides, as no provision had been made, by any law or ordinance, for binding orphans arrived at between fourteen and eighteen years of age; and as the Directors had asked the attention of the City Councils to that omission, the committee were disposed to await the action of those bodies.

These observations are made in order to account for the apparent tardiness of the committee in making the report, which the Directors provided for in October last. Instead of admitting that there has been any unnecessary delay on their part, the committee would not even now present a report, if an impression, which they consider an erroneous one, did not prevail in the College, namely, that orphans who are fourteen years of age, are to go out in the spring. If this is an erroneous impression, it ought to be at once removed, for it disturbs the feelings and minds not only of the orphans, but of their mothers and friends: and on the other hand, if orphans of the age of fourteen years are to be bound out in the spring, the change ought to be announced by those who are competent to make it.

The committee, therefore, without awaiting the decision of the City Councils, as to the mode of binding out orphans, proceed to perform the duty which was assigned to them.

On the 1st of January, 1848, the Girard College was opened, and preparatory to that event, about one hundred orphans between the ages of six and ten years, were enrolled as admitted, to be maintained and educated as directed by the founder of the institution. Subsequently, about two hundred other orphans, between the ages of six and ten years, were from time to time admitted. None of the orphans, therefore, who were admitted within the four years commencing in December, 1847, having, until December 1851, attained the age of fourteen years; the attention of the Directors of the College had been until then confined to the maintenance and education only of the pupils; and no necessity had previously arisen for closely examining the provisions of Stephen Girard's will, relative to binding orphans to suitable occupations.

In the autumn of 1851, however, although there had been no action, as to binding out orphans, on the part of the Directors, suggestions were made in other quarters, and doubts arose, which were well calculated to create embarrassment. By some it seemed and still seems to be supposed, that the operation of binding the orphans may be regulated according to their ages: Others appear to regard the age of fourteen as the proper period for binding them: And so confident is even the President of the College, on the subject, that, in his report to the Directors, made on the 12th of February, he says, "I deem it important that situations should be engaged, with as little delay as possible, for the boys who are to go out in the spring."

Therefore, although there really may be no present necessity for inquiring what were the actual intentions of the founder of the College, or what may be the positive duties of the Directors, as to binding out orphans over the age of fourteen years, it is discreet to consider what is the true character of those intentions and duties, so that doubt may no longer exist, and that future operations may be advisedly conducted.

Accordingly, the Committee, under the sanction of the resolution of the 8th of October last, above referred to, proceed to inquire what were the intentions of the founder of the College, and what measures ought the Directors to adopt, as to binding out orphans between the ages of fourteen and eighteen years?

If the committee truly understand Stephen Girard's will, no particular age or precise time was prescribed by the testator for binding orphans who may be above the age of fourteen years. His chief and, it may be said, his sole design was to maintain and educate poor orphans; that is, so to train them morally, physically, and intellectually, in boyhood, that they might become covetable apprentices, and at last virtuous, useful and happy men. To this object he devoted his immense estate: and while he necessarily left to his trustees the details for organizing the College, and for perfecting his design, he took especial care to declare and establish the main principles and means, according to which that design should be carried into execution. He left nothing which he regarded as an essential part of his plan, to the discretion of his trustees or their agents. His own directions in all matters of importance, are given not merely in clear, but mandatory terms; and his trustees, in accepting his estate, solemnly undertook to execute their duty according to those terms. If, therefore, the orphans who may be capable of receiving a thorough education, shall not be thoroughly educated, and if those orphans, whose faculties may be so limited that they cannot acquire a thorough education, shall not receive all the instruction which they may be capable of, the trustees will be accountable.

Thus, as to moral training, the testator says, "I desire that all instructors and teachers in the College shall take pains to instill into the minds of the scholars, the purest principles of morality; so that, on their entrance into active life, they may from inclination and habit, evince benevolence towards their fellow-creatures, and a love of truth, sobriety and industry, adopting, at the same time, such religious tenets as their matured reason may enable them to prefer."

In regard to physical training, he directs that "the orphans shall be fed with plain but wholesome food, clothed with plain but decent apparel, (no distinctive dress to be worn) and lodged in a plain but safe manner: Due regard shall be paid to their health; and to this end their persons and clothes shall be kept clean, and they shall have rational exercise and recreation."

And, as to intellectual improvement, he says--"The orphans shall be instructed in the various branches of a sound education, comprehending reading, writing, grammar, arithmetic, geography, navigation, surveying, practical mathematics, astronomy, natural and experimental philosophy, the French and Spanish languages, (I do not forbid, but I do not recommend, the Greek and Latin languages,) and such other learning and science as the capacities of the several scholars may merit or warrant."

Having thus provided for the moral, physical and mental training of the orphans, in terms more uniformly positive than those used in any other part of his will, the testator defined and fixed the time within which the orphans should be thus educated. He was aware that, for such an education as he directed, much time would be required; but, as he could not foresee how much time would in each case be needful, he on that point took care that his Trustees should have no excuse for any neglect on their part. He formed a sliding scale between the ages of six and eighteen years, so that every orphan between those ages might profit by instruction, according to his capacity and the pains taken to improve it. It may be presumed that he adopted the full scope of twelve years, because there is as great a diversity in the dispositions and capacities of children as there is in their features; and because, while the faculties of some children may be easily developed, the influence of training for several years is essential to the improvement of the minds of others. As, therefore, he could not fix or limit the time which ought to be devoted to the instruction of each orphan, he made the time within which every orphan might remain in the College so ample, that all might be educated according to their respective capacities and wants. Thus, a child admitted at the age of six years, may be retained in the institution for twelve years, if so long a term shall be necessary; or orphans, entering at a later period of childhood, may still have as much time as may be sufficient for preparing them for apprenticeship and manhood.

Orphans between the ages of six and ten years, and no others, are admissible. No orphan can be bound until after he shall have become fourteen years old. Consequently, every orphan admitted into the College at the age of six years is entitled to education for eight years positively, if not removed for malconduct. On the other hand, every orphan, entering the College just before the age of ten years, may have instruction for the like term of eight years: As any such orphan may have had valuable instruction before he entered the College, he may not need further education for eight years; but if he shall not have been well instructed before he entered the College, he is entitled to full instruction there. Consequently, if, without defining any precise time for the education of each orphan, Stephen Girard has at all indicated a preference for any particular term of instruction, that term may be fairly declared to be eight years.

Besides it is not to be supposed that he desired to favor some orphans more than others; or that he wished that some orphans should be positively entitled to maintenance and education for eight, seven or six years, and that others should partake of his bounty for four years only: And yet there would be such an inequality--there would be such an injustice, if an orphan admitted just before his arrival at the age of ten years, should in four years thereafter be bound out. The Trustees have, indeed, the power to bind any orphan between fourteen and eighteen years of age, whatever may have been the time of his admission; but the right to exercise that power is dependent upon the true answers to these questions--has the orphan been fully instructed? if not fully instructed can he be rightfully bound? and, if not rightfully bound, may not the orphan have redress--will not the trust be violated? In order to bring the question more distinctly before the directors, let the cases of the first six orphans, who became fourteen years old be considered. Naming them alphabetically, they were William Ascndorpf, W. Z. Harbert, W. H. Hinsey, George W. Jackson, R. H. Smith and George Summers. These orphans were all admitted just before they were ten years old, and arrived at the age of fourteen years in December last. The instruction of five of them commenced in January, 1848, and that of W. Z. Harbert commenced in April, 1848. So that at fourteen years of age, five of them had received, up to December last, instruction for four years only, and Harbert will not have had instruction for four years until April next. Has any of these orphans, (has George W. Jackson, for instance, who is one of the best scholars in the College,) had the instruction "in the various branches of a sound education," so specifically defined by the founder of the College? What progress has any of them made in practical mathematics, astronomy, natural and experimental philosophy, in the French or Spanish languages, or other learning or science? Is the College, even at this late day, furnished with the philosophical and experimental apparatus and instruments, which, its founder anticipated, would be provided at the opening of the Institution? Are there not on the files of the directors appeals from instructors for the means needful for the performance of their duty? And have those means been provided?

The Directors have before them the suggestions, which were made to them on the 7th of October last, by Professor Stevens. Those suggestions have an important bearing upon the subject considered in this report. Mr. Stevens appears to have heard, but from what quarter he does not state, that some of the orphans in the College were to be bound out, on their arrival at the age of fourteen years; and, in consequence, he makes some remarks well worthy of the attention of the Directors. He does not make them as an opponent to the binding out, which he seems to think is contemplated, but simply as an inquirer with regard to his own future duties and to the performance of them.

Alluding to the orphans about to become fourteen years old, he says:--"The elder classes in this school are now reaching the age and the period in study, when boys can first be expected to have an insight into the value of education; and this incentive will, of course, gain strength as they advance to the practical scientific studies, which are a leading feature in Mr. Girard's requirements." Such is the declaration of the principal teacher in the College. The boys about to become fourteen years old, says he, are just approaching the period, when they will for the first time, begin to understand the true value of education; and their knowledge of its value will increase, as they advance to those practical studies which Mr. Girard especially provided for. Such, we repeat, are the sentiments which Professor Stevens considered it his duty officially to express. And yet it is just as the oldest orphans are for the first time beginning to know what education is, and what its value is; it is when, for the first time, they manifest an anxiety to receive what the founder of the College said they "shall" have, that it is not only proposed by the President of the College to bind them, but considered by him as decided that they are to be bound out in the ensuing spring!

Professor Stevens, we repeat, appears to apprehend, that the orphans, who may be fourteen years old, may be so bound out; and, therefore, it may be, that he ventured to contrast the present and the future of the High School of Philadelphia, with the present and the future of Girard College. "The ages of the pupils, when admitted into the High School," says he, "average more than fourteen years, although they comprise the selected talent of the city schools."

It seems, therefore, that the intelligent fathers of the pupils in the High School agree with Stephen Girard, not only in the anxiety to give a sound education, but as to what a sound education is; and it further appears, that in sustaining the High School, the community in which it exists sanctions the principles on which it is conducted. The fathers of the pupils in it, although their sons may be above the age of fourteen years, wisely prefer to have them fully instructed, to binding them out, when half instructed, to occupations, for which, owing to ignorance, they may be unfit. They do not stop their sons when in pursuit of knowledge, because they may be above the age of fourteen years; but they cheer and encourage them in their course. And yet, although the founder of the Girard College provided for at least such an instruction of the orphans therein, as may be had in the High School, Professor Stevens appears to doubt, whether it may not be the desire of Stephen Girard's Trustees, or of the Directors of the College, to make the College a mere grammar or primary school!

Whence this doubt? Can it be the design of the Trustees, or of the Directors, to convert the doubt into reality? Are they of opinion, that when the orphans pass the age of fourteen years, they are to be no longer instructed? Have the Trustees, or Directors, a right so to decide? Would not any such decision be a violation of their duty, and morally wrong? In fine, has the age of an orphan, whether fourteen, or fifteen, or sixteen years old, anything to do with binding him out, if he shall not at that age have had as full instruction as his faculties may enable him to receive? Are not the true inquiries these? Is A. B. capable of receiving the instruction "in the various branches of a sound education," to which he is legally entitled, according to the requirements of Stephen Girard's will? If he has a capacity to receive that instruction, has he had it? And, if he has not had it, (whether he is at the age of fourteen, or fifteen, or sixteen, or seventeen years,) who has a right to say, he shall not receive it, but be bound out?

Without doubt, there may be instances in which the utmost care fully to develop and improve the faculties of orphans may be abortive. Yet, even in such cases, there ought not to be a hasty decision; on the contrary, before a determination, that must affect the whole future of an orphan, should be arrived at, a fair and full trial of his powers should be made. If, after such a trial, his faculties should be found defective, then, and not until then, may arrive the period for binding him out to some occupation, which may not demand the existence and exercise of much mental ability.

The committee conceive, that the observations which they have thus made, have naturally arisen out of the subject, into which they were directed to make an inquiry. That inquiry is, what measures ought the Directors to adopt, respecting orphans, arriving from time to time, between the ages of fourteen and eighteen years? At the outset, the committee considered it a duty to ascertain, as clearly as they could, the views of the founder of the College, and they have expressed their opinion on that head; and in doing so, they have been mindful, that they were not submitting that opinion for a present purpose only, but with a view to the future course of the Directors.

The conclusions at which the committee have arrived, are these:--

1st. The requirements of the founder of the College, should be faithfully complied with. 2nd. The time at which an orphan, above the age of fourteen years, should be bound to some suitable occupation, should be determined, not according to his age but to his fitness for the change. 3d. A register should be provided and carefully kept in the College, showing the capacity and acquirements of every orphan, at any and every time, after his arrival at the age of fourteen years, in order that a just and deliberate decision may be made by the Directors of the College, as to the proper period for binding out the orphan, as well as the occupation most suitable for him. 4th. All orphans, capable of receiving a thorough education, should be thoroughly educated. 5th. Orphans found, after a patient and full trial, incapable of receiving the instruction specifically prescribed by the founder of the College, should, therefore, be the more carefully educated in the branches of study which they may be able to master. 6th. Whenever and as often as orphans may be deemed prepared to become apprentices, pains should be taken to provide suitable places for them.

In an inquiry like the present, which is initiative only, entire accuracy or insight as to needful measures could not have been anticipated. The Girard College is an institution of a peculiar character. From the opening of it unto the present time, the Directors have been advancing slowly, because on ground before almost untrodden; and, as in all human undertakings, time and experience will be the only safe guides for the future. The committee have stated what they think ought to be now done; and, in order to ascertain the judgment of the Directors, they submit the annexed resolutions.

They will not, however, close their report, without briefly adverting to an obstacle in the way of binding out orphans to suitable occupations, which the founder of the College could not have foreseen. Formerly the operation of binding apprentices by indenture was almost universally adopted in Pennsylvania. The home of the apprentice was in the house of the master; who not only instructed the apprentice in his operative duties, but was the conservator of his morals. Within the twenty years which have elapsed since the death of Stephen Girard, however, the relationship previously existing between masters and apprentices has been almost wholly superseded, in the city and districts of Philadelphia at least, by a practice, which the committee believe to be highly injurious not only to the parties immediately concerned, but to society at large. Owing to the selfishness of masters, to combinations among journeymen, and to the necessities of unfortunate parents, the ancient and useful operation of binding by indenture has been almost abandoned. Masters in general, in order to be released from the responsibility of providing homes for apprentices, and of making the apprentices good workmen, hire boys from their parents at weekly or monthly wages, and the parents assent to those loose bargains, through ignorance of the consequences to their children, or under the pressure of a sad necessity. The committee trust that this practice is not long to prevail, and that in other parts of Pennsylvania it is unknown. But if these hopes are unfounded, still the committee do not despair of finding in Pennsylvania, masters willing to take apprentices by indenture from the Girard College. The orphans of that institution, if the injunctions of its founder shall be faithfully followed by his Trustees, will have had such a moral, physical and scholastic training, as to render them acceptable apprentices to all masters who truly understand their own true interest, and who at the same time have a just sense of their duty to society. Let the Trustees and Directors act their own parts well, and the future may be awaited without responsibility or apprehension.

The resolutions which the committee respectfully ask the Directors to adopt, are the following:

1st. Resolved, that all orphans, who are capable of receiving the sound education defined in the seventh clause of the twenty-first article of Stephen Girard's Will, shall be instructed according to his requirements.

2d. Resolved, that orphans, whose faculties may not qualify them to receive the full education contemplated in the clause aforesaid, shall nevertheless be fully instructed in all the branches of education, which they may be able to master.

3d. Resolved, that the time, at which an orphan between fourteen and eighteen years of age should be bound out as an apprentice, should be determined not according to his age, but to his fitness for the change.

4th. Resolved, that a book suitable for a register shall be provided and carefully kept in the College; that in it, from time to time, the names of orphans, as they shall severally arrive at the age of fourteen years, shall be entered; and that thereafter a faithful record shall be kept of the capacity, progress and standing of each of the said orphans as a scholar, as well as of his morals and health.

APPENDIX F

SIXTH ANNUAL REPORT OF THE BOARD OF DIRECTORS OF THE GIRARD COLLEGE FOR ORPHANS FOR THE YEAR 1853

[pp. 5-6]

The Principal Department of the College has been recently somewhat modified, agreeably to a plan proposed, and earnestly recommended by the Faculty of the College, with a view of a more systematic method of apprenticing the pupils of the College, of better defining the time they are to remain in the Institution, and of harmonizing it with the Instruction and Discipline of the College. Accordingly the Board has adopted the following plan:

First.--That a Course of Study be arranged for the Principal Department in such form that the scholars "shall be instructed in the various branches of a sound education, comprehending Reading, Writing, Grammar, Arithmetic, Geography, Navigation, Surveying, Practical Mathematics, Astronomy, Natural, Chemical and Experimental Philosophy, the French and Spanish Languages, and other learning and science as their capacities may merit or warrant."

Second.--That the candidates for promotion from the Primary to the Principal Department, be required to pass a satisfactory examination in Reading, Writing, Geography, History, English Grammar, Arithmetic, as far as Involution, and Algebra through Equations of the first degree.

Third.--That the scholars who shall be admitted to the Principal Department be placed on a course of study which shall occupy three years; but that no pupil over the age of fourteen years shall be admitted to a full course in the said Department.

Fourth.--That there be six classes in the Principal Department, and that one class shall graduate every six months, say in the months of March and September.

Fifth.--That the first regular Commencement for graduating a class be held on the first Wednesday of March, 1854, and that a suitable testimonial be prepared for the graduates.

Sixth.--That public notice be given by advertisement in the newspapers previous to each Commencement, that after date of said Commencement a certain number of orphans will be bound out by the Directors, and the following notice be given to each orphan, and to his mother or next friend:--"You are hereby notified that the Board of Directors of Girard College have instructed their Committee on Discharge to procure a situation for A--- B---, and to bind him in accordance with the Will of Stephen Girard. The Committee, anxious to consult your wishes so far as is proper, are willing to wait a reasonable time, (not exceeding one month,) hoping that you will aid the Committee in finding a suitable place, either with those who apply to the College for boys, or with others, but if unsuccessful, then the Committee will select a place for A--- B---, and proceed to bind him."

Seventh.--That during the time which shall intervene between graduation and binding, or going out on trial, the graduates shall continue to reside in the College, and shall be usefully employed, or shall pursue such studies as may be assigned to them; and such orphans as have not the capacity or application to prepare themselves for admittion to the Principal Department before the age of fourteen years, and such pupils of this Department as do not merit its advantages by application and good conduct, shall, at the direction of the Directors, be bound out after they become fourteen years of age without graduation.

APPENDIX G

SEVENTH ANNUAL REPORT OF THE BOARD OF DIRECTORS OF THE GIRARD COLLEGE FOR ORPHANS FOR THE YEAR 1854

[pp. 25-27]

CATALOGUE OF APPRENTICES.

APPRENTICE.	MASTER.	BUSINESS.	RESIDENCE.
Benj. P. Wrigley,	R. G. Warren	Mariner,	Philadelphia.
Geo S. Graham,	John F. Lush,	Carpenter	Do.
Joseph Dittus	R. & R. S. Smith,	Ornamental Carvers,	Do.
Chas. Lawrence,	Alfred Wright,	Painter and Glazier,	Do.
Chas. F. Herring,	Saml. Pincott,	Manufactu'r Piano Keys,	Do.
Jno. F. Garrett,	Jas. W. Newberry,	Watch Maker,	Do.
Jno. Lyons,	Jos. Conrad,	Boot and Shoe Maker,	Do.
Cornelius Barnes,	Saml. Powell,	Tinsmith,	Do.
George Sykes,	W. P. Painter,	Drug Store,	Muncy, Lycoming co.
Wm. Field,	Thos. H. Marston,	Painter and Glazier,	Philadelphia.
Geo. Armstrong,	Saml. B. Reed,	Cabinet Maker,	Do.
Lawrence Tobin,	King & Baird,	Printers,	Do.
Geo. W. Jackson,	Thos. R. Reynolds,	Merchant,	Bellefonte.
Jno. R. Brown,	Jos. M'Cartney,	Tanner,	Kittanning.
Jno. Bussinger,	Jas. A. Montgomery,	Farmer,	Chester county.
Jno. Robinson,	Jas. M. Brown,	Farmer and Miller,	Franklin county.
Jas. M'Ginn,	Jos. Harvey,	Turner in Ivory, &c.,	Philadelphia.
Jno. A. Cope,	W. E. Hamill,	Farmer,	Philadelphia county

APPRENTICE.	MASTER.	BUSINESS.	RESIDENCE.
Benj. W. Dunham,	Jos. Harvey,	Turner in Ivory,	Philadelphia.
Jas. Foster,	Robt. Lyle,	Farmer and Paper Maker,	Chester county.
Stephen Ebert,	Robt. Buist,	Horticulturist,	Philadelphia county.
Benj. D. Hartle	Slote & Mooney,	Stereotypers,	Philadelphia.
Ervin Scheetz,	Saml. S. Addams,	Farmer,	Cumberland county.
W. Wallace Clark,	Jno. W. Donnelly,	Manuf'r Boots & Shoes,	Philadelphia.
Norton Lindsay,	Saml. Pincott,	Manufactu'r Piano Keys,	Do.
Wm. Ward,	Young S. Walter,	Printer,	Chester.
David Chambers,	Alex. M'Clure,	Do.	Chambersburg.
G. H. Bartram	Henry Homer,	Brass Founder,	Philadelphia.
Saml. E. Conrad,	Jno. W. M'Bride,	Cooper,	Carlisle.
Chas. Devlin,	Henry Homer,	Brass Founder,	Philadelphia.
Edw. Eisenbeis,	G. W. Pearce,	Printer,	West Chester.
Thos. Riley,	Dechert & Co.,	Do.	Chambersburg.
Fred. Noble,	Bennet Chalfont,	Machinist,	Chester county.
Jno. Ward,	W. M. Reilly,	Druggist,	Philadelphia.
W. B. Linn,	W. White,	Do.	Do.
Jno. T. Carpenter,	David A. Roberts,	Tinsmith,	Germantown.
Geo. Gorman,	Jas. Halsey,	Man'r Tailors' Trimmings,	Philadelphia.
W. E. Littleton,	Thos. S. Mitchell,	Conveyancer,	Do.
J. F. Anderson,	Geo. Black,	Plasterer,	Do.
Jno. Fitzpatrick,	Jas. Harper,	Hatter,	Do.
W. H. Govett,	French & Richards,	Druggists,	Do.
Geo. Lithgow,	Do.	Do.	Do.
Chas. C. Smith,	Ed. Franciscus,	Do.	Jersey Shore, Lycoming, Pa.

APPRENTICE.	MASTER.	BUSINESS.	RESIDENCE.
W. Sullivan,	Lacey & Phillips,	Saddlers,	Philadelphia.
W. J. M'Girr,	Hall & Boardman,	Manufa'rs Britannia Ware,	Do.
Jos. Bewley,	Geo. Charles,	Stereotyper,	Do.
Jas. S. Everton,	James Bispham,	Druggist,	Do.
W. Edwards,	Jesper Harding,	Printer,	Do.
W. Dunn,	Do.	Do.	Do.
W. Davidson,	Jesse Williamson,	Druggist,	Do.
David Vetter,	Ernst Werner,	Fresco Painter,	Do.
Jno. Lewis,	Jno. M'Bride,	Cooper,	Carlisle.
David Stockton,	Lacey & Phillips,	Saddlers,	Philadelphia.
Jno. Loyd,	Jno. O. Mead & Co.,	Silver Platers,	Do.
Thos. Tompkins,	Jas. Greenfield,	Wheelwright,	Chester county.
Geo. Summers,	Jno. M'Arthur,	Architect,	Philadelphia.
Saml. White,	Krider & Co.,	Silver Chasers,	Do.
Chás. H. Dougherty,	Geo. Sharp,	Silversmith,	Do.
Jno. Harlay,	Charles D. Harlay,	Barber,	Do.
Ed. J. Lilly,	J. Lewis Crew,	Druggist,	Do.
Thos P. Wynkoop,	Robt. S. Bower,	Do.	Do.
Jos. T. Newell,	Chas. White,	Painter and Glazier,	Do.
Chas. H. Byrnes,	W. H. M'Dowell,	Engraver,	Do.
Saml. K. Dilley,	Tillinghast Collins,	Printer,	Do.
M. O'Brien,	Gerardus W. Lanning,	Coach Maker,	Do.
Sol. G. Smith,	Saml. L. Sentman,	Farmer and Tanner,	Franklin county.
Stephen M. Sherman,	Do.	Do.	Do.
Jno. Tobin,	D. W. Baxter,	Wood Engraver,	Philadelphia.
Chas. J. Hill,	W. Dunlap,	Coach Maker	Do.

APPRENTICE.	MASTER.	BUSINESS.	RESIDENCE.
G. W. Klemm,	Wagner & M'Guigan,	Lithographers,	Do.
Jas. Kilroy,	Geo. B. Sloan,	Coach Maker,	Chester county.
Jno. J. Stell,	Bullock & Crenshaw,	Chemists,	Philadelphia.
Chas. Milligan,	L. C. Francis,	Philosoph. Inst. Maker,	Do.
Wm. Guest,	Joseph Pusey,	Farmer,	Chester county.
James Lawton,	Cornelius Hall,	Chair Maker,	Philadelphia.
Henry McClay,	E. G. Roddy,	Merchant,	Fayette county.
Jas. Behring,	Bishop & Simons,	Mariner,	Philadelphia.
Jno. T. Worthington,	Do.	Do.	Do.
W. Jackson,	C. Sherman,	Printer,	Do.
Wm. Ball,	Jas. Bispham,	Druggist,	Do.
Theo. Harbach,	Anna Harbach,	Confectioner,	Do.
Wm. Miller,	W. Brewster,	Printer,	Huntingdon.
Jno. W. Bayne,	Jno. O. Mead & Co.	Silver Platers,	Philadelphia.
Wm. Kilpatrick,	Ewing Brownfield,	Merchant,	Fayette county.
Rich. Overdeer,	P. Krider,	Silver Chaser,	Philadelphia.
W. M'Main,	Jno. Hancock,	Druggist,	Do.
Chas. Weed,	A. Iseminger,	Carpenter,	Do.
Fred. Krumschield,	Stouch & Christman,	Printers,	Washington, Penna.
Hugh M'Clenagin,	Do.	Do.	Do.

APPENDIX II

REPORT [BOARD OF DIRECTORS OF THE GIRARD COLLEGE FOR ORPHANS]. February 23, 1858. [pp. 30-32]

Trusting that the views we have now expressed will commend themselves to the judgment of the Board, and with a view to reduce them, in substance and effect, to the test of experience, the following resolutions are offered:--

1. Resolved, That measures be taken to organize an Infant-school department for the youngest pupils in the College, on the most approved plan, and to secure the services of one or more teachers, of tried skill in that particular branch or method of instruction.

2. Resolved, That in the opinion of this Board it is desirable a building should be erected upon the College premises, of such materials and of such form as may be best adapted to the purpose, for the employment of a portion of the pupils in manual and mechanical labor, to be supplied with the needful furniture and tools, and also with instruction in such labor.

3. Resolved, That some suitable arrangement be made for the temporary board, lodging and employment of such orphans as are obliged to remain in the College after having finished the prescribed course of study, or who shall have left the College in good repute, and, during their apprenticeship are, for any cause, (not involving a fault of their own,) deprived of a home.

4. Resolved, That in the apportionment of time to the different pursuits of the orphans, enough shall be allowed to spelling, reading,

writing, geography, and the simple rules of arithmetic, to secure a thorough knowledge of those branches by the time they arrive at fourteen years of age.

5. Resolved, That it is expedient that all persons employed in the care of the orphans, except the nurses and house-servants, shall be of "tried skill" in the offices of teaching and training--so that a free interchange of official duties in the school-rooms and out of them, may from time to time take place, thus diffusing the influence of each individual and of each department through the whole body; and that the present corps of teachers be enlarged sufficiently to accomplish the end proposed in the present resolution.

6. Resolved, That a department of instruction in the principles of morality, including the sacred rights of conscience, be organized, of which the President, for the time being, shall be the head; said department to have such a place in the arrangements of study and such a portion of the pupil's time, as its importance demands.

7. Resolved, That a general revision of our text-books be instituted as soon as practicable, with a view to a reduction of their number and an improvement in their quality; and that if, in any case, such as are well adapted to our purposes cannot be obtained in the market, arrangements be made to have them prepared.

FRED. A. PACKARD,	HENRY D. GILPIN,
SAMUEL H. PERKINS,	D. M. FOX,
SAMUEL F. FLOOD,	W. J. DUANE,
WILLIAM MARTIN,	JAMES S. WATSON.

APPENDIX I

"COURSE OF STUDY FOR EIGHT YEARS AND SIX MONTHS."
FIFTH ANNUAL REPORT OF THE BOARD OF DIRECTORS OF CITY TRUSTS:
REPORT FOR THE YEAR 1874.
[pp. 109-116]

First School--Studies and Exercises.

Class 1.

ALPHABET--Names and Sounds of Letters.

READING--Primer.

SPELLING--Phonic and Orthographic.

WRITING--Letters, Numbers, from 1 to 100, on slates.

DRAWING.

OBJECT LESSONS--Colors and their shades; Forms, Lines, Surfaces and Solids; Parts, Qualities and Uses of common objects.

Class 2.

READING--First Reader.

SPELLING--Primary Speller.

WRITING--Words and Sentences, on Slates.

DRAWING.

ARITHMETIC--Numeration and Notation. Addition.

OBJECT LESSONS--Inanimate Objects and their qualities.

Class 3.

READING--Second Reader.

SPELLING.

WRITING--On Slates, Numbers to millions. Sentences.

Class 3.--Continued.

DRAWING.

ARITHMETIC--Addition and Subtraction; Multiplication Table.

OBJECT LESSONS--Animals, their habits, forms and uses; Forms, of earth, oceans, continents, islands, &c.

Class 4.

READING--Third Reader

SPELLING.

WRITING--On Slates; Dictation Lessons.

DRAWING.

ARITHMETIC--Simple Multiplication; Table reviewed; Mental Arithmetic commenced; Federal and English Money Tables.

GEOGRAPHY--Outlines of Countries, States, Gulfs, Bays, Coasts, Courses of Rivers.

OBJECT LESSONS--Plants, Fruits, Grains, Flowers, Geographical Figures.

Class 5.

READING--Fourth Reader.

WRITING--On Slates and Paper.

SPELLING.

DRAWING.

GEOGRAPHY--Primary, United States; Outline Maps; Drawing Maps on Slates and Blackboards.

ARITHMETIC--Simple Division, long, short, and by factors. Mental Arithmetic.

OBJECT LESSONS--Birds and other Natural History objects.

Second School--Studies and Exercises.

Class 1.

READING--Selected Books.

Class 1.--Continued.

SPELLING--Words of similar sound but different meaning. Difficult words of one and more syllables.

WRITING--With pen on paper; Dictation Lessons; Roman Numbers.

ARITHMETIC--Reduction of Compound numbers; Tables of Weights and Measures; Mental Arithmetic, continued.

GEOGRAPHY--Primary, North and South America; Drawing Maps on Slates and Blackboards.

DRAWING.

Class 2.

READING--History of the United States; Natural History.

SPELLING--Oral, and by dictation.

GEOGRAPHY--Primary, Europe; Outline Maps; Drawing Maps on Slates and Blackboards; Terrestrial Globe.

ARITHMETIC--Tables of Weights and Measures; Addition and Subtraction of Compound Numbers; Mental Arithmetic, continued.

WRITING--With pen on paper; Dictation Lessons; Roman Numbers reviewed.

DRAWING.

Class 3.

READING--Selected Books.

SPELLING--Pronouncing Speller; Geographical and Historical words that occur in other lessons; Use of Dictionary; Defining.

WRITING--Dictation of words and sentences, and from copies; Abbreviations.

GEOGRAPHY--North and South America and United States reviewed; Drawing Outline Maps on Blackboards; Terrestrial Globe.

HISTORY--United States.

ARITHMETIC--Tables reviewed; Addition, Subtraction and Multiplication of Compound Numbers; Mental Arithmetic, continued.

DRAWING.

Class 4.

READING--Natural History; History of the United States; Selected Books.

WRITING--From copies; Dictation; Defining; Abbreviations, continued.

SPELLING--Including oral definitions.

GEOGRAPHY--Europe; Drawing Outline Maps; Globe.

ARITHMETIC--Multiplication and Division of Compound Numbers; Vulgar Fractions, commenced; Mental Arithmetic.

GRAMMAR--Commenced.

HISTORY--United States.

DRAWING.

Class 5.

READING--History of the United States; Selected Books.

WRITING--Letters to friends on familiar subjects; Words and sentences dictated; Writing from copies.

SPELLING--Pronouncing Speller; Dictionary, with definitions; Dictation lessons.

GEOGRAPHY--Asia and Africa; Australia; Drawing Outline Maps; Use of Globe.

GRAMMAR--Continued; Parsing simple sentences; Practice on the conjugation of verbs.

HISTORY--England; to be read, and questions answered after reading.

ARITHMETIC--Vulgar Fractions, continued; Mental Arithmetic.

DRAWING.

Third School--Studies and Exercises.

Class 1.

READING--History of France; Selected Books.

SPELLING--Oral and Written; Defining.

Class 1.--Continued.

WRITING--From copies; Dictated words and sentences.

GEOGRAPHY--General Review; Drawing Outline Maps; Use of Globe.

GRAMMAR--Analysis and Parsing.

ARITHMETIC--Vulgar Fractions reviewed; Decimal Fractions; Mental Arithmetic finished.

HISTORY--General; United States reviewed.

DEPARTMENT OF ENGLISH.

Class 2.

ORTHOGRAPHY--Written Exercises.

ETYMOLOGY--Prefixes and Suffixes; Derivation of Words.

GRAMMAR--Parsing and Analysis.

ELOCUTION--Reading and Declamation.

COMPOSITION--Construction of Simple and Compound Sentences; Interrogative, Affirmative, Negative, and Conditional Sentences; Epistolary Exercises.

HISTORY--General History, continued.

Class 3.

ORTHOGRAPHY--Written Exercises, continued.

ETYMOLOGY--Roots and their Derivatives.

GRAMMAR--Written Exercises in Parsing; Analysis.

ELOCUTION--Reading and Declamation.

COMPOSITION--Letter Writing and Narratives.

Class 4.

ORTHOGRAPHY--Written Exercises, continued

ETYMOLOGY--Derivatives and combination of words.

GRAMMAR--Parsing and Analysis.

Class 4.--Continued.

HISTORY--Narratives of important events.

CONSTITUTION--of the United States.

COMPOSITION--Descriptions of familiar objects and scenes.

ELOCUTION.

Class 5.

GRAMMAR--Analysis, continued.

CONSTITUTION--of the United States.

READING--Historical.

COMPOSITION--Historical Events and Characters.

ELOCUTION.

Class 6.

GRAMMAR--Correction of false Syntax; Parsing selected extracts.

RHETORIC--Figures of Speech; Style

ELOCUTION--Oratorical and poetical extracts read and recited.

HISTORY--Lessons to be read, and questions thereon.

COMPOSITION--Reports of passing events.

Class 7.

HISTORY--Written Biographical Sketches prepared for recitation.

RHETORIC--Parts of discourse; Arguments and their arrangement.

COMPOSITION--Descriptive.

ELOCUTION.

DEPARTMENT OF FRENCH.

Class 2.--Elementary Lessons; Pronunciation.

Class 3.--Verbs, 1st Conjugation; Reading.

Class 4.--Verbs, 2nd Conjugation; Nouns, Reading.

Class 5.--Verbs, 3rd Conjugation; Irregular Verbs; Reading.

Class 6.--Verbs; Irregular Verbs, continued; Personal and Demonstrative Pronouns; Reading.

Class 7.--All the Parts of Speech; All the Conjugations; Irregular Verbs, continued; Reading and Translation.

DEPARTMENT OF SPANISH.

Class 3.--Sounds of the Alphabet; Pronunciation of words; Reading; Grammar, to Verbs.

Class 4.--Reading and Translating; Written Exercises; Grammar, Verbs.

Class 5.--Reading and Translating; Dictation Lessons; Grammar, Regular and Irregular Verbs; Questions and Answers in Spanish.

Class 6.--Reading and Translating; Grammar, continued; Spanish conversation.

Class 7.--Reading and Translating; Grammar; Parsing and Analysis of Sentences; Spanish conversations; Translation from English to Spanish.

DEPARTMENT OF NATURAL HISTORY.

Class 2.--Common things; Sights and sounds, and what they mean, &c.

Class 3.--NATURAL HISTORY.
ELEMENTS OF PHYSIOLOGY.

Class 4.--NATURAL HISTORY.
ANATOMY AND PHYSIOLOGY.

Class 5.--NATURAL HISTORY.
PHYSICAL GEOGRAPHY.

Class 6.--COMPARATIVE PHYSIOLOGY.
BOTANY.

Class 7.--GEOLOGY
PRINCIPLES OF ZOOLOGY.

DEPARTMENT OF GENERAL PHYSICS.

Class 2.--Conversations on Natural Philosophy.

Class 3.--NATURAL PHILOSOPHY; Definitions, Mechanical Powers; Lectures and Illustrations.

Class 4.--NATURAL PHILOSOPHY; The Pendulum; Uniform, Accelerated, and Retarded Motion; Falling Bodies, Specific Gravity; Lectures.

CHEMISTRY; Recitations and Lectures, with experiments.

Class 5.--CHEMISTRY; Recitations and Lectures.

NATURAL PHILOSOPHY; Hydrostatics, Hydraulics, Pneumatics; Lectures, with illustrations.

Class 6.--CHEMISTRY; Recitations and Lectures, with experiments.

NATURAL PHILOSOPHY; Optics, Heat; Lectures, with illustrations.

ASTRONOMY.

Class 7.--CHEMISTRY; Recitations and Lectures, with experiments.

NATURAL PHILOSOPHY; Electricity and Magnetism; Lectures, with illustrations.

ASTRONOMY.

DEPARTMENT OF MATHEMATICS.

Class 2.--ARITHMETIC; Analysis; Simple Proportion; Square Root.

Class 3.--ARITHMETIC; Square Root; Compound Proportion; Partnership; Percentage and its applications.

ALGEBRA, to Fractions.

Class 4.--ARITHMETIC; Simple and Compound Interest; Discount; Cube Root.

ALGEBRA; Fractions; Equations of the first degree.

Class 5.--GEOMETRY Four Books.

ALGEBRA; Equations of the second degree.

ARITHMETIC, Reviewed.

Class 6.--PLANE TRIGONOMETRY, with use of Instruments.

ARITHMETIC, Reviewed.

Class 7.--SURVEYING; Field Operations.

NAVIGATION.

ARITHMETIC, Reviewed.

DEPARTMENT OF GRAPHICS.

Class 2.--Writing; Linear drawing.

Class 3.--Writing; Card drawing.

Class 4.--Writing, drawing from cards and objects. Book-keeping.

Class 5.--Drawing from cards and objects; Linear perspective. Book-keeping; Writing.

Class 6.--Plain and ornamental writing; Drawing from cards and objects; Geometrical perspective; Mechanical drawing; Book-keeping.

Class 7.--Drawing from Objects; Geometrical perspective; Mechanical Drawing; Book-keeping; Plain and ornamental writing.

APPENDIX J

[GIRARD COLLEGE] COURSE OF STUDY FOR EIGHT YEARS

[January 1882]

PRIMARY SCHOOL.

Classes 1^1 1^2 1^3

ALPHABET.--Names and Sounds of Letters.

READING.--Primer.

SPELLING.--Phonic and Orthographic.

WRITING.--Letters, Numbers, on Slates.

DRAWING.--On Slates.

ARITHMETIC.--Numeration, Notation, Addition.

OBJECT LESSONS.--Colors and their shades; Forms, Lines, Surfaces and Solids; Parts, Qualities and Uses of common objects.

Classes 1^4 1^5 1^6

READING.--First Reader--Phonic Chart.

SPELLING.--Primary Speller.

WRITING.--Words and Sentences, on Slates.

DRAWING.

ARITHMETIC.--Subtraction, Multiplication, Multiplication Table, Mental Arithmetic commenced.

OBJECT LESSONS.--Inanimate Objects and their qualities.

Classes 1^7 1^8 1^9

READING.--Second Reader--Phonic Chart.

SPELLING.

WRITING.--On slates, Numbers, Sentences, &c.

DRAWING.

ARITHMETIC.--Short and Long Division; Division by Factors; Tables of Weights and Measures; Roman Numerals; Mental Arithmetic continued.

GEOGRAPHY.--Outlines of Countries, States, Gulfs, Bays, Coasts; Courses of Rivers.

OBJECT LESSONS.--Animals, their habits, forms and uses; Forms of Earth, Oceans, Continents, &c.

SECOND SCHOOL.

Classes 2^1 2^2 2^3

READING.--Third Reader.--Phonic Chart.

SPELLING.--Words of three and four syllables.

WRITING.--On slates, Dictation Lessons.

DRAWING.

ARITHMETIC.--Simple Numbers reviewed; Reduction of Compound Numbers, with converse operations; Tables of Weights and Measures; Mental Arithmetic continued.

GEOGRAPHY.--Primary Geography completed; Drawing Outline Maps.

OBJECT LESSONS.--Natural History Objects, both Vegetable and Animals.

Classes 2^4 2^5 2^6

READING.--Fourth Reader; Selected Books.

SPELLING.--Words of similar sound but different meaning; Difficult Words of one and more syllables.

WRITING.--With pen on paper; Dictation Lessons.

ARITHMETIC.--Reduction reviewed; Addition and Subtraction of Compound Numbers; Combining Roman Numerals; Tables of Weights and Measures; Mental Arithmetic continued.

GEOGRAPHY.--Common School Geography; Geographical Definitions; Maps of the Hemispheres; Outline Maps, &c.

OBJECT LESSONS.--Birds, their forms, habits, &c.

DRAWING.

THIRD SCHOOL.

Classes 3^1 3^2

READING.--Selected Books.

SPELLING.--Pronouncing Speller; Oral and by Dictation.

WRITING.--Dictation Lessons, and from Copies.

GEOGRAPHY.--North and South America; United States, Mexico, Central America and West Indies.

DRAWING.

ARITHMETIC.--Multiplication; Short and Long Division of Compound Numbers; Tables Reviewed; Mental Arithmetic continued.

HISTORY.--United States; Explorations; Settlements; French and Indian War.

Classes 3^3 3^4

READING.--Selected Books.

SPELLING.--Pronouncing Speller; Geographical and Historical Words that occur in other lessons; Use of Dictionary; Defining.

WRITING.--Dictation Lessons and from Copies; Abbreviations.

GEOGRAPHY.--Europe; Drawing Outline Maps; Terrestrial Globe.

HISTORY.--United States; the American Revolution.

ARITHMETIC.--Compound Numbers reviewed with Applications and Converse Operations; Vulgar Fractions commenced; Mental Arithmetic continued.

DRAWING.

Classes 3^5 3^6

READING.--Natural History; Selected Books.

WRITING.--Dictation Lessons, and from Copies. Abbreviations.

SPELLING.--Pronouncing Speller, Dictionary with Definings.

GEOGRAPHY.--Asia, Africa, Australia; Drawing Outline Maps; Use of Globe.

ARITHMETIC.--Vulgar Fractions continued; Decimal Fractions; Mental Arithmetic continued.

GRAMMAR.--Commenced.

HISTORY.--United States, completed.

DRAWING.

Classes 3^7 3^8

READING.--History of England; Selected Books.

WRITING.--Letters to friends on familiar subjects; Dictation Lessons; Writing from Copies.

ETYMOLOGY.--Prefixes and Suffixes.

GEOGRAPHY.--General Review: Drawing Outline Maps; Use of Globes.

HISTORY.--United States reviewed.

ARITHMETIC.--Analysis; Simple Proportion; Square Root.

GRAMMAR.--Parsing Simple Sentences; Practice on the Conjugation of Verbs.

DRAWING.

FOURTH SCHOOL.

Class 4^1

READING.--Selected Books.

ETYMOLOGY.--Prefixes, Suffixes and Roots.

WRITING.--From Copies; Dictation Lessons.

GEOGRAPHY.--Commence Physical Geography.

GRAMMAR.--Continued, Analysis and Parsing.

ARITHMETIC.--Cube Root; Compound Proportion; Discount; Percentage and its applications; Simple and Compound Interest.

HISTORY.--England.

DRAWING.

DEPARTMENT OF ENGLISH.

Class 4^2

ORTHOGRAPHY.--Written Exercises; Spelling of Technical Words; Attention to Marks Indicating Accent and Pronunciation; the Dictionary.

ETYMOLOGY.--Roots and their Derivatives.

GRAMMAR.--Oral and Written Exercises in Analysis and Parsing.

HISTORY.--England.

COMPOSITION.--Important General Principles and Rules for Punctuation; Letter Writing and Business Communications.

Class 4^3

ORTHOGRAPHY.--Dictation Exercises; Attention to Spelling in every exercise.

ETYMOLOGY.--Derivations and Combinations of Words.

GRAMMAR.--Analysis and Parsing.

HISTORY.--General History commenced.

COMPOSITION.--Historical Events and Character.

Class 4^4

GRAMMAR.--Analysis; Parsing; Correction of False Syntax.

CONSTITUTION --of the United States.

HISTORY.--General History Continued.

COMPOSITION.--Reports of Passing Events.

Class 4^5

GRAMMAR.--Correction of False Syntax; Parsing Selected Extracts.

CONSTITUTION--of the United States, continued.

HISTORY.--General History continued.

COMPOSITION.--Abstracts from Reading and other lessons; Transposition from Poetry to Prose.

Class 4^6

RHETORIC.--Commenced.

HISTORY.--General History continued.

COMPOSITION.--Study of Synonyms; Descriptions.

Class 4^7

RHETORIC.--Continued.

HISTORY.--Ancient History--Greece and Rome.

ENGLISH LITERATURE.

COMPOSITION.--Biographical and Historical Sketches; Compositions on Abstract Subjects.

DEPARTMENT OF FRENCH.

Class 4^2--Pronunciation; Nouns; Numerals; Auxiliary and Regular Verbs.

Class 4^3--Adjectives; Personal Pronouns; Contraction of Articles and Prepositions; Multiplication Table; Five Irregular Verbs; Translation from French to English.

Class 4^4--Relative Pronouns; Possessive and Demonstrative Adjectives and Pronouns; Comparison of Adjectives; Participles of All Primitive Irregular Verbs; Translation from French to English--English to French; Oral Practice.

Class 4^5--Comparison of Adverbs; Conjugation of Irregular Verbs; Impersonal Verbs; Translation from English to French--French to English; Dictation; Oral Practice.

Class 4^6--Irregular Verbs continued; Use of Subjunctive; Translation from French to English--English to French; Dictation; Oral Practice.

Class 4^7--Syntax; Translations continued; Dictation; Recitation in French of French History; Conversation.

DEPARTMENT OF SPANISH.

Class 4^3--Sounds of the Alphabet; Pronunciation of Words; Reading; Grammar, to Verbs.

Class 4^4--Reading and Translating; Written Exercises; Grammar, Verbs.

Class 4^5--Reading and Translating; Dictation Lessons; Grammar, Regular and Irregular Verbs; Questions and Answers in Spanish.

Class 4^6--Reading and Translating; Grammar continued; Spanish Conversations.

Class 4^7--Reading and Translating; Grammar; Parsing and Analysis of Sentences; Spanish Conversations; Translating from English to Spanish.

DEPARTMENT OF NATURAL HISTORY.

Class 4^2--Common things; Sights and Sounds, and what they mean, etc.

Class 4^3--NATURAL HISTORY
ELEMENTS OF PHYSIOLOGY.

Class 4^4--NATURAL HISTORY.
ANATOMY AND PHYSIOLOGY.

Class 4^5--NATURAL HISTORY.
PHYSICAL GEOGRAPHY.

Class 4^6--COMPARATIVE PHYSIOLOGY.
BOTANY.

Class 4^7--GEOLOGY.
PRINCIPLES OF ZOOLOGY.

DEPARTMENT OF GENERAL PHYSICS.

Class 4^2--CONVERSATIONS on Natural Philosophy.

Class 4^3--NATURAL PHILOSOPHY; Definitions; Mechanical Powers; Lectures and Illustrations.

Class 4^4--NATURAL PHILOSOPHY; The Pendulum; Uniform, Accelerated and Retarded Motion; Falling Bodies; Specific Gravity; Lectures.
CHEMISTRY; Recitations and Lectures, with Experiments.

Class 4^5--CHEMISTRY; Recitations and Lectures.
NATURAL PHILOSOPHY; Hydrostatics; Hydraulics; Pneumatics; Lectures, with illustrations.

Class 4^6--CHEMISTRY; Recitations and Lectures, with experiments.
NATURAL PHILOSOPHY; Optics; Heat; Lectures, with illustrations
ASTRONOMY.

<u>Class 4⁷</u>--CHEMISTRY; Recitations and Lectures, with experiments.
NATURAL PHILOSOPHY; Electricity and Magnetism Lectures, with illustrations.
ASTRONOMY.

DEPARTMENT OF MATHEMATICS.

Class 4^2--Review the whole subject of Arithmetic.

Class 4^3--ALGEBRA, through Simple Equations.

Class 4^4--ALGEBRA; Quadratic Equations.
GEOMETRY; Three Books.

Class 4^5--GEOMETRY; Mensuration.

Class 4^6--TRIGONOMETRY.

Class 4^7--SURVEYING; Navigation.

Extra Class--ANALYTICAL GEOMETRY; Calculus; Civil Engineering, &c.

DEPARTMENT OF GRAPHICS.

Class 4^2--WRITING; Linear Drawing.

Class 4^3--WRITING; Card Drawing.

Class 4^4--WRITING; Drawing from Cards and Objects.
BOOK-KEEPING.

Class 4^5--DRAWING from Cards and Objects; Linear Perspective.
Book-keeping. Writing.

Class 4^6--WRITING, Plain and Ornamental; Drawing from Cards and Objects; Geometrical Perspective; Mechanical Drawing; Book-keeping.

Class 4^7--DRAWING from Objects; Geometrical Perspective; Mechanical Drawing; Book-keeping; Plain and Ornamental Writing.

APPENDIX K

[GIRARD COLLEGE] CURRICULUM OF THE DEPARTMENT OF MECHANICAL INSTRUCTION [1904]

THE MACHINE TOOL LABORATORY

This Department occupies a well lighted and ventilated room 49x95 ft. in size, including a 16x20 ft. printing room, and a 10x32 ft. lavatory. There is a test and exhibit table with appliances for live and exhaust steam, water, gas, etc. This is surrounded by a nickel plated railing and occupies a space of 12x23 ft. Next to this is a show case, 12 ft. long, 12 ft. high, and 2 ft. wide, for the display of the work of the pupils.

This department is equipped with a ten horse power electric motor, with a clutch device on main shafting, capable of driving the machinery of the Wood Department, in case of accident to their motor.

The machine tools used are the same that would be found in any first class jobbing or repair shop; viz.,

1 Slotting Machine.
1 Planing Machine.
1 Universal Milling Machine.
1 20" Lathe.
1 16" Lathe.
1 Drill Press.
1 Shaping Machine.
1 Double Emery Wheel for grinding tools.
1 Grinding Machine for grinding cutters, reamers, &c.
1 Polishing or Buffing Machine.
6 10" Reed Lathes.

The bench equipments are:

10 Vise benches with two vises each.
1 Vise bench, with one vise, for the Instructor.
1 Vise bench, with five vises, for the Trade Class.

In addition to this there is a complete tool room, 14x18 ft. with a vise bench on two sides, and three large sized tool racks, equipped with all kinds of tools, such as, taps, dies, reamers, drills, boring bars, cutters, counter bores, milling cutters, files, scrapers, chisels, squares, gauges, templates, jigs, and devices of various kinds for tools and tool making.

There are also an air pump and a reservoir, for pneumatic experiments, and a brazing furnace.

COURSE OF INSTRUCTION.

FIRST YEAR. FIRST TERM.

Classes 3-1, 3-2, 3-3.

(Ages of pupils range from ten to thirteen.)

The use of the hammer, cold and cape chisels. Chipping plane surfaces; first, the parallelopipedon. Description of files, and the uses thereof. Use of the square in testing the chipping and filing of a straight surface or of one at right angles to another. Use of the straight edge in testing the filing of straight surfaces.

Having done the above, the boys are then given a cube, to finish. They also receive other exercises, comprising a repetition of former exercises on shorter surfaces. Extra figure, the lozenge.

Time 15 hours.

FIRST YEAR. SECOND TERM.

Classes 3-4, 3-5, 3-6.

Hammerhead. Chipping, filing, calipering, laying out, chamfering, draw-filing and polishing, drilling, and filing out the eye.

Extra figure, a surface plate. Finish all over and scrape to bearing.

Time 15 hours.

SECOND YEAR. FIRST TERM.

Classes 3-7, 3-8, 3-9.

Vise work. Small anvil, finishing complete.

Lathe work: Names of different parts of the lathe. Centering, drilling, countersinking, facing off, turning of plane cylindrical piece, turning down ends, leaving filleted shoulders, grooving and recessing, taper turning, turning to different sizes on one piece, to test the ability of the pupil.

Time 15 hours.

SECOND YEAR. SECOND TERM.

Classes 3-10, 3-11.

Chipping and filing to gauge. Hexagonal and octagonal figures of small surfaces.

Lathe work: Cutting screw threads; the V thread, the U. S. S. thread, the square thread, the worm thread, the double thread, and the right and left hand threads.

Time 15 hours.

THIRD YEAR. FIRST TERM.

Class 4-1.

Vise Work: Fitting rabbit block in piece to template.

Fitting dove-tail in pieces to template.

Lathe Work: Chuck work; facing; drilling; boring and counterboring; recessing and cutting internal thread.

Time 30 hours.

THIRD YEAR SECOND TERM.

Class 4-2.

Vise Work: Making an octahedron.

Machine Work: On planer, slotter, drill press, large lathes and milling machines. See separate curriculum for each machine.

Time 12 hours.

FOURTH YEAR. FIRST TERM.

Class 4-3.

Vise Work: Making fulcrum and fitting to block.

Machine Work: Continuation of machine curriculum.

Time 12 hours.

FOURTH YEAR. SECOND TERM.

Class 4-4.

Vise Work: Making bench vise. Machine work on this figure to be done by pupils when on machine.

Machine Work: Continuation of machine curriculum.

Time 9 hours.

FIFTH YEAR. FIRST TERM

Class 4-5.

Vise Work: Finishing up bench vise.

Machine Work: Advanced machine curriculum.

Time 12 hours.

FIFTH YEAR. SECOND TERM.

Class 4-6.

Review of previous lessons. Explanation and illustrations of steam boilers and engines, hydraulic powers, gas and pneumatic machinery.

Time 12 hours.

Machine Curriculum.

Lathe:

Turning work on centers.
Turning work in chuck.
Turning work chuck and steady rest.
Turning work on center and steady rest.
Use of boring bar with work clamped to carriage of machine.

Planing Machine:

Horizontal planing.
Vertical planing.
Round planing.
Angular planing.

Shaping Machine:

Plane and irregular surfaces.

Milling Machine:

Plane milling.
Grove milling.
Irregular and surface milling.
Use of index plate and centers.
Milling of gear teeth straight and bevel.

Slotting Machine:

Cutting key board
Straight, round and angular slotting.

Different Metals Used:

Tool, or cast, steel.
Wrought iron.
Brass, rolled, sawed, and cast.
Aluminum.
Copper.
Tin.
Cold rolled, or soft, steel.
Cast iron.
Lead.
Zinc.
Bronze.

EXTRA CLASS OR TRADE BOYS.

MACHINE WORK.

First Year.

Lathe Work:

Turning to different sizes on practice piece.
Calipers set to scale.
Calipers set to inside calipers.
Calipers set to standard outside gauge.
Running fit.
Driving fit.
Shrink fit.
Taper fit.

Taper Turning:

Turning to scale.
Turning to size.
Turning to fit holes.
Thread Cutting: U. S. S. V., and square threads of various pitches.

Chuck Work: Making small bolts, studs, pins, screws, nuts, washers, bushings, bosses, etc.; facing, reaming, counter-boring, recessing, and cutting internal threads, on 10" and 16" lathes; also boring taper by use of the cant rest on a 16" lathe; the use of hand tools employed in turning. All this work is done so as to impress it on the pupil's mind and at the same time to show how to work quickly.

Drilling: Drilling small holes by use of the 10" lathe; drilling accurately to lines and holes laid out.

Drilling by drill press, as follows: Device for clamping work on table; drilling to gauge plates, and on parallel strips, so as to avoid making holes in the table of the machine; drills for tapping, reaming and clearance; the use of boring bars in drill press, when supported by holes and bushings in the table; counter-boring, and boring with single end cutter.

Second Year.

Work on 10" Lathe: Thread cutting; double, triple, quadruple, external and worm threads, of different pitch, lead and turn per inch.

Planer Work: Planing plane surfaces, rough cut and finish cut.

Planing surfaces at different angles with each other.

Planing concave and convex surfaces.

Describing different ways of holding work in a planer, clamping and holding light work without springing.

Milling: Milling plane surfaces.

Work held in vise.

Work clamped on bed.

Different devices for holding work in milling machine; use of center and dividing attachment in milling taps, reamers, gear wheels, etc., and also in cutting straight gears, bevel gears, worm wheels, and counter-boring, facing and grooving.

Work on 20" Lathe: Facing off large work.

Boring and turning at the same time.

The use of the boring bar with the travelling head, work being clamped to carriage of lathe or to the shears.

Facing off large work held in the same manner.

Blocking up lathe for large dimensions.

Turning work in lathe, when work is longer than lathe bed.

Slotting and Shaping Machines: Repetition of planer work curriculum.

VISE WORK.

Each of the boys serves one month in the tool room, to learn the names and uses of the tools, and how to take proper care of them, and at the same time he is doing the following vise work:

Making Cubes: Chip, file and scrape; all sides are to be straight and at right angles with adjacent sides, parallel with opposite side, and to caliper alike in every way.

Hexagonal Nut: To be chipped, filed, and scraped to a given size; the angle of each side to be 120° to adjacent side, and at right angles to the face; also to caliper alike across the flats.

Lay out, chip, and file a rectangular hole in a practice piece of round iron, preparatory to doing same in two boring bars with taper shanks, and filed flat at the end to fit slot in drill sockets. Making cutters and keys for boring bars, filing the cutting edges, hardening, tempering, and testing in machine, to show that the work is properly done.

Chip, file and scrape square a piece of iron to gauge, lay out and drill; chip and file square another piece of iron, to fit the square piece just made, so as to be interchangeable. Chip, file and scrape two pieces, male and female, to fit each other.

Chip, file and scrape two half round pieces, male and female, to fit each other.

APPENDIX L

[GIRARD COLLEGE] COURSE IN SLOYD [1904]

COURSE IN SLOYD.

This Course is two years in length and is given to the eight Classes of the Second and Third Grades, Second School. Each Class receives instruction two hours per week.

FIRST YEAR.

Knife work; whittling.

Measuring with rule.

Naming tools and parts of bench.

Joinery; the making of eight models, involving the use of sixteen different tools.

Reading working drawings.

Correct position while working.

SECOND YEAR.

Joinery; the making of ten models, involving the use of seven new tools.

Naming tools.

Reading working drawings.

Names of all wood used.

Sharpening knife and chisel.

Correct position while working.

APPENDIX M

[GIRARD COLLEGE] HIGH SCHOOL CURRICULUM [1912]

HIGH SCHOOL CURRICULUM.

FIRST YEAR.

Subject.	Periods per Week.
English	5
Algebra	4
English History	4
Physical Geography	4
French	4
General Mechanical Instruction	4
Study	5
Total	30

SECOND YEAR.

Subject.	Periods per Week.
English	4
Algebra	$2\frac{1}{2}$
English and European History	3
General Biology	4
French	5
Bookkeeping	$2\frac{1}{2}$
General Mechanical Instruction	4
Study	5
Total	30

THIRD YEAR.

Subject.	Periods per Week.
English	5
Geometry	5
Modern European History	3
Chemistry, or	5)
Spanish	5)
Bookkeeping (5), Commercial Arithmetic (2), and Shorthand and Typewriting (5)	12
or	
Trade Instruction	17 $\frac{1}{2}$
Total, Commercial	30
Trade	35 $\frac{1}{2}$

FOURTH YEAR.

Subject.	Periods per Week.
English	5
American History and Government	4
Mathematics and Surveying	4)
or Economics	4)
Physics, or	5)
Spanish	5)
Commercial Geography (2 $\frac{1}{2}$), Commercial Law (2 $\frac{1}{2}$) and Shorthand and Typewriting (5)	10
or	
Trade Instruction	17 $\frac{1}{2}$
Military Science and Tactics, or Study	2
Chorus	2
Total, Commercial	32
Trade	37 $\frac{1}{2}$

APPENDIX N

[GIRARD COLLEGE] COURSE OF STUDY; MECHANICAL SCHOOL INSTRUCTION

Development of Industrial Training in Girard College. Stephen Girard wished to have the boys of Girard College taught "facts and things" rather than "words and signs." So, from the beginning, those who directed the policy of Girard College have kept pace with developing ideas and practice in the field of practical education. Thus, during the early fifties when Cooper Union and Mechanics' Institute were established in New York, Franklin Union and Spring Garden Institute in Philadelphia, and Ohio Mechanics' Institute in Cincinnati, the reports of the Board of Directors of Girard College urged the need for practical education.*

As early as 1848 boys were used in the industrial operation of Girard College. At the Centennial Exhibition of 1876 displays of hand work instruction from the schools of Russia and Sweden made a profound impression on American educators. While courses in tool instruction were being introduced in Massachusetts Institute of Technology in 1877 and the first manual training school was being founded in St. Louis by Professor Woodward, the Board of Directors of Girard College were planning extensions of mechanical training. In 1882 a department of mechanical instruction and workshops was started in the basement of Building Seven under the superintendency of Mr. T. Mason Mitchell. This work was so successful that a Mechanical School Building was completed in 1884 and two hundred and fifty boys were enrolled in this department. The course was expanded by

---

*History of Girard College by Cheesman A. Herrick, Chap. VIII.

the introduction of mechanical drawing and foundry work in 1885, electrical work in 1891 and plumbing and blacksmithing in 1893.

In 1924-25 the Mechanical School Building was doubled in size, much new equipment was installed, and two additional shops, for auto-mechanics and painting and finishing, were added. Soon after work in sheet-metal was introduced.

During the years in which these developments occurred in Girard College, the theory and practice of industrial education in American schools became definite, first with regard to the relation of industrial education to general education, and second, with regard to the objectives of three types of industrial education--manual training, prevocational shop work, and training for the mechanical trades. In these respects the present procedure in Girard College is as follows:

Present Procedure. Two types of training. A Girard College boy who completes the course of study laid down by the College has received two distinct types of training. First, he has pursued the usual academic studies--English, mathematics, science, history and modern languages--necessary to meet the College Entrance Board requirements of fifteen units for entrance to college. Many of these subjects are elective, so that the boy has been enabled to follow the line of his interests, and to prepare for any particular type of college work he may plan to take. Second, he has received adequate training in a selected trade or in a selected commercial course as a vocational preparation.

Three phases of industrial training. Instruction in manual arts and mechanical trades falls in three phases. The first consists of general elementary manual arts pursued by every boy from the second term of the fourth grade to the end of the sixth grade.

The second phase consists of prevocational courses from the seventh grade through the second year of high school. During this period each boy receives training in the fundamentals of some half dozen basic trades. The purpose of this training is to test the boy's ability, skill and interests against the requirements of a number of trades in order that he may be helped to discover his own aptitudes. This try-out period culminates in the second term of the second year of high school in a tentative selection either of one mechanical trade or of the commercial course.

The third phase, for the boy who chooses a mechanical trade, consists of two years of intensive trade training designed to accomplish two aims:--(a) to enable the boy to enter industry on a self supporting basis:--to get a job; and (b) to lay a foundation from which the boy can build toward advancement in trade skill and further study and training in technical subjects:--to win promotion.

Throughout this training stress is laid on the development of those qualities needed for success in industrial work, such as dependability, regard for safety, industry, good personality, honesty and truthfulness.

A guidance program. Guidance in Girard College is a blending of many activities. During the first year of high school, guidance is stressed in the study of civics. In the first term of the second year all boys have a course in study of occupations with special stress on choice of opportunities in the commercial and mechanical school courses. At the same time they pursue try-out courses in commercial work, consisting of business writing and informational junior business training. Meantime they are engaged in prevocational or try-out courses in mechanical work. These are supplemented by tests for aptitude.

At the end of this term, each boy is called for a personal interview, at which time his record in his try-out work, his personal tastes and plans, his opportunities for employment in his own community, and the advice of his parent, teachers and friends, are discussed with him. With this information the boy then makes a preliminary choice of either the mechanical or commercial school course.

During the second term, the boy who elects the mechanical school course adds to experiences gained in earlier prevocational courses, learns the elements of the proper care and operation of the principal machines used in the trade selected by him, progresses in the use and care of hand tools, and receives training in the fundamental operations of the trade. Similarly, a further study of commercial work is made by boys who select the commercial course.

At the end of this term a boy is allowed to change courses if, in the opinion of his teachers and vocational advisers, such change will be to his advantage. Otherwise he remains in the trade selected and receives intensive trade instruction during the junior and senior years.

Thus training and guidance cover broad vocational fields at first, gradually become more specialized, and finally focus on training for a specific occupation. At the completion of the course elected, a boy is prepared to enter on a pay-roll in a specific line of business or industry.

Placement of the boy in his first job and the maintaining of helpful contact with him through this and subsequent jobs or promotions, are functions of the Girard College Department of Admission and Discharge.

Names of Classes. In Girard College normal progress takes a boy through the Elementary School course in seven years and through the High School course in four years. Each school year is divided into two terms, and promotions are made at the end of each term. In the Elementary School the lower grade or term of any class is B grade, the higher is A. Thus, Grade 6-A indicates the class enrolled for the work of the higher or second term of the sixth grade.

In the High School the four classes or years, beginning with the entering class, are called, respectively, One, Two, Junior and Senior; and in each year the lower grade or term is One and the higher is Two. Thus, Class 2-2 indicates the class enrolled for the work of the higher or second term of the second year of High School; and Senior-Two, or S-2, indicates the class in the last term of the senior year.

GENERAL ORGANIZATION OF CLASSES AND CONTENT OF INSTRUCTION

The Sloyd Shops. The shops for elementary manual arts, located on the third floor of the Middle School building, consist of three woodworking shops, a print shop, supply rooms, and a machine tool room. Here boys of the fourth, fifth and sixth grades receive instruction in woodwork, light ornamental metal work, basketry and printing. A close correlation is maintained with instruction in other departments, especially in Art and English.

The Sloyd group. These boys learn the beginnings of how to handle tools and bench equipment. They satisfy a desire inherent in most boys, to convert ideas into objects. They have practice in receiving directions which they must carry out concretely. The evidence of their success lies before them in the shape of well-made, or of badly-made, products. They have an experience in worthwhile service when they send the best of their toys and projects at Christmas time to some hospital, or take them home as gifts to others. The character of their interest and the quality of their hand-work may furnish some evidence as to their vocational aptitude, but in the main this experience is simply part of their general education, not all of which can be derived from books or from academic instruction. The work in the last term, 6-A, for this group, in their own Print Shop, is essentially prevocational, and prepares for entrance to the prevocational shop work.

The Mechanical School. The forge shop and foundry are in a detached building near the North Gate. The other shops, class rooms and offices are in the Mechanical School Building. Two wings enclose an inner court floored with concrete and completely roofed over. A driveway leads into the enclosed court and makes it possible for a truck to drive into the building and unload material on the concrete floor. A balcony running around the court on the level of the second floor provides easy access to the classrooms and shops on that level.

Each shop contains from 1500 to 2500 square feet of floor space, with tool rooms and supply rooms, and most of them contain an office set off with glass partitions for the instructor. The lower floor contains the shops for painting, auto-mechanics, machine, carpentry and pattern work. The second floor contains shops for printing, mechanical drawing, trade drafting, electrical work, prevocational woodwork, and three class rooms.

All machines have unit or group motor drive and are guarded by the latest devices for assuring safety: Conduits under the floors provide for the installing of electric wiring, and an under-floor suction system removes sawdust and shavings.

The prevocational group. This consists of boys in the seventh grade and in the first two years of high school. They come to the Mechanical School four, six or eight hours each week, and go through a series of shop experiences designed to give them some definite information as to how the industrial work of the world is performed, and to help them to discover their own vocational interests and aptitudes. Their instructors are practical trade-trained and skilled mechanics. The machines and tools with which they work, or, if there is an element of danger involved, with which they see their instructors or the older boys work, are the man-sized equipment of the various trades. Some exercise work is necessary for purposes of instruction, but so far as possible, their efforts are expended on products which are useful and, again so far as possible, which are usefully consumed in the College. Thus for five terms, these boys acquire experience in the elementary wood-working, printing, (in the Sloyd group,) electrical, forge and sheet metal, foundry, machine and mechanical drawing courses. At the end of this period, that is, in the middle of the second year of high school, and after advice from relatives and instructors, each boy makes a tentative choice between the commercial course and the mechanical course.

The vocational industrial trade group. This consists of boys of the junior and senior high school classes who have chosen a trade course in the Mechanical School. These boys pursue the regular high school academic studies each morning, but spend their afternoons in the shops. The boy's intention is to go out at the end of his course as a helper or operator in some branch of industry for which training is provided in the courses in the forge and sheet metal, foundry, trade drafting, printing, electrical, machine, auto-mechanics, painting, carpentry or pattern-making shops, or by assignment as helper in plumbing, pipe-fitting, or power plant practice in the Engineer's Department. Shifting from one course to another is permitted only in decidedly exceptional cases, because concentrated effort is needed if the boy is to go out as a qualified workman at the end of his course. Obviously during this period the work done should be of a most practical nature. Herein, conditions in the College are very favorable. There seems to be no end to the practical demands which the College makes on the Mechanical School.

The Elementary Industrial and Intermediate High School groups. These consist of boys who for one reason or another have not kept up with the regular academic work in the elementary or high school, or of those who, because of their age, cannot complete the regular high school course before reaching the age limit of eighteen years. These are organized into a younger group called Elementary Industrial boys. In general they are boys who are retarded in academic instruction, though they may be boys of good personality and of good mechanical skill. For these boys the Mechanical School provides both academic and shop instruction. In general they spend three-fourths of their school time in the shops. The academic instruction is based as closely as possible on their shop interests and on fundamentals of mathematics, English, civics and hygiene. Every effort is made to give them instruction suited to their individual needs. No great difficulty is encountered in the shops in having each boy go as far and as fast as he is capable. In the academic classes, individual instruction is much more difficult, but the intimate personal knowledge of each boy, which the instructors have, accomplishes much in surmounting even this difficulty.

Some of the boys of this group, about a dozen during normal years, are placed in employment on a co-operative plan, whereby two boys are assigned to one job with a firm outside the College. For two weeks one boy attends classes and shop work in the Mechanical School, while the other works every day. During the next two weeks the assignment to school and to work is reversed. This arrangement gives a boy valuable working experience and paves the way toward a full time job when he leaves the College.

SUMMARY

For the groups just described, the shop assignments and time allotments are summarized in the following outline:

Subject and Time Allotment of Industrial Courses

Sloyd or General Manual Arts Courses

(450-500 boys)

Fourth Grade, Second Term

Woodworking, basketry 2*

Fifth Grade, First Term	Fifth Grade, Second Term
Woodworking 2	Woodworking 3

Sixth Grade, First Term	Sixth Grade, Second Term
Woodworking, ornamental metal work 3	Printing or ornamental metal work 3

Prevocational or Try-Out Industrial Courses

(400-425 boys)

Seventh Grade, First Term

Woodworking 6

Seventh Grade, Second Term

Elementary foundry practice . . . 4

High School, First Year
First Term

Forge and sheet metal practice 4

Mechanical drawing 4

High School, First Year
Second Term

Electricity 4

Mechanical drawing 4

High School, Second Year
First Term

Machine shop practice 4

High School, Second Year
Second Term

Vocational shop elective 4

Vocational Industrial Trade Courses

Daily, 1-4 P. M.

Junior and Senior Years, Four Terms

(130-140 boys)

One of the courses listed is elected and followed for two full years.

Automobile practice
Carpentry and cabinet making
Trade drafting
Electricity
Forge and sheet metal practice
Foundry practice
Machine shop practice
Painting
Pattern-making
Printing
Plumbing, pipe fitting, or elementary power plant practice

Elementary Industrial Courses

(Prevocational)

Daily, 9 A. M. to 4 P. M.

(20-25 boys)

One Year, Two Terms

First Term

Subject	
Mathematics	5
English, Hygiene, Civics	5
Machine shop practice	4
Forge and sheet metal practice	8
Woodwork	8
Library	1
Recreation	9
Total	40

Second Term

Subject	
Mathematics	5
English, Hygiene, Civics	5
Machine shop practice	6
Forge and sheet metal practice	6
Foundry practice	8
Library	1
Recreation	9
Total	40

Intermediate High School Courses

Daily, 9 A. M. to 4 P. M.

Two Years, Four Terms

(40-50 boys)

Subject	Periods	Subject	Periods
Mathematics	5	Industrial trade course	16†
English, Hygiene, Civics	5	Library	1
Science	2	Recreation	7
Mechanical Drawing	4	Total	40

*

The figures placed after the subjects in the foregoing outline indicate the number of periods per week. A period is one hour for the Sloyd group and forty-five minutes for the other groups. No shop assignments above the sixth grade are less than double periods.

The list of trades from which one is elected is the same as that for high school juniors and seniors, excepting automobile practice. During the second term of the second year boys may be assigned to co-operative work.

BIBLIOGRAPHY

I. BIBLIOGRAPHICAL AND GENERAL REFERENCES

Barzun, Jacques, and Henry F. Graff. *The Modern Researcher.* 2nd ed. New York: Harcourt, Brace and Company, 1970. pp. xiii + 386.

Brickman, William W. *Guide to Research in Educational History.* New York: New York University Bookstore, 1949. pp. ix + 220. [Reissued, Philadelphia: Norwood Editions, 1973].

Campbell, William G. *Form and Style in Thesis Writing.* Rev. ed. Boston: Houghton Mifflin Company, 1974. pp. vi + 114.

Cordasco, Francesco, and Elliot S. M. Gatner. *Research and Report Writing.* Rev. ed. New York: Barnes & Noble, 1974. pp. viii + 142.

Dictionary of American Biography. Published under the auspices of the American Council of Learned Societies. New York: C. Scribner's Sons, 1928-1936. 20 vols. and Supplements I (1943), II (1958).

Ebel, Robert L. (ed.). *Encyclopedia of Educational Research.* 4th ed. New York: The Macmillan Company, 1969. pp. xxix + 1564 + xlvii.

Good, Carter V. (ed.). *Dictionary of Education.* New York: McGraw-Hill Book Co., 1959. xxvii + 676.

Good, Carter V., and Douglas E. Scates. *Methods of Research.* New York: Appleton-Century-Crofts, Inc., 1954. pp. xx + 920.

Gottschalk, Louis. *Understanding History.* New York: Alfred A. Knopf, 1956. pp. xx + 298 + vi.

Monroe, Paul (ed.). A Cyclopedia of Education. 5 vols. New York: Macmillan, 1911-1913; also Lee C. Deighton, ed. The Encyclopedia of Education. 10 vols. New York: Macmillan, 1971.

Park, Joe. (ed.). The Rise of American Education: An Annotated Bibliography. Evanston: Northwestern University Press, 1965. pp. xi + 216.

Sears, William P., Jr. "Analytical Procedures for Scientific Research," Research in Industrial Arts Education. Ninth Yearbook of the American Council on Industrial Arts Teacher Education. Bloomington, Illinois: McKnight and McKnight Publishing Company, 1960. pp. 50-79.

U.S. Department of Health, Education and Welfare. Research in Industrial Education: Summaries of Studies, 1930-1955. Vocational Division Bulletin No. 264. Trade and Industrial Series No. 65. Washington: U.S. Government Printing Office, 1957. pp. vii + 527.

U.S. Department of Health, Education and Welfare. Research in Industrial Education: Summaries of Studies, 1956-1959. OE-84016. Vocational Division Bulletin No. 293. Trade and Industrial Education Series No. 72. Washington: U.S. Government Printing Office, 1961. pp. vii + 148.

U.S. Department of Health, Education and Welfare. Research in Industrial Education: Summaries of Studies, 1960-61. OE 84016-61. Vocational Division Bulletin No. 299. Trade and Industrial Education Series No. 75. Washington: U.S. Government Printing Office, 1962. pp. iv + 34.

II. PRIMARY SOURCE MATERIALS

City of Philadelphia. Journal of the Common Council of the City of Philadelphia. 1831-1848. (Philadelphia: Various publishers. Unpublished manuscripts deposited at the Department of Archives, Philadelphia City Hall.)

City of Philadelphia. Journal of the Select Council of the City of Philadelphia. 1831-1848. (Philadelphia: Various publishers. Unpublished manuscripts deposited at the Department of Archives, Philadelphia City Hall.)

Girard College. Anniversary Addresses of the Opening of Girard College for Orphans. [Annual]

Girard College. Catalogue of Staff and Students. 1848-1965. [Annual] Catalogues for 1848-69 in Report of the College's Board of Directors; for 1870-1914 in Report of the Philadelphia Board of Directors of City Trusts; for 1914-1965 in Report of the President of the College.

Girard College. Course of Study. [Annual, irregular, 1848 to the present] Sometimes these appear as appendices to the Reports of the President, the Board of Directors, the Directors of City Trusts.

Girard College. Report of the Board of Directors of the Girard College for Orphans. 1848-1869. [Annual]

Girard College. Report of the Committee on Admission and Discharge Relative to Binding Orphans to Suitable Occupations. [1852]

Girard College. Report of the Committee on Moral and Religious Instruction and Discipline. [1852?]

Girard College. *Report of the Philadelphia Board of Directors of City Trusts.* 1870-1958. [Annual]

Girard College. *Report of the President.* [Annual, 1848 to the present. Sometimes appears in *Report* of the College's Board of Directors; or in Report of the Philadelphia Board of Directors of City Trusts].

Girard College. *A Sketch of Girard College and of The Girard Estate.* Printed by order of the Board of Directors of City Trusts. Philadelphia: J Spencer Smith [Appeared irregularly; cf. *Report* for 1887].

III. GENERAL SECONDARY REFERENCES

1. *Institutional and General Histories of Girard College*

Arey, Henry W. *The Girard College and Its Founder.* Philadelphia: C. Sherman, Printer, 1856. pp. 85.

Cunningham, Ernest. *Memories of Girard College.* Philadelphia: Girard College, 1942. pp. xiv + 454.

Herrick, Cheesman. *History of Girard College.* Philadelphia: Girard College, 1935. pp. xi + 390.

2. *General Histories of American Education*

Butts, R. Freeman, and Lawrence A. Cremin. *A History of Education in American Culture.* New York: Holt, Rinehart & Winston, 1953. pp. x + 628.

Cubberley, Ellwood P. *Public Education in the United States.* Cambridge: Houghton Mifflin Company, 1947. pp. xviii + 782.

Edwards, Newton, and Herman G. Richey. _The School in the American Social Order._ Boston: Houghton Mifflin Company, 1963. pp. xiii + 694.

Good, H. G., and James D. Teller. _A History of American Education._ 3rd ed. New York: The Macmillan Company, 1973. pp. x + 610.

Meyer, Adolphe E. _An Educational History of the American People._ 2nd ed. New York: McGraw-Hill Book Company, 1967. pp. xx + 444.

Monroe, Paul. _Founding of the American Public School System._ Vol. I. New York: Macmillan Company, 1940. pp. xiv + 520.

Potter, Robert E. _The Stream of American Education._ New York: American Book Co., 1967. pp. 551.

Rippa, S. Alexander. _Education in a Free Society: An American History._ 2nd ed. New York: David McKay, 1971. pp. 392.

3. General Histories of Manual and Industrial Education

Anderson, Lewis F. _History of Manual and Industrial School Education._ New York: D. Appleton and Company, 1926. pp. xi + 251.

Bennett, Charles A. _History of Manual and Industrial Education Up to 1870._ Peoria: The Manual Arts Press, 1926. pp. 461.

Bennett, Charles A. _History of Manual and Industrial Education 1870 to 1917._ Peoria: The Manual Arts Press, 1937. pp. 566.

Hawkins, Layton S., Charles S. Prosser and John C. Wright. _Development of Vocational Education._ Chicago: American Technical Society, 1951. pp. ix + 656.

McGrath, William J. "History of Vocational Education." Unpublished Ph.D. dissertation, New York University, 1913. pp. 4 + vii + 154 + 2.

Roberts, Roy W. _Vocational and Practical Arts Education._ New York: Harper & Bros., 1957. pp. x + 637.

Sears, William P., Jr. _The Roots of Vocational Education._ New York: John Wiley & Sons, 1931. pp. xii + 310.

Smith, Ross H. _Development of Manual Training in the United States._ Lancaster: Intelligencer Printing Co., 1914. pp. 90. (Originally, Ph.D. dissertation, University of Pennsylvania, 1913).

Swanson, Chester J. _Development of Federal Legislation for Vocational Education._ Chicago: American Technical Society, 1962. pp. 110.

4. Selected Miscellaneous Materials

American Council of Industrial Arts Supervisors of the American Industrial Arts Association. _Industrial Arts Education._ Bloomington, Illinois: McKnight & McKnight Publishing Company, 1963. pp. 32.

American Vocational Association. _Studies in Industrial Education: A Bibliography of Studies in Industrial Education with a Classified Index._ American Vocational Association Bulletin No. 4. Washington: American Vocational Association, 1949. pp. 160.

Arnold, Walter K., and Russell K. Britton. "Fifty Years of Progress in Trade and Industrial Education," _American Vocational Journal_, Vol. 31, No. 9 (December, 1956), 83-90, 104.

Arnstein, George E. "Vocational Education," The Bulletin of the National Association of Secondary-School Principals, Vol. 48, No. 295 (November, 1964), 56-72.

Ashley, L. F. "Chronological Development of the Industrial Arts Concept," IAVE, Vol. 26, No. 10 (October, 1937), 309-312.

Bache, Alexander D. Report on Education in Europe, to the Trustees of the Girard College for Orphans. Philadelphia: Lydia R. Bailey, 1839. pp. xiv + 666.

Banes, Charles E. Manual Training and Apprenticeship Schools in 1890. Philadelphia: George H. Buchanan and Company, 1890. pp. 81.

Bawden, William T. Leaders in Industrial Education. Milwaukee: Bruce Publishing Co., 1950. pp. 196.

Beck, James M. "Stephen Girard, Merchant and Mariner." An oration delivered at the unveiling of a statue to Stephen Girard on the West Plaza of the City Hall, Philadelphia, on May 20, 1897. Philadelphia: J. B. Lippincott Company, 1897. pp. 24.

Binder, Frederick M. The Age of the Common School, 1830-1865. New York: John Wiley, 1974. pp. 191.

Binzen, Peter H. "Philadelphia's Negroes Challenge a Will," The Reporter, Vol. 33, No. 7 (October 21, 1965), 43-45.

Brown, B. Frank, ed. The Reform of Secondary Education: A Report to the Public and the Profession. New York: McGraw-Hill, 1973. pp. 188.

Brumbaugh, Martin G. "Educational Setting of Stephen Girard's Benefaction." An Address Delivered in the Chapel of Girard College, Philadelphia on Founder's Day, May 20, 1902. Philadelphia: Press of Allen, Lane & Scott, 1902. pp. 8.

Carlton, Frank T. _Economic Influences Upon Educational Progress in the United States, 1820-1850._ Madison: University of Wisconsin, 1908. pp. 135.

Chittenden, Russell H. _History of the Sheffield Scientific School of Yale University 1846-1922._ 2 Vols. New Haven: Yale University Press, 1928. pp. x, x + 610. (paged consecutively)

Coates, Charles P. _History of the Manual Training School of Washington University._ Department of the Interior, Bureau of Education, Bulletin No. 3. Washington: Government Printing Office, 1923. pp. 86.

Commission on Industrial Education. _Report of the Commission on Industrial Education Made to the Legislature of Pennsylvania._ Harrisburg: Edwin K. Meyers, State Printer, 1889. pp. 592.

Commissioner of Labor. _Industrial Education in the United States._ Twenty-Fifth Annual Report of the Commissioner of Labor. Washington: U.S. Government Printing Office, 1911. pp. 822.

Conant, James B. _The American High School Today._ New York: McGraw-Hill Book Company, 1959. pp. xiii + 140.

Conant, James B. _Slums and Suburbs._ New York: McGraw-Hill Book Company, 1961. pp. vii + 147.

Cremin, Lawrence A. _The American Common School._ New York: Teachers College, Columbia University, 1951. pp. xi + 248.

Cremin, Lawrence A. _The Transformation of the School_. New York: Alfred A. Knopf, 1961. pp. xi + 387 + xxiv.

Curti, Merle. _The Social Ideas of American Educators_. Totowa, N. J.: Littlefield Adams & Co., 1961. pp. xx + 613.

Douglas, Paul H. _American Apprenticeship and Industrial Education_. New York: Columbia University, 1921. pp. 348.

Duane, Morris. "The Writing of the Will of Stephen Girard," _Educational Outlook_, Vol. XXIII, No. 1 (November, 1948), 13-18.

Duane, Russell. "Who Wrote Stephen Girard's Will?" _The Pennsylvania Magazine of History and Biography_, Vol. LIV, No. 1 (January, 1930), 1-31.

Evans, Owen D. "Institutional Training of Children for Vocations," _Atlas Social Service Exchange_, Vol. I, No. II (March, 1928), 1-5.

Evans, Owen D., and Raymond I. Haskell. (comps. and eds.). _Proceedings of the Girard College Centennial_. Philadelphia: Girard College Print Shop, 1948. pp. viii + 249.

Everett, Edward. _The Importance of Practical Education and Useful Knowledge_. New York: Harper & Bros., 1847. pp. 419.

Fales, Roy G. "Fifty Years of Progress in Industrial Arts Education," _American Vocational Journal_, Vol. 31, No. 9 (December, 1956), 75-82, 111.

Fee, Edward M. _The Origin and Growth of Vocational Industrial Education in Philadelphia to 1917_. Philadelphia: Westbrook Publishing Co., 1938. pp. viii + 258.

Fink Eugene D. "History of the Development of Industrial Education and of Industrial Arts Education at the Oswego State Normal School." Unpublished M.A. thesis, New York University, 1938. pp. ix + 758.

Fish, Carl R. _The Rise of the Common Man, 1830-1850_. New York: The Macmillan Company, 1927. pp. xix + 391.

Fox, Deyo B. "European Influence on the Industrial Education in the United States," _IAVE_, Vol. 33, No. 8 (October, 1944), 305-307.

Gillette, John M. _Vocational Education_. New York: American Book Co., 1910. pp. viii + 303.

[Girard College] "Alexander Urges Suit to Open Girard Gate," _The Philadelphia Inquirer_, May 23, 1965, pp. 1, 5.

[Girard College] The Building Committee of the Girard College for Orphans. _Proceedings on Laying the Corner Stone of the Girard College for Orphans together with an address on that occasion by Nicholas Biddle_. Philadelphia: Lydia R. Bailey, 1833. pp. 23.

[Girard College] "Eight Men Seized Near Girard College Wall," _The Evening Bulletin_ [Philadelphia], May 4, 1965, p. 3.

[Girard College] "Girard Rings with Singing Inside, Outside," _The Philadelphia Inquirer_, May 23, 1965, pp. 1, 4.

[Girard College] "1,000 Police Bar 'Invasion' of Girard College," _The Philadelphia Inquirer_, May 2, 1965, pp. 1, 38.

[Girard College] Weart, William G. "A Private School is N.A.A.C.P. Target," _New York Times_, January 17, 1965, p. 74.

[Girard, Stephen] Board of Directors of City Trusts [Philadelphia]. _Will and Codicils of the Late Stephen Girard Esq. Together with the Acts of Assembly and Decisions Relating Thereto_. Philadelphia: 1892. pp. 59.

Gordon, George F. "Report of The Committee of Visitation on Girard College for the Month of October, 1858," Presented to the Common Council, November 11, 1858. Philadelphia: City of Philadelphia, 1858, pp. 23.

Gordon, Milton M. "The Girard College Case: Desegregation and a Municipal Trust," _The Annals of the American Academy of Political and Social Science_, Vol. 304 (March, 1956), 53-61.

Graham, Patricia A. _Community and Class in American Education, 1865-1918_. New York: John Wiley, 1974. pp. 256.

Grayson, Theodore J. "Stephen Girard," _Leaders and Periods of American Finance_. New York: John Wiley & Sons, 1932. pp. 115-127.

Grizzell, E. Duncan. "The Place of Girard College Among Educational Institutions," _Educational Outlook_, Vol. XXIII, No. 1 (November, 1948), 32-38.

Gumbert, Edgar B., and Joel H. Spring. _The Superschool and the Superstate: American Education in the Twentieth Century, 1918-1970_. New York: John Wiley, 1974. pp. 214.

Ham, Charles H. _Manual Training_. New York: Harper & Bros., 1886. pp. xxii + 403.

Hardin, Robert A. "Our Evolving Philosophy of Industrial Arts," _IAVE_, Vol. 39, No. 5 (May, 1950), 179-182; _Ibid_., Vol. 39, No. 5 (June, 1950), 223-226.

Harris, Norman C. "Redoubled Efforts and Dimly Seen Goals," Phi Delta Kappan, Vol. XLVI, No. 8 (April, 1965), 360-365.

Haskell, Raymond I. Girard College: A Pioneer American School. Centennial Edition Series. Philadelphia: Girard College Print Shop, 1948. pp. 7.

Haskell, Raymond I. "Stephen Girard as an Educational Pioneer," Educational Outlook, Vol. XXIII, No. 1 (November, 1948), 19-24.

Henry, Hugh T. "Stephen Girard," Catholic Historical Review, Vol. IV (1918), 277-303.

Herrick, Cheesman A. Stephen Girard, Founder. Philadelphia: Girard College Trade School, 1923. pp. ix + 203.

Hornbake, R. Lee, and C. Kenneth Beach. "Industrial Education," Review of Educational Research, Vol. XX, No. 4 (October, 1950), 309-321.

Hug, Elsie A. Seventy-Five Years in Education: The Role of the School of Education, New York University, 1890-1965. New York: New York University Press, 1965. pp. xii + 276.

Ingram, Henry A. The Life and Character of Stephen Girard. Philadelphia: E. Stanley Hart, 1885. pp. 185.

Janssen, Peter A. "1830 Humanitarian Who's Out of Step With 1965," New York Herald Tribune, December 19, 1965, p. 19.

Jordan, Thomas F. The Problem of Vocational Education and the Catholic Secondary School. Washington: The Catholic University of America Press, 1942. pp. xii + 185.

Karnes, John W., Jr. "Industrial Education," Review of Educational Research, Vol. XXXII, No. 4 (October, 1962), 402-410.

Keller, Franklin J. The Comprehensive High School. New York: Harper & Bros., 1955. pp. xv + 302.

Keller, Franklin J. Principles of Vocational Education. Boston: D. C. Heath & Company, 1948. pp. vi + 402.

Knight, Edgar W., and Clifton L. Hall. Readings in American Educational History. New York: Appleton-Century-Crofts, Inc., 1951. pp. xxi + 799.

Lee, Edwin A. (ed.). Objectives and Problems of Vocational Education. New York: McGraw-Hill Book Co., 1938. pp. x + 476.

Lieber, Francis. A Constitution and Plan of Education for Girard College for Orphans, with an Introductory Report Laid Before the Board of Trustees. Philadelphia: Carey, Lea and Blanchard, 1834. pp. 227.

London, Hoyt H. "Industrial Education," Review of Educational Research, Vol. XXVI, No. 4 (October, 1956), 379-387.

Macy, S. Herman. "The Plan, Philosophy, and Objectives of Girard College," Educational Outlook, Vol. XXIII, No. 1 (November, 1948), 3-12.

MacAlister, James. Manual Training in the Public Schools of Philadelphia. New York: New York College for the Training of Teachers, March, 1890. pp. 56.

Madsen, David L. Early National Education, 1776-1830. New York: John Wiley, 1974. pp. 162.

Mays, Arthur B. Essentials of Industrial Education. New York: McGraw-Hill Book Co., 1952. pp. ix + 248.

Mays, Arthur B. "Fifty Years of Progress in Vocational and Practical Arts Education," American Vocational Journal, Vol. 31, No. 9 (December, 1956), 29-38, 105.

Mays, Arthur B. An Introduction to Vocational Education. New York: The Century Co., 1930. pp. x + 323.

McCarthy, John A. Vocational Education: America's Greatest Resource. Chicago: American Technical Society, 1950. pp. 387.

McLure, David. A System of Education for the Girard College for Orphans. Philadelphia: 1838. pp. 16 + 48. Includes also, A Brief Exposition of the Philosophic Principles Upon Which the System of Education for the Girard College for Orphans is Founded. Philadelphia: Isaac Ashmead & Co., 1838. pp. 363.

McMaster, John B. The Life and Times of Stephen Girard, Mariner and Merchant. 2 Vols. Philadelphia: J. B. Lippincott Company, 1918. pp. xi + 469 + 481.

Melchior, D. Montford. "The Contributions of Girard College to Education," Educational Outlook, Vol. XXIII, No. 1 (November, 1948), 25-31.

Minnigerode, Meade. "Stephen Girard, The Merchant Banker," Certain Rich Men. New York: G. P. Putnam's Son, 1927. pp. 3-30.

Mulhern, James. A History of Secondary Education in Pennsylvania. Philadelphia: Published by the Author, 1933. pp. xvi + 714.

[National Society for the Study of Education] Industrial Education: Typical Experiments Described and Interpreted. The Eleventh Yearbook of The National Society for the Study of Education, Part I. Chicago: University of Chicago Press, 1912. pp. 124.

[National Society for the Study of Education] Social Forces Influencing American Education. The Sixtieth Yearbook for the Study of Education, Part II. Chicago: University of Chicago Press, 1961. pp. x + 252 + xcv.

[National Society for the Study of Education] Vocational Education. The Forty-Second Yearbook of The National Society for the Study of Education, Part I. Chicago: University of Chicago Press, 1943. pp. xvi + 494.

[National Society for the Study of Education] Vocational Education. The Sixty-Fourth Yearbook of the National Society for the Study of Education, Part I. Chicago: University of Chicago Press, 1965. pp. x + 301 + vi.

Novak, Benjamin J. "Origins of Public Industrial Education in Philadelphia," IAVE, Vol. 43, No. 2 (February, 1954), 39-42; Ibid., Vol. 43, No. 3 (April, 1954), 132-135; Ibid., Vol. 43, No. 4 (May, 1954), 165-167.

Odgers, Merle M. Alexander Dallas Bache. Philadelphia: University of Philadelphia Press, 1947. pp. vii + 223.

Odgers, Merle M. "Bache As An Educator," Proceedings of the American Philosophical Society, Vol. 2, No. 2 (May, 1941), 161-171.

Odgers, Merle M. "A Message From The President," Educational Outlook, Vol. XXIII, No. 1 (November, 1948), 2.

[Office of Science and Technology. Executive Office of the President] Youth: Transition to Adulthood. Report of the Panel on Youth of the President's Science Advisory Committee. Washington: Government Printing Office, 1973. pp. 190.

Parton, James. "Stephen Girard and His College," Famous Americans of Recent Times. Boston: Ticknor & Fields, 1867. pp. 223-257.

Perkinson, Henry J. The Imperfect Panacea: American Faith in Education, 1865-1965. New York: Random House, 1968. pp. 239.

Prosser, Charles A., and Thomas H. Quigley. Vocational Education in a Democracy. Chicago: American Technical Society, 1949. pp. ix + 575.

Reigart, John F. The Lancastrian System of Instruction in the Schools of New York City. New York: Columbia University, Teachers College, 1916. pp. vi + 105 + i.

Reisner, Edward H. The Evolution of the Common School. New York: The Macmillan Co., 1930. pp. x + 590.

Rupp, George P. (ed.). Semi-Centennial of Girard College, 1848-1898. Philadelphia: Girard College, 1898. pp. 182.

Russell, John D., and Associates. Vocational Education. Staff Study No. 8. Prepared for the Advisory Committee on Education. Washington: U.S. Government Printing Office, 1938. pp. x + 325.

Salmon, David. _Joseph Lancaster_. London: Longmans, Green & Co., 1904. pp. vi + 76.

Salmon, David, ed. _The Practical Parts of Lancaster's Improvements and Bell's Experiment_. Cambridge: Cambridge University Press, 1932. pp. li + 112.

Shaplin, Judson T. "An Alumnus Looks Back a Century," _Educational Outlook_, Vol. XXIII, No. 1 (November, 1948), 39-43.

Siljestrom, P. A. _The Educational Institutions of the United States_. Translated from the Swedish by Frederica Brown. London: John Chapman, 1853. pp. xvi + 411.

Simpson, Stephen. _Biography of Stephen Girard_. Philadelphia: Thomas L. Bonsal, 1832. pp. 281 + 35.

Smith, Edgar F. "Franklin and Girard." An oration delivered in the Chapel of Girard College, Philadelphia, on Founder's Day, May 19 (20), 1906. Philadelphia: Press of Ware Bros. Company, 1907. pp. 10.

Smith, Herbert E. "The Historical Development of Technical Education in the First Nine Colleges Founded in the United States 1636-1862." Unpublished Ph.D. dissertation, New York University, 1940. pp. vi + 424.

Snedden, David P. _The Problem of Vocational Education_. Boston: Houghton Mifflin Co., 1910. pp. vii + 86.

Snedden, David. _Vocational Education_. New York: Macmillan Company, 1920. pp. xi + 587.

Stombaugh, Ray M. _A Survey of the Movements Culminating in Industrial Arts Education in Secondary Schools_. New York: Teachers College, Columbia University, 1936. pp. vi + 192.

Struck, F. T. Foundations of Industrial Education. New York: John Wiley & Sons, 1930. pp. ix + 492.

Thayer, V. T. Formative Ideas in American Education. New York: Dodd, Mead and Co., 1965. pp. xii + 394.

[U.S. Department of Health, Education and Welfare] Education for a Changing World of Work, Appendix III. OE-80026. U.S. Government Printing Office, 1963. pp. v + 91.

[U.S. Department of Health, Education and Welfare] Education for a Changing World of Work. OE-80021. Washington: U.S. Government Printing Office, 1963. pp. xx + 296.

[U.S. Department of Health, Education and Welfare] Improving Industrial Arts Teaching. OE-33022. Washington: U.S. Government Printing Office, 1962. pp. v + 67.

Walsh, Louise G., and John M. Walsh. History and Organization of Education in Pennsylvania. Indiana, Pa.: R. S. Grosse Print Shop, 1930. pp. xvi + 412.

Wendt, Erhard F. "Brief History of Industrial Arts and Vocational Education," IAVE, Vol. 35, No. 4 (April, 1946), 151-154; Ibid., Vol. 35, No. 5 (May, 1946), 202-203.

Wenrich, Ralph C., Gordon I. Swanson and Rupert N. Evans. "Vocational, Technical, and Practical Arts Education," Review of Educational Research, Vol. XXXII, No. 4 (October, 1962), 367-376.

Wert, James E., and Charles O. Neidt. "Education for Work Movement," Review of Educational Research, Vol. XVII, No. 3 (June, 1947), 202-208.

White, James D. "The Needs and Problems of Girard College Graduates." Unpublished Ph.D. dissertation, University of Pennsylvania, 1949. pp. 122.

Whitesel, John A. "Industrial Education," *Review of Educational Research*, Vol. XVII, No. 3 (June, 1947), 222-230.

Wickersham, James P. *A History of Education in Pennsylvania*. Lancaster: Inquirer Publishing Co., 1886. pp. xxiv + 683. [Reissued, New York: Arno Press, 1969]

Wilber, Gordon O. *Industrial Arts in General Education*. Scranton: International Textbook Co., 1948. pp. xiii + 362.

Wildes, Harry E. *Lonely Midas*. New York: Farrar & Rinehart, Inc., 1943. pp. xii + 372.

Wolcott, Wilfred B. *Background of the Educational Provisions of the Will of Stephen Girard*. Philadelphia: University of Pennsylvania, 1948. pp. v + 75.

Woodward, Calvin M. *The Manual Training School*. Boston: D. C. Heath & Co., 1887. pp. vii + 366.

AMERICAN ETHNIC GROUPS: THE EUROPEAN HERITAGE

An Arno Press Collection

Allswang, John Myers. **The Political Behavior of Chicago's Ethnic Groups, 1918–1932**. 1980

Appel, John J. **Immigrant Historical Societies in the United States, 1880–1950**. 1980

Bayer, Alan E. **The Assimilation of American Family Patterns by European Immigrants and Their Children**. 1980

Berger, Morris Isaiah. **The Settlement, the Immigrant and the Public School**. 1980

Berman, Myron. **The Attitude of American Jewry Towards East European Jewish Immigration, 1881-1914**. 1980

Buxbaum, Edwin Clarence. **The Greek-American Group of Tarpon Springs, Florida**. 1980

Castelli, Joseph Roy. **Basques in the Western United States**. 1980

Costantakos, Chrysie Mamalakis. **The American-Greek Subculture**. 1980

Dahlie, Jorgen. **A Social History of Scandinavian Immigration, Washington State, 1895–1910**. 1980

Dickinson, Joan Younger. **The Role of the Immigrant Women in the U.S. Labor Force, 1890–1910**. 1980

Dobbert, Guido Andre. **The Disintegration of an Immigrant Community**. 1980

Farrell, John Joseph. **The Immigrant and the School in New York City**. 1980

Ferroni, Charles D. **The Italians in Cleveland**. 1980

Gabriel, Richard. **The Irish and Italians**. 1980

Glasco, Laurence Admrial. **Ethnicity and Social Structure**. 1980

Gobetz, Giles Edward. **Adjustment and Assimilation of Slovenian Refugees**. 1980

Hansen, Judith Friedman. **We Are a Little Land**. 1980

Harper, Richard Conant. **The Course of the Melting Pot Idea to 1910**. 1980

Hill, Robert F[red]. **Exploring the Dimensions of Ethnicity**. 1980

Hosay, Philip M[yron]. **The Challenge of Urban Poverty**. 1980

Iorizzo, Luciano John. **Italian Immigration and the Impact of the Padrone System.** 1980

Juliani, Richard N. **The Social Organization of Immigration.** 1980

Knoche, Carl Heinz. **The German Immigrant Press in Milwaukee.** 1980

Kolm, Richard. **The Change of Cultural Identity.** 1980

Kraus, Harry P. **The Settlement House Movement in New York City, 1886–1914.** 1980

Leder, Hans Howard. **Cultural Persistence in a Portuguese-American Community.** 1980

Leonard, Henry Beardsell. **The Open Gates.** 1980

Lindberg, Duane Rodell. **Men of the Cloth and the Social-Cultural Fabric of the Norwegian Ethnic Community in North Dakota.** 1980

Matulich, Loretta. **A Cross-Disciplinary Study of the European Immigrants of 1870 to 1925.** 1980

Mondello, Salvatore. **The Italian Immigrant in Urban America, 1880–1920, as Reported in the Contemporary Periodical Press.** 1980

Mostwin, Danuta. **The Transplanted Family.** 1980

Nam, Charles B[enjamin]. **Nationality Groups and Social Stratification.** 1980

Neuringer, Sheldon Morris. **American Jewry and United States Immigration Policy, 1881–1953.** 1980

Newton, Lewis William. **The Americanization of French Louisiana.** 1980

Obidinski, Eugene Edward. **Ethnic to Status Group.** 1980

Olson, Audrey L. **St. Louis Germans, 1850–1920.** 1980

Romano, Louis A. **Manual and Industrial Education at Girard College, 1831–1965.** 1980

Scarpaci, Jean Ann. **Italian Immigrants in Louisiana's Sugar Parishes.** 1980

Schelbert, Leo. **Swiss Migration to America.** 1980

Scherini, Rose Doris. **The Italian American Community of San Francisco.** 1980

Scourby, Alice. **Third Generation Greek Americans.** 1980

Spengler, Paul A. **Yankee, Swedish and Italian Acculturation and Economic Mobility in Jamestown, New York, from 1860 to 1920.** 1980

Stein, Howard F[inn]. **An Ethno-Historic Study of Slovak-American Identity.** 1980

Theriault, George French. **The Franco-Americans in a New England Community.** 1980

Thompson, Bryan. **Cultural Ties as Determinants of Immigrant Settlement in Urban Areas.** 1980

Ulrich, Robert James. **The Bennett Law of 1889.** 1980

Wilhelm, Hubert G.H. **Organized German Settlement and Its Effects on the Frontier of South-Central Texas.** 1980